Collins

NEW MATHS FRAMEWORKING

Matches the revised KS3 Framework

Kevin Evans, Keith Gordon, Trevor Senior, Brian Speed

Contents

Introduction

This is the main teaching text for Year 8. It accompanies *New Maths Frameworking* Year 8 Pupil Book 2 and caters for pupils working at Levels 5–6. Pupils who are working at a level below this (Levels 4–5) are catered for by Pupil Book 1 and Teacher's Pack 1 and those working at a level above this (Levels 6–7) are catered for by Pupil Book 3 and Teacher's Pack 3. The topics and their sequence are the same across all three books but are handled at different levels, allowing for sensitive differentiation in mixed-ability classes.

New Maths Frameworking has been based on the revised Mathematics Programme of Study for Key Stage 3 (KS3). The detailed lesson plans in this book deliver core material from the revised *Framework for Teaching Mathematics: Year 8*. We have produced just under 90 one-hour lessons to cover all the material you need to deliver the new KS3 Maths Curriculum. This should give some flexibility to include tests, extended activities and revision classes to the teaching programme, and allows for the normal events that disrupt teaching time. For further help in mapping lessons and producing your scheme of work, please consult the Contents pages and the Framework Objectives Matching Chart given in this book.

Chapter Overview

Each chapter starts with an outline of the content being covered in the entire chapter, explaining clearly how the lesson plans cover the National Curriculum and at what attainment level. Its features are listed below.

- **Overview** shows the topics covered in each section at a quick glance.

- **Context** provides a summary of the work pupils will encounter. It offers a context for key mathematical ideas explored in the chapter.

- **National Curriculum references** identify the key learning outcomes.

- **Key concepts** show the applications and implications of mathematics.

- **Key processes** indicate essential skills and processes in mathematics that pupils need to make progress.

- **Route mapping chart** for each exercise displays the National Curriculum level for each question in the Pupil Book. The chart will show, for example, that questions 1–2 in Exercise 1A are set at around Level 5.

Lesson Plans

Each lesson plan focuses on a Strand of Progression in the new Framework, making it easy to deliver the new Framework. Every plan follows the same format making it easy to prepare for and use. Its features are listed below.

- **Framework objectives** identify the key learning outcomes from the Framework.

- Engaging **Oral and mental starter** activities involve the whole class and are designed to work with minimal specialised equipment.

- **Main lesson activity** helps you to lead pupils into exercise questions.

- **Plenary** offers guidance to round off the three-part lesson.

- **Functional Maths icons** highlight questions and activities that correspond to Functional Maths exercises in the Pupil Book.

- **Key words** highlight when to introduce Framework Vocabulary terms.
- Extra **Homework questions** consolidate and extend learning. All questions have been graded with a National Curriculum level.
- **Answers** are provided for all Pupil Book, Homework and National Test questions.

Functional Maths notes

These notes offer guidance on how to use the **Functional Maths activities** that can be found at the end of 10 chapters in the Pupil Book. These activities make it easy to embed Functional Maths into your lessons and put maths into real-life contexts. They also help to prepare pupils for Functional Mathematics exams at GCSE.

Levelled Learning Checklists

The one-per-chapter checklists can be found at the end of the book and can be easily copied and distributed to the class, so pupils can use them for self-assessment to gauge what level they are currently working at and how to improve.

Practice Book answers

Answers to the accompanying *New Maths Frameworking* Year 8 Practice Book 2 can be found at the end of the book.

PLUS

The **free, easy-to-use CD-ROM** that comes with this Teacher's Pack contains Word documents as well as PDFs of all the overviews, lesson plans, Functional Maths notes, learning checklists and Practice Book answers. Depending on the need, this will allow you to easily customise your lessons, incorporate extra material into ICT exercises and produce individual teaching programmes for pupils.

Functional Maths Introduction

Rationale

Following the 14–19 Education and skills White Paper (February 2005) and the Skills White Paper (March 2005), the DfES gave QCA a remit to develop functional skills in English, ICT and Mathematics. Functional skills are practical skills that allow individuals to gain the most out of work, education and everyday life.

Programme of Study for Mathematics

The new Programme of Study for Mathematics requires that students can use and apply Maths. A major part of this is the development of functional skills. Functional Maths requires students to use mathematics in ways that enable them to operate confidently in life and work in a wide range of contexts.

Students are expected to have the skills and confidence to apply, combine and adapt their mathematical knowledge to new situations. The necessary mathematical knowledge can be classified as 'Competency' and 'Functionality'.

Competency

Competency is the basic skills needed for real-life mathematics, for example:

- Using the four rules with integers and decimals up to two decimal places
- Using fractions, percentages and decimals and knowing the equivalences between them
- Using simple formulae expressed in words
- Recognising simple 2-D and 3-D shapes and knowing their properties
- Working out perimeters, areas and volumes in practical situations
- Reading scales and using metric and imperial measures
- Interpret data represented in a variety of ways
- Represent data and find the mean and range of data
- Use basic ideas of chance

This is not a comprehensive list but as the majority of work in this book and accompanying Pupil Book covers material that can be defined as 'competency' this is not flagged up.

Functionality

Functionality is the ability to do some or all of the following as appropriate when faced with a real-life problem:

- Representing: Making sense of a problem and how to represent it
  - Understand the situation
  - Devise a strategy to tackle the problem
- Analysing: Processing and using mathematics
  - Use mathematics to model the situation
  - Use basic mathematics (competency) to solve the problem

● Interpreting: Interpreting and communicating the results

  ○ Interpret and check results

  ○ Evaluate the strategy used

  ○ Explain the result

Questions that involve functionality are flagged throughout the accompanying Pupil Book with the icon given in the margin.

In addition there are 10 Functional Maths activities in the Pupil Book which develop a theme in more detail giving students the chance to apply a range of mathematical techniques in the context of a real-life situation. This Teacher's Pack contains notes on those activities and the answers.

Progression

As the students work through the New Maths Frameworking series they will meet more work on Functional Mathematics. By the time students have reached the end of Book 9.2 they should be prepared for the Level 2 'Certificate of Functional Mathematics'. This is the basic standard that the government wants all citizens to achieve so that they become 'effective and involved as citizens, able to operate confidently in life, and to work in a wide range of contexts'.

Framework Objectives Matching Chart

This chart matches the renewed framework of objectives from the Secondary National Strategy to specific lesson plans contained in this Teacher's Pack. The objectives are taken from the year 8 Strands and Sub-strands of Progression.

Objectives	Chapter title	Lesson number and title
1 Mathematical processes and applications		
1.1 Representing		
Identify the mathematical features of a context or problem; try out and compare mathematical representations; select appropriate procedures and tools, including ICT.	Number and Algebra 1 Number 2 Algebra 3 Algebra 5 Solving problems Geometry and Measures 4	1.7 Solving problems FM Blackpool Tower FM Going on holiday FM M25 FM Timetable 14.2 Using algebra, graphs and diagrams to solve problems FM Photographs
1.2 Analysing – use reasoning		
Visualise and manipulate dynamic images; conjecture and generalise; move between the general and the particular to test the logic of an argument; identify exceptional cases or counter-examples; make connections with related contexts.	Solving problems	14.3 Logic and proof
1.3 Analysing – use procedures		
Within the appropriate range and content: make accurate mathematical diagrams, graphs and constructions on paper and on screen; calculate accurately, selecting mental methods or calculating devices as appropriate; manipulate numbers, algebraic expressions and equations, and apply routine algorithms; use accurate notation, including correct syntax when using ICT; record methods, solutions and conclusions; estimate, approximate and check working.	Solving problems	14.1 Number and measures
1.4 Interpreting and evaluating		
Use logical argument to interpret the mathematics in a given context or to establish the truth of a statement; give accurate solutions appropriate to the context or problem; evaluate the efficiency of alternative strategies and approaches.	Algebra 2 Number 4 Solving problems	FM M25 FM Shopping for bargains 14.3 Logic and proof
1.5 Communicating and reflecting		
Refine own findings and approaches on the basis of discussions with others; recognise efficiency in an approach; relate the current problem and structure to previous situations.	Number 2 Algebra 5	4.1 Fractions and decimals 13.1 Expand and simplify
2 Number		
2.1 Place value, ordering and rounding		
Read and write positive integer powers of 10; multiply and divide integers and decimals by 0.1, 0.01.	Number 3	8.1 Powers of 10
Order decimals.	Number 2	4.1 Fractions and decimals
Round positive numbers to any given power of 10; round decimals to the nearest whole number or to one or two decimal places.	Number 3	8.1 Powers of 10 8.2 Large numbers
2.2 Integers, powers and roots		
Add, subtract, multiply and divide integers.	Number and Algebra 1	1.1 Multiplying and dividing negative numbers
Use multiples, factors, common factors, highest common factors, lowest common multiples and primes; find the prime factor decomposition of a number, for example, $8000 = 2^6 \times 5^3$.	Number and Algebra 1	1.2 HCF and LCM 1.4 Prime factors

Objectives	Chapter title	Lesson number and title
Use squares, positive and negative square roots, cubes and cube roots, and index notation for small positive integer powers.	Number and Algebra 1	1.3 Powers and roots
2.3 Fractions, decimals, percentages, ratio and proportion.		
Recognise that a recurring decimal is a fraction; use division to convert a fraction to a decimal; order fractions by writing them with a common denominator or by converting them to decimals.	Number 2	4.1 Fractions and decimals
Add and subtract fractions by writing them with a common denominator; calculate fractions of quantities (fraction answers); multiply and divide an integer by a fraction.	Number 2 Number 4	4.2 Adding and subtracting fractions 4.3 Multiplying and dividing fractions 12.2 Adding and subtracting fractions
Interpret percentage as the operator 'so many hundredths of' and express one given number as a percentage of another; calculate percentages and find the outcome of a given percentage increase or decrease.	Number 2 Number 3 Geometry and Measures 4	4.4 Percentages 4.5 Percentage increase and decrease FM Going on holiday FM Taxes FM Photographs
Use the equivalence of fractions, decimals and percentages to compare proportions.	Number 2 Number 4	4.5 Percentage increase and decrease 12.1 Fractions
Apply understanding of the relationship between ratio and proportion; simplify ratios, including those expressed in different units, recognising links with fraction notation; divide a quantity into two or more parts in a given ratio; use the unitary method to solve simple problems involving ratio and direct proportion.	Geometry and Measures 3 Solving Problems Geometry and Measures 4	9.5 Shape and ratio 14.4 Proportion 14.5 Ratio FM Photographs
2.4 Number operations		
Understand and use the rules of arithmetic and inverse operations in the context of integers and fractions.	Number 4	12.2 Adding and subtracting fractions
Use the order of operations, including brackets, with more complex calculations.	Number 4	12.3 Order of operations
2.5 Mental calculation methods		
Recall equivalent fractions, decimals and percentages; use known facts to derive unknown facts, including products involving numbers such as 0.7 and 6, and 0.03 and 8.	Number 2	4.6 Real-life problems
Strengthen and extend mental methods of calculation, working with decimals, fractions, percentages, squares and square roots, and cubes and cube roots; solve problems mentally.	Number 3	8.1 Powers of 10
Make and justify estimates and approximations of calculations.	Number 3	8.3 Estimations
2.6 Written calculation methods		
Use efficient written methods to add and subtract integers and decimals of any size, including numbers with differing numbers of decimal places.	Number 3	8.4 Adding and subtracting decimals
Use efficient written methods for multiplication and division of integers and decimals, including by decimals such as 0.6 or 0.06; understand where to position the decimal point by considering equivalent calculations.	Number 3 Number 4	8.6 Multiplying and dividing decimals 12.4 Multiplying decimals 12.5 Dividing decimals
2.7 Calculator methods		
Carry out more difficult calculations effectively and efficiently using the function keys for sign change, powers, roots and fractions; use brackets and the memory.	Number 2 Number 3	FM Going on holiday 8.5 Efficient calculations
Enter numbers and interpret the display in different contexts (extend to negative numbers, fractions, time).	Solving Problems	14.4 Proportion
2.8 Checking results		
Select from a range of checking methods, including estimating in context and using inverse operations.	Number 3	8.3 Estimations

Objectives	Chapter title	Lesson number and title
3 Algebra		
3.1 Equations, formulae, expressions and identities		
Recognise that letter symbols play different roles in equations, formulae and functions; know the meanings of the words *formula* and *function*.	Algebra 2	5.1 Algebraic shorthand
Understand that algebraic operations, including the use of brackets, follow the rules of arithmetic; use index notation for small positive integer powers.	Algebra 2	5.3 Expanding brackets 5.4 Using algebra with shapes 5.5 Use of index notation with algebra
Simplify or transform linear expressions by collecting like terms; multiply a single term over a bracket.	Algebra 2 Algebra 5	5.2 Like terms 5.3 Expanding brackets 5.4 Using algebra with shapes 13.1 Expand and simplify 13.6 Change of subject
Construct and solve linear equations with integer coefficients (unknown on either or both sides, without and with brackets) using appropriate methods (for example, inverse operations, transforming both sides in same way).	Algebra 4 Algebra 5	10.1 Solving equations 10.2 Equations involving negative numbers 10.3 Equations with unknowns on both sides 13.2 Solving equations 13.3 Constructing equations to solve
Use graphs and set up equations to solve simple problems involving direct proportion.	Solving Problems	14.2 Using algebra, graphs and diagrams to solve problems
Use formulae from mathematics and other subjects; substitute integers into simple formulae, including examples that lead to an equation to solve; substitute positive integers into expressions involving small powers, for example, $3x^2 + 4$ or $2x^3$; derive simple formulae.	Algebra 4 Geometry and Measures 4	10.4 Substituting into expressions 10.5 Substituting into formulae 10.6 Creating your own expressions and formulae 15.6 Circumference and area of a circle
3.2 Sequences, functions and graphs		
Generate terms of a linear sequence using term-to-term and position-to-term rules, on paper and using a spreadsheet or graphics calculator.	Number and Algebra 1	1.5 Sequences 1
Use linear expressions to describe the nth term of a simple arithmetic sequence, justifying its form by referring to the activity or practical context from which it was generated.	Number and Algebra 1	1.6 Sequences 2
Express simple functions algebraically and represent them in mappings or on a spreadsheet.	Algebra 3	7.1 Linear functions 7.2 Finding a function from its inputs and outputs
Generate points in all four quadrants and plot the graphs of linear functions, where y is given explicitly in terms of x, on paper and using ICT; recognise that equations of the form $y = mx + c$ correspond to straight-line graphs.	Algebra 3 Algebra 5	7.3 Graphs from functions 7.4 Gradient of a straight line (steepness) 13.4 Problems with graphs
Construct linear functions arising from real-life problems and plot their corresponding graphs; discuss and interpret graphs arising from real situations, for example, distance–time graphs.	Algebra 3 Algebra 5	7.5 Real-life graphs 13.5 Real-life graphs
4 Geometry and measures		
4.1 Geometrical reasoning		
Identify alternate angles and corresponding angles; understand a proof that: the angle sum of a triangle is 180° and of a quadrilateral is 360°; the exterior angle of a triangle is equal to the sum of the two interior opposite angles.	Geometry and Measures 1	2.1 Alternate and corresponding angles 2.2 Angles in triangles and quadrilaterals 2.3 Geometric proof
Solve geometrical problems using side and angle properties of equilateral, isosceles and right-angled triangles and special quadrilaterals, explaining reasoning with diagrams and text; classify quadrilaterals by their geometrical properties.	Geometry and Measures 1	2.4 The geometric properties of quadrilaterals
Know that if two 2-D shapes are congruent, corresponding sides and angles are equal.	Geometry and Measures 3	9.1 Congruent shapes
Visualise 3-D shapes from their nets; use geometric properties of cuboids and shapes made from cuboids; use simple plans and elevations.	Geometry and Measures 4	15.1 & 15.2 Plans and elevations
4.2 Transformations and coordinates		
Identify all the symmetries of 2-D shapes.	Geometry and Measures 3	9.1 Congruent shapes
Transform 2-D shapes by rotation, reflection and translation, on paper and using ICT.	Geometry and Measures 3	9.2 Combinations of transformations

Objectives	Chapter title	Lesson number and title
Try out mathematical representations of simple combinations of these transformations.	Geometry and Measures 3	9.2 Combinations of transformations
Understand and use the language and notation associated with enlargement; enlarge 2-D shapes, given a centre of enlargement and a positive integer scale factor; explore enlargement using ICT.	Geometry and Measures 3 Geometry and Measures 4	9.3 & 9.4 Enlargements FM Photographs
Make scale drawings.	Geometry and Measures 4	15.3 Scale drawings
Find the midpoint of the line segment AB, given the coordinates of points A and B.	Geometry and Measures 4	15.4 Finding the mid-point of a line segment

4.3 Construction and loci

Objectives	Chapter title	Lesson number and title
Use straight edge and compasses to construct: the midpoint and perpendicular bisector of a line segment; the bisector of an angle; the perpendicular from a point to a line; the perpendicular from a point on a line; a triangle, given three sides (SSS).	Geometry and Measures 1 Geometry and Measures 4	2.5 Constructions 15.5 To construct a triangle given three sides
Use ICT to explore these constructions.	Geometry and Measures 4	15.5 To construct a triangle given three sides
Find simple loci, both by reasoning and by using ICT, to produce shapes and paths, for example, an equilateral triangle.		

4.4 Measures and mensuration

Objectives	Chapter title	Lesson number and title
Choose and use units of measurement to measure, estimate, calculate and solve problems in a range of contexts; know rough metric equivalents of imperial measures in common use, such as miles, pounds (lb) and pints.	Number 2 Geometry and Measures 2 Geometry and Measures 4	FM Going on holiday 6.1 Area of a triangle 6.2 Area of a parallelogram 6.3 Area of a trapezium 6.4 Volume of a cuboid 6.5 Imperial units FM Photographs
Use bearings to specify direction.	Geometry and Measures 4	15.7 Bearings
Derive and use formulae for the area of a triangle, parallelogram and trapezium; calculate areas of compound shapes.	Geometry and measures 2 Geometry and Measures 4	6.1 Area of a triangle 6.2 Area of a parallelogram 6.3 Area of a trapezium FM Photographs
Know and use the formula for the volume of a cuboid; calculate volumes and surface areas of cuboids and shapes made from cuboids.	Geometry and Measures 2 Geometry and Measures 4	6.4 Volume of a cuboid 15.8 A cube investigation

5 Statistics

5.1 Specifying a problem, planning and collecting data

Objectives	Chapter title	Lesson number and title
Discuss a problem that can be addressed by statistical methods and identify related questions to explore.	Statistics 3	16.1 Frequency tables
Decide which data to collect to answer a question, and the degree of accuracy needed; identify possible sources; consider appropriate sample size.	Statistics 3	16.1 Frequency tables
Plan how to collect the data; construct frequency tables with equal class intervals for gathering continuous data and two-way tables for recording discrete data.	Statistics 3	16.1 Frequency tables
Collect data using a suitable method (for example, observation, controlled experiment, data logging using ICT).	Statistics 1 Statistics 3	3.5 Experimental probability 16.1 Frequency tables

5.2 Processing and representing data

Objectives	Chapter title	Lesson number and title
Calculate statistics for sets of discrete and continuous data, including with a calculator and spreadsheet; recognise when it is appropriate to use the range, mean, median and mode and, for grouped data, the modal class.	Statistics 2 Statistics 3	11.1 Stem-and-leaf diagrams FM Football attendances 16.2 Assumed mean and working with statistics 16.5 Which average to use? FM Questionnaire
Construct graphical representations, on paper and using ICT, and identify which are most useful in the context of the problem. Include: pie charts for categorical data; bar charts and frequency; diagrams for discrete and continuous data; simple line graphs for time series; simple scatter graphs; stem-and-leaf diagrams.	Statistics 2 Statistics 3	11.1 Stem-and-leaf diagrams 11.3 More about pie charts 11.4 Scatter graphs 11.5 More about scatter graphs 16.3 Drawing frequency diagrams

Objectives	Chapter title	Lesson number and title
5.3 Interpreting and discussing results		
Interpret tables, graphs and diagrams for discrete and continuous data, relating summary statistics and findings to the questions being explored.	Number 2 Statistics 2 Statistics 3 Geometry and Measures 4	FM Going on holiday 11.2 Pie charts 11.4 Scatter graphs 11.5 More about scatter graphs FM Photographs 16.4 Comparing data
Compare two distributions using the range and one or more of the mode, median and mean.	Statistics 3	16.4 Comparing data
Write about and discuss the results of a statistical enquiry using ICT as appropriate; justify the methods used.	Statistics 3	16.6 Experimental and theoretical probability
5.4 Probability		
Interpret the results of an experiment using the language of probability; appreciate that random processes are unpredictable.	Statistics 1 Statistics 3	3.1 Probability FM Fun in the fairground FM Questionnaire
Know that if the probability of an event occurring is p, then the probability of it not occurring is $1 - p$; use diagrams and tables to record in a systematic way all possible mutually exclusive outcomes for single events and for two successive events.	Statistics 1	3.2 Probability scales 3.3 Mutually exclusive events 3.4 Calculating probabilities
Compare estimated experimental probabilities with theoretical probabilities, recognising that: if an experiment is repeated the outcome may, and usually will, be different; increasing the number of times an experiment is repeated generally leads to better estimates of probability.	Statistics 1 Statistics 3	3.5 Experimental probability FM Fun in the fairground 16.6 Experimental and theoretical probability

New Maths Frameworking Year 8
Lesson Plans

For use with New Maths Frameworking Year 8 Pupil Book 2

Number and Algebra **1**

Overview

Context

This chapter recalls addition and subtraction of negative numbers and moves on to multiplying and dividing negative numbers. Highest Common Factor (HCF) and Lowest Common Multiple (LCM) are introduced. The chapter then moves on to powers and roots, with or without a calculator. The pupil is then introduced to prime factors, and their relationship with HCF and LCM is briefly explored. Previous work on sequences is revisited and extended to include multiplicative sequences. Finally, two investigations encourage thinking skills and the use of algebra to represent general solutions to a practical problem.

National Curriculum references

Framework objectives

1.1   Add, subtract, multiply and divide integers.

1.2   Use multiples, factors, common factors, highest common factors, lowest common multiples and primes.

1.3   Use squares, positive and negative square roots, cubes and cube roots, and index notation for small positive integer powers.

1.4   Find the prime factor decomposition of a number, for example, $8000 = 2^6 \times 5^3$.

1.5   Generate terms of a linear sequence using term-to-term and position-to-term rules.

1.6   Use linear expressions to describe the nth term of a simple arithmetic sequence, justifying its form by referring to the activity or practical context from which it was generated.

1.7   Identify the mathematical features of a context or problem; try out and compare mathematical representations; select appropriate procedures and tools, including ICT.

    Identify the mathematical features of a context or problem; try out and compare mathematical representations; select appropriate procedures and tools, including ICT.

Key concepts

Applications and implications of mathematics

- Understand the relationships between numbers, their factors and multiples and other types of numbers such as prime numbers
- Use algebra to represent general solutions of problems

Key processes

Representing

- Breaking numbers down into prime factors to investigate their structure and connections with other numbers
- Simplifying the situation or problem in order to represent it mathematically, using the appropriate variables, symbols, diagrams and models

Analysing

- Breaking down a number into prime factors
- Finding the HCF and LCM of pairs of numbers
- Using algebra and sequences to investigate problems

Communicating and reflecting

- Showing results in a variety of forms and showing the connection between these
- Checking that results fit the initial data

Route mapping

Exercise	Levels			
	4	5	6	7
1A		1–2	3–11	
1B	1–3	4–5	6–7	
1C		1–8	9–10	
1D			1–8	
1E		1–8		
1F		1–2	3–9	10
1G			1–3	

Framework objectives – Multiplying and dividing negative numbers
Add, subtract, multiply and divide integers.

Oral and mental starter

● Use a number line drawn on the board or a 'counting stick' with 10 divisions marked on it. State that the right end is the number 0.

0

● Point out that as the students look at the line, the values to the left of zero are negative.
● Give a value to each segment, say –3 and as a group or with an individual pupil count down the line in steps of –3 from zero. Pupils can have the positions pointed out to them on the line until the end is reached, then continue without prompts.
● Repeat with other values for the segments, such as –4, –2, –1.5, etc.
● Now give a value to each segment, say –6 and point at a position on the stick, say, the fourth division asking what value it represents.
● Repeat with other values for each segment and different positions on the stick.
● Explain that there is an easy way of finding the value at any position on the stick without counting down in steps. This leads on to the main lesson activity.

Main lesson activity

● Draw a number line on the board and mark it from –10 to +10.
● First of all, recall rules for dealing with directed number problems using the number line. It is important to recall that two signs together can be rewritten as one sign, that is + + is +, + – is –, – + is – and – – is +. Another way of emphasising this is to say that if the signs are the same, then the overall sign is plus and if they are different it is minus.
● Demonstrate this by using the number line to work out $7 + -3$ (= +4) and $-4 - -5$ (= +1).
● Now ask for the answer to $-2 + -2 + -2 + -2 + -2$ (= –10). Ask if there is another way to write this, that is 5×-2 (recall that multiplication is repeated addition).
● Repeat with other examples, such as $- -4 - -4 - -4 = -3 \times -4$ (= +12).
● Ask pupils if they can see a quick way to work out products such as $-2 \times +3$ or -5×-4 or $+7 \times +3$.
● They should come up with the rule that it is the product of the numbers combined with the rules we have met earlier about combining signs.
● The $- \times - = +$ can cause problems. Ask pupils to complete this pattern:
$$+2 \times -3 = -6$$
$$+1 \times -3 = -3$$
$$0 \times \ldots = \ldots$$
$$-1 \times \ldots = \ldots \text{ , and so on.}$$
● This can then be linked to division. For example, if $-3 \times +6 = -18$, then $-18 \div -3 = +6$, if $+5 \times -3 = -15$, then $-15 \div +5 = -3$.
● Ask pupils to explain a quick way of doing these. As for multiplication, the numbers are divided as normal and the sign of the final answer depends on the combination of signs in the original division problem.

● **The class can now do Exercise 1A from Pupil Book 2.**

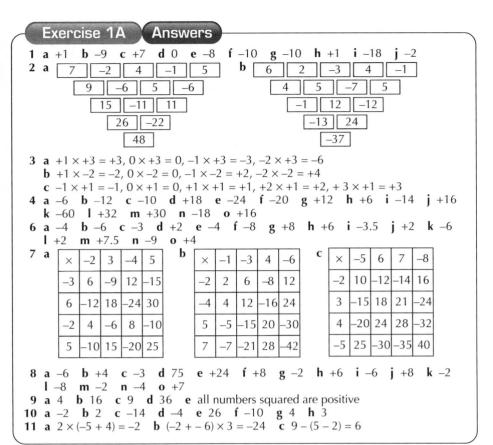

Exercise 1A **Answers**

1 a +1 **b** –9 **c** +7 **d** 0 **e** –8 **f** –10 **g** –10 **h** +1 **i** –18 **j** –2

2 a

7		–2		4		–1		5
9		–6		5		–6
15		–11		11
26		–22
48

b

6		2		–3		4		–1
4		5		–7		5
–1		12		–12
–13		24
–37

3 a +1 × +3 = +3, 0 × +3 = 0, –1 × +3 = –3, –2 × +3 = –6
b +1 × –2 = –2, 0 × –2 = 0, –1 × –2 = +2, –2 × –2 = +4
c –1 × +1 = –1, 0 × +1 = 0, +1 × +1 = +1, +2 × +1 = +2, +3 × +1 = +3

4 a –6 **b** –12 **c** –10 **d** +18 **e** –24 **f** –20 **g** +12 **h** +6 **i** –14 **j** +16
k –60 **l** +32 **m** +30 **n** –18 **o** +16

6 a –4 **b** –6 **c** –3 **d** +2 **e** –4 **f** –8 **g** +8 **h** +6 **i** –3.5 **j** +2 **k** –6
l +2 **m** +7.5 **n** –9 **o** +4

7 a

×	–2	3	–4	5
–3	6	–9	12	–15
6	–12	18	–24	30
–2	4	–6	8	–10
5	–10	15	–20	25

b

×	–1	–3	4	–6
–2	2	6	–8	12
–4	4	12	–16	24
5	–5	–15	20	–30
7	–7	–21	28	–42

c

×	–5	6	7	–8
–2	10	–12	–14	16
3	–15	18	21	–24
4	–20	24	28	–32
–5	25	–30	–35	40

8 a –6 **b** +4 **c** –3 **d** 75 **e** +24 **f** +8 **g** –2 **h** +6 **i** –6 **j** +8 **k** –2
l –8 **m** –2 **n** –4 **o** +7

9 a 4 **b** 16 **c** 9 **d** 36 **e** all numbers squared are positive

10 a –2 **b** 2 **c** –14 **d** –4 **e** 26 **f** –10 **g** 4 **h** 3

11 a 2 × (–5 + 4) = –2 **b** (–2 + – 6) × 3 = –24 **c** 9 – (5 – 2) = 6

Extension **Answers**

3c; 9, –14, 11; 4, 2, 0; –7, 18, –5; –6, –1, –8; –7, –5, –3; –2, –9, –4

Plenary

● Ask some mental questions, such as:
　　How many negative fours make negative sixteen?
　　What is: 6 – 9; –5 – +3; –4 – 3; –2 × +7; –32 ÷ –8; –3 squared?
● Encourage pupils to 'say the problem to themselves', for example, for
+7 – –2, say 'plus seven minus minus two'.
● Make sure the confusion about 'two negatives make a positive' is
overcome. For example, pupils will often say that '–6 – 7 = +13'.

Key words

- positive
- negative
- multiply
- divide
- inverse operation

6

Homework

1 Work out the answer to each of these:

　a 5 × –4 **b** –2 × 4 **c** –6 × 3 **d** –3 × –3 **e** –2 × 9 **f** 5 × –11 **g** 9 × 2 **h** –12 × –3
　i –5 × –2 × –2 **j** –3 × 5 × –2 **k** 15 ÷ –5 **l** –24 ÷ 3 **m** –8 ÷ 2 **n** –9 ÷ –3 **o** –40 ÷ 5
　p 50 ÷ –10 **q** 16 ÷ 4 **r** –9 ÷ –2 **s** –6 × –4 ÷ –3 **t** –2 × 8 ÷ –4

2 Find the missing number:

　a 5 × –3 = ☐ **b** –2 × ☐ = –10 **c** 3 × ☐ = –12 **d** 6 × –4 ÷ ☐ = –12 **e** –10 × ☐ ÷ –2 = –10
　f ☐ × –3 ÷ –2 = 15

Homework Answers

1 a –20 **b** –8 **c** –18 **d** 9 **e** –18 **f** –55 **g** 18 **h** 36 **i** –20 **j** 30 **k** –3 **l** –8 **m** –4 **n** 3
　o –8 **p** –5 **q** 4 **r** 4.5 **s** –8 **t** 4
2 a –15 **b** 5 **c** –4 **d** 2 **e** –2 **f** 10

LESSON 1.2

Framework objectives – HCF and LCM

Use multiples, factors, common factors, highest common factors, lowest common multiples and primes.

Oral and mental starter

- Pupils should use a number fan or a white board to write down answers.
- They should not hold this up until requested to avoid weaker pupils copying.
- Ask for an example of: an even number; a multiple of 6; a factor of 12; a prime number; a square number; a number that is a multiple of 3 and 4 at the same time; a triangle number; etc.
- Go around the class each time, checking each pupil's answer.
- If necessary, discuss and define what was required.
- Particularly emphasise factors and multiples, as these will be used in the main lesson activity.

Main lesson activity

- Keeping the fans or cards, ask pupils if they can write down a number that is a multiple of 3 and 4 (this was asked in the oral and mental starter).
- Write on the board all the answers shown. Ask for a few more suggestions if many answers are the same.
- Hopefully, 12 have will been written up and the pupils should be asked what is special about this. Emphasise that it is the lowest common multiple or LCM.
- Repeat for a common multiple of 4 and 5.
- Now ask for the lowest common multiple of 3 and 5.
- Now ask for the lowest common multiple of 4 and 6.
- Many pupils will answer 24, as they will have spotted that previous answers were the product of the two numbers in question.
- Make sure that they understand that in fact 12 is the LCM of 4 and 6.
- If pupils are having trouble at this stage, then they should be encouraged to write out the multiples for the two numbers and look for the first common value in each list. For example, for the LCM of 4 and 5:

  | 4 | 8 | 12 | 16 | ⑳ | 24 | 28 | ... |
  | 5 | 10 | 15 | ⑳ | 25 | 30 | 35 | ... |

- Now ask pupils to show a number that is a factor of 12 and a factor of 18.
- Once again, write all the numbers shown onto the board. It is likely that all possibilities will be shown (1, 2, 3, 6, plus a few that are incorrect).
- Make sure pupils understand the idea, and if any factors are missing ask what is needed to complete the set.
- Ask: 'What is special about 6?' Emphasise that it is the highest common factor or HCF.
- Repeat for the common factors of 30 and 50.
- Now ask for the highest common factor of 16 and 20.
- Repeat for 15 and 30. (5 is a likely answer here – make sure that pupils understand the HCF is 15)
- Repeat for 7 and 9.
- Ask why the answer is 1.

● Prime numbers should have been defined in the oral and mental starter.
  If not, define prime numbers.

● **The class can now do Exercise 1B from Pupil Book 2.**

Exercise 1B   Answers

1 a 10, 4, 18, 8, 72, 100   **b** 18, 69, 81, 33, 72   **c** 10, 65, 100   **d** 18, 81, 72
2 a 4, 8, 12, 16, 20, 24, 28, 32, 36, 40   **b** 5, 10, 15, 20, 25, 30, 35, 40, 45, 50
  c 8, 16, 24, 32, 40, 48, 56, 64, 72, 80   **d** 15, 30, 45, 60, 75, 90, 105, 120, 135, 150
  e 20, 40, 60, 80, 100, 120, 140, 160, 180, 200
3 a 1, 3, 5, 15   **b** 1, 2, 4, 5, 10, 20   **c** 1, 2, 4, 8, 16, 32   **d** 1, 5, 7, 35
  e 1, 2, 3, 4, 5, 6, 10, 12, 15, 20, 30, 60
4 a 40   **b** 20   **c** 60   **d** 120
5 a 5   **b** 15   **c** 20   **d** 4
6 a 45   **b** 25   **c** 24   **d** 12   **e** 24   **f** 60   **g** 63   **h** 77
7 a 3   **b** 4   **c** 2   **d** 4   **e** 2   **f** 2   **g** 9   **h** 1

Extension   Answers

1 a 6 and 8   **b** 6 and 9   **c** 15 and 20
2 a i 1 and 35   **ii** 1 and 12   **iii** 1 and 22   **b** $x \times y$
3 a i 5 and 10   **ii** 3 and 18   **iii** 4 and 20   **b** y

Plenary

● Write numbers on the board (or have prepared cards) such as
    1, 2, 3, 4, 6, 8, 10, 12, 15, 20, 24, 25, 30, 35, 40, 48.
● Ask the pupils to pick out one card and then:
      if a low-value card is chosen, ask for the first 10 multiples;
      if a high-value card is chosen, ask for all the factors.
● Ask pupils to pick out two cards. Ask for the LCM if both cards are low-
  value, ask for the HCF if both are high-value, or ask for the product (or
  quotient and remainder) if one is high and one low.
● Alternatively, ask for a card that is the lowest common multiple of 5 and
  6 or the highest common factor of 15 and 20, etc.

Key words

☐ **multiple**
☐ **factor**
☐ **prime**
☐ **highest common factor (HCF)**
☐ **lowest common multiple (LCM)**

Homework

1 Find the LCM of:

  a 6 and 10   **b** 6 and 21   **c** 4 and 10   **d** 6 and 27   **e** 8 and 18
  f 12 and 27   **g** 15 and 25   **h** 9 and 11

2 Find the HCF of:

  a 16 and 20   **b** 15 and 20   **c** 8 and 12   **d** 6 and 10   **e** 3 and 18
  f 8 and 20   **g** 15 and 25   **h** 9 and 11

3 a Two numbers have an LCM of 30 and an HCF of 3. What are they?
  b Two numbers have an LCM of 12 and an HCF of 2. What are they?

6

7

Homework Answers

1 a 30   **b** 42   **c** 20   **d** 54   **e** 72   **f** 108   **g** 75   **h** 99
2 a 4   **b** 5   **c** 4   **d** 2   **e** 3   **f** 4   **g** 5   **h** 1
3 a 6 and 15   **b** 4 and 6

LESSON

1.3

Framework objectives – Powers and roots

Use squares, positive and negative square roots, cubes and cube roots, and index notation for small positive integer powers.

Oral and mental starter

- Use a target board, such as the one shown.
- Assign values to a and b. These need to be squares, say $a = 1$ and $b = 4$
- Randomly select pupils and ask them to evaluate the expressions.
- Repeat with other values for a and b, say $a = 4$ and $b = 9$.

a^2	$\sqrt{a}$	$2b^2$	$\sqrt{b}$
$3\sqrt{b}$	$3a^2$	$\frac{\sqrt{a}}{2}$	$2a^2$
b^2	$3\sqrt{b}$	$\frac{a^2}{2}$	$2\sqrt{a}$
$\frac{\sqrt{b}}{2}$	$\frac{b^2}{2}$	$2\sqrt{b}$	$3b^2$

Main lesson activity

- Following on from the oral and mental starter, one of the problems asked earlier was 'If $a^2 = 9$, what is a?'
- It is likely that the pupils will only have identified 3. If so, ask if there is another solution. Obtain the answer –3.
- Another problem asked earlier was 'What is $\sqrt{9}$?' Is there another answer to this? Again, it is unlikely that –3 will have been given earlier.
- Emphasise that a square root is generally accepted as the positive square root, but that the solution to the equation $a^2 = 9$ can be positive or negative. This is a subtle point that is difficult to explain.
- Ask pupils what we mean by a^3.
- If $a = 2$, what is a^3? If $a = 3$, what is a^3? If $a = 4$, what is a^3? If $a = 5$, what is a^3?
- Pupils should have the mental skill to work out up to 5^3, but may find 6^3 difficult. If possible, continue to obtain cubes or write out the sequence 1, 8, 27, 64, 125, 216, 343, 512, 729, 1000, etc.
- If $a^3 = 729$, what is a? It is likely that answers of –9 and 9 will be given. Demonstrate that $-9 \times -9 \times -9 = -729$. Hence only one answer is possible for $a^3 = 729$.
- Introduce the notation of cube root, $\sqrt[3]{729} = 9$.
- What is $\sqrt[3]{64}$? What is $\sqrt[3]{125}$?
- Ask the students what 2^4 means. What is the value of 2^4? (= 16)
- What about 3^5? (Calculator may be needed here, = 243.)

- **The class can now do Exercise 1C from Pupil Book 2.**

Exercise 1C Answers

1 Area, 1, 4, 9, 16, 25, 36, 49, 64, 81, 100; cubes, 1, 8, 27, 64, 125, 216, 343, 512, 729, 1000
2 **a** 2 **b** 8 **c** 9 **d** 10 **e** 5 **f** 3 **g** 5 **h** 10 **i** 8 **j** 9
3 **a** ±6 **b** ±11 **c** ±12 **d** ±1.5 **e** ±14 **f** ±2.4 **g** ±1.6 **h** ±60
4 **a** 169 **b** 2197 **c** 225 **d** 3375 **e** 441 **f** 9261 **g** 1.96 **h** 5.832
   i 12.167 **j** 20.25 **k** 1728 **l** 3.375
5 **a** 16 **b** 243 **c** 81 **d** 32 **e** 256 **f** 625 **g** 2401 **h** 512 **i** 128 **j** 512
   k 1024 **l** 59 049
6 **a** 400 **b** 27 000 **c** 125 000 **d** 3 200 000 **e** 4900 **f** 8 000 000
7 10^4, 10^5, 10^6, 10^7
8 **a** 1 **b** 1 **c** 1 **d** 1 **e** 1 **f** 1
9 **a** 1 **b** –1 **c** 1 **d** –1 **e** 1 **f i** –1 **ii** 1
10 **a** $729 = 27^2$ **b** $16^3 = 4096 = 64^2$ (cubes of square numbers)

Extension Answers

204 squares = 1 + 4 + 9 + 16 + 25 + 36 + 49 + 64

Plenary

Key words
☐ square
☐ square root
☐ cube
☐ cube root
☐ power
☐ index

Quick factual recall test of squares, cubes, etc.

1 What is the cube root of 64?
2 What is 1000 as a power of 10?
3 What is 3 cubed?
4 What is the square root of 196?
5 What is the cube root of 1000?
6 What is 5 cubed?
7 What is 1 million as a power of 10?
8 What is –2 squared?
9 If x squared equals x cubed, what is x?
10 What are the values of x if $x^2 = 25$?

Answers **1** 4 **2** 10^3 **3** 27 **4** 14 **5** 10 **6** 125 **7** 10^6 **8** 4 **9** 1 (or 0) **10** ±5

Homework

1 Without using a calculator, write down the following:
   a $\sqrt{1}$ **b** $\sqrt{64}$ **c** $\sqrt[3]{8}$ **d** $\sqrt[3]{27}$ **e** $\sqrt[3]{64}$
2 Use a calculator to find the value of:
   a 17^2 **b** 17^3 **c** 25^3 **d** 6^4 **e** 3^7 **f** 8^5
3 Given that $0.1^2 = 0.01$, $0.1^3 = 0.001$, $0.1^4 = 0.0001$, write down the answers to **a** 0.1^5 **b** 0.1^8

Homework Answers

1 **a** 1 **b** 8 **c** 2 **d** 3 **e** 4
2 **a** 289 **b** 4913 **c** 15 625 **d** 1296 **e** 2187 **f** 32 768
3 **a** 0.000 01 **b** 0.000 000 01

LESSON

1.4

Framework objectives – Prime factors
Find the prime factor decomposition of a number, for example, $8000 = 2^6 \times 5^3$.

Oral and mental starter

- Using a target board like the one shown, point at a number and ask a pupil picked at random to give the factors of the number.
- Recall the rule for factors – that is, they come in pairs, except for square numbers.
- 1 and the number itself are always factors.
- Prime numbers only have two factors.

25	36	70	64	75
81	18	50	20	45
30	63	80	92	16
32	15	10	28	60

Main lesson activity

- Ask for the answer to $2 \times 3 \times 3$ (= 18).
- What about $2 \times 2 \times 5$ (= 20), $3 \times 5 \times 5$ (= 75), $3 \times 3 \times 7$ (= 63)?
- What can you say about the numbers in the multiplication? Establish that they are all prime.
- This is the prime factor form of a number (the number broken down into a product of primes).
- How can we find this if we start with the number, 30, say?
- Explain the tree method: split 30 into a product such as 2×15, then continue splitting any number in the product that is not a prime.
- This can easily be seen in the form of a 'tree'.
  Example: Find the prime factors of 120.

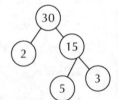

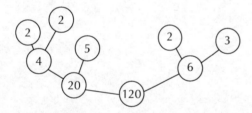

- An alternative is the division method where the number is repeatedly divided by any prime that will go into it exactly.
- Demonstrate this with 50. Continue to divide by primes until the answer is 1.

$$
\begin{array}{r|r}
2 & 50 \\
5 & 25 \\
5 & 5 \\
\hline
 & 1
\end{array}
$$

- Repeat with 96 ($2 \times 2 \times 2 \times 2 \times 2 \times 3$), 60 ($2 \times 2 \times 3 \times 5$).
- At this stage, it may be useful to introduce the index notation, that is
  $96 = 2^5 \times 3$, $60 = 2^2 \times 3 \times 5$.

- **The class can now do Exercise 1D from Pupil Book 2.**

Exercise 1D Answers

1 **a** 12 **b** 90 **c** 36 **d** 270 **e** 150
2 **a** 2^3 **b** 2×5 **c** 2^4 **d** $2^2 \times 5$ **e** $2^2 \times 7$ **f** 2×17 **g** 5×7 **h** $2^2 \times 13$
　i $2^2 \times 3 \times 5$ **j** $2^2 \times 3^2 \times 5$
3 **a** $2 \times 3 \times 7$ **b** 3×5^2 **c** $2^2 \times 5 \times 7$ **d** 2×5^3 **e** $2^5 \times 3 \times 5$
4 2, 3, 2 × 2, 5, 2 × 3, 7, 2 × 2 × 2, 3 × 3, 2 × 5, 11, 2 × 2 × 3, 13, 2 × 7, 3 × 5,
　2 × 2 × 2 × 2, 17, 2 × 3 × 3, 19, 2 × 2 × 5
5 **a** 2, 3, 5, 7, 11, 13, 17, 19 **b** prime numbers
6 **a** $2^3 \times 5^2$ **b** 2×5^2 **c** $2^3 \times 5^3$ **d** $2^6 \times 5^6$
7 **a** $2 \times 5 = 10$ **b** $2 \times 3 \times 5 = 30$
8 **a** 2^5 **b** 2^6 **c** 2^7 **d** 2^{10}

Extension Answers

1 **a** HCF = 6　LCM = 360 **b** HCF = 10　LCM = 450 **c** HCF = 12　LCM = 336
2 HCF = 30　LCM = 600
3 HCF = 30　LCM = 630

Plenary

- Choose a number, say 70.
- Find the factors (1, 2, 5, 7, 10, 14, 35, 70) and the prime factors (2 × 5 × 7).
- Choose another number and repeat, say 90. The factors are 1, 2, 3, 5, 6,
  9, 10, 15, 18, 30, 45, 90, and the prime factors are $2 \times 3^2 \times 5$.
- Ask pupils if they can spot a connection. This is simply that only the
  prime numbers in the list of factors appear in the prime factors.
- Discuss how to find the HCF and LCM of 70 and 90 (HCF 10, LCM 630).
- Repeat with 48 and 64 (HCF 16, LCM 192).

Key words

- factors
- prime
- highest common factor (HCF)
- lowest common multiple (LCM)
- powers

Homework

1 These are the prime factors of some numbers. What are the numbers?

　a $2 \times 3 \times 5$　　**b** $2 \times 2 \times 3 \times 5$　　**c** $2^3 \times 5^2$

2 Using a prime factor tree, work out the prime factors of:

　a 44　　　　**b** 120　　　　**c** 250

3 Using the division method, work out the prime factors of:

　a 84　　　　**b** 125　　　　**c** 240

4 The prime factors of 100 are 2 × 2 × 5 × 5. The prime factors of 150 are 2 × 3 × 5 × 5.

　Use this information to work out the HCF and LCM of 100 and 150.

6

Homework Answers

1 **a** 30 **b** 60 **c** 200
2 **a** $2^2 \times 11$ **b** $2^3 \times 3 \times 5$ **c** 2×5^3
3 **a** $2^2 \times 3 \times 7$ **b** 5^3 **c** $2^4 \times 3 \times 5$
4 HCF 50, LCM 300

LESSON 1.5

Framework objectives – Sequences 1
Generate terms of a linear sequence using term-to-term and position-to-term rules.

Oral and mental starter

- This activity can be played as a game between teams.
- Ask a pupil to give the first two terms of a sequence. For example 1, 5.
- Ask another pupil (from the other team, if a game is played) to carry on the sequence. For example, 1, 5, 9. Then another (from the first team) to carry on the sequence. For example, 1, 5, 9, 13, …
- Once it becomes obvious that there is a well-defined sequence, stop and ask another pupil to give the first two terms of a sequence and so on. (Alternate the starting team.)
- Points are scored when:
  a Once you decide a sequence is obvious, a pupil from the starting team can describe the rule.
  b At any time pupils from the opposing team may challenge the last pupil to justify the term they have given and score a point if it is wrong or the rule is incorrect.
  c A pupil is unable to carry on the sequence (other team scores).
- Do not allow bizarre rules, although pupils should be encouraged to make sequences hard to spot. For example, 1, 5, 25 (× by 5), or 1, 2, 3, 5, 8 (Fibonacci), or 98, 97, 95, 92, … (subtract 1, 2, 3, …).
- If a score is kept, do not declare a winning team yet.

Main lesson activity

- Write some sequences on the board such as:
  a 2, 5, 8, 11, 14,   **b** 4, 8, 16, 32, 64,   **c** 100, 99, 97, 94, 90,
- Ask the pupils to describe how these are building up, that is 'What is the rule', and what the next two terms are.
- Ask pupils to make up a number sequence of their own (if number cards are available, pupils can lay out their pattern on the desk).
- Go round the class and pick some sequences to write on the board.
- When at least five sequences are collected, ask the rest of the class to say what the next two terms are and also to describe the rule for developing the sequence. Introduce the idea of a term-to-term definition.
- Repeat the exercise, but this time encourage (or write up) some 'odd rules', for example:
  1, 2, 3, 5, 7, 11, 13, 17, … (the prime numbers)
  1, 2, 4, 5, 7, 8, 10, 11, 13, … (miss out multiples of 3)
  1, 2, 5, 10, 20, 50, 100, 200, … (currency in circulation in Britain)
  O, T, T, F, F, S, S, E, … (first letters of the numbers)
- Draw this flow diagram on the board or OHP:

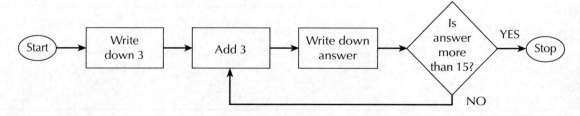

- Briefly explain the parts of the diagram [start/stop boxes (oval), action boxes (rectangular), decision boxes (diamonds)].
- Work through the diagram to give:
  - 3, 6, 9, 12, 15, 18, the multiples of 3 up to 18.

- **The class can now do Exercise 1E from Pupil Book 2.**

Exercise 1E   Answers

1 **a** 3, 8, 13, 18, 23, 28, 33, 38, 43   **b** 1, 4, 9, 16, 25, 36, 49, 64, 81, 100, 121
   c 10, 100, 1000, 10 000, 100 000, 1 000 000, 10 000 000
2 square numbers
3 powers of 10
4 **a** goes up by 3   **b** multiply by 4   **c** increases by 3, 4, 5, 6, 7, ...
   d goes up by 3, 5, 7, 9, ...
6 **a** increases 1, 2, 3, 4, 5, ... 61, 68   **b** goes down 1, 2, 3, 4, ... 69, 62
   c increases 2, 4, 6, 8, 10, ... 43, 57   **d** increases 4, 6, 8, 10, 12, ... 56, 72
7 **a** 1, 3, 9, 27, 81, 243   **b** 2, 4, 8, 16, 32, 64   **c** 1, −1, 1, −1, 1, −1
   d 1, $\frac{1}{2}$, $\frac{1}{4}$, $\frac{1}{8}$, $\frac{1}{16}$, $\frac{1}{32}$,   **e** 2, 0.8, 0.32, 0.128, 0.0512, 0.02048
   f 1, 0.3, 0.09, 0.027, 0.0081, 0.002 43
8 **a ii** 25, 36, 49, 64   **b ii** 15, 21, 28, 36   **c ii** 16, 32, 64, 128
   d ii 30, 42, 56, 72

Extension   Answers

1.66, 1.6, 1.625, 1.615, 1.619; The sequence is heading towards 1.61803. (This is known as the 'Golden ratio'.)

Plenary

- Repeat the introductory activity, but this time *you* start the sequences off and use the same two starting numbers until no more sequences can be suggested. For example:
  - 1, 2, 4, 8, ...   1, 2, 3, 4, ...   1, 2, 4, 7, 11, 16, ...   1, 2, 5, 10, 17, ...
  - 1, 3, 9, 27, ...   1, 3, 5, 7, 9, ...   1, 3, 6, 10, ...   1, 3, 7, 13, ...
- If a 'score' has been kept from the mental and oral starter, then this can be used to decide the winning team.

Key words

- sequence
- term
- rule
- flow diagram
- generate
- consecutive

1 Write down four sequences beginning 1, 2, ..., and explain how each of them is generated.
2 Describe how each of the following sequences is generated and write down the next two terms
   a 50, 48, 46, 44, 42, 40, ...   **b** 9, 12, 18, 27, 39, 54, ...   **c** 1, 3, 6, 10, 15, 21, ...
   d 2, 6, 8, 14, 22, 36, ...
3 You are given a starting number and a multiplier. Write down at least the first six terms.
   a start 1, multiplier 4   **b** start 2, multiplier −1   **c** start 20, multiplier 10
   d start 40, multiplier $\frac{1}{2}$

2 **a** decreases in 2s, 38, 36   **b** increases by 3, 6, 9, 12, 15, ..., 72, 93
   c increases by 2, 3, 4, 5, ..., 28, 36   **d** add previous two terms, 58, 94
3 **a** 1, 4, 16, 64, 256, 1024   **b** 2, −2, 2, −2, 2, −2   **c** 20, 200, 2000, 20 000, 200 000, 2 000 000
   d 40, 20, 10, 5, $2\frac{1}{2}$, $1\frac{1}{4}$

LESSON
1.6

Framework objectives – Sequences 2

Use linear expressions to describe the nth term of a simple arithmetic sequence, justifying its form by referring to the activity or practical context from which it was generated.

Oral and mental starter

- Explain to pupils that they have to make you say a number, say 25.
- They do this by giving you a number. You apply a secret rule to it and respond with the number. For example, if the rule is 'add 2', pupils may say 7 and you reply 9, they say 16 and you reply 18; eventually a pupil will say 23 to which you reply 25.
- This is a fairly easy rule. Other rules (and the answer to make you say '25') are 'square, 5', '$3n + 1$, 8', 'multiply by 5, 5' and so on.
- To tie in with the main lesson activity the rules should be of the type $ax \pm b$.

Main lesson activity

- Given a rule, can you generate the sequence? For example, the first term is 5 and the rule is add 3 to the previous term. What sequence is found? 5, 8, 11, 14, 17, ...
- Other examples: first term 1, multiply each term by 5 (1, 5, 25, 125, 625, ...); first term 2 multiply by –3 (2, –6, 18, –54, 162, ...).
- Discuss the difference between this type of term-to-term definition and the type of rule used in the mental and oral starter (a position-to-term definition). For example, in the first sequence above, any term is given by multiplying the term number by 3 and adding 2.
- Demonstrate that this rule works: the first term is $3 \times 1 + 2 = 5$, the second term is $3 \times 2 + 2 = 8$, and the third term is $3 \times 3 + 2 = 11$.
- How can we write this rule down? For example, 3 × term number + 2, which can be shortened to $3n + 2$. This is the algebraic definition, which gives the nth term of the sequence.
- Example: each term of a sequence is given by $2n - 1$. What are the first five terms of the sequence?
    $2 \times 1 - 1 = 1, 2 \times 2 - 1 = 3, 2 \times 3 - 1 = 5, 2 \times 4 - 1 = 7, 2 \times 5 - 1 = 9$
- Example: each term of a sequence is given by $4n + 4$. What are the first five terms of the sequence?
    $4 \times 1 + 4 = 8, 4 \times 2 + 4 = 12, 4 \times 3 + 4 = 16, 4 \times 4 + 4 = 20, 4 \times 5 + 4 = 24$
- Point out that the sequences have a *constant difference* between terms. Such sequences are called *arithmetic sequences*. The expression for their nth term is always of this general form ($an \pm b$).
- Refer back to the paving slabs pattern at the beginning of this section in Pupil Book 2. The rule for this is $4n + 4$.
- How can we use this rule to find out how many slabs are around a $100 \times 100\,\text{m}^2$ pond?
- Put the sequence 3, 7, 11, 15, 19, ... on the board.
- Ask the class if they know what the nth term of this sequence is. It is unlikely, but someone may spot that it is $4n - 1$. If not, write this up as the nth term.
- Explain that $4n - 1$ is known as the general term or nth term of the sequence.
- Ask the class if they know the nth term of 7, 12, 17, 22, 27, ...
- Establish that it is $5n + 2$.
- Leave the nth terms and the sequences visible and ask the class to see if they can spot any connections.
- Now put another sequence on the board for example 2, 5, 8, 11, 14, ... Ask if anyone knows what the nth term is.
- If a pupil knows this ($3n - 1$), get them to explain how they found it.

- If not, or if the explanation does not cover this, make sure that the class can see that the '*n*' term is generated by the difference. Use the examples already seen to emphasise this.
- Also, make sure the class can see that the constant term is the first term minus the difference. Use the examples already seen to emphasise this.
- Put other sequences on the board and get the class to use the rules to generate the *n*th terms.

- **The class can now do Exercise 1F from Pupil Book 2.**

Exercise 1F **Answers**

1 **a** $a = 4, d = 5$ **b** $a = 1, d = 2$ **c** $a = 3, d = 6$ **d** $a = 5, d = -2$
2 **a** 1, 8, 15, 22, 29, 36, … **b** 3, 5, 7, 9, 11, 13, … **c** 5, 9, 13, 17, 21, 25, …
   d 0.5, 2, 3.5, 5, 6.5, 8, … **e** 4, 1, –2, –5, –8, –11, … **f** 2, 1.5, 1, 0.5, 0, –0.5, …
3 **a** 1 000 000, 100 000, 10 000, 1000, 100, 10, 1 **b** 1, 4, 9, 16, 25, 36, 49, 64, 81, 100, 121, 144, 169, 196, 225
   c 1, 2, 4, 8, 16, 32, 64, 128, 256, 512, 1024 **d** 10, 5, 0, –5, –10, –15, –20, –25
   e 3, 5, 7, 9, 11, 13, 15, 17, 19, 21, 23 **f** 1, –2, 4, –8, 16, –32, 64, –128, 256, –512, 1024
   g 48, 24, 12, 6, 3, 1.5, 0.75 **h** 1, 3, 7, 15, 31, 63 **i** 2, 5, 14, 41, 122, 365 **j** 0, 1, 3, 6, 10, 15, 21, 28, 36, 45, 55
4 **a** 1, 3, 5, 7, 9 **b** 5, 7, 9, 11, 13 **c** 4, 6, 8, 10, 12 **d** 3, 5, 7, 9, 11 **e** 2
5 **a** 4, 7, 10, 13, 16 **b** 5, 8, 11, 14, 17 **c** 1, 4, 7, 10, 13 **d** 2, 5, 8, 11, 14 **e** 3
6 **a** 4, 9, 14, 19, 24 **b** 7, 12, 17, 22, 27 **c** 1, 6, 11, 16, 21 **d** 8, 13, 18, 23, 28 **e** 5
7 **a i** 2, 3, 4 **ii** 101 **b i** 2, 5, 8 **ii** 299 **c i** –1, 1, 3 **ii** 197 **d i** 3, 8, 13 **ii** 498
   e i 1, 5, 9 **ii** 397 **f i** 10, 19, 28 **ii** 901 **g i** $1\frac{1}{2}$, 2, $2\frac{1}{2}$ **ii** 51 **h i** 7, 13, 19 **ii** 601 **i i** 1, $2\frac{1}{2}$, 4 **ii** $149\frac{1}{2}$
8 **a i** $4n + 1$ **ii** 201 **b i** $5n + 1$ **ii** 251 **c i** $3n - 1$ **ii** 149 **d i** $7n + 1$ **ii** 351
9 **a** $6n - 2$ **b** $3n + 6$ **c** $6n + 3$ **d** $3n - 1$ **e** $7n - 5$ **f** $2n + 6$ **g** $4n + 6$ **h** $8n - 5$ **i** $10n - 1$ **j** $9n - 5$
10 Some of these are examples. Other answers are possible:
   a $A = 2$, add 2 **b** $A = 1$, add 2 **c** $A = 5$, add 5 **d** $A = 1$, add 2, 3, 4, etc.
   e $A = 1$, add 10 **f** $A = 1$, add 3 **g** $A = 1$, multiply by –1

Extension **Answers**

a i 8, 18, 32 **ii** 20 000 **b i** 0, 3, 8 **ii** 9800 **c i** 3, 6, 10 **ii** 5050

Plenary

Key words

- Ask for the meaning of 'generalisation'. How does the *n*th term demonstrate the nature of a pattern?
- Why is it more useful than the term-to-term rule?
- Ask what these generalisations generate:
   $2n$ (even numbers) $n + 1$ (consecutive integers from 2)
   $2n - 1$ (odd numbers) $6n$ (multiples of 6)
- Try some non-linear generalisations such as n^2 or $n(n + 1)$.

☐ arithmetic
   sequence
☐ constant
   difference
☐ first term
☐ *n*th term

Homework

1 Given the first term a and the constant difference d, write down the first 6 terms of each of these sequences:
   a $a = 2, d = 6$ **b** $a = 0.5, d = 2$ **c** $a = -8, d = 3$

2 The *n*th term of a sequence is given by each of the rules below. Use this to write down the first six terms of each sequence:
   a $6n - 1$ **b** $10n + 3$ **c** $4n + 1$ **d** $8n - 3$

3 Write down the *n*th terms of these sequences:
   a 4, 9, 14, 19, 24, … **b** 6, 13, 20, 27, 34, … **c** 1, 5, 9, 13, 17, … **d** –3, 2, 7, 12, 17, … **e** 7, 15, 23, 31, 39, …

Homework Answers

1 **a** 2, 8, 14, 20, 26, 32 **b** 0.5, 2.5, 4.5, 6.5, 8.5, 10.5 **c** –8, –5, –2, 1, 4, 7
2 **a** 5, 11, 17, 23, 29, 35 **b** 13, 23, 33, 43, 53, 63 **c** 5, 9, 13, 17, 21, 25 **d** 5, 13, 21, 29, 37, 45
3 **a** $5n - 1$ **b** $7n - 1$ **c** $4n - 3$ **d** $5n - 8$ **e** $8n$

5
6

Framework objectives – Solving problems

Identify the mathematical features of a context or problem; try out and compare mathematical representations; select appropriate procedures and tools, including ICT.

Oral and mental starter

- There is no oral and mental starter, as the investigations take considerable time to set up and do.

Main lesson activity

- This is a lesson on investigations, building on work done in Year 7, such as 'mathematical mice'. The objective is to concentrate on breaking down a problem into easier, more manageable steps. There are three problems in the exercise.
- The main lesson activity is to go through the problem first encountered at the start of the last section, 'Sequences 2'.
- This is outlined in the pupil book and reproduced here in part.

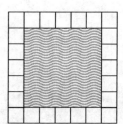

At the start of the last section you were asked to say how many 1 metre square slabs would be needed to go round a $100 \times 100 \, \text{m}^2$ pond. To solve this problem you need to:

    Step 1, break the problem into simple steps;

    Step 2, set up a table of results;

    Step 3, predict and test a rule;

    Step 4, use your rule to answer the question.

Step 1 is already done with the diagrams given.

Step 2

Pond size	Number of slabs
1	8
2	12
3	16
4	20

Step 3

    Use the table to spot how the sequence is growing.

    In this case it is increasing by 4 each time.

    So we can say that a 5×5 pond will need 24 slabs.

    We can show this by a sketch.

    We can also say that the numbers of slabs is 4 times the pond size plus 4, which we can write as:

        $S = 4P + 4$

There are many other ways to write this rule and many ways of showing that it is true. For example:

4P + 4   2(P + 2) + 2P   4(P + 1)

Step 4

We can now use any of the rules to say that for a 100 × 100 pond, $4 \times 100 + 4 = 404$ slabs will be needed.

● **The class can now try the investigations in Exercise 1G of Pupil Book 2.**

Exercise 1G **Answers**

1 If the sides are *a* and *b*, the rule is $S = 2a + 2b + 4$.
2 If the final score is *a–b*, the number of possible half-time scores is $S = (a + 1)(b + 1)$.
3 There are 377 ways of going up the 13 stairs. The sequence is 1, 2, 3, 5, 8, 13, 21, 34, 55, 89, 144, 233, 377 (Fibonacci type sequence).

Plenary

● There is no plenary to this lesson, although if desired one or more solutions to the problems in Exercise 1G could be discussed.

Key words

☐ **investigation**
☐ **table**
☐ **rule**
☐ **test**
☐ **predict**

Homework

Write up one of the investigations for a wall display, and include:

● the problem;

● your working;

● the table of results;

● your rule;

● the answer.

6

National Tests **Answers**

1 **a** 6, 18   **b** 8, 10   **c** $n \div 5$, $n - 20$, $\sqrt{n}$
2 Various answers, for example, $-5 + -3$, $-11 - -3$.
3 **a** 5, -3 **b** -5, 3   **c** -5
4 $2n + 4$, $n + 2$, n
5 **a** 3^2, 2^4, 5^2, 3^3 **b** 78 125
6 **a** $4n + 2$ **b** $3n + 3$ **c** $10n - 6$
7 **a** $4n \rightarrow 4, 8, \ldots$; $(n + 1)^2 \rightarrow 4, 9, \ldots$; $n^2 + 3 \rightarrow 4, 7, \ldots$; $n(n + 3) \rightarrow 4, 10, \ldots$
   b 4, 10, 18, 28, ...

Functional Maths – Blackpool Tower

Framework objectives

Identify the mathematical features of a context or problem; try out and compare mathematical representations; select appropriate procedures and tools, including ICT.

Oral and mental starter

Look at the information on the Blackpool Tower activity on page 20 of Pupil Book 2. Ask the pupils some questions relating to it. Topics could include:

- Periods of time (when did it open, how long since the foundation stone was laid?)
- Conversion factors (imperial to metric, square metres to square centimetres)
- Data from the internet (search for 'Blackpool Tower')

Main lesson activity

- Encourage the pupils to suggest possible questions. They could do these in small groups or individually, then present these to the class for others to answer. This is particularly useful if they have access to the internet.

- **The class can now work through the questions on pages 20–21.**

FM Activity | Answers

1 1994
2 2 years and 8 (or 9) months
3 16 times (by 2008)
4 1974
5 Approx. 7100 (7111 gallons)
6 Approx. 24°C (23.9°C)
7 a $\frac{1}{40}$ b $2\frac{1}{2}$p
8 Approx. 1800 (1786)
9 a Eiffel Tower costs £8.89 so is 61p cheaper   b Approx. 2 (2.07)
   c Approx. 10 (10.3)   d 5 years
10 96
11 158.1 m
12 14
13 Approx. 800 (793)
14 Approx. 3600 (3579)
15 437 cm²
16 Approx. £80 000 (£77 760)
17 a 190 000 000   b 6.57m
18 No, as $\sqrt{(13 \times 120)} = 39.5 < 42$

Plenary

- When the pupils reach questions 14 onwards, it will be useful to discuss some of the mathematics and strategies needed to work them out. Pupils may also need help using brackets on a calculator in questions 17 and 18.

Homework

Both the Eiffel Tower and the Blackpool Tower are called 'lattice' towers.

This table shows the heights of the world's tallest lattice towers.

Tower	Country	Height (metres)	When built
Kiev Tower	Ukraine	385	1973
Dragon Tower	China	336	2000
Tokyo Tower	Japan	332.6	1958
WITI TV tower	USA	329	1962
WSD TV tower	USA	327.6	1957
Eiffel Tower	France	324	1889
KCTV tower	USA	317.6	1956
Atlanta TV tower	USA	314.3	1980
Yerewa TV tower	Armenia	311.7	1977
St Petersburg TV tower	Russia	311.2	1962

1 The Blackpool Tower is 158m tall. How much taller is the Kiev Tower?

2 For how many years was the Eiffel Tower the tallest in the world?

3 For how many years was the Tokyo Tower the tallest in the world?

4 What is the difference in height between the WITI tower and the Atlanta tower?

5 The Kiev tower is not open to the public. The first $\frac{4}{7}$ are accessible by elevator. How much of the tower is **not** accessible by elevator? Give your answer in metres.

6 An approximate formula for how far you can see, D kilometres, when you are m metres above the ground is:

$$D - \sqrt{13m}$$

   a How far, in kilometres, can you see from the top of the Eiffel Tower? Give your answer to the nearest kilometre.

   b What is the difference between the distance you can see from the Kiev Tower and the distance you can see from the St Petersburg Tower? Give your answer to the nearest kilometre.

Homework Answers

1 227 m
2 68 years
3 15 years
4 14.7 m
5 165 m
6 a 65 km   b 7 km

Geometry and Measures **1**

Overview

2.1 Alternate and corresponding angles

2.2 Angles in triangles and quadrilaterals

2.3 Geometric proof

2.4 The geometric properties of quadrilaterals

2.5 Constructions

Context

This chapter introduces pupils to the angles formed in parallel lines, and then leads on to finding exterior angles in triangles and quadrilaterals. Pupils are then introduced to simple geometric proofs and the geometric properties of quadrilaterals. Finally, pupils are shown four important geometric constructions using a ruler and compasses.

National Curriculum references

Framework objectives

2.1 Identify alternate angles and corresponding angles.

2.2 Understand that: the angle sum of a triangle is 180° and of a quadrilateral is 360°; the exterior angle of a triangle is equal to the sum of the two interior opposite angles.

2.3 Understand a proof that: the angle sum of a triangle is 180° and of a quadrilateral is 360°; the exterior angle of a triangle is equal to the sum of the two interior opposite angles.

2.4 Solve geometrical problems using side and angle properties of special quadrilaterals, explaining reasoning with diagrams and text; classify quadrilaterals by their geometrical properties.

2.5 Use a straight edge and compasses to construct: the mid-point and perpendicular bisector of a line segment; the bisector of an angle; the perpendicular from a point to a line; the perpendicular from a point on a line.

Key concepts

Applications and implications of mathematics

- Understand how angles can be calculated from diagrams
- Understand the concept of geometric proof
- Understand the importance of geometric construction

Key processes

Representing

- Using geometric knowledge to solve problems
- Using mathematical equipment to draw accurate diagrams

Analysing

- Recognising and explaining how to calculate angles in diagrams
- Identifying and classifying shapes by their geometrical properties

Communicating and reflecting

- Explaining the method when calculating angles in diagrams
- Explaining the different properties of quadrilaterals
- Explaining the importance of a geometric proof

Route mapping

Exercise	Level 5	Level 6
2A		1–2
2B	1–2	3–6
2C		1–4
2D	1–4	5–8
2E		1–6

LESSON 2.1

Framework objectives – Alternate and corresponding angles
Identify alternate angles and corresponding angles.

Oral and mental starter

- Use a target board, such as the one shown. This activity can be repeated using different sets of numbers or different rules, but the theme is supplementary and complementary angles (which sum to 180° and 90°, respectively).
- Ask the pupils to choose a number from the board, and subtract it from 180.
- Ask the pupils to find two numbers that add up to 180.
- Ask the pupils to add two numbers together to give a total less than 180, and subtract the result from 180.
- Ask the pupils to find two numbers that add up to 90.
- Ask the pupils to find three numbers that add up to 180.

90	70	50	30	60	58	73
45	105	32	17	127	15	165
63	87	25	120	148	20	3
163	135	75	110	130	65	40

Main lesson activity

- Draw a letter Z (with a rotational symmetry order of two) on a piece of card. Tell the class that the main activity involves finding angles. Ask the pupils what happens to the letter Z when the card is rotated through 180°. Ask them to be specific about what happens to the two angles.
- Demonstrate, by using an acetate sheet with a tracing of the letter on it, that the top and bottom angles are equal.
- Now ask the class what happens to the two angles if a letter Z is drawn without the top and bottom lines being parallel.
- You could use geo-strips to demonstrate this. Ensure that the class recognise that if the lines are parallel, then the angles are equal, but if they are not parallel, then the angles will be different.
- Point out that some people call these angles Z angles, but the correct name is alternate angles.
- Now use geo-strips or a letter F drawn on a piece of card or the board to establish the rules for corresponding angles.
- Point out that some people call these angles F angles, but the correct name is corresponding angles.
- **The class can now do Exercise 2A from Pupil Book 2.**

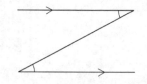

Exercise 2A **Answers**

1 a *e* **b** *f* **c** *g* **d** *h* **e** *d* **f** *c* **g** *o* or *s* **h** *q* or *m* **i** *p* or *t* **j** *v* or *j*
k *k* or *w* **l** *v* or *j*
2 a $a = 70°$ **b** $b = 125°$ **c** $c = 160°$ **d** $d = 48°$ **e** $e = 75°$ **f** $f = 57°$

Plenary

- Summarise the lesson by pointing out that in questions with many parallel lines, often many of the angles will be the same and many others will be the supplement of the first angle.
- Remind the class that they need to be able to work out angles and remember the correct terminology.

Key words

- corresponding angles
- alternate angles
- supplementary angles
- complementary angles
- interior angle
- exterior angle
- parallel
- perpendicular

6

Homework

Work out the size of the lettered angles in these diagrams:

1

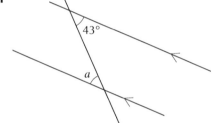

2

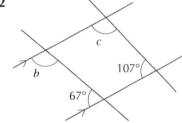

3

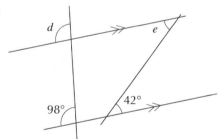

4

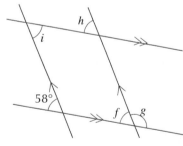

5

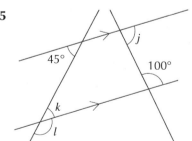

6

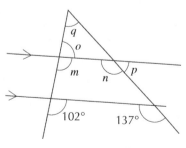

Framework objectives – Angles in triangles and quadrilaterals

Understand that: the angle sum of a triangle is 180° and of a quadrilateral is 360°; the exterior angle of a triangle is equal to the sum of the two interior opposite angles.

Oral and mental starter

- Draw a table on the board as shown below. Ask the class to tell you how many of each type of angle each shape has, and also any special properties of the shape. Fill in the table.
- For different triangles and quadrilaterals, for example, instead of writing the word in the left column, insert a sketch.

	Acute	Obtuse	Reflex	Right angles	Special properties
Equilateral triangle					
Square					
Rectangle					
Parallelogram					
	2	2	0	0	One pair of parallel sides

- You could reverse the problem by inserting numbers or properties in the table and asking the class for the name or a sketch of the shape (as on the final row).
- Extend the table or change the column labels to facts about sides in order to extend the task.

Main lesson activity

- Tell the class that the aim of the lesson is to learn about angles in triangles and quadrilaterals.
- Draw a triangle on the board. Ask the class to tell you what they know about its interior angles (for example, they add up to 180°).
- Draw a straight line with two angles on the board. Ask the class to tell you what they know about these two angles (for example, they add up to 180°).
- Now draw a triangle with an exterior angle divided by a line parallel to the opposite side on the board. Fill in the interior opposite angles and ask the class to tell you the third angle and then the exterior angle.
- Ask them if they can see any connection between the exterior angle and the interior opposite angles. Repeat this for different angles, if necessary.
- Use the words exterior and interior opposites to reinforce their vocabulary.
- Check also that they know that the angles of a quadrilateral add up to 360° and that this can be shown by dividing the quadrilateral into two triangles.
- **The class can now do Exercise 2B from Pupil Book 2.**

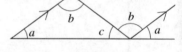

Exercise 2B   Answers

1 a $a = 80°$ **b** $b = 110°$ **c** $c = 55°$ **d** $d = 40°$
2 a $a = 80°$ **b** $b = 139°$ **c** $c = 108°$ **d** $d = 50°$
3 a $a = 136°$ **b** $b = 71°$ **c** $c = 158°$ **d** $d = 136°$ **e** $e = 101°$ **f** $f = 139°$ **g** $g = 109°$ **h** $h = 115°$
4 a $a = 38°$ **b** $b = 25°$ **c** $c = 51°$ **d** $d = 29°$
5 a $a = 82°$ **b** $b = 64°$ **6 a** $k = 35°$ **b** $l = 52°$ **c** 180°

Plenary

- Summarise the lesson by emphasising that there are often many ways to find out the values of angles, but usually it is easier to work on copies of the diagram. Advise the class to write in any angle that they know, as this will lead them to the required angle.
- Remind the class that it is important to know the key words, so that they can explain their answers.
- If time permits give them a few key words (for example, exterior or sum) and ask them to give you a definition.

Key words

- sum
- prove
- proof
- triangle
- quadrilateral
- vertex
- vertices
- angles

Homework

6

1 Work out the size of the lettered angles in these diagrams:

a    **b**    **c**

d 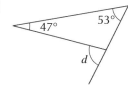   **e** 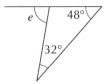   **f**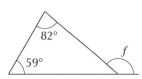

g 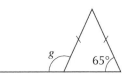   **h**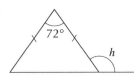

2 Work out the size of the lettered angles in these diagrams:

a 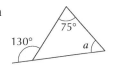   **b**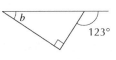

c 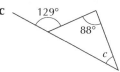   **d**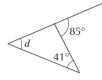

3 Work out the size of the lettered angles in these diagrams:

a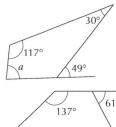

b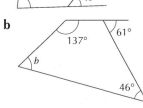

LESSON 2.3

Framework objectives – Geometric proof

Understand a proof that: the angle sum of a triangle is 180° and of a quadrilateral is 360°; the exterior angle of a triangle is equal to the sum of the two interior opposite angles.

Oral and mental starter

- Imagine two equilateral triangles of the same size.
- Place them together, edge to edge.
- Ask the class to give the name of the shape that is formed (a rhombus).
- Ask them to explain why the answer is always the same (the same shape is formed no matter which edges are placed together).
- This can be repeated using three or four equilateral triangles.

Main lesson activity

- Explain to the class that the lesson is about proof.
- Remind the class that the sum of the angles of a triangle is 180°. Ask them how can they show this.
- Their answer will probably be, 'draw a triangle and measure the three angles.'
- Explain that this is not accurate and shows only that the rule works by drawing examples.
- Explain that you can demonstrate that the rule works by cutting off the corners of a triangle and placing the three angles together to form a straight line. Show the class this demonstration to remind them how it works.
- Explain that this demonstration only shows the rule, but there could be triangles for which the rule may not work. This is why we need a proof to convince us that the rule works for every triangle. A proof usually involves using algebra.
- Show the class a proof that the sum of the angles of a triangle is 180°:

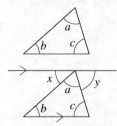

To prove $a + b + c = 180°$, draw a line parallel to one side of the triangle. Let x and y be the other two angles formed on the line with a, then $x = b$ (alternate angles), $y = c$ (alternate angles), and $a + x + y = 180°$ (angles on a line), so $a + b + c = 180°$.

- Show the class a proof that the exterior angle of a triangle is equal to the sum of the two interior opposite angles: x is an exterior angle of the triangle.

To prove $a + b = x$, let the other interior angle of the triangle $= c$. Then $a + b + c = 180°$ (angles in a triangle) and $x + c = 180°$ (angles on a straight line), so $a + b = x$.

- **The class can now do Exercise 2C from Pupil Book 2.**

Exercise 2C   Answers

1 $a + b + 90° = 180°$ (angles in a triangle), so $a + b = 90°$.

2 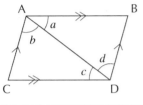 The quadrilateral can be split into two triangles with $a + b + c = 180°$ and $d + e + f = 180°$. The sum of these angles makes the four angles of the quadrilateral, so the sum of the angles in the quadrilateral is 360°.

3 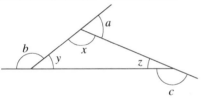 Let the angle adjacent to x be z, then $x + z = 180°$ (angles on a line) and $z = y$ (corresponding angles), so $x + y = 180°$.

4 Draw in the diagonal AD. Then $a = c$ (alternate angles) and $b = d$ (alternate angles), so $a + b = c + d$ and $\angle A = \angle D$.

Extension   Answers

1 Let the three interior angles of the triangle be x, y and z. Then $a + x = 180°$, $b + y = 180°$ and $c + z = 180°$, so $a + x + b + y + c + z = 540°$. Also, $x + y + z = 180°$. So $a + b + c + 180° = 540°$, and hence $a + b + c = 360°$.

2 Split the pentagon into three triangles. The sum of the angles of the pentagon is then $3 \times 180° = 540°$.

Plenary

- Ask the class to explain the difference between a demonstration and a proof.

Key words

- exterior angle
- interior angle
- proof, prove

Homework

1 Write out a proof to show that the sum of the angles of a triangle is 180°.

2 Write out a proof to show that the exterior angle of a triangle is equal to the sum of the two interior opposite angles.

6

LESSON 2.4

Framework objectives – The geometric properties of quadrilaterals

Solve geometrical problems using side and angle properties of special quadrilaterals, explaining reasoning with diagrams and text; classify quadrilaterals by their geometrical properties.

Oral and mental starter

- Mainly a revision exercise on quadrilaterals.
- Tell the class to imagine a quadrilateral that has only two lines of symmetry:
  Ask a pupil to draw one possible shape on the board with its name;
  Ask another pupil to draw another example that is possible.
  (The possible shapes are a rectangle and a rhombus.)
- Tell the class that the shape now has equal sides, and ask them which of the two quadrilaterals satisfies both conditions (the rhombus does).
- This activity can be repeated using different quadrilaterals.

Main lesson activity

- Explain to the class that the lesson is about looking at the properties of all the special quadrilaterals. Draw each of the following shapes on the board or on an overhead projector (OHP). Ask the class to describe all the mathematical properties of each one. Write all the properties below each and tell the pupils to copy these into their books.

Square
- Four equal sides
- Four right angles
- Opposite sides parallel
- Diagonals bisect each other at right angles
- Four lines of symmetry
- Rotational symmetry of order four

Rhombus
- Four equal sides
- Two pairs of equal angles
- Opposite sides parallel
- Diagonals bisect each other at right angles
- Two lines of symmetry
- Rotational symmetry of order two

Rectangle
- Two pairs of equal sides
- Four right angles
- Opposite sides parallel
- Diagonals bisect each other
- Two lines of symmetry
- Rotational symmetry of order two

Kite
- Two pairs of adjacent sides of equal length
- One pair of equal angles
- Diagonals intersect at right angles
- One line of symmetry

Parallelogram
- Two pairs of equal sides
- Two pairs of equal angles
- Opposite sides parallel
- Diagonals bisect each other
- No lines of symmetry
- Rotational symmetry of order two

Arrowhead or Delta
- Two pairs of adjacent sides of equal length
- One pair of equal angles
- Diagonals intersect at right angles outside the shape
- One line of symmetry

Trapezium
- One pair of parallel sides
- Some trapeziums have one line of symmetry

● **The class can now do Exercise 2D from Pupil Book 2**.

Exercise 2D **Answers**

1

No lines of symmetry	One line of symmetry	Two lines of symmetry	Four lines of symmetry
Parallelogram Trapezium	Kite Arrowhead	Rectangle Rhombus	Square

2

Rotational symmetry of order one	Rotational symmetry of order two	Rotational symmetry of order four
Kite Arrowhead Trapezium	Rectangle Parallelogram Rhombus	Square

3 Rectangle
4 Parallelogram
5 Wrong, it could be a rhombus.
6 Wrong, it could be a parallelogram or a rhombus.
7 Parallelogram, rhombus

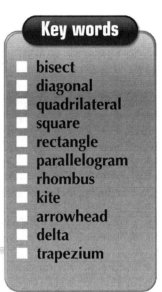

Key words

☐ **bisect**
☐ **diagonal**
☐ **quadrilateral**
☐ **square**
☐ **rectangle**
☐ **parallelogram**
☐ **rhombus**
☐ **kite**
☐ **arrowhead**
☐ **delta**
☐ **trapezium**

Plenary

● Ask individual pupils to draw on the board one of the special
quadrilaterals they have met during the lesson and then explain to the rest
of the class all the mathematical properties of the shape they have chosen.

Homework

1 Copy and complete the table:

	Square	Rectangle	Parallelogram	Rhombus
Number of lines of symmetry	4			
Order of rotational symmetry		2		
All sides equal			No	
All angles equal				No
Opposite sides parallel	Yes			

2 a Which quadrilaterals have diagonals that bisect each other?

b Which quadrilaterals have diagonals that intersect at right angles?

3 The instructions below are to draw the rectangle shown.

REPEAT TWICE
[FORWARD 5
TURN RIGHT 90°
FORWARD 12
TURN RIGHT 90°]

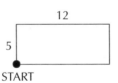

START

Write down a set of similar instructions to draw a rectangle that has sides twice the length of those
on the diagram.

Homework Answers

1

	Square	Rectangle	Parallelogram	Rhombus
Number of lines of symmetry	4	2	0	2
Order of rotational symmetry	4	2	2	2
All sides equal	Yes	No	No	Yes
All angles equal	Yes	Yes	No	No
Opposite sides parallel	Yes	Yes	Yes	Yes

2 a square, rectangle, parallelogram, rhombus   **b** square, rhombus, kite, arrowhead
3 REPEAT TWICE, [FORWARD 10, TURN RIGHT 90°, FORWARD 24, TURN RIGHT 90°]

Framework objectives – Constructions

Use a straight edge and compasses to construct: the mid-point and perpendicular bisector of a line segment; the bisector of an angle; the perpendicular from a point to a line; the perpendicular from a point on a line.

Oral and mental starter

- Write on the board, '180 DIAT'. Explain to the class that this is an acronym for 180 degrees in a triangle.
- Ask the class to solve the following geometric acronyms:

     90 DIARA (90 degrees in a right angle)

     180 DOASL (180 degrees on a straight line)

     360 DIACT (360 degrees in a complete turn)

     3 SIAT (three sides in a triangle)

     4 SIAQ (four sides in a quadrilateral)
- Ask the class to make up their own geometric acronyms.

Main lesson activity

- For this lesson the pupils will need a sharp pencil, a ruler, compasses and a protractor.
- Show the class how to complete the four constructions in Examples 1 to 4 below.
- Explain that these constructions are very accurate when done with a sharp pencil, which is why they are used in other subjects such as Design and Technology.

Example 1

To construct the mid-point and the perpendicular bisector of the line AB.
- Draw a line segment AB of any length.
- Set compasses to any radius greater than half the length of AB.
- Draw two arcs, with the centre at A, above and below AB.
- With compasses set at the same radius, draw two arcs with the centre at B, to intersect the first two arcs at C and D.
- Join C and D to intersect AB at X.
- X is the mid-point of the line AB.
- The line CD is the perpendicular bisector of the line AB.

A ———————————— B

Example 2

To construct the bisector of the angle ABC.
- Draw an ∠ABC of any size.
- Set compasses to any radius and, with the centre at B, draw an arc to intersect BC at X and AB at Y.
- With compasses set to any radius, draw two arcs with the centres at X and Y, to intersect at Z.
- Join BZ.
- BZ is the bisector of the ∠ABC.
- The ∠ABZ = ∠CBZ.

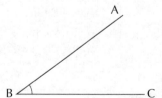

Example 3

To construct the perpendicular from a point P to a line segment AB:

- Set compasses to any suitable radius and draw arcs from P to intersect AB at X and Y.
- With compasses set at the same radius, draw arcs with the centres at X and Y to intersect at Z below AB.
- Join PZ.
- PZ is perpendicular to AB.

Example 4

To construct the perpendicular from a point Q on a line segment XY:

- Set compasses to a radius that is less than half the length of XY and, with the centre at Q, draw two arcs on either side of Q to intersect XY at A and B. (The line XY may sometimes need to be extended).
- Set compasses to a radius that is greater than half the length of XY and, with the centres at A and B, draw arcs above and below XY to intersect at C and D.
- Join CD.
- CD is the perpendicular from the point Q.

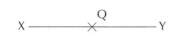

- **The class can now do Exercise 2E from Pupil Book 2**.

Extension Answers

1 Bisect an angle of 60° to obtain an angle of 30° and bisect this angle to obtain an angle of 15°.

Plenary

- Briefly summarise the four constructions completed during the lesson.

Key words

- bisect, bisector
- compasses
- construction
- construction lines
- mid-point
- perpendicular bisector
- straight edge

Homework

1 Draw a line XY 8cm in length. Using compasses, construct the perpendicular bisector of the line.

2 Draw an acute angle of any size. Using compasses, construct the angle bisector.

3 Explain how to draw an angle of 45° without having to use a protractor.

Homework Answers

3 Draw a line of any length and, using compasses, construct the perpendicular bisector. Using compasses, bisect one of the 90° angles formed to obtain an angle of 45°.

National Tests Answers

1 $a = 50°$, $b = 130°$, $c = 20°$
2 **a** Alternate angles of 75° at top of diagram **b** 50°
3 **a** $a = 110°$ **b** $b = 70°$ **c** $c = 50°$ **d** $d = 130°$
4 **a** $k = 110°$ **b** $m = 50°$
5 47°, 50°, 125°, 138°
6 $a = 10°$
7 $p = 140°$

Statistics **1**

Overview

3.1 Probability

3.2 Probability scales

3.3 Mutually exclusive events

3.4 Calculating probabilities

3.5 Experimental probability

(FM) Fun in the fairground

Context

This chapter builds on previous knowledge of probability and extends this first to see how probability is applied differently to theory and experiments, and then to being able to compare the two results critically.

National Curriculum references

Framework objectives

3.1 Interpret the results of an experiment using the language of probability; appreciate that random processes are unpredictable.

3.2 Know that if the probability of an event occurring is p, then the probability of it not occurring is $1 - p$.

3.3 Use diagrams and tables to record in a systematic way all possible mutually exclusive outcomes for single events and for two successive events.

3.4 Use diagrams and tables to record in a systematic way all possible mutually exclusive outcomes for single events and for two successive events.

3.5 Collect data using a suitable method (for example, observation, controlled experiment, data logging using ICT). Compare estimated experimental probabilities with theoretical probabilities, recognising that: if an experiment is repeated the outcome may, and usually will, be different; increasing the number of times an experiment is repeated generally leads to better estimates of probability.

(FM) Interpret the results of an experiment using the language of probability. Compare estimated experimental probabilities with theoretical probabilities, recognising that: if an experiment is repeated the outcome may, and usually will, be different; increasing the number of times an experiment is repeated generally leads to better estimates of probability.

Key concepts

Critical understanding

- Use mathematical ideas and models to explore real-world issues and problems, recognising that solutions may need to take account of wider factors

Creativity

- Pose questions and developing appropriate lines of enquiry

Key processes

Representing

- Identifying the mathematical aspects of the situation or problem

Analysing

- Using knowledge of related problems

Communicating and reflecting

- Communicating findings in a range of forms

Route mapping

Exercise	Levels 5	Levels 6
3A	1–3	4–5
3B		1–6
3C		1–4
3D	1	2–5
3E		1–3

Framework objectives – Probability

Interpret the results of an experiment using the language of probability; appreciate that random processes are unpredictable.

R	R	R	R	R
B	B	B	G	G

R	R	R	R	B
G	G	G	Y	Y

Oral and mental starter

- Use two boards marked with grids, as shown on the right.
- The letters could be replaced by colours:
  R, red; B, blue; G, green; Y, yellow.
- Hold up the first grid and ask the pupils what fraction of the grid is formed by red, blue and green sections. You could, at this stage, mention giving fractions in their simplest form.
- Now repeat with the second grid.
- You could now increase the level of difficulty by putting one grid beneath the other, as shown, and making the fractions out of 20. Then, by covering columns up, the fraction could be in sixteenths, say, and so on.
- Now follow the fraction work by asking what the *probability* of picking red is. Stress that you want the answer as a fraction.

Main lesson activity

- Explain that the lesson is about chance and using the words associated with probability.
- Start off by asking the class to give you any words about probability that they have met before. Ask them to spell the words and/or define them. Try to ensure that the key words are covered.
- Draw on the board a probability scale with seven dividing marks, but not labelled.
- Write one word on the scale (for example, impossible).
- Ask the class to fill in the gaps.
- Now ask them to think of events that are impossible. Discuss the idea that some things are almost impossible, but could still happen.
- Try to encourage them to give you events that are both mathematical and non-mathematical.
- Use the key words when talking about their answers. For example, ask them what bias means.

- **The class can now do Exercise 3A from Pupil Book 2.**

Exercise 3A Answers

1 There are many valid answers for events that are **a** certain, **b** impossible, **c** a fifty–fifty chance, **d** very unlikely, **e** likely, **f** very likely, **g** unlikely.

2 **a** triangle from Grid 2   **b** square from Grid 2
   c circle from Grid 1 or Grid 2, or square from Grid 1   **d** rectangle from Grid 1
   e triangle from Grid 1.

3 **a** Bag B (8 out of 10 is a bigger proportion than 10 out of 20)
   b Bag A (5 out of 20 is a bigger proportion than 2 out of 10)
   c Bag A (Bag B has no green marbles).

4 Either biased because six more than expected, or not biased because 36 is quite near to 30, or hard to tell because it is necessary to carry out more trials.

5 Yes: there are more ways to get a score higher than 6 than a score lower than 6.

Plenary

- Point out that different words are sometimes used to mean the same thing (for example, fifty–fifty chance and even chance).
- Reinforce to the class that the work they have done is often based on experiments or expectation and therefore the results, although probably reliable, may not happen every time.
- Tell them that the next step will be to use the number scale rather than words.

Key words

- event
- theory
- sample
- sample space
- biased

Homework

1 Draw a probability scale and label it with words. Under each word put a number value from 0 for impossible to 1 for certain.

2 A bag contains 10 counters. How many red counters are in the bag if the chance of picking out a red counter is:

   a fifty–fifty   **b** impossible   **c** certain

3 10 cards are numbered from 1 to 10. Describe in words the chance of picking:

   a an odd number   **b** a number less than 11   **c** a number greater than 3

Homework Answers

1 A seven-number scale, in ascending order, from 0 to 1, including $\frac{1}{2}$.

2 **a** 5 **b** 0 **c** 10

3 **a** fifty–fifty   **b** certain   **c** likely or very likely

5

LESSON 3.2

Framework objectives – Probability scales
Know that if the probability of an event occurring is p, then the probability of it not occurring is $1 - p$.

Oral and mental starter

- Write 10 numbers on the board or OHP. Tell the class to try to memorise as many as possible. Give them about 15 seconds.
- Now cover the numbers up and see how many numbers the pupils can recall. This could be a timed exercise, which could be repeated in another lesson.
- Now write 10 fractions and/or decimals on the board or OHP.
- Again, see how many the pupils can recall after, say, 20 seconds.
- This time, return to the 10 fractions and/or decimals and ask the class what is needed to make each one add up to 1. Write the correct answer on the board or OHP. To help them, you may wish to use a number line drawn on the board or a 'counting stick' with 10 divisions marked on. Mark it at one end with 0 and at the other end with 1.

0   1

- Tell the pupils that they now have 30 seconds to memorise the answers.

Main lesson activity

- Ask the class to tell you some events that are opposite or exclusive of each other. You may need to give them an example, such as red playing card, black playing card.
- Now tell them an event and ask them what the opposite is, for example, even number, vowel, wears glasses, doesn't wear glasses.
- Now ask one pupil to give you a probability as a decimal and ask another pupil for the probability of that event not happening. This could be repeated several times.
- This could now be repeated with simple fractions.
- In pairs, pupils could now test each other by making up their own probabilities in turn, and writing them into two columns in their books.
- Introduce the idea that we say the probability of something happening is p, so the expression for the probability of it **not** happening is $1 - p$.
- Remind the class of the method used to calculate probabilities (introduced in Year 7):

$$\text{The probability of an event } (p) = \frac{\text{Number of outcomes in the event}}{\text{Total number of all possible outcomes}}$$

- **The class can now do Exercise 3B from Pupil Book 2.**

Exercise 3B   Answers

1 A′ at 0.8, B′ at 0.7, C′ at 0.4, D′ at 0
2 $\frac{3}{4}$, $\frac{2}{3}$, $\frac{1}{4}$, $\frac{9}{10}$, $\frac{13}{15}$, $\frac{1}{8}$, $\frac{2}{9}$
3 a $\frac{1}{2}$ b $\frac{1}{13}$ c $\frac{12}{13}$ d $\frac{1}{4}$ e $\frac{3}{4}$ f $\frac{12}{13}$ g $\frac{10}{13}$ h $\frac{12}{13}$ I $\frac{1}{2}$ j $\frac{8}{13}$ k $\frac{51}{52}$
4 a $\frac{1}{4}$ b $\frac{3}{5}$ c $\frac{3}{4}$ d 0 e $\frac{3}{4}$ f $\frac{2}{5}$ g $\frac{1}{4}$ h 1
5 24
6 a 0.25 b 0.2 c 0.4 d 0.1 e 0.05

Plenary

Key words

- probability
- event
- outcome
- random

- Remind the class that they should never have an answer greater than 1.
- Point out that sometimes decimals are easier to use and at other times fractions are easier.
- Look at the problem of tossing two coins and obtaining at least one head. Ask them to explain what we mean by 'at least one'. Now point out that 'at least one' is the opposite of 'none', so there are two approaches to this type of question, but the quickest way is to use $1 - \frac{1}{4}$.

Homework

1 The probabilities of different events happening are given. Write down the probability of these events **not** happening:

a 0.1   b 0.25   c 0.5   d 0.6   e 0.85   f 0.91   g 0.001

h 1   i $\frac{1}{5}$ j $\frac{1}{4}$ k $\frac{1}{10}$ l $\frac{2}{3}$ m $\frac{9}{10}$ n $\frac{4}{7}$

2 There are eight outcomes when throwing three coins. Make a list of all the outcomes. Write down the probability of obtaining:

a three heads   b at least one tail   c three tails   d at least one head

Homework Answers

1 a 0.9 b 0.75 c 0.5 d 0.4 e 0.15 f 0.09 g 0.999 h 0 i $\frac{4}{5}$ j $\frac{3}{4}$ k $\frac{9}{10}$ l $\frac{1}{3}$ m $\frac{1}{10}$ n $\frac{3}{7}$
2 HHH, HHT, HTH, THH, HTT, THT, TTH, TTT
   a $\frac{1}{8}$ b $\frac{7}{8}$ c $\frac{1}{8}$ d $\frac{7}{8}$

6

Framework objectives – Mutually exclusive events
Use diagrams and tables to record in a systematic way all possible mutually exclusive outcomes for single events and for two successive events.

Oral and mental starter

8	5	$\frac{1}{2}$	0.4
$\frac{3}{4}$	7	0.2	$\frac{1}{5}$
0.25	9	1	$\frac{2}{3}$

- To show the class outcomes that overlap, use a target board and ask the class to sort the values into groups. They will probably go for integers, fractions and decimals.
- Try to direct the class to ensure that the groups selected do not overlap.
- Now ask them to take, say, the group of integers and break them into two sub-groups. They may, for example, go for odd and even.
- They can then do this with the fractions, for example, numerators of 1 and numerators other than 1.
- They can also do this for decimals, for example, 0.2 with 0.4 (one decimal place) and 0.25 (two decimal places).
- Keep insisting that no value must occur in more than one group (no overlap).
- Now say to the class that you will give them two groups from the target board and ask them which values do overlap. Give then, for example, prime and odd or the third column and the second row.
- Ask the class to give you two groups for which no values overlap.

Main lesson activity

- Ask the class how many results there are when tossing a coin twice. Make the point that head-then-tail is different from tail-then-head.
- Now ask them to write the combinations in their books. Ask them to record the results in different ways (this could be done as a group activity). Compare the results for each group. Make sure that everyone records the different methods, such as list, abbreviated list, sample space, diagrams of coins.
- Ask the class to give you an advantage or disadvantage of one particular method. Which method best ensures that they don't miss any possible outcomes?
- Ask the class to imagine four people, John, Jane, Ramesh and Avril in a room. Tell them that two people leave the room, and start writing down the possibilities for this: '2 boys'; '2 girls'; 'Ramesh and Jane'; '1 boy and 1 girl'. Ask for more suggestions.
- Now ask if this particular list is the best method for working out probabilities. Hopefully someone will point out that some of the outcomes in the list overlap, which means that some events will have been counted more than once (for example, 'Ramesh and Jane' coming out is included in '1 boy and 1 girl' coming out). The pupils may also point out that not all possibilities have been included in the list.
- Introduce the phrase 'mutually exclusive' as referring to outcomes which do not overlap. That is to say, when you carry out a trial (like 2 people coming out of a room), two events that are mutually exclusive cannot both happen. In our example, 'Ramesh and Jane' and 'Ramesh and John' are mutually exclusive outcomes.
- Get the pupils to help you rewrite an exhaustive list using only mutually exclusive outcomes.
- Give some other examples of mutually exclusive events, but try to avoid using all events that are exact opposites of each other (for example, use rain, snow or fine, rather than rain and not rain). This is to avoid confusion with exhaustive events.
- The class could write some examples down in their books.

- **The class can now do Exercise 3C from Pupil Book 2.**

Exercise 3C   Answers

1 a mutually exclusive
  b not mutually exclusive
  c not mutually exclusive
  d not mutually exclusive
  e not mutually exclusive
  f not mutually exclusive
  g not mutually exclusive
  h not mutually exclusive
  i not mutually exclusive
  j mutually exclusive
  k not mutually exclusive
  l not mutually exclusive

2 a Not necessarily, as there are other beads that have not been seen
  b **i** and **iii**

3 a There are 64 different combinations.
  b More likely, as there are more ways of getting over 40p.

4 a

Spinner 1	Spinner 2	Total score
+2	0	2
+2	−1	1
+2	+1	3
−3	0	−3
−3	−1	−4
−3	+1	−2
+4	0	4
+4	−1	3
+4	+1	5

  b i Yes, as there are more positive totals.
   ii No, as there are more odd totals than even.

Extension   Answers

2 horses – Ways to finish = 2! (2 × 1) = 2
3 horses – Ways to finish = 3! (3 × 2 × 1) = 6
4 horses – Ways to finish = 4! (4 × 3 × 2 × 1) = 24
n horses – Ways to finish = *n*!

Plenary

● Tell the class that they are expected to know all the different methods of recording outcomes for two events. Reinforce the fact that there is not a right or wrong way, but that some methods are better for some questions than others.

● Let them know that, now they have a good understanding of how to record, next time you will be able to look at more complicated probability questions involving more than one event.

● Remind them that when making lists the order matters sometimes, but not always. For example, it does not matter in which order the six lottery balls are picked out if they are your numbers. Also, say the class needs to be systematic when making long lists.

Key words

- event
- mutually exclusive
- equally likely
- chance
- outcome

Homework

1 A coin is tossed and a die is rolled:
  a Make a list of all the possible outcomes   **b** Make a table of all the possible outcomes

2 There are three pets in a house: a cat, a dog and a hamster. There are also three children, Mark, David and Paul, who each own one of the pets. Make a table of all the possibilities of who owns each pet.

3 Five girls, Bev, Val, Lynne, Sarah and June, go to the cinema. Bev wants to sit next to Val and June wants to sit on the end. Make a list of the possible seating arrangements.

Homework Answers

1 a Head 1, Head 2, Head 3, Head 4, Head 5, Head 6, Tail 1, Tail 2, Tail 3, Tail 4, Tail 5, Tail 6
  b

	1	2	3	4	5	6
Head	H,1	H,2	H,3	H,4	H,5	H,6
Tail	T,1	T,2	T,3	T,4	T,5	T,6

2

Cat	M	M	P	P	D	D
Dog	D	P	M	D	P	M
Hamster	P	D	D	M	M	P

3 Note: Each order could also be reversed (24 combinations altogether):
June, Bev, Val, Lynne, Sarah
June, Val, Bev, Lynne, Sarah
June, Bev, Val, Sarah, Lynne
June, Val, Bev, Sarah, Lynne
June, Sarah, Val, Bev, Lynne
June, Sarah, Bev, Val, Lynne
June, Lynne, Val, Bev, Sarah
June, Lynne, Bev, Val, Sarah
June, Lynne, Sarah, Bev, Val
June, Lynne, Sarah, Val, Bev
June, Sarah, Lynne, Bev, Val
June, Sarah, Lynne, Val, Bev

6

LESSON 3.4

Framework objectives – Calculating probabilities
Use diagrams and tables to record in a systematic way all possible mutually exclusive outcomes for single events and for two successive events.

Oral and mental starter

- Write a number on the board, say 36. Ask the class to give you two numbers that add up to 36, two numbers with a difference of 36, two numbers with a product of 36 and, finally, two numbers that divide to give an answer of 36.
- Now change the number and repeat.
- Next take a piece of A4 paper and tell the class that you are going to fold it in various ways. They have to work out how many pieces the folds divide it into.
- First of all fold it in half horizontally and vertically. Ask them how many pieces there are.
- Now fold it in half again to obtain eight sections. Ask them if it makes any difference to the answer if you fold horizontally rather than vertically.
- Start with a fresh sheet of paper and fold it in half vertically and then into thirds (so that there are six columns) and then make one horizontal fold. Ask them how many sections there are. (This could be used later for the coin and dice example.)

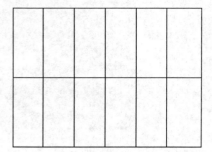

Main lesson activity

- Tell the class about the person who wanted three flavours on his ice cream cornet: vanilla, strawberry and chocolate. The scoops are placed on top of each other. Ask them to tell you the different orders that he could have.
- Prompt them to give you different ways of recording the information: words, abbreviations or diagrams. Ask them to give you the advantages or disadvantages of each method.
- Now give them a different problem. For example, a boy and a girl each choose an apple or an orange. Ask them to record the different combinations in their books.
- At this stage introduce sample spaces.
- You can now use the paper from the starter to show the class a sample space for a coin and a dice. Ask them to copy the 12 sections and label them.

| H, 1 | H, 2 | H, 3 | H, 4 | H, 5 | H, 6 |
| T, 1 | T, 2 | T, 3 | T, 4 | T, 5 | T, 6 |

- When this is done, tell them you are thinking of one of these sections. Introduce the idea of the probability of them choosing the same section.

- **The class can now do Exercise 3D from Pupil Book 2.**

Exercise 3D — Answers

1 a $\frac{1}{2}$ b $\frac{1}{10}$ c $\frac{7}{25}$ d $\frac{3}{10}$ e $\frac{4}{25}$ f $\frac{7}{50}$ g $\frac{9}{50}$ h $\frac{3}{25}$ i $\frac{3}{25}$

2 a BB, BG, GB, GG b It should be $\frac{1}{4}$

3 AA, AB, AP, BB, BP, PP

4 a PB, CP, CC, CB, BP, BC, BB
 b i $\frac{1}{3}$ ii $\frac{1}{3}$ iii $\frac{1}{9}$ iv $\frac{1}{9}$ v $\frac{1}{9}$ vi $\frac{1}{3}$ vii $\frac{4}{9}$ viii $\frac{2}{3}$

5

	1	2	3	4	5	6
1	2	3	4	5	6	7
2	3	4	5	6	7	8
3	4	5	6	7	8	9
4	5	6	7	8	9	10
5	6	7	8	9	10	11
6	7	8	9	10	11	12

a 7 b i $\frac{1}{12}$ ii $\frac{1}{9}$ iii 0 iv $\frac{1}{36}$ v $\frac{5}{12}$ vi $\frac{7}{12}$ vii $\frac{1}{6}$ viii $\frac{1}{2}$ ix $\frac{5}{18}$ x $\frac{13}{18}$

Plenary

- Write an empty sample space on the board and ask the pupils to tell you how to fill it in.
- Then ask them to give a few probabilities from it. Delete or add extra lines to change the sample space and the probabilities.

Key words

- single events
- successive events
- sample space
- table
- dice

Homework

1 Two four-sided dice are thrown and the scores added together. Copy and complete the table of scores:

	1	2	3	4
1	2	3		
2				
3				
4				

Write down the probability of:

a 3 b 4 c 8 d less than 4

e greater than 5 f an even number g a prime number h a square number

i a multiple of 3

2 A room is painted using two different colours. The colours can be chosen from red, green, blue and yellow. Make a list of the six different combinations that could be chosen. Write down the probability of choosing:

a red and green b green with any other colour c no red

Homework — Answers

1

	1	2	3	4
1	2	3	4	5
2	3	4	5	6
3	4	5	6	7
4	5	6	7	8

a $\frac{1}{8}$ b $\frac{3}{16}$ c $\frac{1}{16}$ d $\frac{3}{16}$ e $\frac{3}{8}$ f $\frac{1}{2}$ g $\frac{9}{16}$ h $\frac{3}{16}$ i $\frac{5}{16}$

2 a $\frac{1}{6}$ b $\frac{1}{2}$ c $\frac{1}{2}$

Framework objectives – Experimental probability

Collect data using a suitable method (for example, observation, controlled experiment, data logging using ICT).

Compare estimated experimental probabilities with theoretical probabilities, recognising that: if an experiment is repeated the outcome may, and usually will, be different; increasing the number of times an experiment is repeated generally leads to better estimates of probability.

Oral and mental starter

- Use a multiplication table or write the first five rows on the board or OHP:

1	2	3	4	5	6	7	8	9	10
2	4	6	8	10	12	*14*	16	18	20
3	6	9	12	15	18	*21*	24	27	30
4	8	12	16	20	24	28	32	36	40
5	10	15	20	25	30	35	40	45	50

- Ask a pupil to pick two numbers from the same column (for example, 14 and 21, as shown in italic).
- Now ask the class to say them as a fraction (fourteen twenty-firsts).
- Now tell the class to look at the beginning of the rows chosen and say what fraction they see (two-thirds).
- Ask them if they can tell you anything about these fractions (they are equivalent).
- Point out that this always works, for example $\frac{9}{36} = \frac{1}{4}$.
- Now pick out your own fractions and ask them to tell you an equivalent fraction.
- You could then work this backwards by giving them a fraction in its simplest form and asking for an equivalent fraction. You could say, 'I want $\frac{3}{4}$ changed into sixteenths.'

Main lesson activity

- Explain to the class that you want to be able to predict whether the next person who comes through the door will have brown hair. Ask them to tell you how you could collect the information you need.
- Note on the board any key words that are given (for example, tally, observation sheet, survey, sample).
- Conduct a survey of the class by recording data about their hair colour.
- Now use the result to obtain the experimental probability. Allow the class time to put this information into their books.
- Ask them, in pairs or groups, to make a list of the types of information that they could collect to estimates probabilities. You may need to prompt them with a few examples, such as the number of times a six is thrown to test the fairness of a dice, the number of times the school bus is late this month, the sex of shoppers at a supermarket, etc.
- **The class can now do Exercise 3E from Pupil Book 2.**

Exercise 3E — Answers

1 a Point up, as this happens more times (for example, 175 out of 250)

b Last result, more trials.   **c** $\dfrac{\text{Number pointing up}}{\text{Number of drawing pins}}\left(\dfrac{175}{250}\right)$ **d** $\dfrac{7}{10}$

e More trials

2 a Yes, for example twice as many 2s as 1s   **b** More trials   **c** $\frac{1}{10}$ **d** $\frac{1}{4}$

3 d The more trials, the closer the P(H) gets to 0.5.

Plenary

- Ask the class what the difference is between theoretical probability and experimental probability.
- Remind them that experiments are prone to errors, but the more trials carried out, the more reliable the results tend to be.
- If appropriate, introduce the term 'relative frequency'.

Key words
- data
- theoretical probability
- experimental probability
- different outcomes
- estimate of probability

Homework

This homework is connected to the extension work, which some pupils may already have started.

1 Having decided on an experiment of your own, collect your data. Try to collect as much as possible.

2 Write a brief report about the data you have collected.

3 Work out an experimental probability for your data.

6

National Tests — Answers

1 a $\frac{1}{3}$ **b** 3

2 a $\frac{1}{4},\frac{1}{2}$ **b** $0,\frac{2}{3}$

3 a $\frac{1}{20}$ **b** green

4 a $\frac{4}{5}$ **b** 4   **c** 8   **d** 20 (altogether) − 12 (green) − 1 (blue) = 7

Functional Maths – Fun in the fairground

> ## Framework objectives
> Interpret the results of an experiment using the language of probability.
> Compare estimated experimental probabilities with theoretical probabilities,
> recognising that: if an experiment is repeated the outcome may, and usually will,
> be different; increasing the number of times an experiment is repeated generally
> leads to better estimates of probability.

Oral and mental starter

Look at the information on the fairground activity on page 48 of the corresponding Pupil
Book. This Functional Maths activity can be introduced once you have covered the previous
work on probability.

- Write a fraction on the board, say $\frac{1}{2}$.
- Ask for other fractions that are the same as $\frac{1}{2}$. You are expecting answers such as $\frac{2}{4}$, $\frac{5}{10}$, $\frac{50}{100}$, etc.
- Ask the pupils to explain how they are getting the answers.
- Ask the class for something that has a probability of $\frac{1}{2}$. You will expect examples like:
    rolling a dice and getting a head
    cutting a pack of cards and getting a red card
    having a baby and it being a girl
    rolling a dice and getting an even number.
- Now put $\frac{1}{5}$ on the board and ask for fractions equivalent to that. You are
    expecting answers such as $\frac{2}{10}$, $\frac{3}{15}$, $\frac{10}{50}$.
- Ask the class for something that has a probability of $\frac{1}{5}$. You might start with suggestions
    such as:
    choosing one school-day of the week at random
    selecting a blue marble from a bag containing 5 marbles and only 1 is blue.

Main lesson activity

- Discuss with the pupils the subject of fairgrounds and the different stalls they have. Quite a few of the
    stalls rely on the good chances that you will lose, but that someone will win a prize every now and again.
    Tell them that this activity illustrates just two of those types of stalls.
- The data handling expected in this spread is:
    reading from a table
    probability
    expectations.
- Before starting the activity put on the board a table similar to:

	Number of throws	Times hit target
Bull's eye	40	2
20	10	3
A double	50	5

- Explain that someone was throwing darts at a dartboard for practice and kept a count of what
    they were aiming at and how many times they were successful.
- Ask the pupils simple questions such as:
  1 How many darts were thrown altogether? (100)

2 What is the probability of throwing a dart at and hitting a:
 a Bull's eye? ($\frac{2}{40} = \frac{1}{20}$)
 b 20? ($\frac{3}{10}$)
 c a double? ($\frac{5}{50} = \frac{1}{10}$)

3 If 100 darts were thrown at the number 20, how many times would you expect them to have hit the target? ($100 \times \frac{3}{10} = 30$ times)

4 How many darts should be thrown at the bull to expect to have hit it once? ($\frac{40}{2} = 20$ times)

● **The class can now work through the questions on pages 48–49.**

FM Activity **Answers**

1 £160
2 a $\frac{1}{40}$ **b** $\frac{1}{60}$ **c** $\frac{1}{320}$
3 a $\frac{7}{640}$ **b** $\frac{35}{640} = \frac{7}{128}$
4 a £6.25 **b** $\frac{25}{60} = \frac{5}{12}$
5 a £1 notes – 8, £10 notes – 16, watches – 4 **b** £625 **c** £385
6 a $\frac{1}{45}$ **b** $\frac{1}{15}$ **c** $\frac{7}{9}$
7 a $\frac{10}{45} = \frac{2}{9}$
8 a 5 **b** £2
9 a 250 **b** 5 or 6 **c** 50
10 a 625 **b** 486 **c** 125 **d** 14 **e** £137.94

Plenary

● Ask the pupils whether they feel that they have a chance of winning prizes in a fairground. The answer should be yes, but not the star prize many times.
● Ask whether they think the Hook a Duck game seems fair.
● How would they change that game to make even more profit?

Homework

Make a game using a grid of twenty-five 5 cm squares, with £1 written on 5 of the squares and £5 written on just one square.

10p coin is rolled onto the grid. If it lands completely in a square with £1 or £5 written on it, you win the amount of money.

 a Roll a 10p coin 100 times and keep a tally of:
  ● the number of times you landed on the £5 square
  ● the number of times you landed on a £1 square
  ● the number of times you lost.

 b If this was a stall in a fairground, would you have made a profit?

 c Can you change the game in order to make it:
  i more attractive to players?
  ii more profitable?

Homework **Answers**

Answers will vary.

Number 2

Overview

4.1 Fractions and decimals

4.2 Adding and subtracting fractions

4.3 Multiplying and dividing fractions

4.4 Percentages

4.5 Percentage increase and decrease

4.6 Real-life problems

FM Going on holiday

Context

This chapter reinforces the links between fractions, decimals and percentages and introduces the phrases 'terminating decimal' and 'recurring decimal'. The idea is introduced of using the lowest common multiple as the common denominator to add and subtract fractions efficiently. This is then extended to multiplication and division of fractions with whole numbers, and then to increasing and decreasing quantities by a percentage using real contexts.

National Curriculum references

Framework objectives

4.1 Refine own findings and approaches on the basis of discussions with others; recognise efficiency in an approach; relate the current problem and structure to previous situations. Order decimals. Recognise that a recurring decimal is a fraction; use division to convert a fraction to a decimal; order fractions by writing them with a common denominator or by converting them to decimals.

4.2 Add and subtract fractions by writing them with a common denominator; calculate fractions of quantities (fraction answers).

4.3 Multiply and divide an integer by a fraction.

4.4 Interpret percentage as the operator 'so many hundredths of' and express one given number as a percentage of another.

4.5 Calculate percentages and find the outcome of a given percentage increase or decrease. Use the equivalence of fractions, decimals and percentages to compare proportions.

4.6 Recall equivalent fractions, decimals and percentages; use known facts to derive unknown facts, including products involving numbers such as 0.7 and 6, and 0.03 and 8.

FM Identify the mathematical features of a context or problem. Calculate percentages and find the outcome of a given percentage increase or decrease. Carry out more difficult calculations effectively and efficiently. Know rough metric equivalents of imperial measures in common use. Interpret tables and diagrams.

Key concepts

Applications and implications of mathematics

● Understand that basic process skills, for example, using fractions, decimals and percentages, can be used to solve real life problems and different approaches and techniques can be used to solve a single problem

Key processes

Representing

● Deciding on the appropriate method to use in given situations

Analysing

● Finding results and solutions to problems

Communicating and reflecting

● Interpreting results and solutions giving answers to an appropriate level of accuracy

Route mapping

Exercise	Levels		
	5	6	7
4A		1–7	8–10
4B	1	2–6	
4C	1–2	3–6	
4D		1–10	
4E	1–8		
4F		1–11	

Framework objectives – Fractions and decimals

Refine own findings and approaches on the basis of discussions with others; recognise efficiency in an approach; relate the current problem and structure to previous situations.

Order decimals.

Recognise that a recurring decimal is a fraction; use division to convert a fraction to a decimal; order fractions by writing them with a common denominator or by converting them to decimals.

Oral and mental starter

- This is an exercise in adding and subtracting integers.
- Using a target board, such as the one shown, explain that the object is to add the first three values in a column and then subtract the final value.
- Ask an individual pupil to do this or ask the class to note totals on a piece of paper (totals here are 87, 91, 45, 33, 34).
- This can be repeated for the rows by adding the first three and subtracting the last two (totals here are 55, 44, 62, 5).
- To make the activity easier, the bottom row can be covered and the first two numbers in each column added, and then the third number subtracted (totals are 95, 2, –15, 39, 6).
- Similarly, the last one or two columns can be covered.

	60	38	7	22	28
+	48	16	14	26	8
+	13	52	36	9	30
–	34	15	12	24	32
	+	+	–	–	

Main lesson activity

- The pupils will need a calculator for this lesson.
- Recall methods for writing a decimal as a fraction (for example, $0.34 = \frac{34}{100} = \frac{17}{50}$, after cancelling by 2).
- Repeat with 0.4 ($= \frac{4}{10} = \frac{2}{5}$) and 0.875 ($= \frac{875}{1000} = \frac{7}{8}$).
- Recall methods for converting fractions to decimals (for example, $\frac{17}{20} = 0.85$, dividing the numerator by the denominator).
- Repeat with $\frac{7}{10}$ ($= 0.7$) and $\frac{8}{25}$ ($= 0.32$, for which an alternative method is to make the denominator into 100).
- Now ask for the decimal equivalent to $\frac{1}{3}$. Pupils should recall this is 0.333 33, or they can work it out.
- Ask for the difference between this answer and previous answers.
- Define (or recall) the definition of a terminating decimal and a recurring decimal.
- Ask pupils to find the decimal equivalent to $\frac{452}{999}$ (0.452 452 452 ...).
- Introduce the recurring decimal notation of a 'dot' over the recurring digits or the first and last digit of a recurring cycle (for example, $0.\dot{3}$, $0.\dot{4}5\dot{2}$).
- Now ask pupils to write each of the following as a terminating decimal or a recurring decimal:

    $\frac{11}{20}$ ($= 0.55$), $\frac{3}{7}$ ($= 0.\dot{4}2857\dot{1}$), $\frac{3}{8}$ ($= 0.375$), $\frac{5}{16}$ ($= 0.312\,5$), $\frac{2}{3}$ ($= 0.\dot{6}$), $\frac{5}{12}$ ($= 0.41\dot{6}$).

- Note that in the last answer only the 6 recurs.
- Ask pupils which of the fractions $\frac{5}{8}$ and $\frac{3}{5}$ is larger.
- How could we find out?
- Either convert them into fractions with the same denominator ($\frac{25}{40}$ and $\frac{24}{40}$) or turn them into decimals (0.625 and 0.6).
- Discuss the advantages and/or disadvantages of each method. The conversion into fractions with a common denominator needs good table skills and the ability to spot a common denominator. Turning them into decimals is much easier if a calculator is available.

- **The class can now do Exercise 4A from Pupil Book 2.**

Exercise 4A — Answers

1 a $\frac{6}{25}$ b $\frac{9}{20}$ c $\frac{1}{8}$ d $\frac{87}{250}$ e $\frac{4}{5}$ f $\frac{111}{200}$ g $\frac{11}{20}$ h $\frac{7}{8}$

2 a 0.6 b 0.375 c 0.65 d 0.72

3 a 0.5 b 0.25 c 0.2 d 0.125 e 0.1 f 0.0625 g 0.05 h 0.04
   i 0.025 j 0.02

4 a 0.$\dot{3}$ b 0.1$\dot{6}$ c 0.$\dot{1}$42 85$\dot{7}$ d 0.$\dot{1}$ e 0.$\dot{0}\dot{9}$ f 0.08$\dot{3}$ g 0.$\dot{0}$769 2$\dot{3}$
   h 0.0$\dot{7}$1 428 $\dot{5}$ i 0.0$\dot{6}$ j 0.0$\dot{5}$

5 a 0.$\dot{6}$ b 0.8 c 0.$\dot{4}$28 57$\dot{1}$ d 0.$\dot{2}$ e 0.1875 f 0.625 g 0.58$\dot{3}$
   h 0.7$\dot{8}$5 714 $\dot{2}$ i 0.2$\dot{6}$ j 0.78

6 a $\frac{7}{20}$ b $\frac{5}{9}$ c $\frac{7}{8}$ d $\frac{2}{3}$

7 a $\frac{2}{9}$, $\frac{6}{25}$, $\frac{1}{4}$, $\frac{13}{50}$ b $\frac{3}{5}$, $\frac{5}{8}$, $\frac{2}{3}$, $\frac{17}{25}$

8 $\frac{1}{9}$ = 0.$\dot{1}$, $\frac{2}{9}$ = 0.$\dot{2}$, $\frac{3}{9}$ = 0.$\dot{3}$, $\frac{4}{9}$ = 0.$\dot{4}$, $\frac{5}{9}$ = 0.$\dot{5}$, $\frac{6}{9}$ = 0.$\dot{6}$, $\frac{7}{9}$ = 0.$\dot{7}$, $\frac{8}{9}$ = 0.$\dot{8}$

9 The sevenths always have the same six digits recurring, 142857, and they always recur in the same cyclic order.

10 The elevenths have the 9 times table as the recurring digits, 0.090 909, 0.181 818 …, etc.

Extension — Answers

a The number has factors that divide into 10, 100, 1000, etc.
b The denominator has factors that do not divide exactly into 10, 100, 1000, etc.

Plenary

● Write many fractions on the board in a random order, such as:
  $\frac{7}{10}$, $\frac{3}{4}$, $\frac{5}{13}$, $\frac{6}{25}$, $\frac{2}{9}$, $\frac{3}{5}$, $\frac{2}{3}$, $\frac{13}{18}$, $\frac{9}{14}$, etc.
● Ask the pupils to identify the terminating and recurring decimals.
● Ask the pupils to give you the decimal equivalents, and/or put them in order.
● Some they should know ($\frac{3}{4}$, $\frac{3}{5}$, $\frac{2}{3}$), and some they will need to work out with a calculator.
● Discuss the recurring decimal notation:
  $\frac{3}{14}$ (= 0.214 285 $\dot{7}$), $\frac{2}{9}$ (= 0.$\dot{2}$), $\frac{6}{25}$ (= 0.24), $\frac{7}{20}$ (= 0.35), $\frac{5}{13}$ (= 0.$\dot{3}$84 61$\dot{5}$),
  $\frac{3}{5}$ (= 0.6), $\frac{2}{3}$ (= 0.$\dot{6}$), $\frac{13}{18}$ (= 0.72$\dot{2}$), $\frac{3}{4}$ (= 0.75)

Key words

- numerator
- denominator
- terminating decimal
- recurring decimal
- simplest form

Homework

1 Write the following decimals as fractions with a denominator of 10, 100 or 1000 and then cancel to their simplest form if possible:

   a 0.44 b 0.78 c 0.625 d 0.928

2 Use a calculator to work out (or write down) the following terminating decimals:

   a $\frac{17}{20}$ b $\frac{3}{4}$ c $\frac{4}{5}$ d $\frac{11}{50}$ e $\frac{9}{10}$

3 Use a calculator to work out (or write down) the following recurring decimals:

   a $\frac{2}{3}$ b $\frac{5}{6}$ c $\frac{2}{7}$ d $\frac{6}{11}$ e $\frac{5}{12}$

4 In each of these pairs of fractions, which is larger?

   a $\frac{9}{20}$ and $\frac{4}{9}$ b $\frac{5}{8}$ and $\frac{31}{50}$

6

Homework Answers

1 a $\frac{11}{25}$ b $\frac{39}{50}$ c $\frac{5}{8}$ d $\frac{116}{125}$
2 a 0.85 b 0.75 c 0.8 d 0.22 e 0.9
3 a 0.$\dot{6}$ b 0.8$\dot{3}$ c 0.$\dot{2}$85 71$\dot{4}$ d 0.5$\dot{4}$ e 0.41$\dot{6}$
4 a $\frac{9}{20}$ b $\frac{5}{8}$

Framework objectives – Adding and subtracting fractions

Add and subtract fractions by writing them with a common denominator; calculate fractions of quantities (fraction answers).

Oral and mental starter

- Use a number line drawn on the board, or a 'counting stick'. Mark or state that one end is the number 0 and the other end is the number 4, as shown:

0   4

- Ask the pupils to identify the rest of the marks on the stick.
- As a group, or with an individual pupil, count in units of 0.4.
- Pupils can have the positions pointed out to them on the line or stick until the end is reached, when they have to continue without prompts.
- Repeat, possibly with different individuals to establish a class 'record'.
- Repeat the activity with the line or stick marked with 0 and 7, as shown:

0   7

- Alternatively, count down from 4 or 7 to 0.

Main lesson activity

- Write the following problem on the board: $\frac{1}{2} + \frac{1}{3}$.
- Ask the pupils to think of the answer, or write it down. The majority will give $\frac{2}{5}$.
- Get the correct answer and discuss the processes used to add fractions with a different denominator.
- Pupils have met this before and should recall the need to use the same denominator.
- Work through the original example in some detail: $\frac{1}{2} + \frac{1}{3} = \frac{3}{6} + \frac{2}{6} = \frac{5}{6}$.
- Repeat with $\frac{3}{8} + \frac{5}{12} = \frac{9}{24} + \frac{10}{24} = \frac{19}{24}$, and $\frac{4}{5} + \frac{3}{4} = \frac{16}{20} + \frac{15}{20} = \frac{31}{20} = 1\frac{11}{20}$.
- Recall the need to write top-heavy fractions as mixed numbers.
- Now ask for the answer to $\frac{2}{3} - \frac{1}{4} = \frac{8}{12} - \frac{3}{12} = \frac{5}{12}$.
- The method is basically the same, but with the top two numbers subtracted rather than added.
- Repeat with $\frac{4}{5} - \frac{2}{3} = \frac{12}{15} - \frac{10}{15} = \frac{2}{15}$, and $\frac{5}{12} - \frac{3}{8} = \frac{10}{24} - \frac{9}{24} = \frac{1}{24}$.

- **The class can now do Exercise 4B from Pupil Book 2.**

Exercise 4B **Answers**

1 a 12 **b** 30 **c** 15 **d** 6 **e** 20 **f** 4 **g** 18 **h** 12

2 a $\frac{11}{12}$ **b** $\frac{17}{30}$ **c** $\frac{11}{15}$ **d** $\frac{5}{6}$ **e** $\frac{9}{20}$ **f** $\frac{3}{4}$ **g** $\frac{17}{18}$ **h** $\frac{5}{12}$

3 a $\frac{1}{12}$ **b** $\frac{7}{30}$ **c** $\frac{1}{15}$ **d** $\frac{1}{6}$ **e** $\frac{3}{20}$ **f** $\frac{1}{4}$ **g** $\frac{13}{18}$ **h** $\frac{1}{12}$

4 a $\frac{7}{12}$ **b** $\frac{1}{2}$ **c** $\frac{11}{20}$ **d** $\frac{23}{24}$ **e** $\frac{17}{30}$ **f** $1\frac{17}{24}$ **g** $\frac{5}{6}$ **h** $1\frac{7}{12}$ **i** $\frac{13}{24}$ **j** $\frac{1}{2}$ **k** $\frac{1}{20}$ **l** $\frac{13}{18}$ **m** $\frac{1}{6}$
  n $\frac{1}{24}$ **o** $\frac{1}{3}$ **p** $\frac{7}{12}$

5 a $\frac{11}{24}$ **b** $3\frac{5}{21}$ **c** $3\frac{11}{12}$ **d** $2\frac{7}{15}$

6 $\frac{1}{6}$

Extension **Answers**

1 a $\frac{1}{8}+\frac{1}{4}$ **b** $\frac{1}{2}+\frac{1}{4}$ **c** $\frac{1}{2}+\frac{1}{12}$ **d** $\frac{1}{2}+\frac{1}{6}$

2 a $\frac{1}{2}+\frac{1}{4}+\frac{1}{8}$ **b** $\frac{1}{2}+\frac{1}{6}+\frac{1}{6}$ **c** $\frac{1}{4}+\frac{1}{4}+\frac{1}{8}$ **d** $\frac{1}{2}+\frac{1}{3}+\frac{1}{8}$

Plenary

- Write some fractions on the board, including some mixed numbers (for example, $\frac{1}{7}$, $\frac{3}{8}$, $\frac{3}{14}$, $\frac{5}{6}$, $2\frac{1}{3}$, $1\frac{2}{5}$).
- Ask the pupils to add and subtract combinations of these.
- Make sure they are aware of the need to convert mixed numbers to top-heavy fractions or to do the integer part separately.

Key words

☐ common
   denominator
☐ top-heavy
   fraction
☐ mixed number

Homework

1 Convert the following fractions to equivalent fractions with a common denominator, and then work out the answer, cancelling down or writing as a mixed number, if appropriate:

a $\frac{1}{5}+\frac{2}{7}$ **b** $\frac{5}{6}+\frac{2}{3}$ **c** $\frac{7}{10}+\frac{3}{4}$ **d** $\frac{1}{4}+\frac{2}{3}+\frac{7}{12}$ **e** $\frac{2}{3}-\frac{1}{7}$

f $\frac{5}{8}-\frac{1}{3}$ **g** $\frac{7}{10}-\frac{1}{4}$ **h** $\frac{3}{5}+\frac{2}{3}-\frac{3}{4}$

2 Convert the following fractions to equivalent fractions with a common denominator, and then work out the answer, cancelling down or writing as a mixed number if appropriate:

a $2\frac{1}{2}+\frac{3}{5}$ **b** $3\frac{3}{4}-2\frac{1}{3}$

Homework Answers

1 a $\frac{17}{35}$ **b** $1\frac{1}{2}$ **c** $1\frac{9}{20}$ **d** $1\frac{1}{2}$ **e** $\frac{11}{21}$ **f** $\frac{7}{24}$ **g** $\frac{9}{20}$ **h** $\frac{31}{60}$

2 a $3\frac{1}{10}$ **b** $1\frac{5}{12}$

51

Framework objectives – Multiplying and dividing fractions

Multiply and divide an integer by a fraction.

Oral and mental starter

● Display a target board as shown:

10	15	20	25	30	35
6	12	18	24	36	42
22	48	56	80	72	100

● Ask the pupils to give, for example, halves of the numbers in the bottom row, thirds of the numbers in the middle row, fifths of the numbers in the top row.
● Now ask the pupils to give two-thirds of the numbers in the middle row. Discuss how to do this by working out one-third then doubling.
● Extend to other non-unit fractions, for example two-fifths.

Main lesson activity

● Following on from the starter, reinforce that, for example, $\frac{2}{5}$ of 30 is the same as $\frac{2}{5} \times 30$.
● Encourage pupils to use mental arithmetic rather than a calculator.
● Now ask for the answer to $\frac{4}{5}$ of 45.
● Recall the method to do this: find $\frac{1}{5}$ of 45 (= 9) and then multiply by 4 (= 36).
● Repeat with $\frac{3}{4}$ of £28 (= £21), $\frac{2}{7}$ of 35 kg (= 10 kg).
● Ask for the answers to $3 \times \frac{4}{7}$ ($= \frac{12}{7} = 1\frac{5}{7}$) and $5 \times \frac{4}{5}$ ($= \frac{20}{5} = 4$).
● Ask for the answers to $\frac{3}{4} \div 3$ ($= \frac{3}{12} = \frac{1}{4}$) and $\frac{2}{7} \div 5$ ($= \frac{2}{35}$).
● Use further examples if more practice is needed.

● **The class can now do Exercise 4C from Pupil Book 2.**

Exercise 4C — Answers

1 a 4 **b** 12 **c** 8 **d** 24 **e** 5 **f** 15 **g** 30 **h** 100
2 a £20 **b** 12 kg **c** £30 **d** 200 cm **e** £24 **f** 36 grams **g** £27 **h** 36 km
3 a $3\frac{3}{4}$ **b** $5\frac{3}{5}$ **c** 6 **d** $3\frac{1}{2}$ **e** $7\frac{1}{5}$ **f** $2\frac{4}{7}$ **g** $7\frac{1}{2}$ **h** $7\frac{1}{2}$
4 a $\frac{3}{20}$ **b** $\frac{1}{10}$ **c** $\frac{1}{9}$ **d** $\frac{5}{63}$ **e** $\frac{2}{35}$ **f** $\frac{4}{9}$ **g** $\frac{3}{35}$ **h** $\frac{7}{48}$
5 smaller
6 smaller

Extension — Answers

a $36 \times \frac{1}{4}$ $\quad$ $35 \times \frac{2}{7}$ $\quad$ $24 \times \frac{5}{8}$
b $\frac{2}{7} \div 5$ $\quad$ $\frac{1}{4} \div 3$ $\quad$ $\frac{3}{8} \div 4$

Plenary

- Introduce the use of the fraction button on the calculator.
- Ensure that pupils can convert between mixed fractions and improper fractions using the calculator.
- Ask pupils to check their own answers to Exercise 4C using a calculator.

Key words

- fraction
- half
- third
- quarter
- fifth
- multiply
- improper fraction
- mixed number

5

Homework

1 Work out:

$\quad$ **a** $\frac{4}{9}$ of £36 $\qquad$ **b** $\frac{3}{7}$ of 49 kg

2 Work out, cancelling down or writing as mixed numbers, as appropriate:

$\quad$ **a** $3 \times \frac{5}{9}$ $\qquad$ **b** $4 \times \frac{3}{8}$ $\qquad$ **c** $\frac{3}{8} \div 6$ $\qquad$ **d** $\frac{4}{7} \div 8$

Homework Answers

1 a £16 **b** 21 kg
2 a $1\frac{2}{3}$ **b** $1\frac{1}{2}$ **c** $\frac{1}{16}$ **d** $\frac{1}{14}$

LESSON 4.4

Framework objectives – Percentages
Interpret percentage as the operator 'so many hundredths of' and express one given number as a percentage of another.

Oral and mental starter

- Ask the pupils to think of products that make 100 (for example, 1×100, 2×50, 4×25, 5×20, 10×10).
- If possible, also establish $40 \times 2\frac{1}{2}$ and $8 \times 12\frac{1}{2}$.
- Now use a target board like the one shown, and ask the pupils to give the percentage equivalent to each fraction.
- Discuss how to do this, by multiplying the denominator to make 100 and doing the same to the numerator.
- Answers for the grid are shown below:

$\frac{1}{2}$	$\frac{3}{10}$	$\frac{7}{20}$	$\frac{2}{5}$	$\frac{13}{25}$
$\frac{11}{20}$	$\frac{7}{40}$	$\frac{43}{50}$	$\frac{3}{8}$	$\frac{7}{10}$
$\frac{1}{5}$	$\frac{1}{4}$	$\frac{1}{20}$	$\frac{12}{25}$	$\frac{1}{8}$
$\frac{9}{25}$	$\frac{9}{50}$	$\frac{31}{40}$	$\frac{7}{8}$	$\frac{3}{4}$

50%	30%	35%	40%	52%
55%	17½%	86%	37½%	70%
20%	25%	5%	48%	12½%
36%	18%	77½%	87½%	75%

Main lesson activity

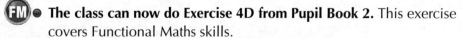

- This follows on from the oral and mental starter above.
- Ask the pupils for the percentage of 40 that is 32.
- Discuss ways of doing this, firstly without a calculator.
- Establish the fraction $\frac{32}{40}$ and multiply the top and bottom by $2\frac{1}{2}$ to give $\frac{80}{100}$, which is 80% (or cancel first to $\frac{4}{5}$).
- Also write on the board that 32 out of 40 is the same as 80 out of 100.
- Repeat the process with 55 out of 200 ($27\frac{1}{2}$%) and 3 out of 8 ($37\frac{1}{2}$%).
- Now discuss the calculator method to find, say, the percentage of 65 that is 13 (20%).
- This is the fraction $\frac{13}{65}$, which can be converted to a percentage by dividing through and multiplying by 100.
- Repeat the process with 24 out of 80 (30%) and 55 out of 69 (80% when rounded off).
- Ask the pupils how they would compare two sets of exam marks, such as 38 out of 60 and 45 out of 70.
- Converting both to percentages gives 63.3% and 64.3%, so 45 out of 70 is a better percentage mark.

FM • **The class can now do Exercise 4D from Pupil Book 2.** This exercise covers Functional Maths skills.

Exercise 4D — Answers

1 **a** 64% **b** 85% **c** 60% **d** 64% **e** 61% **f** 31% **g** 64% **h** 72%
2 **a** 55% **b** 23% **c** 33% **d** 40% **e** 47% **f** 56% **g** 18% **h** 37%
3 Maths 65%, English 60%, Science 67½%; Trevor did best in Science.
4 Number 14%, Algebra 43%, Shape 29%, Data Handling 15%. The total is 101% because 3 of the values are rounded up.
5 **a** £72 **b** 60%
6 **a** £500 **b** 9%
7 Electricity 40%, gas 35%, oil 25%
8 Internet 29%, long distance 53%, local 18%
9 Food 59%, drink 32%, cleaning products 8%. The total is 99% because all the values are rounded down.
10 B roads 13%, A roads 59%, motorways 28%.

Extension — Answers

1 20
2 24
3 £120
4 £96

Plenary

- Write four quantities on the left-hand side of the board, such as 45, 60, 56 and 12.
- Write four other quantities on the right-hand side of the board, such as 120, 300, 200 and 160.
- Match the quantities, one from the left-hand side and one from the right-hand side.
- Calculate, with or without a calculator as appropriate, the percentage that the left value is of the right value.
- Some pairs are obvious, such as 12 and 120.
- Some are clearly non-calculator, such as 45 out of 300.
- Some have whole-number answers, but are not obvious, such as 56 out of 160 (35%).
- Discuss the appropriate methods to use for these.

Key words

- equivalent fraction
- denominator
- rounding off

Homework

1 Without using a calculator, work out what percentage the first quantity is of the second:

   a 45 out of 50   **b** 13 out of 20   **c** 22 out of 40   **d** 16 out of 200

2 Use a calculator to work out what percentage the first quantity is of the second (round off to the nearest percent if necessary):

   a 21 out of 60   **b** 28 out of 80   **c** 35 out of 75   **d** 46 out of 85

3 In the Year 10 exams, Tamsin scored 84 out of 120 in Maths, 54 out of 75 in English and 64 out of 90 in Science. Convert these scores into percentages. Which test did Tamsin do best in?

Homework — Answers

1 **a** 90% **b** 65% **c** 55% **d** 8%
2 **a** 35% **b** 35% **c** 47% **d** 54%
3 Maths 70%, English 72%, Science 71%; Tamsin did best in English.

6

Framework objectives – Percentage increase and decrease

Calculate percentages and find the outcome of a given percentage increase or decrease. Use the equivalence of fractions, decimals and percentages to compare proportions.

Oral and mental starter

- Use a target board such as the one shown:
- Recall the mental method for multiplying a two-digit number by a single-digit number (partitioning), such as $7 \times 23 = 7 \times 20 + 7 \times 3 = 140 + 21 = 161$.
- Roll a dice (preferably a 10-sided dice). Ask the pupils to multiply the numbers on the grid in turn by the number on the dice.
- Do this with individual pupils or ask the class to write down the answers (some jotting could be allowed).

28	38	17	22	60
18	16	14	26	48
30	52	36	19	13
32	15	12	24	34

Main lesson activity

- Ask the pupils what they understand by percentage increase or decrease.
- Ask where such things occur in everyday life (for example, sales, increases from inflation, pay rises, and so on).
- Give an example, such as a cooker is reduced by 15% in a sale. If its original price was £320, what is its sale price? (Pupils may need to be introduced to the vocabulary of cost price, sale price, selling price, etc.)
- Work through the example. First calculate 15% of £320 (= £48) and then deduct this from the original price, £320 – £48 = £272.
- Now calculate 85% of £320 (= £272). Can the pupils explain why this gives the same answer as deducting 15%? Show that decreasing a value by 15% is the same as finding 85% of the value (100 – 15 = 85), using a diagram like the one below.

- Give another example, such as a plumber adds VAT at $17\frac{1}{2}$% to her bills. How much will she add to a bill of £90? What will the final bill be? ($17\frac{1}{2}$% of £90 is £15.75, so the final bill will be £90 + £15.75 = £105.75.
- Now ask the class what the final bill is as a percentage of the original, that is £105.75 as a percentage of £90 (= $117\frac{1}{2}$%). Explain this by writing £90 + £15.75 = £105.75 on the board again. Ask what £90 is as a percentage of £90 (100%, write this underneath). Ask what £15.75 is as a percentage of £90 ($17\frac{1}{2}$%, as just worked out). Add the percentages to give $117\frac{1}{2}$%. Illustrate the concept with the diagram shown, if necessary.

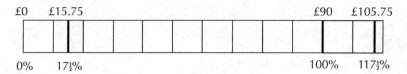

● Give another example, such as the depth of water in a swimming pool is measured every day as it is filled up slowly. The depths are given in this table:

Day	1	2	3	4	5
Depth (m)	1	2	4	–	0

● What is the percentage increase in depth between day 1 and day 2? (The answer is 100%.) What about between day 1 and day 3? (The answer is 300%.) Make the distinction that 4 m is 400% of 1 m, but that this is only a 300% increase.
● If the depth increases by 150% between day 3 and day 4, then what is the depth on day 4? (The answer is 10 m.)
● Lastly, explain that the swimming pool sprang a leak on day 5 and all the water escaped. What is the percentage decrease in depth between day 4 and day 5? (The answer is 100%.)
● Repeat with more examples if any of the pupils are still not happy with percentages over 100.

● **The class can now do Exercise 4E from Pupil Book 2**. This exercise covers Functional Maths skills.

Exercise 4E **Answers**

1 a 12 bats **b** 52 bats **2 a** 9000 midges **b** 11,000 midges **c** 55%
3 a £49.50 **b** £43.20 **c** £144 **d** £72 **e** £74.75 **f** £93.50 **g** £312.50
h £225 **i** £22.78 **j** £4.59 **4 a i** £14.79 **ii** £22.10 **iii** £44.88 **iv** £62.90
b i £241.50 **ii** £136.50 **iii** £404.25 **iv** £103.95
5 a 552 bacteria **b** 2952 bacteria **6 a** 108 rabbits **b** 122 rabbits **c** 53%
7 a €72.80 **b** €55.90 **c** €153.72 **d** €381.60 **e** €220.40 **f** €22.08
g €527.85 **h** €345.22 **i** €22.92 **j** €3.89 **8 a i** £20.56 **ii** £57.75
iii £49.70 **iv** £108.50 **b i** £293.75 **ii** £211.50 **iii** £333.70 **iv** £233.83

Extension **Answers**

a £5.95 **b** £7.70 **c** £9.80 **d** £13.13 **e** £21 **f** £33.25

Key words

- percentage increase/decrease
- reduction
- value added tax (VAT)
- sale price
- original price
- selling price

Plenary

● Put a variety of percentages on the board, such as 5%, 10%, 20%, 25%, and a variety of quantities, such as £32, 58 kg, 200 km and £150.
● Apply each percentage value to the different quantities and calculate a percentage increase or decrease, as appropriate.
● Most of these can be done without a calculator.

Homework

Do not use a calculator for Questions 1 and 2.
1 A car has a top speed of 130 miles per hour. After tuning, the top speed increases by 15%.
  a How many miles per hour faster is the car now?
  b What is the new top speed of the car?
2 Work out the final amount when:
  a £44 is increased by 20%   **b** £58 is decreased by 10%
  c £140 is increased by 25%   **d** £80 is decreased by 20%
3 Work out the final amount when:
  a £48 is increased by 12%   **b** £62 is decreased by 8%
  c £235 is decreased by 15%   **d** £88 is decreased by 32%

Homework Answers

1 a 19.5 mph **b** 149.5 mph
2 a £52.80 **b** £52.20 **c** £175 **d** £64
3 a £53.76 **b** £57.04 **c** £199.75 **d** £59.84

5

Framework objectives – Real-life problems

Recall equivalent fractions, decimals and percentages; use known facts to derive unknown facts, including products involving numbers such as 0.7 and 6, and 0.03 and 8.

Oral and mental starter

- Recall methods of multiplying integers and decimals expressed to one significant figure (for example, $0.7 \times 6 = 4.2$, $0.03 \times 8 = 0.24$).
- Use this to ask for answers to a variety of similar questions.
- As these can be hard to verbalise and for pupils to conceptualise, a grid, as shown, could be used.
- Particular squares could be pointed at and individual pupils asked for the product.
- Reverse the process by asking for the missing number in $0.4 \times ? = 0.32$ (0.8) or the answer to $0.048 \div 0.6 = ?$ (0.08).
- Repeat this process with $0.04 \div ? = 0.08$ (0.5), $0.5 \times ? = 0.035$ (0.07), etc.

×	0.8	0.3	9	0.6
0.7				
5				
0.02				
0.01				

Main lesson activity

- This is a lesson on practical situations in which percentages are used.
- Introduce two real-life situations, such as buying goods on credit and paying tax.
- Ask the pupils what they know about buying goods on credit.
- Establish that usually a deposit is required, followed by so many monthly payments. For example, a bike that normally sells for £299 can be bought for a 20% deposit followed by 12 monthly payments of £24. How much will it cost buying by credit? What percentage of the original cost is the extra cost?

    Deposit = 20% of £299 = £59.80;
    monthly payments = 12 × £24 = £288;
    total = £59.80 + £288 = £347.80.
    Extra cost = £347.80 – £299 = £48.80.
    £48.80 as percentage of £299 is 48.80 ÷ 299 × 100 = 16.3%

- Ask pupils what they know about income tax.
- Establish that people have a tax allowance (the amount they can earn before tax).
- After the allowance is deducted, the rest is the taxable income.
- Tax is paid at 10% for some of the taxable income, 22% for some more of the taxable income and 40% if the taxable income is higher than a certain amount.
- This is quite a complicated idea for pupils to take in, so it may be easier to concentrate on tax allowance and one rate of tax for taxable income. For example, Mr Brown earns £25 000 a year. His tax allowance is £5000 and he pays tax at 22%.

    a What is his taxable income?
    b How much tax does he pay?

        Taxable income = £25 000 – £5000 = £20 000
        Tax paid = 22% of £20 000 = £4400.

- **FM** **The class can now do Exercise 4F from Pupil Book 2.** This exercise covers Functional Maths skills.

Exercise 4F Answers

1 Plan A: **a** £624 **b** 130%
   Plan B: **a** £480 **b** 100%
   Plan C: **a** £696 **b** 145%
2 20%
3 29.3%
4 a £7296.25 **b** 4.3%
5 Ada £4466
   Bert £6675
   Carmine £922.50
   Derek £1760
   Ethel £15,200
6 20%
7 a £9 **b** £8.10 **c** £8.00
  d John is incorrect. A 20% decrease followed by a 15% decrease, is actually the
     same as a 32% decrease overall.
8 a £360 **b** 7.5%
9 a £5170 **b** £330
10 a £180 **b** £22.50
11 Scheme A costs £1344 and Scheme B costs £1017.75, so Scheme B is cheaper.
   Scheme A might be preferred if the buyer does not have enough money for the
   deposit.

Key words

- deposit
- percentage profit
- percentage loss
- credit
- cost price
- selling price

Plenary

- Discuss some of the aspects of percentages in real life [for example, tax,
  National Insurance, tax allowances (vary with circumstances), tax bands,
  higher rate tax, credit, hire purchase, bank loans, etc.].

Homework

1 A scooter that normally costs £1599.99 can be bought using two different plans:

Plan	Deposit	Number of payments	Each payment
A	20%	24	£65
B	50%	12	£66.67

  a Work out how much the scooter costs using each plan.

  b Work out the percentage of the original price that each plan costs.

2 A shop buys a table for £62 and sells it for £86.80. Work out the percentage profit made by the shop.

3 Work out the tax paid by the following people:

Person	Income	Tax allowance	Tax rate
Xavier	£35 000	£4600	22%
Yves	£52 000	£5300	35%

Homework Answers

1 Plan A: **a** £1880 **b** 117.5%
   Plan B: **a** £1600 **b** 100%
2 40%
3 Xavier £6688 Yves £16345

National Tests Answers

1 a 40, 4, 0.8 **b** 44.8
2 a 8.4, 4.2, 2.1 **b** £98.70
3 $\frac{1644}{21\,842} \times 100 = 7.5\%$
4 a 120, 84 **b** 38.8, 61.2

Functional Maths – Going on holiday

Oral and mental starter

Look at the information on the going on holiday activity on page 62 of the corresponding Pupil Book. This Functional Maths activity consolidates topics previously covered on reading and interpreting data from tables and scales, exchange rates, imperial units and percentage change.

● Draw the following table on the board or OHP.

08:00	17:00	18:05	23:20
00:30	20:20	8 am	6:05 pm
5 pm	15:15	9:05 am	12:30 am
09:05	11:20 pm	3:15 pm	8:20 pm

● Ask pupils to match up the equivalent pairs of times.

Main lesson activity

● Encourage pupils to suggest questions which might arise from the data on page 62, for example, the reasons why there may not be flights everyday and why there are two flights on Friday.
● Discuss check-in times at airports and the reasons why people need to check in a long time before the flight departure, for example. passport control, security checks and time to check in perhaps over 200 people. Pupils may want to discuss their own experiences at airports.
● Discuss exchange rates before starting question 2. For example, the rates may change on a daily basis, some banks may charge commission and others even advertise 0% commission. Mention that banks only issue notes and the smallest euro note is €5 and all transactions are therefore usually rounded to the nearest €5.
● Discuss the conversion scale before starting question 3. Ask pupils why people still use imperial units.
● Discuss the benefits of hiring a car before you go on holiday, for example, able to pick up the car at the airport, often cheaper as there are usually special offers, particularly on the internet.

● **The class can now work through the questions on pages 62–63.**

FM Activity   Answers

1 a Tue, Fri, Sat   b LS225, return LS224   c 4 hours 45 minutes and 4 hours 35 minutes   d 05.15   e £998   f £1058.28
2 a €565   b €75   c £40
3 a No, more than 20 kg   b About $12\frac{1}{2}$ stones
   c Yes, 1st and 6lb is less than 10 kg.
4 Ka £57.60, Clio £72, Astra £96

Plenary

- Sum up by asking the pupils what areas of mathematics they have used during the lesson. They could do this individually by writing them on the board or on a flip-chart.

Homework

Mrs Green works in London and often goes on business to Newcastle.

The tables show the times of the flights she can catch.

From London Gatwick to Newcastle

Flight	M	T	W	T	F	S	S	From	Departs	To	Arrives
LS102	✈	✈	✈	✈		✈		London Gatwick	08:30	Newcastle	09:45
LS104	✈	✈	✈	✈	✈			London Gatwick	15:20	Newcastle	16:35
LS108	✈	✈	✈	✈			✈	London Gatwick	19:00	Newcastle	20:15

From Newcastle to London Gatwick

Flight	M	T	W	T	F	S	S	From	Departs	To	Arrives
LS101						✈		Newcastle	06:40	London Gatwick	07:55
LS101	✈	✈	✈	✈				Newcastle	06:40	London Gatwick	08:00
LS103	✈	✈	✈	✈	✈			Newcastle	13:35	London Gatwick	14:50
LS107	✈	✈	✈	✈			✈	Newcastle	17:05	London Gatwick	18:20

1 How long is the scheduled flight time from Gatwick to Newcastle?
2 In the table, there are two LS101 flights. Explain the difference between them. Give a possible reason for the difference.
3 **a** Flight LS101 flies to Gatwick and then returns to Newcastle as Flight LS102. How long is the turn-round time?
   b Give other examples of the flight numbers where there are also possible turn-round flights.
4 Mrs Green has a three-hour meeting in Newcastle on a Monday. She allows herself 40 minutes to travel between the airport and the meeting venue. Which flights will she travel on? Give the flight number and the departure time for her outward journey and the flight number and arrival time for her return journey.
5 One week Mrs Green has a two-day meeting in Newcastle which starts at 10 am on Wednesday and finishes at 5 pm on Thursday. She decides to fly to Newcastle on Tuesday evening and fly back to London on Friday. Give the flight numbers and the departure times for her flights.

Homework Answers

1 1 hour 15 minutes
2 The Saturday flight is five minutes shorter. It is possibly not so busy at the airports on a Saturday.
3 **a** 30 minutes (35 minutes on Saturday)   **b** LS104 and LS107, LS103 and LS104, LS107 and LS108
4 outward: LS102, dep 08:30, return: LS107, arrive 18:20
5 outward: LS108, dep 19:00, return: LS103, dep 13:35

Algebra **2**

Overview

5.1 Algebraic shorthand

5.2 Like terms

5.3 Expanding brackets

5.4 Using algebra with shapes

5.5 Use of index notation with algebra

Context

This chapter builds on previously learned algebraic techniques and moves to more advanced method of algebraic manipulation. These include multiplication and division of algebraic terms, expanding brackets with negative coefficients, combining (using addition and subtraction) linear expressions and index notation.

National Curriculum references

Framework objectives

5.1 Recognise that letter symbols play different roles in equations, formulae and functions.

5.2 Simplify or transform linear expressions by collecting like terms.

5.3 Understand that algebraic operations, including the use of brackets, follow the rules of arithmetic. Multiply a single term over a bracket.

5.4 Understand that algebraic operations, including the use of brackets, follow the rules of arithmetic. Multiply a single term over a bracket.

5.5 Understand that algebraic operations, including the use of brackets, follow the rules of arithmetic; use index notation for small positive integer powers.

Key concepts

Applications and implications of mathematics

● Know that variables can be represented by letters, and how to manipulate algebraic expressions

● Know that manipulation of algebraic expressions will, in general, produce another expression, but that manipulation of numerical expressions will, in general, produce a numerical value

● Know that the rules of arithmetic apply to variables represented by letters

Key processes

Representing

- Multiplying or adding together algebraic expressions to produce simplified expressions
- Expanding and simplifying expressions involving brackets
- Knowing how to combine powers when multiplied or divided

Analysing

- Using negative values accurately when expanding brackets and collecting terms

Communicating and reflecting

- Correct and accurate algebraic manipulation

Route mapping

Exercise	Levels		
	4	**5**	**6**
5A	1–3	4–5	
5B	1–4		
5C		1	2–6
5D	1		2–5
5E		1–4	5–7

LESSON 5.1

Framework objectives – Algebraic shorthand
Recognise that letter symbols play different roles in equations, formulae and functions.

Oral and mental starter

- Ask the class to do a countdown from 10, 9, 8 to zero.
- Now ask them to do a countdown from 10, but in steps of a half: ten, nine-and-a-half, nine, eight-and-a-half to zero.
- Now ask for a countdown from ten in steps of 0.4: 10, 9.6, 9.2, 8.8 to zero.
- If this proves very difficult mentally, write the numbers on the board as the pupils respond.
- With the pupils in pairs (or individually), sort out a sequence, such as down a class row then back up, and ask them to do an individual countdown, such as from 10 in steps of 0.3, etc.
- You can extend the countdown to start from 100 and use steps of numbers like $2\frac{1}{2}$.

Main lesson activity

- Show the pupils some well-known symbols, such as road signs, and ask them what they each mean.
- Ask what is meant by the symbols $+$, $\times$, $\div$, $-$, which are shorthand for our arithmetic operations.
- Tell them that it is a very powerful tool to be able to use a letter to stand for a number, as this has its own shorthand, which is what we need to be able to recognise.
- Explain that one of these is to miss out the multiplication sign. Ask the pupils if they know why (because x is widely used in algebra so to use it may cause great confusion; it is also easier to write the expression). Show them how to write the favoured 'curly' style x.
- Introduce these conventions:
    $5 \times m$ is written $5m$ (leave out $\times$ signs);
    $m \times 5$ is written $5m$; $b \times 2a$ is written $2ab$ (numbers come to the left of letters);
    $1x$ is written x;

    $a \div b$ is written $\frac{a}{b}$; $2 \div (a + 1)$ is written $\frac{2}{a + 1}$;   (write division as a fraction)

- Now simplify some expressions involving multiplication and division:
    $2 \times m \times 3 = 2 \times 3 \times m = 6 \times m = 6m$; $3 \times a \times 2b = 3 \times 2 \times a \times b = 6ab$;
    $\frac{3a}{3} = a$ (for example, a third of three apples is one apple)

- **The class can now do Question 1 of Exercise 5A from Pupil Book 2.**
- Now talk about the $=$ sign, and explain that we use it to mean 'has the same value as', and not 'is exactly the same as'. For example, in $3 + 4 = 4 + 3$ each side has the same value, but they are not exactly the same as they are written a different way round.
- Explain that we can use algebra to help us recognise useful, general patterns and properties of our operations in arithmetic. For example, $a + b = b + a$ illustrates that we can always add two numbers the other way round and get the same answer.
- Ask the class if the same thing works for subtraction. For example, is $a - b = b - a$? (It is not.)
- Ask them if it works for multiplication. For example, is $ab = ba$? You may need to show a few examples of this before all the class are convinced, for example $3 \times 4 = 4 \times 3$. Contrast this with division.

- Explain to the class that it is very easy to misuse the equals sign, and we must be careful not to do that. Lead them through solving the equation $3x + 2 = 23$ on the board.
- Write out each stage explicitly, emphasising that they must always do the same thing to BOTH sides, in order to keep them equal.
- Show clearly the way to set the whole solution out, with equals signs in a column, to end up with $x = 7$.

- **The class can now do the rest of Exercise 5A from Pupil Book 2.**

Exercise 5A **Answers**

1 a $3n$ **b** $5n$ **c** $7m$ **d** $8t$ **e** ab **f** mn **g** $5p$ **h** $6m$ **i** $a(b + c)$ **j** $m(p + q)$
  k $c(a + b)$ **l** abc **m** $\dfrac{m}{3}$ **n** $\dfrac{5}{n}$ **o** $\dfrac{(a + b)}{c}$ **p** $\dfrac{7}{(m + n)}$ **q** $2fg$ **r** $5ej$
  s $b(a + 3)$ **t** $\dfrac{(5 + g)}{3}$

2 a $4hp$ **b** $4st$ **c** $8mn$ **d** $25wx$ **e** $9bc$ **f** $24bcd$ **g** $12afg$

3 a $m \times n = mn$ **b** $q - p = -p + q$ **c** $a \div b = \dfrac{a}{b}$ **d** $6 + x = x + 6$
  e $3y = 3 \times y$

4 a $x = 5$ **b** $x = 2$ **c** $x = 3$ **d** $x = 7$ **e** $x = 1.5$ **f** $x = 2.5$ **g** $x = 0.5$
  h $x = 7.5$ **i** $x = 15$ **j** $x = 11$ **k** $x = 13$ **l** $x = 8$

5 a, **b** and **e**

Extension **Answers**

a 2 is not true **b** 1, 3 and 4 may be true

Plenary

- Go through the shorthand routines of algebra, and ask the pupils why they are useful to us. Also, discuss misuse of the equals sign, such as:
    $$2x + 3 = 18 = 2x = 15 = x = 7.5$$
- Discuss with the class why this is wrong.

Key words
- symbol
- operation
- equal

Homework

1 Write each of these expressions in as simple a way as possible:

  a $5 \times p$ **b** $2 \times t$ **c** $8 \times q$ **d** $k \times t$ **e** $m \times (a - c)$
  f $t \times (5 + d)$ **g** $(a - b) \times d$ **h** $m \times n \times p$ **i** $m \div 3$ **j** $5 \div n$
  k $(a + b) \div m$ **l** $5 \div (q - n)$

2 Solve the following equations, making correct use of the equals sign:

  a $4x + 1 = 21$ **b** $3x - 3 = 18$ **c** $5x + 4 = 29$ **d** $3x + 1 = 13$ **e** $7x + 3 = 17$
  f $8x - 3 = 13$ **g** $10x + 9 = 12$ **h** $2x - 7 = 10$

3 Show which of the statements below are true (not all are):

  a $b - c = d + e$ is the same as $d - e = b + c$ **b** $p - b = 6$ is the same as $6 = p - b$
  c $5t = t + 3$ is the same as $t = 5t + 3$

Homework Answers

1 **a** $5p$ **b** $2t$ **c** $8q$ **d** kt **e** $m(a - c)$ **f** $t(5 + d)$ **g** $d(a - b)$ **h** mnp **i** $\frac{m}{3}$ **j** $\frac{5}{n}$ **k** $\frac{(a + b)}{m}$ **l** $\frac{5}{(q - n)}$
2 **a** $x = 5$ **b** $x = 7$ **c** $x = 5$ **d** $x = 4$ **e** $x = 2$ **f** $x = 2$ **g** 0.3 **h** $x = 8.5$
3 Only **b** can be shown to be possibly true

LESSON 5.2

Framework objectives – Like terms
Simplify or transform linear expressions by collecting like terms.

Oral and mental starter

- This activity is about using rules.
- You are going to ask pupils for a number and give them a number back, and they have to guess the rule.
- The idea is to see who can guess the rule first.
- Start with the rule 'double and add 1'.
- Ask pupils in turn for a number, say 7, and give them the reply after you have applied the rule (in this case, 15).
- Use other rules, such as 'take away from 50', 'add 3 and double'.
- You can ask some pupils to think of a rule and have other pupils give them numbers.
- This can develop into a team game, with one half of the class versus the other half. Each takes it in turn to think of the rule and then to guess. The rule has to be found within so many turns, or a score is kept of how many guesses had to be made, or of how many numbers had to be processed.
- Let no-one write anything down, as this should all be mental maths.

Main lesson activity

- Ask the class for a quick way of writing $2 + 2 + 2$ (3×2). Replace 2 by a and show that $a + a + a$ can be written more concisely as $3 \times a$ or $3a$.
- Write $3a + 2a$, $3d + e - 2f$ and $\frac{x}{4} + x^2$ on the board.

  Use these to remind the class of the meanings of 'expression' and 'term'. (An algebraic expression is made up of individual terms.)
- Write the expression $3a + 2a$ and ask for its terms ($2a$, $3a$). Ask how the terms are alike (both: contain a; are multiples of a). Demonstrate how like terms can be combined to simplify an expression, for example, $3a + 2a$ can be simplified to $5a$ (use the analogy of adding three apples and two apples).
- Show how to simplify some other expressions containing like terms, for example, $2a + 3a + 4a$, $2ab + 3ab$.
- Write the expression $3a + 2b$ and ask if it can be simplified. Describe the terms $3a$ and $2b$ as 'unlike', which means they cannot be combined, so the expression cannot be simplified. (Use the analogy of adding three apples and two bananas.)
- Go through some more examples of unlike terms:

  $3ab + 2a$ (like terms must have exactly the same letters)
  $3a^2 + 2a$ ($3a^2 = 3 \times a \times a$)
- Simplify some more expressions containing like and unlike terms, for example,

  $4e + 3e + 5f = 7e + 5f$
  $4x - x = 3x$ (remind pupils that x can be written $1x$)
  $2b - 7b = -5b$ (because $2 - 7 = -5$)
  $-a - a = -2a$
  $4x + 2y - 3x = 4x - 3x + 2y = x + 2y$ (group like terms together before combining)

$$7 + 2ab + 3ab = 7 + 5ab$$
$$-2x^2 + 7x^2 + 4x = 5x^2 + 4x$$

● **The class can now do Exercise 5B from Pupil Book 2.**

Exercise 5B **Answers**

1 a $4a, 2d, -6c$ **b** $5x, -3, 7$ **c** $3x^2, 4x, 5$ **d** $9, -2u, -7$
2 a $11h$ **b** $5p$ **c** $6u$ **d** $-5b$ **e** $5j$ **f** $-12r$ **g** $6k$ **h** $8y$ **i** $10d$ **j** $7i$ **k** $3b$
   l $-4b$ **m** $9xy$ **n** $11p^2$ **o** $-5ab$ **p** $4a^?$ **q** $-10fg$
3 a $8h + 5g$ **b** $2g + 8m$ **c** $8f + 10d$ **d** $11x + 5y$ **e** $6q + 2r$ **f** $4 + 2s$ **g** $3c + 3$
   h $14b + 7$ **i** $14w - 7$ **j** $6bf + 5g$ **k** $7d + 3d^2$ **l** $4st + 5t$ **m** $-3s + 2t$
   n $-2h + 2i$ **o** $4y - 9w$
4 a $13e + 9f$ **b** $6u + 7t$ **c** $4b + 3d$ **d** $7a + 7c$ **e** $6f + 5g$ **f** $2h + 6i$ **g** $p + 5q$
   h $19j + 4k$ **i** $2t - 2u$ **j** $5s - 4t$ **k** $-2p + q$ **l** $-6d - 4e$

Extension **Answers**

1 If the first number is n, the next will be $(n + 1)$, and the product of these two is
$n(n + 1)$. Either n is odd and $n + 1$ is even, or vice versa, so $n(n + 1)$ is odd × even or
even × odd, both of which are even.

2 Any three consecutive integers will always consist of one multiple of 3 and at least
one even number. Let the three numbers be $3x$, $2y$ and z. Then $3x \times 2y \times z = 6xyz$
which is a multiple of 6.

Plenary

Key words

● Write a range of like and unlike terms on the board, for example:
   $5x, 2a, 4x^2, 3ab, 6a, 9y, 2x, 3xy$ etc.
   Ask pupils to identify the like terms, and add them together at the board.
● Quiz pupils on why certain terms are unlike, for example, $5x$ and $4x^2$.

- **algebraic expressions**
- **like terms**
- **simplify**

Homework

1 Make a list of the terms in each of the following.

   a $2y - 3c$ **b** $6 + m + \frac{g}{4}$ **c** $4a = 24$ **d** $9 = 3b^2 - 2b$

Simplify the expressions in Questions 2, 3 and 4.

2 a $2u + 4u$ **b** $9k - 3k$ **c** $5t - 7t$ **d** $-m - 2m$
   e $4n + 2n + 7n$ **f** $9r - 2r - 3r$ **g** $4xy - 2xy$ **h** $3m^2 + 8m^2 - 6m^2$

3 a $2h + 5h + 4g$ **b** $5y - 3y + 2z$ **c** $8a + 3b - 20b$ **d** $4i - 7j + 2j$
   e $2bc + 5bc + 3b$ **f** $9f^2 - 2f - 5f^2$

4 a $4w + 3w + 2x + 3x$ **b** $9p - 3p + 7q - 9q$ **c** $3d + 2e + 5d + e$
   d $4f + 6g - 2g + 3f$ **e** $5m + 3n - 2m - 8n$ **f** $-3a + 2b + 4a - b$

4

Homework **Answers**

1 a $2y, -3c$ **b** $6, m, \frac{g}{4}$ **c** $4a, 24$ **d** $9, 3b^2, -2b$
2 a $6u$ **b** $6k$ **c** $-2t$ **d** $-3m$ **e** $13n$ **f** $4r$ **g** $2xy$ **h** $5m^2$
3 a $7h + 4g$ **b** $2y + 2z$ **c** $8a - 17b$ **d** $4i - 5j$ **e** $7bc + 3b$ **f** $4f^2 - 2f$
4 a $7w + 5x$ **b** $6p - 2q$ **c** $8d + 3e$ **d** $7f + 4g$ **e** $3m - 5n$ **f** $a + b$

LESSON 5.3

Framework objectives – Expanding brackets

Understand that algebraic operations, including the use of brackets, follow the rules of arithmetic. Multiply a single term over a bracket.

Oral and mental starter

- This is about approximations.
- Ask the pupils what the approximate answer is to 314×78.
- Put the suggested answers on the board, but do not accept any calculated answers (the correct answer is 24 492).
- Talk about the guesses, and say that those of more than two significant figures are not approximations.
- Show how we estimate by rounding off to a suitable number and then multiplying, for example, $300 \times 80 = 24\,000$.
- Ask if we can tell whether or not this estimate is definitely too large or too small.
- We do not know, because we rounded the 314 down and the 78 up.
- Repeat this for the estimation of 298×67.
- This time, if we round both numbers up, our estimate is $300 \times 70 = 21\,000$, which we know to be too big as we rounded both numbers up.
- Talk about what would happen with the estimation of 508×42.
- We would probably round both numbers down and hence are certain of an estimate that is too small.

Main lesson activity

- Remind the class that the shorthand for $6 \times y$ is $6y$ and the shorthand for $3 \times (t + 4)$ is $3(t + 4)$.
- Put on the board $5(3 + 4)$ and ask the class what value this has. When someone suggests 35, ask them how they calculated it (hopefully 5×7).
- Now show that we could have multiplied it out separately as $5 \times 3 + 5 \times 4$, which is $15 + 20 = 35$. So we can see that $5(3 + 4) = 5 \times 3 + 5 \times 4$.
- This process is also called expanding.
- Show how we use exactly this technique in algebra to multiply out an expression such as $4(2m + 3)$, by showing that $4(2m + 3) = 4 \times 2m + 4 \times 3 = 8m + 12$.
- Demonstrate expanding some more brackets on the board:

  $3(2a + b) = 6a + 3b$
  $4(x - 2y) = 4x - 8y$
  $a(2b + c) = 2ab + ac$
  $-(a + 2) = -a - 2$ (recall that $-(a + 2) = -1(a + 2)$)
  $-3(a - b) = -3a + 3b$ (note that multiplying a bracket by a negative number changes the sign of each term in the brackets)

- Point out that it will often be possible to simplify an expression further, by combining like terms, once it has been expanded. Show the class some examples:

  $2(3a + 2b) + 4a = 6a + 4b + 4a = 10a + 4b$
  $2(f + 3) + 3(2f + 7) = 2f + 6 + 6f + 21 = 8f + 27$
  $4(2d - 3e) + 3(d - 2e) = 8d - 12e + 3d - 6e = 11d - 18e$

- **The class can now do Exercise 5C from Pupil Book 2.**

Exercise 5C Answers

1 **a** $5p + 5q$ **b** $9m - 9n$ **c** $st + su$ **d** $12d + 8$ **e** $2ab + ac$ **f** $15j - 6k$
  g $5e + 2ef$ **h** $130 - 50n$ **i** $24g + 18h$ **j** $8a + 8b + 8c$
2 **a** $-a - b$ **b** $-q + p$ **c** $-3p - 4$ **d** $-7 + 2x$ **e** $-3g - 6$ **f** $-2d + 2f$
  g $-10h - 15i$ **h** $-24d + 12f$ **i** $6j - 3k$
3 **a** $5w + 2x$ **b** $5d + 7f$ **c** $14h + 15s$ **d** $20x + 12y$ **e** $4m - 14n$ **f** $4p + 9q$
4 **a** $6a + 6b$ **b** $21i + 23j$ **c** $39p + 15q$ **d** $8d + 2f$ **e** $16e + t$ **f** $18x + 2y$
  g $11m - 2x$ **h** $38u - 26k$
5 **a** $5h - 2k$ **b** $4v - t$ **c** $7 - a$ **d** $4p + 5q$ **e** $16 - 3e$ **f** $10a - 5b$
6 **a** $2m + 3n$ **b** $4g + 22h$ **c** $d + 23e$ **d** $6 - 3x$

Extension Answers

1 $a(b + c) + b(a + c) + c(a + b) = ab + ac + ab + bc + ac + bc = 2ab + 2bc + 2ac$
  $2(ab + bc + ac) = 2ab + 2bc + 2ac$

Plenary

Key words
- multiply out
- expand
- BODMAS

● Write up a range of expressions for pupils to expand and simplify at the board:

$3(a - 2b)$; $-4(2x - 5)$; $m(2 - n)$; $4(2i - j) - 3i$; $5(2x + 3) + 3(4x - 5)$; etc.

Homework

1 Expand the following brackets.

  a $5(a - b)$ **b** $d(w + f)$ **c** $4(s + 2t)$ **d** $m(2k - 3n)$ **e** $4(3r - 2t + 4b)$

  f $-(2 + m)$ **g** $-(b - c)$ **h** $-2(x + 5)$ **i** $-3(2i - h)$ **j** $-6(3d + 4h)$

For Questions 2–5, expand the brackets and then simplify the expressions.

2 **a** $2(d + e) + 3d$ **b** $5t + 4(s + 2t)$ **c** $2(3u - 2v) - 8u$

3 **a** $4(m + n) + 2(2m + n)$ **b** $5(2i + 3j) + 4(3i - 3j)$ **c** $5(3b - 2a) + 6(2a - b)$

4 **a** $7p - (2p + 3q)$ **b** $9x - (7x - 2y)$ **c** $4d - (5e - 3d)$

5 **a** $5(s + t) - (2s + 4t)$ **b** $7(a + 3b) - 3(2a - 4b)$ **c** $3(2g - 3h) - 2(4g - h)$

5

6

Homework Answers

1 **a** $5a - 5b$ **b** $dw + df$ **c** $4s + 8t$ **d** $2mk - 3mn$ **e** $12r - 8t + 16b$ **f** $-2 - m$ **g** $-b + c$ **h** $-2x - 10$
  i $-6i + 3h$ **j** $-18d - 24h$
2 **a** $5d + 2e$ **b** $13t + 4s$ **c** $-2u - 4v$
3 **a** $8m + 6n$ **b** $22i + 3j$ **c** $9b + 2a$
4 **a** $5p - 3q$ **b** $2x + 2y$ **c** $7d - 5e$
5 **a** $3s + t$ **b** $a + 33b$ **c** $-2g - 7h$

Framework objectives – Using algebra with shapes
Understand that algebraic operations, including the use of brackets, follow the rules of arithmetic. Multiply a single term over a bracket.

Oral and mental starter

- Work with complements of 10.
- Tell the class that we are working with ten. Complements of numbers you give are the numbers needed to add to those numbers to make 10. For example, the complement of 7 is 3.
- Start with 2.5 (complement of 7.5), and ask in turn for the complements of decimal numbers such as:

  3.5, 8.5, 4.5, 7.2, 8.3, 5.4, 1.7, 9.4

- After a few, stop and ask the pupils how they are trying to find the answer. Some will add on the decimal part to reach the next integer and then build up to 10, while others will use a subtraction method. Explore the diversity of methods, and encourage the pupils to use the technique they see as clear to them. Ask them for a few more examples.
- Then move onto fractions, three and a half, four and two eighths. Again, stop after a few and ask the class how they are doing this – is it the same method as they used for the decimals?
- Finish by asking again for complements of 10, but mix up decimals with fractions; for example, 2.4, three and five eighths, 6.3, five and two fifths, 8.1, seven and five sixths, etc.

Main lesson activity

- Draw the shape shown here onto the board and ask pupils what the perimeter of the shape is.

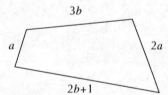

- Add up the lengths to give $a + 3b + 2a + 2b + 1$, which simplifies to $3a + 5b + 1$.

- **The class can now do Questions 1 and 2 of Exercise 5D from Pupil Book 2.**

- Draw the next shape shown on the board, and ask the pupils what the area of the shape is.

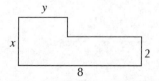

- Show how the shape can be split into two rectangles, parts A $(y \times x)$ and B $[2 \times (8 - y)]$.
- Ask the pupils for the area of part A (xy).
- Ask the pupils for the area of part B $[2(8 - y) = 16 - 2y]$.
- Show that the total area of the shape is given by $xy + 16 - 2y$.

- **The class can now do the rest of Exercise 5D from Pupil Book 2.**

Exercise 5D — Answers

1 **a** $10a$ **b** $6a + 4d$ **c** $7a + k$ **d** $8x + 3y$ **e** $6p + 11t$ **f** $10n + 9k$

2 **a** $14 + kw - 2k$ **b** $45 + gf - 5g$

3 **a** 36 cm^2 **b** $(9 - 3) \times (4 - x) = 6(4 - x) = 24 - 6x$ cm^2
   c i $12 - 3x$ cm^2 **ii** $6x$ cm^2 **iii** $3x$ cm^2 **d** $(24 - 6x) + (12 - 3x) + 6x + 3x = 36$ cm^2

4 $A = 20 - 4x$ cm^2, $B = 40 - 8x$ cm^2, $C = 4$ cm^2, $D = 8x$ cm^2

5 **a** $(2x + 2y)$, $(4x + y)$, $(8x + 7y)$ **b** $(p + 2t)$, $(2p - 4t)$, $(5p + 4t)$
   c $(n - 2c)$, $(n + 6c)$, $8c$ **d** $(2a + 2b)$, $(2a + 3b)$, $4b$

Plenary

Key words
☐ perimeter
☐ area
☐ expansion
☐ simplify

● Talk to the class about how the work they are doing with shapes here looks quite different from the work that involved finding the actual length of perimeters and the actual areas of shapes. Explain that there are times when we have to use algebra like this to help find the actual perimeter or area.

● For example, if we knew that the shape below had an area of 100 m^2, how could we find x? The answer to this will not be dealt with until Year 10 or Year 11.

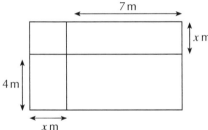

Homework

1 Write down the perimeter of each of the following shapes as simply as possible:

a
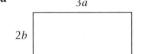
$3a$
$2b$

b
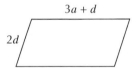
$3a + d$
$2d$

c

$3t$ $3t$
$3k - t$

2 Write down the area of each smaller rectangle in this larger rectangle:

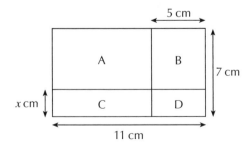

Homework Answers

1 **a** $6a + 4b$ **b** $6a + 6d$ **c** $3k + 5t$
2 $A = 42 - 6x$, $B = 35 - 5x$, $C = 6x$, $D = 5x$

Framework objectives – Use of index notation with algebra

Understand that algebraic operations, including the use of brackets, follow the rules of arithmetic; use index notation for small positive integer powers.

Oral and mental starter

- Ask the class if they can divide 420 by 15 in their heads without writing anything down, or using a calculator.
- It is most unlikely that anyone can (the answer is 28); if anyone does tell you the answer, ask them to tell the class how they did it.
- Explain that you can do this in your head in various ways. One is to divide by 3 and then divide by 5 ($420 \div 3 = 140$, then $\div 5$ to give 28). Another is to divide by 5 and then by 3 ($420 \div 5 = 84$, then $\div 3$ to give 28). Another is to divide by 30, and then double ($420 \div 30 = 14$, then double to give 28). Explain how this works, that to divide by 10 and then double is how you can divide by 5.
- Have the class try out the various techniques by putting a list on the board and asking them all to divide each number by 15. Use the following list: 345 (23), 465 (31), 240 (16), 390 (26), 645 (43), 525 (35), 195 (13), 360 (24), 495 (33), 630 (42), 270 (18), 570 (38).
- After most of the class have used one of the techniques correctly and understand it, ask them how they can tell if a number will divide by 15 before we start dividing. It must be both a multiple of 5 (end in a 5 or a 0) and a multiple of three (digits add up to a multiple of 3).

Main lesson activity

- Ask the class for a quick way of writing $2 \times 2 \times 2$ (2^3) and recall index notation (base = 2, index = 3).
- Replace 2 by a and ask how to write $a \times a \times a$ concisely (a^3).
- Give some more examples for pupils to abbreviate: $m \times m \times m \times m \times m = m^5$; $2a \times a = 2a^2$; $4m \times 3m \times 2m = 24m^3$; $f + f + f + f + f \times f \times f \times f = 4f + f^4$
- Ask the class to tell you the difference between c^5 and $5c$.

- **The class can now do Questions 1, 2 and 3 of Exercise 5E from Pupil Book 2.**

- Write on the board $3(4t - 2)$ and ask the pupils to tell you how to expand it. From previous lessons they should remember this to be $12t - 6$.
- Now write on the board $m(4m - 2)$ and ask the pupils if they can expand this product.
- From the suggestions there is likely to be the correct one of $4m^2 - 2m$; you need to show why the wrong suggestions are not correct. Ensure that each pupil sees the process as identical to the above one, in which numbers are used instead of variables.
- On the board go through a few more similar expansions with the class.
- When they are all confident about these, write on the board $m(3m + 4t)$, and ask the class if they can suggest what this expansion will be.
- Most of the pupils will see the pattern and tell you $3m^2 + 4mt$, but make sure all the class are confident about these expansions, and do a few more on the board with them if necessary.

- **The class can now do Question 4 of Exercise 5E from Pupil Book 2.**

- When they have done this, tell the class they are about to do some difficult algebra, but that they will able to work their way through the expansions and simplifications, if they take care.
- Write on the board $m(m + 3p) - p(2m - 5p)$, and go through the expansion carefully to get $m^2 + 3mp - 2mp + 5p^2$, especially the $-p \times -5p = +5p^2$ step, and then simplify to $m^2 + mp + 5p^2$.
- You may need to go though another example with the class on the board.
- **The class can now complete Exercise 5E from Pupil Book 2**.

Exercise 5E   Answers

1 **a** a^5 **b** r^7 **c** b^9 **d** m^{14} **e** $12a^2$ **f** $2p^2$ **g** $12g^3$ **h** $216k^4$
2 **a** $5f$ **b** w^4 **c** $7c$ **d** k^{11} **e** $6D$
3 $5j = j + j + j + j + j$ $j^5 = j \times j \times j \times j \times j$
4 **a** $d^2 + d$ **b** $4a^2 - 3a$ **c** $4p + p^2$ **d** $6w - 3w^2$ **e** $3f^2 + fg$ **f** $2u^2 - 3us$
  g $qh + 4q^2$ **h** $9AC - 5A^2$
5 **a** $6mn + 3m$ **b** $3i^2 + 4ir$ **c** $5v^2 - 4vt$ **d** $3jk - j^2$ **e** $st + 5s^2$ **f** $-3cq - 3q^2$
6 **a** $d^2 + 2dh + 2h^2$ **b** $3m^2 + 23mn - 4n^2$ **c** $5e^2 + 2ef - 3f^2$
  d $11xy - 2y^2 + 5x^2$ **e** $4k^2 - 5tk - 7t^2$ **f** $j^2 + 16jr - 2r^2$
7 **a** $6d^2 - 5d$ **b** $3a^2 + 4a$ **c** $5t^2 + 2t$ **d** $3w^2 + w$ **e** $2u^2 - 2u$ **f** $5d^2 - 12d$

Extension   Answers

1 **a** d^5 **b** d^6 **c** d^9 **d** d^9
2 **a** Add the indices. **b** $d^m \times d^n = d^{m+n}$
3 **a** d^6 **b** a^{16} **c** e^{45} **d** w^{99} **e** r^{16}
4 **a** $15a^{12}$ **b** $j^{14}k^{10}$ **c** $24m^{15}n^{11}$ **d** $s^{11}t^{14}$

Plenary

- Write a range of expressions for pupils to abbreviate/simplify/expand on the board: $s \times s \times s$; $k + k + k + k + k$; $d \times 3d$; $2i \times i \times i + i + i$; $q(r - q)$; $t(3t - 2)$; $4u^2 + u(3 - u)$; $f(3f - 2g) + g(2f + 7g)$

Key words

- power
- index
- indices

Homework

1 Write the following expressions using index form.
  a $h \times h \times h \times h \times h \times h \times h \times h$ **b** $c \times 3c$ **c** $4d \times d \times d$ **d** $3w \times w \times 2w \times w \times 2w$
2 Write the following expressions as briefly as possible.
  a $i + i + i + i + i$ **b** $eeeee$ **c** $ppppp + q + q + q$
3 Expand the following brackets.
  a $d(d + 5)$ **b** $q(2q + 3p)$ **c** $5t(2k - 5t)$
4 Expand and simplify the following expressions.
  a $v(2t + 3) + 4vt$ **b** $u(3u + h) + 2u^2$ **c** $8jk - j(2k + j)$ **d** $m(m + n) + n(2m + 3n)$
  e $t(7t - 3y) - y(4t - 2y)$ **f** $3b^2 + b(4b + d)$ **g** $w(2w + 5x) + w(4x + 3w)$

Homework   Answers

1 **a** h^8 **b** $3c^2$ **c** $4d^3$ **d** $12w^5$
2 **a** $5i$ **b** e^5 **c** $p^5 + 3q$
3 **a** $d^2 + 5d$ **b** $2q^2 + 3pq$ **c** $10tk - 25t^2$
4 **a** $6vt + 3v$ **b** $5u^2 + uh$ **c** $6jk - j^2$ **d** $m^2 + 3mn + 3n^2$ **e** $7t^2 - 7ty + 2y^2$ **f** $7b^2 + bd$ **g** $5w^2 + 9wx$

National Tests   Answers

1 **a** 13, 12, (5), 2, (10), 18, (15), 8, 7
  b $a = 16, b = 4, c = 9$
2 **a** 8 **b** 3
3 $y = 5, k = 3$
4 $-, \div, +, \times$
5 $8x + 31$
6 No, $14 \times 17 - 51 = 187$
7 $9 + 2k, k^2 + 6k$
8 6.5
9 0.5
10 Answer should be $6a + 3$

Geometry
and Measures **2**

Overview

6.1 Area of a triangle

6.2 Area of a parallelogram

6.3 Area of a trapezium

6.4 Volume of a cuboid

6.5 Imperial units

Context

This chapter initially shows pupils how to deduce and use the formulae to find the area of triangles, parallelograms and trapezia, and then introduces them to the formulae to find the surface area and volume of a cuboid. Finally, pupils are shown how to convert imperial units in daily use to metric units of measurement.

National Curriculum references

Framework objectives

6.1 Choose and use units of measurement to measure, estimate, calculate and solve problems in a range of contexts. Derive and use formulae for the area of a triangle; calculate areas of compound shapes.

6.2 Choose and use units of measurement to measure, estimate, calculate and solve problems in a range of contexts. Derive and use formulae for the area of a parallelogram.

6.3 Choose and use units of measurement to measure, estimate, calculate and solve problems in a range of contexts. Derive and use formulae for the area of a trapezium; calculate areas of compound shapes.

6.4 Choose and use units of measurement to measure, estimate, calculate and solve problems in a range of contexts. Know and use the formula for the volume of a cuboid; calculate volumes and surface areas of cuboids and shapes made from cuboids.

6.5 Choose and use units of measurement to measure, estimate, calculate and solve problems in a range of contexts; know rough metric equivalents of imperial measures in common use, such as miles, pounds (lb) and pints.

Key concepts

Applications and implications of mathematics

● Understand the concept of area for a 2-D shape

● Understand the concepts of surface area and volume for 3-D shapes

● Understand the importance of converting imperial units to metric units of measurement

Key processes

Representing

- Using the correct formula to calculate the area of triangles, parallelograms and trapezia
- Using the formula to calculate the volume of a cuboid

Analysing

- Knowing how to calculate the area of a compound shape
- Recognising the different units used for area and volume
- Identifying the methods used to find the surface area and volume of a cuboid

Communicating and reflecting

- Showing clear methods when calculating the area of 2-D shapes and the volume of a cuboid
- Explaining how to convert an imperial unit of measurement to a metric unit of measurement

Route mapping

Exercise	Levels		
	5	6	7
6A		1–7	
6B		1–6	
6C		1–7	
6D		1–9	10
6E	1–11		

Framework objectives – Area of a triangle

Choose and use units of measurement to measure, estimate, calculate and solve problems in a range of contexts.

Derive and use formulae for the area of a triangle; calculate areas of compound shapes.

Oral and mental starter

- A revision starter on perimeters and areas of rectangles.
- Divide the class into pairs, with each pair having an individual whiteboard or a sheet of A4 paper.
- Ask the class to draw a sketch of a rectangle that has a perimeter of 10 cm and an area of 6 cm² and hold up their solution once they have drawn it.
- The first pair to give the correct answer gains a point.
- Repeat the activity a number of times using different examples to suit the ability of the class.

Main lesson activity

- For this activity the class needs coloured card or gummed paper and scissors.
- Ask the class to cut out two triangles that are exactly the same.
  Cut both triangles into two, as in the diagram.

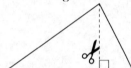

Arrange the four triangles to form a rectangle, which shows that the area of the triangle is equal to half the area of the rectangle:
Area 1 = Area 2 and Area 3 = Area 4
We define the base and the height of a triangle as in the diagram below the rectangle.
The height of the triangle is sometimes referred to as the **perpendicular height.**
The area of a triangle is given by the formula:
$A = \frac{1}{2} \times b \times h = \frac{1}{2}bh$

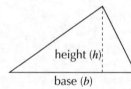

- Show the class an example.

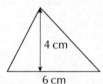

On the diagram above, $b = 6$ cm and $h = 4$ cm. So $A = \frac{1}{2} \times 6 \times 4 = 12$ cm². Explain that this calculation can be worked out in different ways, for example: $(6 \div 2) \times 4 = 12$ or $(6 \times 4) \div 2 = 12$.

- Explain that the height of the triangle is sometimes given outside the triangle. For example, on the diagram to the right $b = 8$ cm and $h = 5$ cm, so $A = \frac{1}{2} \times 8 \times 5 = 20$ cm².

- Show the class how to find the area of a compound shape by dividing it into rectangles and triangles, as in the shape shown.
  Divide the shape into a rectangle and a triangle.

$$\text{Area of A} = \frac{3 \times 4}{2} = \frac{12}{2} = 6 \text{ cm}^2.$$

Area of B = $3 \times 5 = 15$ cm².
So the area of the shape = $6 + 15 = 21$ cm².

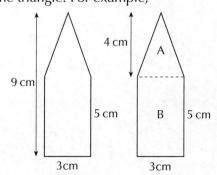

● **The class can now do Exercise 6A from Pupil Book 2.**

Exercise 6A **Answers**

1 a 24 cm² **b** 70 cm² **c** 12.5 cm² **d** 6 m² **e** 28 m²
2 a 15 cm² **b** 60 cm² **c** 270 mm²
3 a 17.5 cm² **b** 30 m² **c** 120 mm²
4 a 10 cm² **b** 7 cm² **c** 22.5 m² **d** 10 mm **e** 7 m
5 a 6 cm² **b** 10 cm² **c** 6 cm² **d** 12 cm²
6 a 6 m² **b** 45 cm² **c** 12 m²
7 2.4 m²

Extension **Answers**

Triangles for which the product of the base and the height is 72 (for example, 1 × 72, 2 × 36, 3 × 24, 4 × 18, 6 × 12).

Key words

☐ area
☐ base
☐ compound shape
☐ perpendicular height
☐ triangle

Plenary

● Ask the class to work in pairs or small groups.
● Ask each group to explain how to find the area of a triangle by drawing diagrams on individual whiteboards or on A4 paper.
● Ask different groups to show their explanation to the rest of the class.

Homework

1 Calculate the area of each of the following triangles:

a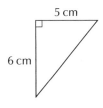
5 cm
6 cm

b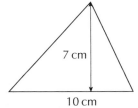
7 cm
10 cm

c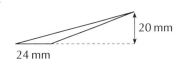
20 mm
24 mm

2 Calculate the area of each of the following triangles:

a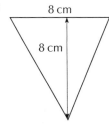
8 cm
8 cm

b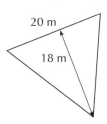
20 m
18 m

c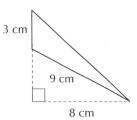
3 cm
9 cm
8 cm

3 Calculate the area of each of the following compound shapes:

a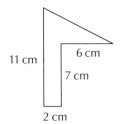
11 cm
6 cm
7 cm
2 cm

b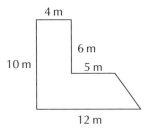
4 m
6 m
10 m
5 m
12 m

Homework Answers

1 a 15 cm² **b** 35 cm² **c** 240 mm²
2 a 32 cm² **b** 180 m² **c** 12 cm²
3 a 30 cm² **b** 66 m²

**LESSON
6.2**

Framework objectives – Area of a parallelogram

Choose and use units of measurement to measure, estimate, calculate and solve problems in a range of contexts.

Derive and use formulae for the area of a parallelogram.

Oral and mental starter

- Draw the grid shown on the board or on an OHP.
- Ask the class to work out the largest number they can make by adding any two adjacent numbers on the grid. Explain that the two numbers can be from any row, column or diagonal.
- Now repeat this, but change the operation to multiplication.
- Repeat the activity, but now use three adjacent numbers from any row, column or diagonal.
- This activity can be extended by using larger numbers or grids of different size.

1	8	5
4	2	7
9	6	3

Main lesson activity

- For this activity, the class needs coloured card or gummed paper and scissors.
- Ask the class to cut out a parallelogram.

Cut off a triangle as in the diagram and place it at the other side. This shows that the area of the parallelogram has the same area as a rectangle with the same base and height. The area of a parallelogram is given by the formula:

$A = b \times h = bh$

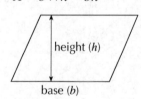

height (*h*)

base (*b*)

- Show the class an example. On the diagram, $b = 8$ cm and $h = 5$ cm, so
$A = 8 \times 5 = 40$ cm^2.

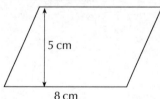

5 cm

8 cm

- **The class can now do Exercise 6B from Pupil Book 2.**

Exercise 6B   Answers

1 a 36 cm² **b** 150 cm² **c** 768 mm²
2 a 80 cm² **b** 49 m² **c** 80 cm²
3 a 88.2 cm² **b** 30 cm²
4 a 32 cm² **b** 204 cm² **c** 40 m² **d** 4 mm **e** 3.5 m
5 a 20 cm² **b** 15 cm² **c** 24 cm²
6 4.5 cm

Extension   Answers

1 6 cm
2 a 38.5 cm² **b** 96 cm² **c** 720 mm²

Plenary

- Ask the class to work in pairs or small groups.
- Ask each group to explain how to find the area of a parallelogram by drawing diagrams on individual whiteboards or on A4 paper.
- Ask different groups to show their explanation to the rest of the class.

Key words

- [ ] **area**
- [ ] **base**
- [ ] **perpendicular height**
- [ ] **parallelogram**

Homework

1 Calculate the area of each of the following parallelograms:

a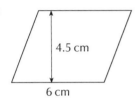
4.5 cm
6 cm

b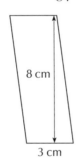
8 cm
3 cm

c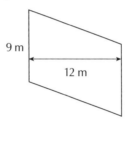
9 m
12 m

2 Calculate the height of each of the following parallelograms:

a Area = 63 cm²
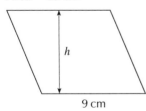
h
9 cm

b Area = 130 m²
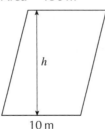
h
10 m

c Area = 400 mm²
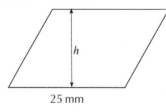
h
25 mm

3 The perpendicular height of a parallelogram is 10 cm and it has an area of 55 cm². Find the length of the base of the parallelogram.

Homework Answers

1 a 27 cm² **b** 24 cm² **c** 108 m²
2 a 7 cm **b** 13 m **c** 16 mm
3 5.5 cm

Framework objectives – Area of a trapezium

Choose and use units of measurement to measure, estimate, calculate and solve problems in a range of contexts.

Derive and use formulae for the area of a trapezium; calculate areas of compound shapes.

Oral and mental starter

- Ask the class to work in pairs or groups for this activity.
- Explain to the class that they have to make as many numbers from 1 to 10 as they can in about 10 minutes by using only four 4s and any of the mathematical operations +, −, ×, ÷, which may be repeated. Allow them to use the rules of BODMAS, but brackets may be used.
- Some examples are:

$$4 \div 4 \times 4 \div 4 = 1 \qquad 4 \div 4 + 4 \div 4 = 2 \qquad (4 + 4 + 4) \div 4 = 3$$

Main lesson activity

- For this activity the class needs coloured card or gummed paper and scissors.
- Ask the class to cut out two trapezia (plural of trapezium can also be trapeziums) that are the same size, and arrange them to form a parallelogram by rotating one by half a turn:

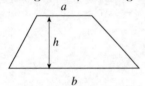 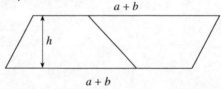

This shows that the area of the trapezium is half the area of a parallelogram. So the area of a trapezium is $\frac{1}{2}$ × sum of the lengths of the parallel sides × the height.

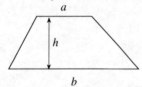

The area of a trapezium is given by the formula:

$$A = \tfrac{1}{2} \times (a + b) \times h = \tfrac{1}{2}(a + b)h$$

- Show the class the example below. On the diagram, $a = 7$ cm, $b = 3$ cm and $h = 4$ cm.

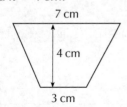

The area is:

$$A = \tfrac{1}{2} \times (3 + 7) \times 4 = \frac{10 \times 4}{2} = 20 \text{ cm}^2$$

- **The class can now do Exercise 6C from Pupil Book 2.**

Exercise 6C — Answers

1 a 35 cm² **b** 56 cm² **c** 8 m² **d** 35 m² **e** 160 mm² **2 a** 15 cm² **b** 66 cm²
c 30 m² **d** 4 cm **e** 10 cm **f** 10 m **3 a** 2 m² **b** 4 m² **4** 30 m² **5** 1480 mm²
6 172 cm² **7** Values of a, b and h with $(a + b) \times h = 16$ and $b > a$ (for example, $a = 3$,
$b = 5$, $h = 2$; $a = 1$, $b = 7$, $h = 2$; $a = 1$, $b = 3$, $h = 4$).

Extension — Answers

1 a 30 cm² **b** 135 cm² **c** 6.24 m²
2 a

Shape	Number of dots on perimeter of shape	Number of dots inside shape	Area of shape (cm²)
i	8	1	4
ii	12	3	8
iii	8	3	6
iv	4	2	3
v	11	3	7.5
vi	14	4	10

b $A = P + I - 1$

Plenary

- A revision exercise to make sure that the pupils know the formulae for the area of different quadrilaterals.
- Draw the following quadrilaterals on the board or OHP: square, rectangle, triangle, parallelogram and trapezium.
- Ask the pupils to write down in their books the formula to find the area of each of the shapes.
- Check their answers by asking individual pupils to write the formula for each quadrilateral on the board.

Key words
- area
- base
- perpendicular height
- trapezium

Homework

1 Calculate the area of each of the following trapezia:

a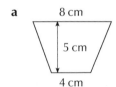

b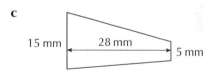

c

2 For each of the following trapezia, calculate:

i its perimeter **ii** its area

a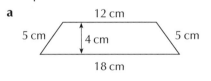

b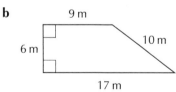

3 Find the height of the trapezium below if it has an area of 100 cm²:

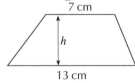

Homework Answers

1 a 30 cm² **b** 10 m² **c** 280 mm²
2 a i 40 cm **ii** 60 cm² **b i** 42 m **ii** 78 m²
3 10 cm

LESSON
6.4

Framework objectives – Volume of a cuboid

Choose and use units of measurement to measure, estimate, calculate and solve problems in a range of contexts.

Know and use the formula for the volume of a cuboid; calculate volumes and surface areas of cuboids and shapes made from cuboids.

Oral and mental starter

- Write the number 12 on the board.
- Ask individual pupils to come up and write on the board three numbers that have a product of 12, allowing repeats. Remind them that 'product' means 'multiply'.
- Examples are: $1 \times 1 \times 12$, $1 \times 2 \times 6$, $1 \times 3 \times 4$, $2 \times 2 \times 3$.
- Repeat the activity using different numbers.

Main lesson activity

- Show the class a cuboid made from multi-link cubes with length = 4 cm, width = 3 cm and height = 2 cm.
- Remind the class how to find the total surface area of the cuboid by finding the area of its six surfaces and adding them together.
- Draw the cuboid shown on the board:
  The formula to find the total surface area of any cuboid is:
  $$A = 2lw + 2lh + 2wh$$
  So the surface area of the multi-link cuboid described above is:
  $$A = (2 \times 4 \times 3) + (2 \times 4 \times 2) + (2 \times 3 \times 2)$$
  $$= 24 + 16 + 12$$
  $$= 52 \text{ cm}^2$$

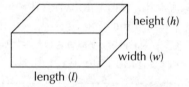

- Explain to the class that **volume** is the amount of space inside a 3-D shape.
- Show the class the multi-link cube and explain that the volume is made from 24 cubes.
- So a quick way to find the volume of a cuboid is to multiply its length by its width by its height.
- Using the same diagram:
  The volume of a cuboid = length × width × height
  $$V = l \times w \times h = lwh$$
- The metric units of volume in common use are:
  the cubic millimetre (mm³)
  the cubic centimetre (cm³)
  the cubic metre (m³)
  So the volume of the multi-link cuboid above is $V = 4 \times 3 \times 2 = 24 \text{ cm}^3$.
- Explain to the class that the **capacity** of a 3-D shape is the volume of liquid or gas it can hold. The metric unit of capacity is the litre (l). The class should then write down the following in their books:
  100 centilitres (cl) = 1 litre
  1000 millilitres (ml) = 1 litre
  Show the class various objects for which capacity is used, such as a 5 ml spoon or a 70 cl wine bottle.
- The following metric conversions for capacity should also be noted:
  $$1 \, l = 1000 \text{ cm}^3$$
  $$1 \text{ ml} = 1 \text{ cm}^3$$
  $$1000 \, l = 1 \text{ m}^3$$

- **The class can now do Exercise 6D from Pupil Book 2.**

Exercise 6D **Answers**

1 **a i** 304 cm² **ii** 320 cm³ **b i** 884 cm² **ii** 1680 cm³ **c i** 40 m² **ii** 16 m³
2 **a** 9 l **b** 1.8 l **c** 0.56 l
3 **a** 24 cm³ **b** 3.84 m³ **c** 3 cm **d** 3 mm **e** 2 m
4 **a** 8 cm³ **b** 125 cm³ **c** 1728 cm³
5 6000 m³
6 96
7 **a** 36 m³ **b** 36 000 l
8 **a** 1080 cm³ **b** 18
9 9600 cm³
10 **a** 16 m³ **b** 11 520 m³

Extension **Answers**

2 $l = 15$ cm, $w = 12$ cm, $h = 4$ cm, $V = 720$ cm³

Plenary

● Draw a cuboid on the board or OHP:

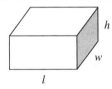

● Ask the class to explain how to find the total surface area of the cuboid.
● Ask the class to explain how to find the volume of the cuboid.

Key words

☐ **capacity:**
  litre
  centilitre
  millilitre
☐ **volume:**
  cubic millimetre
  cubic centimetre
  cubic metre

Homework

1 Find the volume for each of the following cuboids:

  a

  b

  c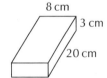

2 Find the volume of a cube with edge length 3 cm.

3 The measurements of the sides of a rectangular water tank are $l = 4$ m, $w = 3$ m and $h = 2$ m.

  a Find the volume of the tank.

  b How many litres of water does the tank hold when it is full?

4 A cube has a surface area of 294 cm².

  a Find the length of an edge of the cube.

  b Find the volume of the cube.

  c Find the capacity of the cube, giving your answer in millilitres.

Homework Answers

1 **a** 48 cm³ **b** 84 cm³ **c** 480 cm³
2 27 cm³
3 **a** 24 m³ **b** 24 000 l
4 **a** 7 cm **b** 343 cm³ **c** 343 ml

Framework objectives – Imperial units

Choose and use units of measurement to measure, estimate, calculate and solve problems in a range of contexts; know rough metric equivalents of imperial measures in common use, such as miles, pounds (lb) and pints.

Oral and mental starter

- A quick method to multiply a two digit number by 11.
- Write on the board: $24 \times 11 = 264$ $53 \times 11 = 583$ $44 \times 11 = 484$
- Ask the class if they can spot a pattern.
- Explain that the answer to the sum is obtained by adding the two digits of the number to be multiplied by 11 and placing the answer between the two digits.
- This method also works if the sum of the two digits is more than 10. In this case, the 1 in the tens column is carried into the hundreds column of the final answer, such as:
     $65 \times 11 = 715$ $46 \times 11 = 506$
- Ask individual pupils to make up their own examples and show these to the rest of the class.

Main lesson activity

- Although imperial units do not appear in the Programme of Study, they are included because of their relevance in real-life situations and to lay a good foundation for Functional Maths. They are also useful for mental and calculator work.
- Explain to the class that the lesson is on the imperial system of measurement, which is still commonly used in Britain, even though we are gradually changing to the metric system.
- Ask the class to give all the different imperial units that they know, and write these on the board as they give them.
- Explain that these units have been used in Britain for centuries and that, in comparison, the metric system is fairly recent. (The metric system was developed in the time of Napoleon at the start of the nineteenth century. Some of today's imperial units were used in Roman times; for example 'oz' is the abbreviation for 'onza', the Latin word for ounce, and 'mile' is derived from the Latin word 'milia', a thousand paces.)
- The class can now copy the imperial units on the right, which are those in common use, into their books. It may be worth mentioning that 'mass' is the word we use for 'weight' in Mathematics and Science. Introduce also, the x' y'' notation for feet and inches.
- Point out that care is needed when using a calculator with imperial units, since (like times) they are not decimal. Work through Pupil Book Examples 6.9 and 6.10 on the board.
- Explain that, although we are gradually changing to the metric system, it is necessary to be able to convert from Imperial units to metric units by using suitable approximations. Better approximations are available and may be required in subjects such as Science and Technology.
- The class can now copy the rough metric equivalents of imperial units on the right into their books (the symbol $\approx$ means 'is approximately equal to').

FM - **The class can now do Exercise 6E from Pupil Book 2.** This exercise covers Functional Maths skills.

Imperial units of length

| 12 inches = 1 foot (ft) |
| 3 feet = 1 yard (yd) |
| 1760 yards = 1 mile |

Imperial units of mass

| 16 ounces = 1 pound (lb) |
| 14 pounds = 1 stone (st) |
| 2240 pounds = 1 ton |

Imperial units of capacity

| 8 pints (pt) = 1 gallon (gall) |

Units of length conversions

| 1 in $\approx$ 2.5 cm |
| 1 yard $\approx$ 1 metre |
| 5 miles $\approx$ 8 km |

Units of mass conversions

| 1 oz $\approx$ 30 g |
| 1 lb $\approx$ 500 g |

Units of capacity conversions

| 1.75 pints $\approx$ 1 l |
| 1 gallon $\approx$ 4.5 l |

Exercise 6E Answers

1 a 74 in b 66 ft c 42 oz d 89 lb e 28 pints
2 a 2 ft 6 in b 6 yd 2 ft c 4 lb 8 oz d 2 st 7 lb e 4 gallons 3 pints
3 a 36 in b 63 360 in 4 a 224 oz b 35 840 oz
5 a 15 cm b 10 m c 40 km d 240 g e 750 g f 4 l g 36 l
6 a 12 in b 600 ft c 50 miles d 5 oz e 6 lb f 10.5 pints g 12 gallons
7 800 m 8 75 miles per hour 9 27 l 10 2000 lb 11 165 cm or 1.65 m

Extension Answers

2 1 furlong = 220 yd ≈ 201 m, 1 fathom = 6 ft ≈ 1.83 m, 1 nautical mile = 6080 ft ≈ 1.853 km
3 11 days 13 hours 46 minutes and 40 seconds

Plenary

- A quiz on imperial units. Divide the class into teams and, using a prepared answer sheet, ask the following 10 questions (the teams are allowed to confer, and repeat each question):
  1 How many inches in 2 feet?
  2 How many feet in 7 yards?
  3 How many ounces in 1½ pounds?
  4 How many pounds in 5 stones?
  5 How many pints in 9 gallons?
  6 Approximately how many centimetres are there in 10 inches?
  7 Approximately how many metres are there in 25 yards?
  8 Approximately how many kilometres are there in 30 miles?
  9 Approximately how many grams are there in 8 ounces?
  10 Approximately how many litres are there in 12 gallons?

Plenary Answers
  1 24 2 21 3 24 4 70 5 72 6 25 7 25 8 48 9 240 10 54

Key words

- capacity:
  litre
  pint
  gallon
- length:
  centimetre
  metre
  kilometre
  foot
  yard
  mile
- mass:
  gram
  kilogram
  tonne
  ounce
  pound

Homework

1 Express each of the following in the unit given in brackets:

  a 3 ft 6 in (in) b 3 yd 2 ft (ft) c 1 lb 14 oz (oz) d 10 st 2 lb (lb) e 3 gallons 7 pints (pints)

2 Express each of the following in the units given in brackets:

  a 47 in (ft and in) b 14 ft (yd and ft) c 42 oz (lb and oz) d 21 lb (st and lb)
  e 36 pints (gallons and pints)

3 Convert the following Imperial quantities into the approximate metric quantity given in brackets:

  a 9 in (cm) b 15 miles (km) c 4 lb (kg) d 5¼ pints (l) e 2 gallons (l)

4 Sam goes on a diet and loses 8 kg. Before he started the diet his weight was 15 stone 4 pounds. After the diet, what is his weight, approximately, in stones and pounds?

5 A cask holds 100 gallons of wine. Approximately how many litre bottles of wine can be filled from the cask?

Homework Answers

1 a 42 in b 11 ft c 30 oz d 142 lb e 31 pints
2 a 3 ft 11 in b 4 yd 2 ft c 2 lb 10 oz d 1 st 7 lb e 4 gallons 4 pints
3 a 22½ cm b 24 km c 2 kg d 3 l e 9 l
4 14 stone 2 pounds 5 450

National Tests Answers

1 8 km 2 a 14–14.2 inclusive b 220–230 inclusive c 35–36 inclusive
3 12 cm, 1.2 m, 0.12 km 4 a height = 4 cm b height = 4 cm
5 a 60 cm³ b 6 cm 5 35 cm²

Algebra **3**

Context

This chapter builds on previous work on mapping diagrams and graphs. Pupils identify input from outputs and vice versa. They identify functions from inputs and outputs (including the inverse function) and relate these to coordinate pairs which are used to draw graphs. The important concept of the gradient of a straight line is introduced, and the form $y = mx + c$ for a straight line is briefly explored. Finally, the concept of the gradient as the change of a variable over time is used in some simple cases of real-life graphs.

National Curriculum references

Framework objectives

7.1 Express simple functions algebraically and represent them in mappings or on a spreadsheet.

7.2 Express simple functions algebraically and represent them in mappings or on a spreadsheet.

7.3 Generate points in all four quadrants and plot the graphs of linear functions, where y is given explicitly in terms of x, on paper and using ICT.

7.4 Recognise that equations of the form $y = mx + c$ correspond to straight-line graphs.

7.5 Construct linear functions arising from real-life problems and plot their corresponding graphs; discuss and interpret graphs arising from real situations, for example, distance–time graphs.

FM Identify the mathematical features of a context or problem; try out and compare mathematical representations; select appropriate procedures and tools, including ICT. Use logical argument to interpret the mathematics in a given context or to establish the truth of a statement; give accurate solutions appropriate to the context or problem; evaluate the efficiency of alternative strategies and approaches.

Key concepts

Applications and implications of mathematics

- Know that relationships can be expressed in words and symbols
- Know that relationships between variables can be shown using mapping diagrams, coordinate pairs and graphs

Key processes

Representing

- Expressing relationships symbolically
- Plotting graphs from equations, functions and mapping diagrams

Analysing

- Measuring gradients
- Using gradients to interpret graphs involving change over time

Communicating and reflecting

- Interpreting graphs that describe real-life situations

Route mapping

	Levels	
Exercise	5	6
7A	1–4	
7B		1–3
7C		1–6
7D		1–3
7E		1–5

Framework objectives – Linear functions

Express simple functions algebraically and represent them in mappings or on a spreadsheet.

Oral and mental starter

- Put onto the board the puzzle shown.

$$\begin{array}{r} \text{C A T S} \\ \text{H A T E} \\ \hline \text{D O G S} \end{array}$$

- Tell the pupils that each letter stands for a different number.
- Ask the pupils what they know about certain letters.
- For example, E = 0, both C and H are less than D, G must be even, and there are a few more sensible observations.
- Ask for a suggestion for C, H and D, then follow this suggestion through and see if it is a possible solution. There are quite a few solutions.
- Once the class has suggested what turns out to be a correct solution, which may be after a few wrong attempts, ask the pupils to work in groups of two, three or four to come up with a different possible solution.
- If you are struggling, one solution is:

$$\begin{array}{r} 4317 \\ 5310 \\ \hline 9627 \end{array}$$

Main lesson activity

- Write on the board ADD 3 and tell the pupils this is a function. For different inputs ask what ADD 3 gives as the outputs.
- Write on the board some functions, such as:

$$2 \rightarrow 5$$
$$4 \rightarrow 9$$

- Use about four inputs suggested by the class, or use 1, 2, 3 and 4.
- Ask the pupils to give you another simple function, but different. (You want one of subtract, multiply or divide).
- Repeat the same idea as above with a simple mapping diagram.
- Introduce the term 'linear function', and explain that this term is used for the four simple functions only (add, subtract, multiply and divide). All the functions the pupils will meet in the next few weeks will be linear functions.
- Introduce the idea of a mapping diagram using two identical, horizontal number lines.
- Use the function $x \rightarrow 2x + 3$, as in Pupil Book 2, page 91, with number lines from –2 to 5.
- Show all the integer values and their images (outputs).
- Ask where some of the fractions would map to, say $\frac{1}{2}$, $-\frac{1}{2}$, $1\frac{1}{2}$, $3\frac{1}{2}$, and then draw these lines in.
- Explain that this number line only represents a much larger line; we use a simple range around 0 to illustrate the mapping.
- Also show the pupils that there are hundreds (infinite) more fractions or decimal values that could be put on the mapping diagram, but it would look rather cluttered.

- **The class can now do Exercise 7A from Pupil Book 2.**

Exercise 7A **Answers**

1 b (−2, 1), (−1, 2), (1, 4) **c** (1.5, 4.5), (0.5, 3.5), (−0.5, 2.5), (−1.5, 1.5)
2 a i {−5, −4, −3, −2, −1, 0, 1, 2, 3, 4, 5, 6, 7, 8} → {−3, −2, −1, 0, 1, 2, 3, 4, 5, 6, 7, 8, 9, 10}
   ii {−3, −2, −1, 0, 1, 2, 3, 4} → {−5, −3, −1, 1, 3, 5, 7, 9}
   iii {−3, −2, −1, 0, 1, 2, 3, 4, 5, 6, 7, 8, 9, 10} → {−5, −4, −3, −2, −1, 0, 1, 2, 3, 4, 5, 6, 7, 8}
   iv {−2, −1, 0, 1, 2, 3, 4, 5} → {−5, −3, −1, 1, 3, 5, 7, 9}
  b i {0.5, 2.5, 3.5} **ii** {−2, 2, 4} **iii** {−3.5, −1.5, −0.5} **iv** {−4, 0, 2}
3 a i {−2, −1, 0, 1, 2, 3, 4} → {−5, −2, 1, 4, 7, 10, 13}
   ii {−1, 0, 1, 2, 3, 4} → {−5, −1, 3, 7, 11, 15}
   iii {−5, −4, −3, −2, −1, 0, 1, 2, 3, 4, 5} → {−5, −3, −1, 1, 3, 5, 7, 9, 11, 13, 15}
   iv {0, 1, 2, 3, 4, 5, 6} → {−5, −2, 1, 4, 7, 10, 13}
  b i {−0.5, 5.5, 8.5} **ii** {−3, 5, 9} **iii** {4, 8, 10} **iv** {−6.5, −0.5, 2.5}
4 All the arrows are parallel within each diagram.

Extension **Answers**

1 d It is because you are actually drawing an enlargement, and this point of intersection is the centre of the enlargement.

Plenary

Key words

☐ **mappings**
☐ **function**
☐ **linear function**
☐ **coefficient**

● Put on the board a function like $x \rightarrow 2x + 17$.
● Show a consecutive input set that contains large numbers such as 123, 124, 125, 126 and ask the pupils what they expect the difference to be between each successive output – this is without working them all out. Lead them to the difference being 2 (as the x coefficient); you may need to talk the pupils through the correct outputs for them to see this pattern.
● Then write on the board a function like $x \rightarrow 7x + 19$, with another large consecutive input set, say 135, 136, 137, 138, and ask what the difference will be between each successive output. Lead them again to the coefficient of x being the difference each time. Again, you may need to lead them through the outputs.
● If need be, then make the examples simpler so that the pupils can see the pattern.

Homework

a Using number lines from −5 to 15, draw mapping diagrams to illustrate the functions:
  i $x \rightarrow 3x + 2$ **ii** $x \rightarrow 4x − 3$ **iii** $x \rightarrow 2x + 3$ **iv** $x \rightarrow 3x − 1$
b In each mapping diagram draw the lines from −2.5, −0.5 and 1.5.

5

Homework Answers

a i {−2, −1, 0, 1, 2, 3, 4} → {−4, −1, 2, 5, 8, 11, 14} **ii** {0, 1, 2, 3, 4} → {−3, 1, 5, 9, 13}
   iii {−4, −3, −2, −1, 0, 1, 2, 3, 4, 5, 6} → {−5, −3, −1, 1, 3, 5, 7, 9, 11, 13, 15}
   iv {−1, 0, 1, 2, 3, 4, 5} → {−4, −1, 2, 5, 8, 11, 14}
  b i {−5.5, 0.5, 6.5} **ii** {−13, −5, 3} **iii** {−2, 2, 6} **iv** {−8.5, −2.5, 3.5}

Framework objectives – Finding a function from its inputs and outputs

Express simple functions algebraically and represent them in mappings or on a spreadsheet.

Oral and mental starter

● Put onto the board the puzzle shown.

BAKED
BEANS
FIBRE

● Tell the pupils that each letter stands for a different number.
● Ask the pupils what they know about certain letters.
● For example, B is either half of F or half of (F – 1), and there are a few more sensible observations.
● Ask for a suggestion for D, S, E, N, etc., and then follow the suggestion given through and see if it is a possible solution. There are quite a few solutions.
● Once the class has suggested what turns out to be a correct solution, which may be after a few wrong attempts, ask the pupils to work in groups of two, three or four to come up with a different possible solution.
● If you are struggling, one solution is:

45 907
40 513
86 420

Main lesson activity

● Ask if any pupil can tell you what a function is. This should create some interesting answers. Try to draw out that it represents a rule for changing numbers and that each input must have only one possible output.
● Write on the board 4 → 8 and ask what function maps 4 to 8.

● You should be given at least two answers, $\boxed{\times 2}$ and $\boxed{+ 4}$.
● There are others that could be suggested, and should be illustrated; two are:

$$\boxed{\times 3} \rightarrow \boxed{-4} \quad \text{and} \quad \boxed{\div 2} \rightarrow \boxed{+6}$$

● Now add on the board 6 → 10; what is the function choice now?

It's clearly $\boxed{+ 4}$.

● Try another pair:
    2 → 11
    3 → 14
● What function are these mapping?
● We can start with some trial and error, such as 2 → 11 could be add 9, but add 9 doesn't work for 3 → 14.

● We could try $\boxed{\times 2} \rightarrow \boxed{+ 7}$, but this also doesn't work for 3 → 14.

● We could try $\boxed{\times 3} \rightarrow \boxed{+ 5}$, which also works for 3 → 14.

● So the function would appear to be $\boxed{x \rightarrow 3x + 5}$.

● Try {0, 1, 2, 3} → {3, 7, 11, 15}.

- We can again use trial and error, or we can start looking for patterns in the data.
- Note the difference of each input is 1, while the difference of the outputs is 4;

  this suggests that part of the function is $\boxed{\times 4}$.
- Notice also that $0 \rightarrow 3$, which suggests that part of the function is $\boxed{+ 3}$.
- If we put the two together, $\boxed{\times 4} \rightarrow \boxed{+ 3}$, we see that this works for all

  the other inputs to the given outputs. So the function is $\boxed{x \rightarrow 4x + 3}$.
- You may need to go through one more example with the class, which could be

  $\{0, 1, 2, 3\} \rightarrow \{-1, 4, 9, 14\}$ from the function $\boxed{x \rightarrow 5x - 1}$.
- Pupils may recall, or can be reminded, that this links with the *n*th term covered
  in chapter 1.
- **The class can now do Exercise 7B from Pupil Book 2.**

Exercise 7B   Answers

1 **a** $x \rightarrow x + 5$ **b** $x \rightarrow x - 1$ **c** $x \rightarrow 2x + 1$ **d** $x \rightarrow 2x + 5$ **e** $x \rightarrow 3x + 5$
2 **a** $x \rightarrow x + 3$ **b** $x \rightarrow x + 7$ **c** $x \rightarrow 2x + 3$ **d** $x \rightarrow 2x - 1$ **e** $x \rightarrow 3x + 1$

3 $\{2, 3, 4, 5\} \rightarrow \boxed{+ 2} \rightarrow \boxed{\times 5} \rightarrow \{20, 25, 30, 35\}$

   $\{2, 3, 4, 5\} \rightarrow \boxed{- 3} \rightarrow \boxed{+ 2} \rightarrow \{1, 2, 3, 4\}$

   $\{2, 3, 4, 5\} \rightarrow \boxed{- 3} \rightarrow \boxed{\times 5} \rightarrow \{-5, 0, 5, 10\}$

   $\{2, 3, 4, 5\} \rightarrow \boxed{\times 5} \rightarrow \boxed{+ 2} \rightarrow \{12, 17, 22, 27\}$

   $\{2, 3, 4, 5\} \rightarrow \boxed{\times 5} \rightarrow \boxed{- 3} \rightarrow \{7, 12, 17, 22\}$

Extension   Answers

1 True
2 True
3 Not true

Plenary

Key word

☐ **function**

- Ask the question 'Does it matter which way round we put two parts of a
  function?' For example, with:

  $\boxed{\times 2}$ and $\boxed{+ 3}$,

  does it matter which we do first?
- Does it always matter which we do first, or does it sometimes not matter?

Homework

What are the functions that generate the following mixed outputs from the given mixed inputs?
(*Hint*: put them into order first.)

a $\{3, 0, 4, 1\} \rightarrow \{9, 1, 13, -3\}$ **b** $\{4, -2, 5, 0\} \rightarrow \{13, -2, -8, 10\}$

c $\{3, -1, 4, 0\} \rightarrow \{-2, 18, 3, 23\}$ **d** $\{5, 0, -1, 6\} \rightarrow \{35, -1, 5, 41\}$

6

Homework Answers

a $x \rightarrow 4x - 3$ **b** $x \rightarrow 3x - 2$ **c** $x \rightarrow 5x + 3$ **d** $x \rightarrow 6x + 5$

LESSON 7.3

Framework objectives – Graphs from functions
Generate points in all four quadrants and plot the graphs of linear functions, where y is given explicitly in terms of x, on paper and using ICT.

Oral and mental starter

- Ask who can divide 420 by 15 in their heads.
- Probably no one can, so tell the class you are going to show them how to divide by 15 in their heads.
- Take the 420, first divide it by 3 (which gives 140), then divide by 10 (which gives 14) and then double, which gives 28. This should be verified with a calculator by one of the pupils.
- Ask the class if they can see why this works, dividing by 3, then 10, then doubling.
- Show them that dividing by 3 and then by 10 is equivalent to dividing by 30, but that doubling the answer is equivalent to dividing by 15.
- Let the class try it out on 312 (104, then 10.4 and finally 20.8); again have this checked by a pupil on a calculator.
- Try this out with a few more numbers, but make sure they are all multiples of 3 or it doesn't work quite so well. Do explain that this is a good shortcut for multiples of 3, but not so good for other numbers.
- Other multiples of 3 to try are 375 (25), 531 (35.4), and 282 (18.8).

Main lesson activity

- Talk about the way we have been writing functions like $x \to 4x + 3$.
- We can write functions in different ways, such as $y = 4x + 3$ which means the same thing.
- This is a simpler way of looking at the function if we want to draw a graph from it.
- We can draw a graph of every function; the coordinates come from the combination of inputs and outputs. Tell the pupils they are going to create some of these graphs.
- Write on the board $\boxed{x \to 3x + 1}$ and show how we can work with $\boxed{y = 3x + 1}$

  as the y simply tells us the output for different input values of x.
- We can create a table of values that combines the inputs and outputs. Write on the board:

x	−2	−1	0	1	2	3
y						

- Show how we use the function $x \to 3x + 1$ to substitute the different values of x as the inputs to find the outputs y. We can use whatever values for x that we want, but it is a good idea to use those around 0.
- Suggest it is best to start with the values 0, 1, 2 and 3 before moving to negative values.
- Go through the substitution with the class to give the values in the table as:

x	−2	−1	0	1	2	3
y	−5	−2	1	4	7	10

- To draw the graph, we need a pair of axes that use all the values in the table, that is x from −2 to 3 and y from −5 to 10.
- Draw the axes on the board, showing the linear scale, and put all the numbers in.

- Remind the pupils how to plot the coordinates from the table and join them up with a straight line.
- Point out that the straight line represents ALL the points that satisfy $y = 3x + 1$. Demonstrate this by choosing any non-integer point, such as $x = 1.5$, go through the calculations $(1.5 \times 3) + 1 \rightarrow 5.5$ and show that $(1.5, 5.5)$ is on the line.
- Show that this works for a few other points also, say $x = 2.2$ (7.6) and $x = -0.5$ (−0.5).

- **The class can now do Exercise 7C from Pupil Book 2.**

Exercise 7C Answers

1 a 1, 2, 3, 4, 5, 6
2 a −4, −3, −2, −1, 0, 1
3 a −7, −3, 1, 5, 9, 13
4 a −9, −5, −1, 3, 7, 11
5 a {1, 3, 5, 7, 9, 11}, {−1, 1, 3, 5, 7, 9}, {−3, −1, 1, 3, 5, 7}, {−5, −3, −1, 1, 3, 5}, {−7, −5, −3, −1, 1, 3}
   d all lines are parallel, and each line intercepts the y-axis at the same number as the single number (called the constant) in the expression for that line
6 a {−2, 1, 4, 7, 10, 13}, {−4, −1, 2, 5, 8, 11}, {−6, −3, 0, 3, 6, 9}, {−8, −5, −2, 1, 4, 7}, {−10, −7, −4, −1, 2, 5}
   d all lines are parallel, and each line intercepts the y-axis at the same number as the single number (called the constant) in the expression for that line

Extension Answers

All four graphs should have the same gradient of 0.5 and intercept the y-axis at −2, 2, −1, and 3, respectively.

Plenary

- Write on the board $y = 5x + 17$ and $y = 5x + 11$.
- Ask what the pupils can tell you about the graphs of these two functions.
- They should be able to tell you that the lines have the same slope (are parallel), and that the first line intercepts the y-axis at a higher number than the second one.

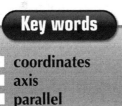

Key words

- [ ] coordinates
- [ ] axis
- [ ] parallel

Homework

Draw the graphs of:

a $y = 4x + 3$ b $y = 4x - 1$ c $y = 4x + 5$ d $y = 4x - 3$

6

Homework Answers

All four lines should be straight with the same gradient of 4, and they should intercept the y-axis at:
a 3   b −1   c 5   d −3

Framework objectives – Gradient of a straight line (steepness)

Recognise that equations of the form $y = mx + c$ correspond to straight-line graphs.

Oral and mental starter

- Ask the class if anyone can tell you a shortcut way to multiply by 29.
- Hopefully, someone will suggest multiplying by 30, and then subtracting one of the number you are multiplying to. There may be other quite valid suggestions also.
- Ask if anyone can multiply 43 by 29:
    $43 \times 30 = (129 \times 10)$ and then $1290 - 43 = 1247$
    (have this checked on a pupil's calculator)
- Ask if anyone can multiply 24 by 29:
    $24 \times 30 = (72 \times 10)$ and then $720 - 24 = 696$
    (have this checked on a pupil's calculator)
- Ask if anyone is up to the three-digit challenge, that is to multiply a three-digit number by 29? At least one pupil should volunteer.
- Ask them to multiply 147 by 29:
    $147 \times 30 = (441 \times 10)$ and then $4410 - 147 = 4263$

Main lesson activity

- Draw a straight line on the board, slanting up towards the top right-hand corner.
- Ask the question, 'How steep is this line?'
- Answers such as 'very steep', or 'quite steep' lead the class towards recognising that steepness needs to be measured in some way.
- Now add to the diagram a pair of axes around the line, so that the line intercepts the y-axis at a positive integer. Label the axes with suitable numbers.

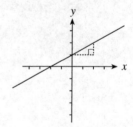

- Draw in a right-angled triangle with a difference of 1 along the x-axis, as shown on the diagram.
- The gradient is 'the increase in the y-ordinate for an increase of 1 in the x-ordinate'.
- Find the increase in the y-ordinate on the triangle; this is the gradient, which is the measure of steepness.
- Every straight line has a gradient that can be found as shown here. Show the class how to find the gradient of a steeper line and show that the gradient is a larger number.
- Explain that **every** linear function gives a straight-line graph of the form $y = mx + c$,
- Where m is the gradient and c is the value at which the y-axis is intercepted.
- So far, you have two straight lines around a pair of axes on the board. Use these to illustrate how to find the equation of these lines by using the gradient for m and the y-axis intercept as c.

- Draw another pair of labelled axes with a straight line (positive gradient).
- Ask the pupils what the gradient is, and go through the procedure with them (gives m).
- Ask the pupils where the line intercepts the y-axis (gives c).
- Hence write down the equation of this straight line.
- **The class can now do Exercise 7D from Pupil Book 2.**

Exercise 7D **Answers**

1 **a** 3 **b** 2 **c** 4 **d** 1
2 **a** $y = 3x + 5$ **b** $y = 2x + 7$ **c** $y = x + 4$ **d** $y = 7x + 15$
3 **a i** 2 **ii** 3 **iii** $y = 2x + 3$
   b i 3 **ii** 1 **iii** $y = 3x + 1$
   c i 4 **ii** 2 **iii** $y = 4x + 2$
   d i 1 **ii** 3 **iii** $y = x + 3$

Extension **Answers**

1 $y = x + 3$
2 $y = 3x + 2$
3 $y = x + 1$
4 $y = 4x - 1$
5 $y = 2x - 1$
6 $y = 3x - 4$

Plenary

Key words

☐ **coefficient**
☐ **gradient**

- Ask the pupils if any of them can tell you what a gradient is. It is a measure of slope, or how much up you have gone for one unit along.
- Put on the board the equation:
    $$y = 6x + 5$$
- Ask what the gradient of the graph is. (It is 6.)
- Ask whereabouts the graph intercepts the y-axis. (It intercepts at 5.)
- Repeat this for a few equations more until everyone can give the correct answer.
- Ask the pupils if the graph drawn from something like $y = 8x + 17$ will always be a straight line. (The answer is yes.)

Homework

On a coordinate grid, plot the points $A(1, 3)$ and $B(2, 5)$.

a Work out the gradient of AB.

b Extend the line AB to intersect the y-axis.

c Write down the equation of the line that passes through AB.

6

Homework Answers

a 2 **b** $(0, 1)$ **c** $y = 2x + 1$

Framework objectives – Real-life graphs

Construct linear functions arising from real-life problems and plot their corresponding graphs; discuss and interpret graphs arising from real situations, for example, distance–time graphs.

Oral and mental starter

- Draw a circle on the board, and write the numbers 36, 25, 7, 3 and 4 inside.
- Also write on the board the number 518 in a box as a target.
- Ask the pupils to suggest a combination of some or all of the numbers in the circle, together with the four operations and brackets, that will give a total as close to the target number as possible.
- This works well with pupils working in small teams of 2, 3 or 4 pupils.
- If you do have specific evenly balanced teams, you can play a few rounds, and keep a score, such as spot on scores 10, closest scores 5, next closest 4 and so on down to 0.
- In the different rounds, choose different targets and change the numbers in the circle.
- The beauty of this game is that you don't need to know the numbers beforehand, as the target number does not have to be achieved exactly.

Main lesson activity

- Ask the pupils where they see graphs the most (TV, papers, adverts, etc.).
- Many of these are what we call travel graphs or time-and-distance graphs.
- Talk the pupils through Example 7.5 in Pupil Book 2 (but do not use the book for this). Tell them the story about picking up a dog from the vet (make the person yourself or a friend).
- Write key information on the board:
    Travel $1\frac{1}{2}$ hours at 60 km/h, so that is 90 km;
    Took 30 minutes to settle the dog, so no distance travelled in that time;
    Came back at 40 km/h (gently for the benefit of the dog), which took $2\frac{1}{4}$ hours.
- Talk about the axes needed – the vertical axis to be 'the distance from home', with the horizontal axis to be 'time'. Draw this pair of axes on the board and label them, with the vertical one from 0 to 100 and the horizontal one from 0 to 5.
- Key coordinates need to be identified to draw up a graph:
    starting off from home (0, 0);
    arrive at the vets $(1\frac{1}{2}, 90)$;
    set off from the vets (2, 90);
    arrive back home $(4\frac{1}{4}, 0)$.
- Draw the graph of the journey, joining point to point with straight lines.
- You will need to explain that the straight lines are to illustrate the average speed travelled (the car did not actually stay at one speed all the time).

- **The class can now do Exercise 7E from Pupil Book 2.**

Exercise 7E Answers

1 **c** 2 PM
2 **c** 60 km/h
3 **b** {0, 40, 100, 160, 200}
5 **a** {5400, 4500, 3600, 2700, 1800, 900, 0}

Extension Answers

1 About 12.18 PM
2 About 11.48 AM

Plenary

- Ask what average speed the pupils walk at to school (for the parts of their journey that they do walk). This is usually between 3 and 4 miles an hour, unless they dawdle.
- Ask if they actually walk at the same speed all the time. Do they walk quicker uphill or downhill? The notion of average speed is exactly what it says, a rough middle-of-the-line speed, which is why it is used on travel graphs.
- Ask a pupil to draw what might be called 'A real travel graph of walking at 4 mph'. This would be a wiggly line that meanders around the straight line.
- Ask for other attempts at a real average 4 mph.
- Discuss with the class why we use one straight line to represent the average speed.

Key words

- travel graph
- average speed

Homework

Dean drove from home at an average speed of 40 km/h for 2 hours. He stopped for 40 minutes to pick up Helen, and then set off back home at an average speed of 60 km/h:

a Draw a travel graph to illustrate this journey.
b How long did the journey take Dean?

6

Homework Answers

b 4 hours

National Tests Answers

1 **a** 0 and 12   **b** 60 seconds
2 **a** 18   **b** 2   **c** $y = x^2$
3 yes because 3 x 25 = 75
4 **a** $x = 0$, line through B and D; $x + y = 2$, line through A and B; $x + y = -2$, line through C and D
  b $x = 1$
  c No, it is $y = x$

Functional Maths – M25

Framework objectives

Identify the mathematical features of a context or problem; try out and compare mathematical representations; select appropriate procedures and tools, including ICT.

Use logical argument to interpret the mathematics in a given context or to establish the truth of a statement; give accurate solutions appropriate to the context or problem; evaluate the efficiency of alternative strategies and approaches.

Oral and mental starter

Look at the information on the M25 activity on page 102 of Pupil Book 2. Ask the pupils some questions relating to it. Topics could include:

- Reading the map (scale, what roads intersect, why some roads are blue)
- Conversion factors (imperial to metric)
- Average traffic flow (per hour, per year)

Main lesson activity

- Encourage pupils to suggest possible questions. They could do these in small groups or individually, then present these to the class for others to answer. This is particularly useful if they have access to the internet.
- **The class can now work through the questions on pages 102–103.**

FM Activity   Answers

1 13 years
2 9 (M1, A1(M), M11, M20, M26, M23, M3, M4, M40)
3 **a** 31   **b** 5   **c** Surrey (9 junctions)
4 **a** 11–13 miles   **b** 18–22 miles
5 **a** 140 000   **b** 73 800 000   **c** 62 000
6 732 miles
7 46.8 miles
8 Approx. 2.4 (2.44)
9 8500
10 1 hour 40 minutes
11 187 km
12 19% (18.8%)

Plenary

- When the pupils reach question 9 it may be useful to discuss some of the mathematics and strategies needed to work it out.

This table shows the lengths of the three longest orbital motorways in the world and the length of the M60, which is the only other orbital motorway in Britain.

City	Country	Road	Length (miles)
Berlin	Germany	B-10	122
London	England	M25	117
Cincinnati	USA	I-275	84
Manchester	England	M60	35

The formula for the radius of a circle given the circumference is $r = \dfrac{C}{2\pi}$.

a Assuming the M25 is a circle with a circumference of 117 miles, what would the radius be?

b Making the same assumption calculate the radii of the other orbital roads.

1 a 18.6 miles
  b B-10 19.4 miles, I-275 13.4 miles, M60 5.6 miles

Number 3

Context

This chapter builds on previous work with decimals, introducing powers of 10 as a lead in to eventually working with standard index form. Estimation is used as a means of teaching whether answers are realistic or sensible. Some of the work is specifically designed to reinforce skills in mental arithmetic, and there is also work on using calculators efficiently.

National Curriculum references

Framework objectives

8.1 Read and write positive integer powers of 10, multiply and divide integers and decimals by 0.1, 0.01. Round decimals to the nearest whole number or to one or two decimal places. Strengthen and extend mental methods of calculation, working with decimals, fractions, percentages, squares and square roots, and cubes and cube roots; solve problems mentally.

8.2 Round positive numbers to any given power of 10; round decimals to the nearest whole number or to one or two decimal places.

8.3 Make and justify estimates and approximations of calculations. Select from a range of checking methods, including estimating in context and using inverse operations.

8.4 Use efficient written methods to add and subtract integers and decimals of any size, including numbers with differing numbers of decimal places.

8.5 Carry out more difficult calculations effectively and efficiently using the function keys for sign change, powers, roots and fractions; use brackets and the memory.

8.6 Use efficient written methods for multiplication and division of integers and decimals, including by decimals such as 0.6 or 0.06; understand where to position the decimal point by considering equivalent calculations.

(FM) Interpret percentage as the operator 'so many hundredths of' and express one given number as a percentage of another; calculate percentages and find the outcome of a given percentage increase or decrease.

Key concepts

Applications and implications of mathematics

- Understand and choose the best approach to tackle problems involving decimals; interpret and check results in context

Key processes

Representing

- Deciding on methods, including whether to use mental arithmetic or a calculator in a given situation

Analysing

- Using appropriate mathematical procedures to find results and solutions

Communicating and reflecting

- Considering the appropriateness and accuracy of results and conclusions

Route mapping

Exercise	Levels 4	5	6
8A		1–3	4–9
8B	1–2	3–4	5–6
8C		1–2	3–8
8D		1–7	
8E			1–5
8F		1–4	

LESSON 8.1

Framework objectives – Powers of 10

Read and write positive integer powers of 10, multiply and divide integers and decimals by 0.1, 0.01.

Round decimals to the nearest whole number or to one or two decimal places.

Strengthen and extend mental methods of calculation, working with decimals, fractions, percentages, squares and square roots, and cubes and cube roots; solve problems mentally.

Oral and mental starter

- Use a target board such as the one shown.
- Recall strategies for rounding to one or two decimal places.
- Point at a number and ask pupils to round it to one or two decimal places, as appropriate.

4.562	2.375	1.071	3.222	0.541
0.082	1.629	14.635	3.999	4.814
3.421	8.525	3.688	9.002	1.035
6.455	1.459	1.291	5.927	2.716

Main lesson activity

- Ask the class for a number, say 63.
- Produce a spider diagram on the board to show what happens if the number is multiplied or divided by 10, 10^2, 10^3.
- Pupils should know the answers to this, but may need to be reminded of the rules about moving digits.
- Ask for the connection between the power and the number of places the digits are moved.
- Ask pupils to complete this pattern:

$$10\,000 = 10^4$$
$$1000 = 10^3$$
$$100 = 10^2$$
$$10 = 10^{\cdots}$$
$$1 = 10^{\cdots}$$

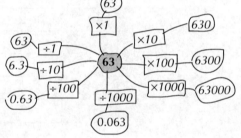

- Ask how the next number down on the left is obtained from the previous line (divide by 10).
- Ask how the pattern of powers on the right-hand side is obtained (powers decrease by 1).
- Ask pupils to write down the next two lines of the pattern:

$$0.1 = 10^{-1}$$
$$0.01 = 10^{-2}$$

- Establish that $\frac{1}{10} = 10^{-1}$ and that $\frac{1}{100} = 10^{-2}$.
- Do a few problems such as $7 \times 0.1 (= 0.7)$, $0.4 \times 0.1 (= 0.04)$, $7 \div 0.1 (= 70)$, $4 \div 0.01 (= 400)$.
- Recall the rules for these or explain how to do them mentally.
- Repeat with other examples.
- Use numbers from the target board above to check that pupils can combine the two activities – for example, multiply 4.562 by 10 and round the answer to one decimal place.

- **The class can now do Exercise 8A from Pupil Book 2.**

Exercise 8A   Answers

1 a i 53   **ii** 530   **b i** 7.9   **ii** 79   **c i** 240   **ii** 2400   **d i** 50.63   **ii** 506.3
   e i 0.03   **ii** 0.3
2 a i 8.3   **ii** 0.083   **b i** 0.41   **ii** 0.0041   **c i** 45.7   **ii** 0.457
   d i 0.604   **ii** 0.006 04   **e i** 3478.1   **ii** 34.781
3 a 31   **b** 678   **c** 560   **d** 0.034   **e** 8.23   **f** 0.009 06   **g** 5789   **h** 0.5789
   i 38   **j** 0.0038   **k** 5000   **l** 0.005 43
4 a i 0.45   **ii** 0.045   **b i** 5.62   **ii** 0.562   **c i** 0.004   **ii** 0.0004   **d i** 40   **ii** 4
   e i 0.07   **ii** 0.007
5 a i 63   **ii** 630   **b i** 3000   **ii** 30 000   **c i** 70   **ii** 700   **d i** 813   **ii** 8130
   e i 290   **ii** 2900
6 a 0.01 cm²   **b** 15, 0.15 cm²   **c** 0.15   **d** 0.5
7 a i 4.7   **ii** 4.72   **b i** 3.1   **ii** 3.10   **c i** 2.6   **ii** 2.63   **d i** 1.9   **ii** 1.93
   e i 0.8   **ii** 0.78   **f i** 1.0   **ii** 0.99   **g i** 4.0   **ii** 4.00   **h i** 2.6   **ii** 2.60
   i i 3.2   **ii** 3.19   **j i** 3.5   **ii** 3.48
8 a i 4.7   **ii** 47.2   **b i** 26.3   **ii** 263.5   **c i** 0.5   **ii** 4.8
9 a i 1.2   **ii** 0.1   **b i** 13.7   **ii** 1.4   **c i** 1.0   **ii** 0.1

Extension   Answers

1 a 50   **b** 700   **c** 8   **d** 63
2 a 0.5   **b** 7   **c** 0.08   **d** 0.63
3 a 50   **b** 700   **c** 8   **d** 63
4 a 0.5   **b** 7   **c** 0.08   **d** 0.63
5 Multiplying by 10 and dividing by 0.1 are the same thing, as are dividing by 10 and
   multiplying by 0.1.
6 Multiply 73 by 100 = 7300.

Plenary

- Write a variety of numbers on the board (for example, 32, 8, 0.09, 0.312,
  48.9, 4598) and ask the pupils to multiply and/or divide them by 10,
  10^2, 0.1, 0.01.
- Discuss the techniques used.

Key words
- ☐ **round**
- ☐ **decimal place**
- ☐ **power of 10**
- ☐ **tenth**
- ☐ **hundredth**

Homework

1 Write down the answers to:

   a 4.8×10 **b** 0.56×10^2 **c** 7.92×10^3 **d** $21 \div 10^3$ **e** $214 \div 10^2$

   f $876 \div 10^3$ **g** 0.007×10^2 **h** $57 \div 10^2$

2 Multiply these numbers by   **i** 0.1, and   **ii** 0.01:

   a 7.9   **b** 652

3 Divide these numbers by   **i** 0.1, and   **ii** 0.01:

   a 0.5   **b** 85

4 Round these numbers to   **i** one decimal place, and   **ii** two decimal places:

   a 2.478   **b** 6.089   **c** 2.997

5

6

Homework Answers

1 a 48   **b** 56   **c** 7920   **d** 0.021   **e** 2.14   **f** 0.876   **g** 0.7   **h** 0.57
2 a i 0.79   **ii** 0.079   **b i** 65.2   **ii** 6.52
3 a i 5   **ii** 50   **b i** 850   **ii** 8500
4 a i 2.5   **ii** 2.48   **b i** 6.1   **ii** 6.09   **c i** 3.0   **ii** 3.00

LESSON 8.2

Framework objectives – Large numbers
Round positive numbers to any given power of 10; round decimals to the nearest whole number or to one or two decimal places.

Oral and mental starter

- This starter is concerned with adding and subtracting 0.1, 0.01 and 0.001 from other decimals and whole numbers.
- For this activity it is useful for the pupils to write on white boards.
- Give pupils an example, such as 'What number is 0.01 more than 6.03?' (= 6.04).
- Now give more examples and ask the pupils to hold up the answer on their white boards.
- Suggested questions are:

  What is 0.001 more than 2.008? (= 2.009)
  What is 0.01 less than 5? (= 4.99)
  What is 0.002 less than 3? (= 2.998)
  What needs to be added to 3.234 to make 3.237? (= 0.003)
  What needs to be subtracted from 4.002 to make 3.997? (= 0.005)

Main lesson activity

- In the previous lesson we dealt with powers of 10, such as 10^2, 10^4 and 10^{-1}.
- Ask the pupils if they can 'name' 10^2 and write it as a multiplication problem. They should come up with 'a hundred' and $10^2 = 10 \times 10$.
- Similarly, name and expand 10^3 (thousand), 10^4 (ten thousand), 10^5 (hundred thousand), 10^6 (million) and 10^9 (a billion). [It may be worth pointing out that this is the internationally accepted version of a billion, which was a million millions (10^{12}) in the UK.]
- Ask pupils if they can think of any other way we use these numbers. They should come up with column headings in place value.
- Put the following table on the board (a version of which is given in Pupil Book 2):

10^6	10^5	10^4	10^3	10^2	10	1
3	7	0	8	4	3	2

- Ask the pupils to read the number (three million, seven hundred and eight thousand, four hundred and thirty two).
- Emphasise that large numbers are read as 'so many millions', 'so many thousands' and finally the last three digits. This is also why large numbers are written in blocks of three, or sometimes with commas between each group of three. However, commas may cause confusion because of the European practice of using a comma as a decimal point.
- Add other large numbers, such as 1 023 708 and 12 007 009, to the table on the board.
- Also give some large numbers in words and ask pupils to write them down, such as:

  Five million, seventy-eight thousand, three hundred and six (5 078 306).
  Two million, nine thousand and sixty three (2 009 063).

 The class can now do Exercise 8B from Pupil Book 2. This exercise covers Functional Maths skills.

Exercise 8B — Answers

1 a Three million, four hundred and fifty-two thousand, seven hundred and sixty three
  b Two million, forty-seven thousand, eight hundred and nine
  c Twelve million, eight thousand, nine hundred and seven
  d Three million, six thousand and ninety-eight
2 a 4 043 207 **b** 19 502 037 **c** 1 302 007
3 Spain 40 million, Germany 77 million, Italy 58 million, France 57 million, Ireland 4 million, Denmark 6 million
4 a i 3 550 000 **ii** 3 500 000 **iii** 4 000 000
  b i 9 720 000 **ii** 9 700 000 **iii** 10 000 000
  c i 3 040 000 **ii** 3 000 000 **iii** 3 000 000
  d i 15 700 000 **ii** 15 700 000 **iii** 16 000 000
5 Both wrong: 'just over 2 million' would mean less than $2\frac{1}{4}$ million, and 'nearly 3 million' would mean over $2\frac{3}{4}$ million.
6 Between 7 500 000 and 8 500 000 people.

Extension — Answers

a 29 000 000 **b** 356 000 **c** 117 000 000 **d** 2 200 000 **e** 950 000 000
f 8 300 000 **g** 23 100 000 000 **h** 504 000

Plenary

- Write a variety of large numbers on the board, such as:
  4 502 611   5 560 097   2 110 009   7 899 911
- Ask the pupils to read out the numbers and round them off to the nearest ten thousand, hundred thousand and million.

Key words
- place value
- column headings
- power
- million
- billion

4

Homework

1 Write the following numbers in words:
  a 5 504 055   **b** 3 089 089
2 Write the following numbers using figures:
  a Two million, one hundred and three thousand, one hundred and six.
  b Eight million, six hundred and seventy thousand and eighty-one.
3 Round off the following numbers to **i** the nearest ten thousand, **ii** the nearest hundred thousand and **iii** the nearest million:
  a 2 578 913   **b** 7 908 688

Homework — Answers

1 a Five million, five hundred and four thousand and fifty-five
  b Three million, eighty-nine thousand and eighty-nine
2 a 2 103 106 **b** 8 670 081
3 a i 2 580 000 **ii** 2 600 000 **iii** 3 000 000
  b i 7 910 000 **ii** 7 900 000 **iii** 8 000 000

LESSON

8.3

Framework objectives – Estimations

Make and justify estimates and approximations of calculations. Select from a range of checking methods, including estimating in context and using inverse operations.

Oral and mental starter

- The pupils can work in small groups. Give the pupils an OHP film and some OHP pens or a large piece of paper and some felt-tip pens.
- Give each group the same five two-digit numbers, say 21, 43, 54, 77 and 12 (use just four values if necessary, and the same five single-digit numbers, say 2, 3, 5, 6 and 9 (use just four values if necessary).
- In a timed session (say 5 minutes), the pupils have to write down as many multiplication problems as possible multiplying a two-digit number by a single-digit number. Calculators are not allowed.
- After the allocated time, stop pupils working and check the answers.
- Allocate a score to see which is the winning group.

×	21	43	54	77	12
2	42	86	108	154	24
3	63	129	162	231	36
5	105	215	270	385	60
6	126	258	324	462	72
9	189	387	486	693	108

Main lesson activity

- Using an OHP calculator or asking a pupil to work them out, obtain the answers to a variety of multiplication problems. For example:
    $12 \times 46 = 552$ $13 \times 23 = 299$ $15 \times 24 = 360$ $19 \times 38 = 722$
- Ask the class if they can spot a way of checking that the answers are right. For example, why must this be wrong: $26 \times 37 = 926$?
- Establish the rule that a correct answer must end in the same digit as that of the product of the original final digits: in this case, 6×7.
- Some pupils may also suggest that an answer can be estimated. For example, $12 \times 46 \approx 10 \times 50 = 500$. (Introduce the notation $\approx$ is approximately equal to.)
- Obtain approximate answers to, say, 13×23. For example:
    10×20, 10×23, 10×25. Which is better?
- Establish that there is no definite way to estimate. Numbers should be chosen that the pupils can deal with mentally. This will depend on their individual numerical skill.
- Now do the following as approximations. (Get pupil suggestions.)
    $304 - 138$ can be $300 - 140$, $300 - 150$, …; 7.5×2.5 can be 7×3, 7×2, 8×3, …
- Rules for dealing with 'halfway' values can be established. Should we go 'one up and one down'? For example:
    $40.8 - 29.7$ can be $40 - 30$, $41 - 30$, …; 8.76×4.79 can be 10×5, 9×5, …
- How can we check whether $510 \div 30 = 17$ is correct?
- Introduce the idea of inverse operations (for example: $510 = 30 \times 17$) which can be checked mentally.
- Similarly, $237 - 43 = 214$. Check if $237 = 214 + 43$. Answer: not correct.
- Addition is the inverse of subtraction and is usually easier to work out. Multiplication is the inverse of division and is almost always easier to work out.
- Using a scale marked with 10 divisions, estimate the value of a given point when the end values are known. For example:

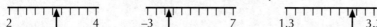

2   4   −3   7   1.3   3.3

© HarperCollins*Publishers* Limited 2008

● Key points: Establish the value of each division. Count on (or back) from one end.
● **The class can now do Exercise 8C from Pupil Book 1.** This exercise covers Functional Maths skills.

Exercise 8C **Answers**

1 a End digit should be 8 **b** Approx $50 \times 70 = 3500$ **c** Approx $100 \div 10 = 10$
d $8 \times 35 = 280$ **e** $323 + 37 = 360$
2 a $2800 - 400 = 2400$ **b** $230 \times 20 = 4600$ **c** $800 : 40 = 20$ **d** $60 \div 15 = 4$
e $400 \times 400 = 160\,000$ **f** $160 \div 40 = 4$ **g** $70 \div 7 = 10$
h top $40 \times 60 = 2400$, bottom $40 - 20 = 20$, $2400 \div 20 = 120$
3 Items are less than £3, £2 and £5, so less than £10 altogether. Change is 35p, 8p and 1p, which is 44p. Not enough
4 Each bottle is less that 50p, so 6 bottles must be less than £3 **5** No: $8 \times 25p = £2$
6 53p entered as £53 **7 a** 2.7 **b** 4.2 **c** −10 **8** Any reasonable estimate.

Extension **Answers**

a The square is larger than a 6×6 square but smaller than an 8×8 square. The area of the square is equal to the central grid squares (4^2) plus the four shaded triangles ($\frac{12}{2}$ each), giving $4^2 + (4 \times \frac{12}{2}) = 16 + 24 = 40$ grid squares
b This square has an area of $6^2 + (4 \times \frac{7}{2}) = 36 + 14 = 50$ grid squares

Plenary

Key words

☐ **inverse operation**
☐ **guess**
☐ **estimate**
☐ **approximate**
☐ **roughly**
☐ **nearly**

● Write the following calculations on the board. Ask why they must be wrong?
   a $56 \times 36 = 2061$ **b** $38 \times 42 = 5196$ **c** $430 \div 6 = 55$
● Make sure the pupils know how to check the last digit, estimate and check using inverse operations.
● Write the following calculations on the board:

   a $\dfrac{39 + 47}{17}$ **b** $169.3 \div 26.4$ **c** 27.8×12.7 **d** $(58.4)^2 + (21.3)^2$

● Ask for an estimate of each. Discuss the 'best' way of approximating. For example:
   a could be $90 \div 15$, $100 \div 20$ or $90 \div 20$ **b** could be $175 \div 25$ or $180 \div 30$
   c could be 30×10, 28×10 or 25×12 **d** is clearly $60^2 + 20^2 = 4000$
● Make sure that the pupils know that there is not always a best approximation. The values should be chosen either for mental calculation or to avoid lengthy calculation.

Homework

1 Explain why these calculations must be wrong.
   a $63 \times 36 = 2286$ **b** $63 \times 36 = 3268$ **c** $714 - 68 = 654$
2 Estimate the answer to each of these calculations.
   a 21.6×38.4 **b** $184 \div 29$ **c** $\dfrac{52.3 + 39.6}{18.6 - 5.4}$ **d** $\dfrac{49.3 \times 61.7}{26.5}$

3 Estimate the number the arrow is pointing to.
   a scale from 5 to 7 **b** scale from −4 to 6 **c** scale from 0.6 to 2.6

5

6

Homework Answers

1 a last digit should be 8 **b** approx $60 \times 40 = 2400$ **c** $654 + 68 = 722$
2 a $20 \times 40 = 800$ **b** $180 \div 30 = 6$ **c** $(50 + 40) \div (20 - 5) = 90 \div 15 = 6$
   d $(50 \times 60) \div 25 = 3000 \div 25 = 120$
3 a 5.5 **b** −0.5 **c** 2.3

LESSON
8.4

Framework objectives – Adding and subtracting decimals
Use efficient written methods to add and subtract integers and decimals of any size, including numbers with differing numbers of decimal places.

Oral and mental starter

- Spellings and definitions of mathematical terms are covered here.
- Point at one pupil and ask her to spell the word 'hundredth', which can be written on the board.
- Point at another pupil and ask him to define 'a hundredth'. (For words that are difficult to define, such as multiply, pupils can give an example.)
- Repeat with other pupils, using suitable words (based on number) such as 'perimeter', 'area', 'square (number)', 'calculator', 'integer', 'digit', 'fraction', 'percentage', 'multiply', 'divide', 'multiplication', 'division', 'addition', 'subtraction', 'decimal', 'tenth', 'thousandth', 'million', etc.

Main lesson activity

- This is a consolidation lesson on adding and subtracting decimals without a calculator.
- A quick recall of methods should be sufficient. Emphasise the need to line up the decimal points and to use zeros to fill in any blank spaces.
- As an example, demonstrate the addition of $64.8 + 213.04 + 91.234$ ($= 369.074$), showing the carry of digits.
- For another example, work out $23 - 6.78 - 8.7$. This will need to be done in two parts: $23 - 6.78 = 16.22$ and $16.22 - 8.7 = 7.52$. Demonstrate the need to 'borrow' and the use of zeros to fill in blank spaces.
- Tell the pupils a package contains two items with masses of 1 kg 542 g and 2 kg 769 g, to which a third item is added to bring the total mass to 6 kg. Show them how to work out the mass of the third item. Demonstrate the need to put the numbers into the same units and to set up both an addition and a subtraction, for example to solve $6 - 1.542 - 2.769$, first do $6 - 1.542 = 4.458$, and then $4.458 - 2.769 = 1.689$. So third item is 1 kg 689 g.
- As another example, find the perimeter of a rectangle with sides of 2.34 m and 76 cm. This could be done by doubling the sides or as an addition problem: $2.34 + 0.76 + 2.34 + 0.76 = 6.2$ m.
- **The class can now do Exercise 8D from Pupil Book 2.**

Exercise 8D Answers

1 **a** 241.718 **b** 32.755 **c** 14.163 **d** 74.73 **e** 5.237 **f** 10.114 **g** 22.657
  h 17.59 **i** 14.482 **j** 15
2 **a** 8.361 km **b** 4.711 km **c** 8.331 km **d** 14.876 km **e** 11.854 km
3 **a** 5.604 kg **b** 2.27 kg
4 0.979 kg
5 5.56 m
6 2.44 m
7 10.98 l

Extension Answers

a 3.7 cm, 37 mm, $3\frac{7}{10}$ **b** 4.4 cm, 44 mm, $4\frac{2}{5}$ **c** 3.8 cm, 38 mm, $3\frac{4}{5}$
d 1.5 cm, 15 mm, $1\frac{1}{2}$ **e** 1.4 cm, 14 mm, $1\frac{2}{5}$ **f** 3.6 cm, 36 mm, $3\frac{3}{5}$

Plenary

- Write an example on the board, such as 23.4 + 5.406 − 3.4 − 1.08 + 2.367. Discuss the methods used and look at alternatives, such as adding all the positive values and 'adding' the negative values before subtracting (for example, 23.4 + 5.406 + 2.367 = 31.173, 3.4 + 1.08 = 4.48 and then 31.173 − 4.48 = 26.693).
- Refer to Question 1 part j, in which the positive numbers total 44.476 and the negative ones total 29.476. The numbers to the right of the decimal points cancel out.
- Discuss advantages of working through such problems in stages or of combining positive numbers and negative numbers.

Key words

- decimal
- hundredths
- tenths
- integer

Homework

1 Work out the following:
  a 1.89 + 32.407 + 601.2 **b** 6.5 + 5 + 12.04 + 2.184
  c 16.23 + 12.39 − 11.18 **d** 51.3 + 18.2 − 28.615
  e 20.07 + 3.4 − 12.35 − 9.92 + 5.8

2 In an experiment, a beaker of water has a mass of 1.256 kg. The beaker alone weighs 0.135 kg. What is the mass of water in the beaker?

3 A rectangle is 1.76 m by 39 cm. What is its perimeter?

Homework Answers

1 **a** 635.497 **b** 25.724 **c** 17.44 **d** 40.885 **e** 7
2 1.121 kg
3 4.3 m

LESSON 8.5

Framework objectives – Efficient calculations

Carry out more difficult calculations effectively and efficiently using the function keys for sign change, powers, roots and fractions; use brackets and the memory.

Oral and mental starter

- As there is much to cover and a variety of makes of calculator are likely to be in use, this lesson does not have an oral and mental starter.

Main lesson activity

- The pupils will need a calculator with square, square root, sign-change keys, a fraction key, cube and cube root (or power), memory and bracket keys.
- This lesson focuses on using a calculator to do problems that involve brackets, fractions, etc.
- The pupils will probably have a variety of makes of calculators, the majority of which will have the keys listed above. The class has met square, square root, sign change, brackets and memory before.
- Do a couple of examples to use these (use your calculator to work them out), such as:

   a $\dfrac{32.3 - 13.1}{14.2 + 12.2}$ $(= 0.7\dot{2})$ **b** $\sqrt{2.3^2 + 2.8^2}$ $(= 3.6)$

- Introduce the new keys. One way of doing this is to get pupils to work in groups, either on the same key or on different keys. Groups can then report back on their findings. Make sure, if this approach is adopted, that the main points below are covered.
- Fraction key, which often looks like [≡] .

- Emphasise that the ability to do simple fraction calculations without a calculator is expected, but that more complicated problems can be done on a calculator.

- Ask pupils to enter: [≡] [4] [▼] [6]

   This will look like $\frac{4}{6}$.

   If pupils now press [=] , the fraction will be cancelled down to $\frac{2}{3}$.

- Now enter: [≡] [1] [7] [▼] [5]

   If [=] is present the display will show $\frac{17}{5}$.

   Now press [SHIFT] [S<->D] and the display will show $3\frac{2}{5}$.

- Note that the calculator gives answers in a mixed number format with simplified form.
- Ask the pupils to enter a fraction, press equals and then press the fraction key again. This will usually change the fraction into a decimal. Pressing the fraction key yet again will usually change the decimal back into a fraction.
- Now ask the pupils to key in the following to check their accuracy of keying:

   a $1\frac{1}{2} \times \frac{3}{4} - \frac{2}{3}$ **b** $\dfrac{2\frac{1}{5} + 1\frac{3}{4}}{1\frac{3}{10} - \frac{1}{2}}$

The answers should be: **a** $\frac{11}{24}$ **b** $4\frac{15}{16}$

- The power key is usually marked as x^y or y^x, either as a separate key or as an inverse function, but on different makes of calculator the power key varies more than any other.
- Note: If calculators have a separate cube and cube-root key, these can be introduced here.
- Make sure pupils can use their power key to do the following:

$$3^4 - 81 \qquad 125^{\frac{1}{3}} = 5 \qquad 9^3 = 729 \qquad {}^3\sqrt{345} \approx 7.013\,58$$

- **The class can now do Exercise 8E from Pupil Book 2.**

Exercise 8E   **Answers**

1 a 3   **b** 4   **c** 6.5
2 a $\frac{73}{80}$ **b** $3\frac{1}{18}$ **c** $\frac{1}{8}$ **d** $12\frac{3}{4}$ **e** $\frac{3}{8}$ **f** $\frac{16}{27}$ **g** $3\frac{1}{16}$ **h** $1\frac{1}{2}$ **i** $4\frac{1}{3}$
3 a 4096   **b** 12.2   **c** 11   **d** 12.0   **e** 1024   **f** 772.4   **g** 155.5   **h** 466.6   **i** 8.3
4 a 6 hours 20 minutes   **b** 1 hour 36 minutes   **c** 7 hours 40 minutes
5 a $\sqrt{2}$ **b** ${}^3\sqrt{10}$ **c** ${}^3\sqrt{40}$ **d** $\sqrt{5}$ **e** $\sqrt{20}$ **f** ${}^3\sqrt{3}$ **g** ${}^3\sqrt{12}$ **h** $\sqrt{30}$

Extension   **Answers**

The $\boxed{x!}$ key is called the factorial key and calculates, for example:

$3! = 3 \times 2 \times 1 = 6$
$7! = 7 \times 6 \times 5 \times 4 \times 3 \times 2 \times 1 = 5040$

The $\boxed{x^{-1}}$ key is called the reciprocal key and divides a number into 1.

For example, $2 \boxed{x^{-1}} = \frac{1}{2}$.

Plenary

- There is no plenary to this lesson as the variety of calculators in use makes it difficult to focus on one area. However, the general characteristics of calculators could be discussed (for example, what the MODE key does and what the SHIFT (INV or 2nd FN) key does).

Key words
- calculator
- display
- fraction button
- power
- brackets
- keys
- square
- square root

Homework

1 Use the fraction key on your calculator to work out each of these (give your answer as a mixed number or a fraction in its simplest form):

a $\frac{1}{4} + \frac{2}{3} + \frac{5}{6}$ **b** $1\frac{2}{3} + 1\frac{1}{8} - \frac{5}{12}$ **c** $\frac{3}{5} \times \frac{5}{9} \div 1\frac{1}{3}$

d $(1\frac{3}{5} + 1\frac{1}{3}) \div \frac{11}{15}$ **e** $\dfrac{2\frac{2}{3} - 1\frac{1}{4}}{1\frac{1}{2} + 1\frac{5}{6}}$

2 Use the power key and/or the cube/cube-root key on your calculator to work out each of these:

a 2^7 **b** 3.2^3 **c** ${}^3\sqrt{2197}$ **d** $\sqrt{3^2 + 2^3}$

Homework Answers

1 a $1\frac{3}{4}$ **b** $2\frac{3}{8}$ **c** $\frac{1}{4}$ **d** 4   **e** $\frac{17}{40}$
2 a 128   **b** 32.768   **c** 13   **d** 4.1231

Framework objectives – Multiplying and dividing decimals
Use efficient written methods for multiplication and division of integers and decimals, including by decimals such as 0.6 or 0.06; understand where to position the decimal point by considering equivalent calculations.

Oral and mental starter

● Have a set of 'Follow me' cards (30 are suggested below) that use multiplication or division by 0.1 or 0.01.

1	**START**. You are 3×0.1	**2**	I am 0.3. You are $5 \div 0.1$
3	I am 50. You are $4 \div 0.01$	**4**	I am 400. You are 6×0.01
5	I am 0.06. You are 11×0.1	**6**	I am 1.1. You are $90 \div 0.1$
7	I am 900. You are 50×0.01	**8**	I am 0.5. You are $6 \div 0.1$
9	I am 60. You are 9×0.01	**10**	I am 0.09. You are 80×0.1
11	I am 8. You are $9 \div 0.1$	**12**	I am 90. You are 23×0.01
13	I am 0.23. You are $49 \div 0.1$	**14**	I am 490. You are 21×0.01
15	I am 0.21. You are $76 \div 0.1$	**16**	I am 760. You are 52×0.1
17	I am 5.2. You are 9×0.1	**18**	I am 0.9. You are 20×0.1
19	I am 2. You are $20 \div 0.1$	**20**	I am 200. You are 8×0.1
21	I am 0.8. You are $18 \div 0.1$	**22**	I am 180. You are 2×0.01
23	I am 0.02. You are $99 \div 0.1$	**24**	I am 990. You are 5×0.01
25	I am 0.05. You are 66×0.1	**26**	I am 6.6. You are 5.2×0.1
27	I am 0.52. You are 7×0.1	**30**	I am 0.7. **END**

Main lesson activity

● This is a consolidation lesson on multiplying and dividing decimals with up to two decimal places.

● A variety of methods can be used, but these are essentially the same as long multiplication and division, which have been met before. It is likely that the pupils will find these concepts difficult. Go through the following examples.

● Work out 17.8×3.5. Firstly, approximate the answer, $20 \times 4 = 80$, and then use a box method:

×	10	7	0.8
3	30	21	2.4
0.5	5	3.5	0.4

Sum of multiplications:

```
   30
   21
   2.4
   5
   3.5
   0.4
  ────
  62.3
```

The answer is 62.3, which agrees with the size of the estimate of 80.

● Work out 32.6×3.7. Do the calculation as 326×37 using standard column methods:

```
      326
   ×   37
   ──────
     2282
     9780
   ──────
    12062
```

The answer has two decimal places as there were two places in the original multiplication (_.6 × _.7 = _._ _). Hence the answer is 120.62.

● Work out $87.4 \div 19$. Firstly, approximate the answer, $90 \div 20 = 4.5$. Then calculate it as a whole-number problem, $874 \div 19$, using chunking, as shown right:

The answer is 4.6.

```
   874
  −380   (20 × 19)
   494
  −380   (20 × 19)
   114
   −76   ( 4 × 19)
    38
   −38   ( 2 × 19)
     0   (46 × 19)
```

- Work out 154 ÷ 2.8. Firstly, approximate the answer, 150 ÷ 3 = 50. Then treat it as a whole-number problem by writing it as 1540 ÷ 28:

```
    1540                          or        1540
   -1120      (40 × 28)                    -1400      (50 × 28)
    ----                                    ----
     420                                     140
    -280      (10 × 28)                     -140      ( 5 × 28)
    ----                                    ----
     140                                       0      (55 × 28)
    -140      ( 5 × 28)
    ----
       0      (55 × 28)
```

The answer is 55.

Point out that the two versions above give the same answer, as the sum of the 'chunks' taken away is the same in both cases. The second version is slightly faster, but using fewer chunks will often involve more difficult mental calculations.

- **The class can now do Exercise 8F from Pupil Book 2.**

Exercise 8F   **Answers**

1 **a** 59.22 **b** 26.1 **c** 7.29 **d** 17.64 **e** 1.95 **f** 4.41 **g** 16.77 **h** 0.1628
2 **a** 5.6 **b** 0.36 **c** 7.5 **d** 3.5 **e** 26 **f** 85 **g** 15 **h** 45
3 £88.56
4 120

Plenary

Key words

- long division
- long multiplication
- column methods
- chunking

- Review methods using examples such as:
  2.3 × 45.6, 136 × 8.7, 456 ÷ 1.9, 34.2 ÷ 8.7
- Discuss estimating answers, counting decimal places, ignoring the decimal points, finding equivalent calculations, etc.

Homework

1 Without using a calculator, and using any method you are happy with, work out:
   a 5.4 × 6.8   **b** 3.82 × 5.5
2 Without using a calculator, and using any method you are happy with, work out:
   a 50.4 ÷ 18   **b** 153 ÷ 3.4
3 Exercise books cost £0.78 each. How much will 88 exercise books cost?
4 Geometry sets cost £1.20 each. How many can be bought for £114?

Homework Answers

1 **a** 36.72   **b** 21.01
2 **a** 2.8   **b** 45
3 £68.64
4 95

National Tests   **Answers**

1 **a** £729 **b** £14
2 80p
3 **a** 9.2, 24 **b** 1140
4 Using 24 photo films costs £56.10. Using 36 photo films costs £61.40. Therefore 24 photo films are £5.30 cheaper for 360 photos.

Functional Maths – Taxes

Oral and mental starter

Look at the information on the taxes activity on page 118 of the corresponding Pupil Book. This spread begins to describe how money is raised through taxes and reinforces work on percentages. This could be split into separate lessons, looking at VAT and income tax as separate topics. The lesson plan deals with the Functional Maths activity as one complete topic.

- Ask pupils to name different types of tax. If answers are not forthcoming, ask pupils what type of tax is paid on money that people earn (income tax) and what type of tax is added to things that people buy (value add tax or VAT).
- Ask the pupils to look at the information on page 118 as a group activity. Tell them that you will be asking questions about it shortly. (Allow about 5 minutes.)
- Now ask the pupils to cover up the information and tell you about, for example direct tax (income tax), indirect tax (VAT). Ask the pupils about the different rates of VAT. Alternatively, simply ask them to tell you facts from the information on taxes without looking at it.

Main lesson activity

- The variety of methods chosen below will vary according to the ability of the group. It may be appropriate with weaker pupils to concentrate on one method, whereas more able groups could look at several methods. It may be helpful to do this work as a group activity throughout.
- Continuing from the oral and mental starter, it would be helpful to discuss the different rates for VAT and look at the various methods of working out 17.5%, for example:
  - the build-up method shown in the example on page 118.
  - the use of tables to read off VAT or total including VAT, where values are rounded to the nearest penny. The table could be displayed and a series of short questions asked, for example how much VAT is payable on an item costing £30 (£5.30).

Amount excluding VAT	£1	£2	£3	£4	10p	25p	50p
VAT	18p	35p	53p	70p	2p	4p	9p
Amount including VAT	£1.18	£2.35	£3.53	£4.70	12p	29p	59p

  - calculator methods (use of the multiplier, for example 0.175 for 17.5% VAT or 1.175 for the total price including 17.5% VAT).
- Then look at income tax, introducing the phrases gross income and net income.

- Explain the principles behind income tax – that generally the more someone earns the more they have to pay in income tax.
- Explain about the taxable allowance and then start by looking at a basic tax rate of 20%. Present examples using simple numbers to begin with, for example a tax allowance of £5000 and an income of £15 000 so that tax is paid on £10 000 at 20% (£2000).
- Use non-calculator methods, calculator methods or tables to calculate the amounts of tax payable.
- There is a good opportunity here to use spreadsheets for the calculations.
- Make sure pupils' have a reasonable understanding.
- **The class can now work through the questions on pages 118–119.**

> **FM Activity** **Answers**
>
> **1** 1 25%
> **2** £16 800
> **3** 5%
> **4** 0%
> **5 a** 5% **b** £94.50
> **6** £305.50
> **7 a** £18 000 **b** £3600
> **8 a** £8400 **b** £12 320
> **9 a** She earns less than she is allowed to earn before she pays tax. **b** £700

Plenary

- Ask each group of pupils to demonstrate how they worked out the answer to one of the questions.
- For the questions on VAT compare the different methods and emphasise that with money, the answers have to be written in the correct form, for example £4.70 not £4.7.
- Display the VAT table, given in the main lesson activity, again.
- Show that using the table can lead to slightly varying answers, for example £2 gives 35p but £1 + £1 gives 36p.

Homework

1 Priya earned £40 000 last year. She spent £20 000 of her earnings on a new car. What percentage of her earnings is this?

2 a Mr Spark receives his electricity bill. What is the rate of VAT that he will have to pay?
b His bill is £120 excluding VAT. How much is the VAT?

3 Miss Sergeant earns £42 000. Her tax allowance is £8000. She pays tax on the rest at 20%.
a How much does she pay tax on?
b How much tax does he pay?

4 Mr Fiddle has a tax allowance is £7200. His income tax is £480.
Show that he earns £9600 altogether if the rate of income tax is 20%.

Homework Answers

1 a 50%
2 a 5% **b** £6
3 a £34 000 **b** £6800
4 He pays tax on £2400. 20% of £2400 = £480

Geometry and Measures **3**

Overview

9.1	Congruent shapes
9.2	Combinations of transformations
9.3 & 9.4	Enlargements
9.5	Shape and ratio

Context

This chapter first shows pupils how to recognise congruent shapes, and then reminds them how to transform a 2-D shape by a reflection, a rotation and a translation. Pupils are then introduced to combining transformations and enlarging a 2-D shape about a given centre of enlargement and scale factor. Finally, pupils are shown how ratio can be used to compare the lengths, areas and volumes of 2-D and 3-D shapes.

National Curriculum references

Framework objectives

9.1	Know that if two 2-D shapes are congruent, corresponding sides and angles are equal. Identify all the symmetries of 2-D shapes.
9.2	Transform 2-D shapes by rotation, reflection and translation, on paper and using ICT. Try out mathematical representations of simple combinations of these transformations.
9.3 & 9.4	Understand and use the language and notation associated with enlargement; enlarge 2-D shapes, given a centre of enlargement and a positive integer scale factor; explore enlargement using ICT.
9.5	Apply understanding of the relationship between ratio and proportion; simplify ratios, including those expressed in different units, recognising links with fraction notation.

Key concepts

Applications and implications of mathematics

- Understand that 2-D shapes can be transformed in different ways
- Understand that shapes transformed by reflections, rotations and translations remain congruent, whereas enlargements do not
- Appreciate the importance of ratio when comparing 2-D and 3-D shapes

Key processes

Representing

- Using the language and notation associated with reflections, rotations, translations and enlargement
- Using ratio to compare lengths, areas and volumes

Analysing

● Identifying the symmetries and different transformations of 2-D shapes

Communicating and reflecting

● Explaining the different properties of reflections, rotations, translations and enlargements

● Showing how ratio can be used in a geometrical context

Route mapping

Exercise	Levels 5	6
9A	1–4	
9B	1–4	5–6
9C		1–6
9D	1–2	3–7

LESSON
9.1

Framework objectives – Congruent shapes
Know that if two 2-D shapes are congruent, corresponding sides and angles are equal. Identify all the symmetries of 2-D shapes.

Oral and mental starter

- Imagine a square.
- Now imagine another square, exactly the same size, that touches the first one along all of one of its sides. What shape are you thinking of? (Answer: a rectangle.)
- Imagine an equilateral triangle.
- Now imagine another equilateral triangle, exactly the same size, that touches the first one along all of one of its sides. What shape are you thinking of? (Answer: a rhombus.)

Main lesson activity

- Remind the class about the different transformations they met in Year 7. The following diagrams can be drawn on the board or on an OHT:

A reflection in a mirror line   A rotation about a point   A translation

- Ask the class to describe what happens to the shapes after any of the three transformations. They should remember that the object and the image are the same shape and size.
- Write on the board:
  'Two shapes are congruent if they are exactly the same shape and size. Reflections, rotations and translations all produce images that are congruent to the original object.'
- Have prepared sets of various congruent triangles and quadrilaterals made from card. With the class working in groups, let them sort the shapes into congruent pairs.
- Make sure the pupils understand that for each pair of congruent shapes the corresponding sides and angles are equal.

- **The class can now do Exercise 9A from Pupil Book 2.**
  Card, scissors and square-dotted paper may be required for this exercise.

Exercise 9A   **Answers**

1 a yes b no c yes d yes e no f yes
2 a and e, b and j, c and k, d and f
3 a and c
4 a two different isosceles triangles, two different parallelograms, a rectangle and a kite
  b a parallelogram and a rhombus c a rhombus

Extension **Answers**

Examples of two congruent shapes:

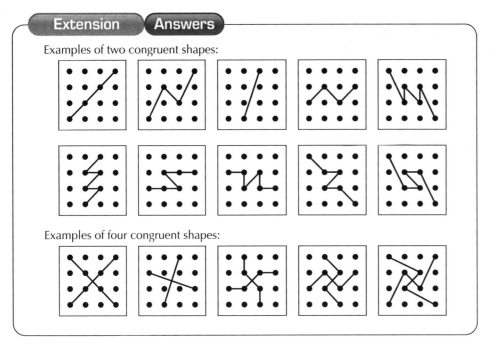

Examples of four congruent shapes:

Plenary

Key words

☐ **congruent**
☐ **congruence**

● Ask the class to explain what congruent shapes are. Invite pupils to draw two congruent shapes on the board or on individual white boards to show the rest of the class.
● Ask the class to describe what would happen if two shapes are the same, but are different in size. This should lead to a discussion on enlargements.

Homework

1 For each pair of shapes below, state whether they are congruent or not:

  a ▱▱   b ◻⌓   c ▽◺   d ○○   e ◻◻

2 Which of the isosceles triangles on the grid below are congruent?

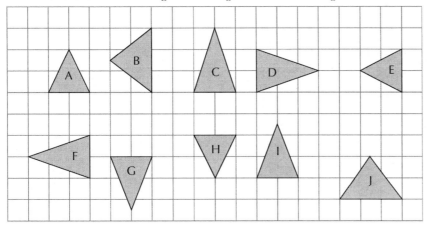

Homework Answers

1 **a** no **b** yes **c** no **d** no **e** yes
2 A, E and H; B and J; C, D and F; G and I

LESSON 9.2

Framework objectives – Combinations of transformations
Transform 2-D shapes by rotation, reflection and translation, on paper and using ICT. Try out mathematical representations of simple combinations of these transformations.

Oral and mental starter

- Draw a large 'T' in the centre of the board.
- Ask a pupil to draw another 'T' anywhere on the board.
- Ask the class which 'T' is the object and which 'T' is the image. Ask them which transformation could have mapped the object to the image?
- Repeat the activity by allowing pupils to draw an image of 'T' in different orientations.

Main lesson activity

- The first part of the lesson is to revise the three single transformations that the pupils have met, with an emphasis on congruency from the previous lesson. The examples can be drawn on the board or on a prepared OHT using a cut-out triangle.

- Reflections

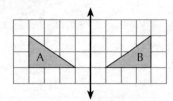

  Triangle A is mapped onto triangle B by a reflection in the mirror line. Triangle A is congruent to triangle B.

- Rotations

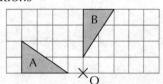

  Triangle A is mapped onto triangle B by a rotation of 90° clockwise about the centre of rotation O. Triangle A is congruent to triangle B.

- Translations

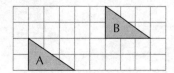

  Triangle A is mapped onto triangle B by a translation of five units right, followed by two units up. Triangle A is congruent to triangle B.

- Combined transformations
  Explain to the class that shapes can be transformed by using a combination of the above transformations. Show the class an example of a combination of two transformations, such as a reflection followed by a translation.

- **The class can now do Exercise 9B from Pupil Book 2.**
  Tracing paper and mirrors will be useful for this exercise.

1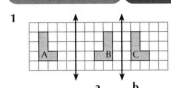

a   b

c translation

2

b   a

c rotation of 180° about their
point of intersection

3

b   a

c rotation about the same centre of
rotation

4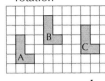

a   b

c translation

5 a i a translation of 3 units right and
3 units up
ii a reflection in the *y*-axis
iii a rotation of 180° about the origin
iv a rotation of 90° clockwise
about the origin

b i for example, a rotation of 90°
anticlockwise about the origin
followed by a translation of
3 units left and 3 units up
ii for example, a rotation of 180°
about the origin followed by a
reflection in the *y*-axis
iii for example, a rotation of 90°
anticlockwise about the origin
followed by a translation of
5 units left and 6 units down
iv for example, a reflection in the
x-axis followed by a reflection in
the *y*-axis

Extension   Answers

The following are possible examples for a combined transformation:
1 a a translation of 1 unit down followed by a reflection in the *x*-axis
b a reflection in the *y*-axis followed by a translation of 6 units down
c a rotation of 90° anticlockwise about the origin followed by a translation of 1 unit down
d a reflection in the *x*-axis followed by a translation of 7 units left and 5 units down
e a rotation of 90° clockwise about the origin followed by a translation of 1 unit left
and 6 units up
f a rotation of 90° anticlockwise about the origin followed by a translation of 6 units
left and 6 units up

Key words
☐ map
☐ tessellation
☐ transformation
☐ reflection
☐ rotation
☐ translation

Plenary

● Ask individual pupils to explain the following terms: a transformation, a
reflection, a rotation, a translation and a combined transformation.

Homework

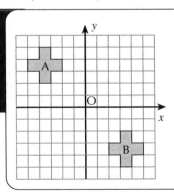

Find three different combinations of two transformations that will
map shape A onto shape B.

6

Homework Answers

Possible answers are:
1 A reflection in the *y*-axis followed by a reflection in the *x*-axis.
2 A rotation of 90° clockwise about the origin followed by a rotation of 90° clockwise about the origin.
3 A translation of 7 units right followed by a reflection in the *x*-axis.

LESSONS
9.3
9.4

Framework objectives – Enlargements

Understand and use the language and notation associated with enlargement; enlarge 2-D shapes, given a centre of enlargement and a positive integer scale factor; explore enlargement using ICT.

Oral and mental starter

- Write on the board, or OHP, a grid similar to the one on the right.
- Ask individual pupils to complete any cell in the multiplication grid. Ask them if they have any particular strategies for working out their answer.
- Discuss some of the strategies used. For example, leave out the decimal point, then multiply and the answer will have one decimal place; to multiply by 4, double the number and then double again.

	×2	×3	×4
1.2			
2.5			
3.4			
5.6			
7.9			

Main lesson activity

- The work in this section involves a good deal of drawing, and so it is suggested that the work should cover two lessons.
- It is a good idea to have some examples of enlargements prepared for the OHP. Showing the class enlargements of photographs will also help the pupils to understand the work.

Lesson 9.3

- Remind the class that the three transformations they have met so far (reflections, rotations and translations) do not change the size of an object. They are now going to look at a transformation that does change the size of an object, an **enlargement.**
- Draw the following diagram on the board or OHT.
- Explain to the class that all the sides of △A′B′C′ are twice as long as the sides of △ABC and that OA′ = 2 × OA, OB′ = 2 × OB and OC′ = 2 × OC. △ABC has been enlarged by a scale factor of two about the centre of enlargement O to give the image A′B′C′. The dotted lines are called the guidelines or rays for the enlargement. Explain to the class that to enlarge a shape a centre of enlargement and a scale factor are needed.

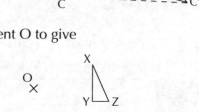

- Show the class how to enlarge the triangle XYZ by a scale factor of two about the centre of enlargement O (shown right). Draw rays OX, OY and OZ. Measure the length of the three rays and multiply each of these lengths by two. Extend each of the rays to these new lengths measured from O and plot the points X′, Y′ and Z′. Join X′, Y′ and Z′.

△X′Y′Z′ is the enlargement of △XYZ by a scale factor of two about the centre of enlargement O.

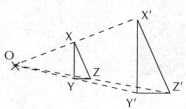

- Now show the class how to enlarge a shape about the origin on a coordinate grid. The rectangle ABCD on the coordinate grid shown is enlarged by a scale factor of three about the origin O to give the image rectangle A′B′C′D′:

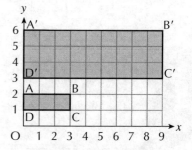

The coordinates of the object are: A(0, 2), B(3, 2), C(3, 1) and D(0, 1).
The coordinates of the image are: A'(0, 6), B'(9, 6), C'(9, 3) and D'(0, 3).
Notice that if a shape is enlarged by a scale factor about
the origin on a coordinate grid, the coordinates of the enlarged shape
are multiplied by the scale factor.

● **The class can now start Exercise 9C from Pupil Book 2.**

Lesson 9.4
● The students can continue with Exercise 9C.
● The class should be encouraged to work in pairs or groups when they start the Extension Work.
● ICT work can also be done using software such as LOGO.

Exercise 9C **Answers**

2 **a** vertices at (8, 6), (8, 2), (4, 2) **b** vertices at (4, 6), (8, 4), (4, 2), (0, 4)
  c vertices at (3, 9), (6, 9), (6, 6), (9, 6), (9, 9), (12, 9), (12, 3), (3, 3)
  d vertices at (0, 8), (8, 8), (8, 12), (12, 6), (8, 0), (8, 4), (0, 4)
3 vertices at (7, 10), (9, 6), (7, 0), (5, 6)
4 **a** A'(3, 7), B'(7, 7), C'(7, 3), D'(3, 3) **b** A"(2, 8), B"(8, 8), C"(8, 2), D"(2, 2)
  c A‴(1, 9), B‴(9, 9), C‴(9, 1), D‴(1, 1)
  d for example, the *x*-coordinate and the *y*-coordinate are the same or they add up to 10
5 **a** 2 **b** (9, 1)
6 **b** 4 cm² **c** 16 cm² **d** 36 cm² **e** 64 cm²
  f the area scale factor is the square of the scale factor **g** yes

Key words

☐ centre of enlargement
☐ enlarge
☐ enlargement
☐ image
☐ object
☐ scale
☐ scale factor

Plenary

● Ask the class to describe which properties of a shape change after an enlargement and which properties remain the same, such as:
  Length of sides change.
  Area changes.
  All angles stay the same size.

Homework

1 Draw copies of the shapes shown and enlarge each one by the given scale factor about the centre of enlargement O:
  a Scale factor 2   **b** Scale factor 3   **c** Scale factor 2

2 Copy the shapes below onto centimetre-squared paper and enlarge each one by the given scale factor about the origin O:
  a Scale factor 2   **b** Scale factor 3

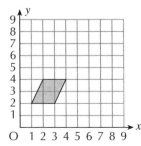   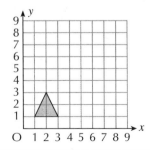

Homework Answers

2 **a** vertices at (4, 8), (8, 8), (6, 4), (2, 4) **b** vertices at (6, 9), (9, 3), (3, 3)

LESSON 9.5

Framework objectives – Shape and ratio
Apply understanding of the relationship between ratio and proportion; simplify ratios, including those expressed in different units, recognising links with fraction notation.

Oral and mental starter

- A revision exercise to remind pupils how to simplify ratios.
- Write the following ratios on the board or OHP and ask the class to give the ratios in their simplest form (the pupils can either give oral answers or show them on individual white boards):

  1 $3:6$ **2** $5:20$ **3** $8:12$ **4** $15:25$ **5** $24:36$

  6 $18:24$ **7** $14:35$ **8** $30:50$ **9** $40:100$ **10** $45:60$

  Answers   **1** $1:2$ **2** $1:4$ **3** $2:3$ **4** $3:5$ **5** $2:3$ **6** $3:4$ **7** $2:5$ **8** $3:5$ **9** $2:5$ **10** $3:4$

Main lesson activity

- The lesson is to show pupils how ratio can be used to solve problems that involve length, area and volume.
- The idea is for pupils to appreciate that the ratio of lengths, areas and volumes is different when comparing 2-D and 3-D shapes.
- Explain the following three examples to the class, reminding them that a ratio is always given in its simplest form.

  Example 1   Find the ratio of the line segment AB to the length of the line segment XY:

  A ——————— B   X ————————————— Y
       80 cm   1.2 m

  Since the lengths are in mixed units, change them to the smallest unit before simplifying the ratio. The ratio is $80\,\text{cm}:1.2\,\text{m} = 80\,\text{cm}:120\,\text{cm} = 2:3$.

  Example 2   Find the ratio of the area of rectangle A to the area of rectangle B:

  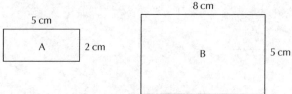

  The ratio is $10\,\text{cm}^2:40\,\text{cm}^2 = 1:4$.

  Example 3   Find the ratio of the volume of cube A to the volume of cube B:

  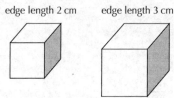

  The ratio is $8\,\text{cm}^3:27\,\text{cm}^3 = 8:27$.

- **The class can now do Exercise 9D from Pupil Book 2.**

Exercise 9D   **Answers**

1 a $2:5$ **b** $1:10$ **c** $4:5$ **d** $1:5$ **e** $1:4$ **2 a** $1:3$ **b** $1:3$ **c** $1:9$
3 a i $1:2:3$ **ii** $1:2:3$ **iii** $1:4:9$ **b** they are enlargements of each other   **4 a** $1:1$ **b** $1:5$ **c** $2:5$ **d** $1:2$
5 a $1:8$ **b** $\frac{1}{8}$ **6 a** $1200\,\text{m}^2$ **b i** $30\,000\,\text{m}^2$ **ii** 3 hectares   **c** $1:5$ **d** $1:25$ **e** $\frac{1}{25}$ **7 a** 24l   **b** 18l   **c** $3:4$

Plenary

- Ask the pupils to write a brief summary of what they have learnt during the lesson.
- Allow them to discuss their summaries in pairs or groups.

Homework

1 Express each of the following ratios in their simplest form:

a 12 cm : 16 cm **b** 40 mm : 5 cm
c 30 cm : 1 m **d** 500 m : 2.5 km
e 500 cm³ : 1 l

2 Rectangle A is 6 cm by 2 cm and rectangle B is 6 cm by 8 cm. Find each of the ratios given below for the two rectangles, giving your answers in their simplest form:

a the perimeter of rectangle A to the perimeter of rectangle B

b the area of rectangle A to the area of rectangle B

3 A rectangle of length 12 cm and width 10 cm has a black square of edge length 2 cm in each corner (four black squares in total). If the four black squares are cut off the rectangle, find the ratio of the area of the black squares to the area of the remaining shape.

Homework Answers

1 a 3:4 **b** 4:5 **c** 3:10 **d** 1:5 **e** 1:2
2 a 4:7 **b** 1:4
3 2:13

1 a 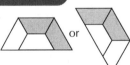 or **b**  or **c** 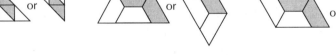 or

2 **a** 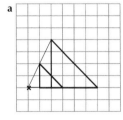 **b**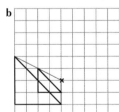

3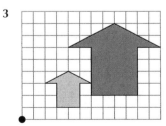

4 90 cm² : 54 cm² = 45 : 27 = 5 : 3

Algebra **4**

Overview

10.1   Solving equations

10.2   Equations involving negative numbers

10.3   Equations with unknowns on both sides

10.4   Substituting into expressions

10.5   Substituting into formulae

10.6   Creating your own expressions and formulae

Context

This chapter builds on previous work on equations and formulae. Pupils learn how to solve increasingly complex equations involving expanding brackets, fractions, negative numbers and the variable appearing on both sides. The last three sections explore increasingly complex formulae and expressions, including formulae involving brackets and fractions. Formulae and expressions are evaluated using negative numbers. Finally, pupils create formulae to represent simple real-life situations and evaluate these using given values.

National Curriculum references

Framework objectives

10.1   Construct and solve linear equations with integer coefficients (unknown on either or both sides, without and with brackets) using appropriate methods (for example, inverse operations, transforming both sides in same way).

10.2   Construct and solve linear equations with integer coefficients (unknown on either or both sides, without and with brackets) using appropriate methods (for example, inverse operations, transforming both sides in same way).

10.3   Construct and solve linear equations with integer coefficients (unknown on either or both sides, without and with brackets) using appropriate methods (for example, inverse operations, transforming both sides in same way).

10.4   Substitute integers into simple formulae, including examples that lead to an equation to solve; substitute positive integers into expressions involving small powers, for example, $3x^2 + 4$ or $2x^3$.

10.5   Substitute integers into simple formulae, including examples that lead to an equation to solve; substitute positive integers into expressions involving small powers, for example, $3x^2 + 4$ or $2x^3$.

10.6   Derive simple formulae.

Key concepts

Applications and implications of mathematics

- Know that relationships can be expressed algebraically using formulae and/or expressions

Key processes

Representing

- Using formulae and expressions to represent practical and real-life situations
- Plotting graphs from equations, functions and mapping diagrams

Analysing

- Solving increasingly complex linear equations
- Interpreting situations and representing them using formulae

Communicating and reflecting

- Making sensible choices for variables and values when setting up and evaluating expressions and formulae

Route mapping

Exercise	Levels	
	5	6
10A	1–4	5–6
10B	1–5	6–8
10C	1	2–4
10D	1–5	
10E	1–6	7–12
10F	1–10	11–12

Oral and mental starter

- This is a puzzle for pupils to work on in twos or threes.
- Draw the diagram shown on the board, or duplicate it and hand it out.
- Show that the sum of the squares of the top two numbers (16 and 2) is given by:
  $$16^2 + 2^2 = 256 + 4 = 260$$
  and the sum of the squares of the opposite two numbers is the same:
  $$14^2 + 8^2 = 196 + 64 = 260$$

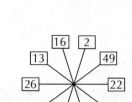

- Tell the pupils that they must now complete the pattern so that the sum of the squares of any two adjacent numbers is equal to the sum of the squares of the two numbers opposite. They aren't allowed to use numbers over 50 nor to use any number more than once.
- Encourage pupils to use calculators to help them.
- You may want to give the following hint to get them started:
  'The differences between the squares of opposite numbers will always be the same (192)'
- The completed diagram is shown on the right. If some pupils are still struggling,
  then you can help by giving them some of the missing numbers one at a time.

Main lesson activity

- Write $3x + 5 = 32$ on the board, and ask the class what this sort of mathematical expression is called.
- The answer you are looking for is 'an equation'. Explain that this is actually a 'linear equation', meaning it only contains terms in x (or another letter) and numbers, rather than terms like x^2, x^3 etc. The only equations they will have to solve are linear ones.
- Tell the class that an equation is like a puzzle – we have to rearrange it so that x appears by itself on one side of the equals sign. This is called solving the equation.
- Explain that x is called an unknown because we don't know its actual value until we have solved the equation.
- Work through the solution with the class on the board:

  subtract 5 from both sides $3x + 5 - 5 = 32 - 5$
  $$3x = 27$$

  divide both sides by 3 $\dfrac{3x}{3} = \dfrac{27}{3}$

  $$x = 9$$

- **The class can now do Questions 1, 2 and 3 of Exercise 10A from Pupil Book 2.**
- Write the equation $3(3x + 1) = 21$ on the board and ask the class how they might start to solve this equation.
- If the pupils suggest multiplying out the bracket first, then put this and the rest of the solution on the board ($x = 2$), asking the class for the next step at each stage.

● Now ask if there was a different way to start the solution. The alternative you are looking for is to start by dividing both sides by 3 to give $3x + 1 = 7$. Work through the solution to this, to obtain the same answer as with the previous method.

● **The class can now complete Exercise 10A.**

Exercise 10A   **Answers**

1 a 7 b 5 c 3 d 8 e 3 f 3 g 2 h 6 i 4 j 11 k 9 l 7
2 a 4 b 5 c 3 d 4 e 4 f 5 g 12 h 1 i 2 j 7 k 9 l 9
3 a 3.5 b 6.5 c 5.5 d 8.5 e 2.5 f 4.5 g 7.5 h 3.5 i 1.5 j 3.5
  k 4.5 l 7.5
4 a 14 b 7 c 4 d 3 e 3 f 2
5 a 5 b 5 c 1 d 2 e 8 f 6
6 a 2 b 5 c 4 d 1 e 3 f 1

Plenary

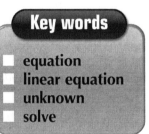
Key words

● Ask if anyone can remember the name of the type of equation they have been looking at today (linear equations).
● Explain that this sort of equation crops up in many different areas of mathematics, science and technology. Being able to solve equations like this (and more complicated ones) is essential in being able to solve problems in these subjects.
● Try to get across the idea that solving equations is just like puzzle solving, but here we are trying to use a logical sequence to help us solve the puzzle, which is guaranteed to give the correct answer every time if we do it correctly.

Key words
- equation
- linear equation
- unknown
- solve

Homework

1 Solve the following equations.
   a $2x + 7 = 13$ b $3x - 8 = 10$ c $2y + 5 = 19$ d $3s - 7 = 17$
   e $4f + 5 = 13$ f $5q - 4 = 16$ g $4p + 7 = 39$ h $5t - 3 = 12$
2 Solve the following equations.
   a $19 - 2t = 7$ b $13 - 3x = 4$ c $17 - 4v = 5$ d $39 - 5z = 4$
   e $15 - 4g = 3$ f $19 - 2x = 5$ g $26 - 3f = 8$ h $11 - 5k = 1$
3 Solve the following equations.
   a $2(5x + 3) = 26$ b $4(3x - 1) = 44$ c $5(2j + 3) = 35$ d $4(4w + 5) = 36$
   e $6(5q - 5) = 30$ f $10(4m - 9) = 30$

5

6

Homework Answers

1 a 3 b 6 c 7 d 8 e 2 f 4 g 8 h 3
2 a 6 b 3 c 3 d 7 e 3 f 7 g 6 h 2
3 a 2 b 4 c 2 d 1 e 2 f 3

Framework objectives – Equations involving negative numbers

Construct and solve linear equations with integer coefficients (unknown on either or both sides, without and with brackets) using appropriate methods (for example, inverse operations, transforming both sides in same way).

Oral and mental starter

- Set the class this puzzle to be solved in groups of two or three.
- A farmer wants to get a chicken, a fox and a bag of grain across a river, but he can only fit one of them at a time in his boat. Also, if he leaves the fox and the chicken by themselves on the riverbank, then the fox will eat the chicken. Similarly, the chicken will eat the grain if left alone with it.
- How can the farmer get all three of them across the river safely?
- The solution is to take the chicken across, then take the fox across and bring back the chicken, then take the grain across and finally take the chicken across.
- If some groups solve this fairly quickly, then you can set them the following slightly harder puzzle.
- The farmer now wants to get two foxes and two rabbits across the river. He has a bigger boat, which can fit any two animals in it at a time. However, if two rabbits are left unattended then they will fight, and if a fox is left with a rabbit then it will eat it. To make this explicit, the following combinations of foxes (f) and rabbits (r) may not be left unattended: rr; fr; ffr; frr.
- One possible solution is shown on the right.

	→	←
ffrr		
	rr	
ff		rr
	r	
ffr		r
	fr	
f		frr
	rr	
frr		f
	fr	
r		ffr
	r	
rr		ff
	rr	
		ffrr

Main lesson activity

- Tell the class that today they are going to look at some equations involving negative numbers.
- If pupils struggle to follow the examples below then you may need to revise working with directed numbers and dividing and multiplying negative numbers.
- Write the equation $4x + 14 = 2$ on the board and go through its solution:
  subtracting 14 from each side gives a negative
  answer on the right-hand side: $\quad 4x = -12$
  dividing both sides by 4 gives $\quad x = -3$
- **The class can now do Questions 1–3 of Exercise 10B from Pupil Book 2.**
- Write $-4x = 8$ on the board. Ask what number you need to divide both sides by to get x by itself (-4). Write out the solution:

$$-4x = 8$$
$$\frac{-4x}{-4} = \frac{8}{-4}$$
$$x = -2$$

- **The class can now do Question 4 of Exercise 10B.**
- Now work through the solution of $9 - 2x = 15$:
  subtract 9 from both sides $\quad 9 - 2x - 9 = 15 - 9$
  $$-2x = 6$$
  divide both sides by -2 $\quad x = 3$
- **The class can now complete Exercise 10B from Pupil Book 2.**

Exercise 10B Answers

1 a –1 **b** –1 **c** –2 **d** –2 **e** 5 **f** –3 **g** –3 **h** –4 **i** –3 **j** 2 **k** –3 **l** –3
2 a –4 **b** –5 **c** –2 **d** –4 **e** 1 **f** –3 **g** 2 **h** –3 **i** –6 **j** –8 **k** –4 **l** –3
3 a –6 **b** –2 **c** –5 **d** –4 **e** –4 **f** 3 **g** –24 **h** –3 **i** –1 **j** –16 **k** –8
  l –9
4 a –5 **b** –2 **c** –6 **d** –9 **e** –6 **f** –3 **g** –11 **h** –4 **i** –13 **j** 4
5 a –2 **b** –1 **c** –3 **d** 3 **e** 3 **f** –5 **g** –3 **h** –4 **i** 5 **j** 3
6 a –1 **b** –3 **c** –2 **d** –3 **e** –1 **f** –7 **g** 6 **h** –2
7 a –2 **b** –3 **c** –1 **d** –1 **e** –2 **f** 7 **g** 4 **h** –3
8 a Error on line 3; $x = -4$ **b** Error on line 2; $x = -4$ **c** Error on line 2; $x = -9$
  d Error on line 7; $x = -2$

Extension Answers

1 a 3 and –8 **b** 6 and –2
2 –6 and –2

Plenary

Key word

☐ **negative**

- Write a few equations, with both positive and negative solutions, up on the board. Ask the class if they can tell you which have positive and which have negative solutions, without writing anything down.
- Discourage them from wild guessing. Attempting to mentally manipulate equations will help them consolidate the order in which steps are done to isolate the unknown.

5

6

Homework

1 Solve the following equations.

  a $3x + 4 = -11$ **b** $4x - 3 = -15$ **c** $3x + 5 = -13$ **d** $2x - 7 = -13$

  e $4x + 5 = -15$ **f** $2x - 5 = -1$ **g** $2x + 7 = -37$ **h** $3x - 7 = -10$

2 Solve the following equations.

  a $19 - 2x = 13$ **b** $11 - 3x = 17$ **c** $13 - 4x = 29$ **d** $27 - 5x = 12$

  e $17 - 4p = 5$ **f** $17 - 2r = 21$ **g** $25 - 3t = 31$ **h** $19 - 5m = 34$

3 Solve the following equations.

  a $2(2x + 8) = 8$ **b** $4(3x - 1) = -16$ **c** $5(4x + 13) = 25$ **d** $4(3q + 7) = 4$

  e $6(2g - 5) = -66$ **f** $10(3y + 19) = 70$

Homework Answers

1 a –5 **b** –3 **c** –6 **d** –3 **e** –5 **f** 2 **g** –22 **h** –1
2 a 3 **b** –2 **c** –4 **d** 3 **e** 3 **f** –2 **g** –2 **h** –3
3 a –2 **b** –1 **c** –2 **d** –2 **e** –3 **f** –4

LESSON

10.3

Framework objectives – Equations with unknowns on both sides

Construct and solve linear equations with integer coefficients (unknown on either or both sides, without and with brackets) using appropriate methods (for example, inverse operations, transforming both sides in same way).

Oral and mental starter

- Tell the class that you want them to make up calculations using any of the following, $+ , - , \times , \div , \sqrt{}$, 5, 55, 555, 5555, ( ), to make as many different integers as possible. They must use the digit 5 exactly four times in each calculation. Write some examples on the board and ask for more suggestions.

  $5 + 5 + 5 + 5 = 20$;

  $(55 + 5) \div 5 = 12$;

  $55 \div 55 = 1$;

  $55 + (5 \div 5) = 56$;

  $\sqrt{55} \times \sqrt{55} = 55$

- Once everyone has grasped the idea, set the task of trying to make as many of the integers from 1 to 10 as possible using this method.
- Possible solutions are:

  $1 = 55 \div 55$

  $2 = (5 \div 5) + (5 \div 5)$

  $3 = 5 - \dfrac{(5 + 5)}{5}$

  $4 = \sqrt{5} \times \sqrt{5} - \dfrac{5}{5}$

  $5 = \sqrt{5} \times \sqrt{5} \times \dfrac{5}{5}$

  $6 = \sqrt{5} \times \sqrt{5} + \dfrac{5}{5}$

  $7 = 5 + \dfrac{(5 + 5)}{5}$

  $8 = \dfrac{(5 + 5 + 5)}{5} + 5$ (8 cannot actually be generated without using five 5s)

  $9 = 5 + 5 - \dfrac{5}{5}$

  $10 = (5 + 5) \times \dfrac{5}{5}$

- Encourage pupils who complete this early to set about trying to generate the integers up to 20.

Main lesson activity

- Write the equation $6x = 20 + 2x$ on the board.
- Ask the class what is different about this equation to those they've met before. Someone should notice that there is an unknown on both sides.

- Explain that we need to get the unknown on to one side only, and so that it ends up as a positive rather than a negative term. To do this here we need to subtract $2x$ from both sides.

$$6x - 2x = 20 + 2x - 2x$$
$$4x = 20$$

We are now back with the familiar type of equation that we can solve to get $x = 5$

- Now write another equation on the board, $5x - 4 = 12 - 3x$, and ask the class what we need to do to solve this equation.
- This time we need to add $3x$ to both sides;

$$5x - 4 + 3x = 12 - 3x + 3x$$
$$8x - 4 = 12$$

Continue the solution to give $x = 2$.

- **The class can now do Exercise 10C from Pupil Book 2.**

Exercise 10C **Answers**

1 a 4 b 6 c 5 d 3 e 19 f 5 g 7 h 5 i 4 j –5 k 4 l –10
2 a 3 b 5 c 2 d 5 e 4 f 4 g 1 h 2 i 3
3 a 2 b 2 c 2 d 2 e 4 f 6 g 3 h 3 i –2
4 a 8 b 2 c 4 d 6 e 7 f 4 g 1 h 3 i 3

Extension **Answers**

1 $x = 8$ 2 $x = 21$ 3 $x = 2.5$ 4 $x = 8.5$

Plenary

Key word

☐ **unknown**

- Invite pupils up to the board to solve some examples of the types of equation covered in this lesson:

$$3x + 4 = x + 16; \quad x - 5 = 8x + 2; \quad 6(x + 1) = 2(2x + 6)$$

- Extend to more complex examples if desired:

$$4(3 + x) = 3(x - 4); \quad 3x + 3 - 2x = 6(x + 3)$$

- Explain to the class that you have just spent three lessons working on different types of linear equations, some harder than others. In the next two lessons they will start to apply this to solving all sorts of real-life problems.

Homework

1 Solve the following equations.

a $5x + 3 = 12 + 2x$ b $7x + 3 = 19 + 3x$ c $6x + 4 = 16 + 2x$ d $7x - 4 = 11 + 2x$

e $6x - 5 = 19 + 2x$ f $7x - 6 = 9 + 2x$ g $7 + 6x = 13 + 3x$ h $4 + 3x = 10 + 5x$

i $6 + 9x = 21 + 4x$

2 Solve the following equations.

a $3(x + 5) = 21 + x$ b $4(2x + 3) = 26 + x$ c $4(3x - 1) = 6 + 7x$

d $5x - 7 = 2(1 + x)$ e $8x + 9 = 3(5 + 2x)$ f $7x - 2 = 2(1 + 3x)$

g $2(4x + 7) = 3(8 + x)$ h $3(8 + 3x) = 4(7 + 2x)$ i $2(5x - 6) = 4(3 + x)$

5

6

Homework Answers

1 a 3 b 4 c 3 d 3 e 6 f 3 g 2 h –3 i 3
2 a 3 b 2 c 2 d 3 e 3 f 4 g 2 h 4 i 4

Framework objectives – Substituting into expressions

Substitute integers into simple formulae, including examples that lead to an equation to solve; substitute positive integers into expressions involving small powers, for example, $3x^2 + 4$ or $2x^3$.

Oral and mental starter

- This is a puzzle that is best done in groups of two or three.
- Write the number 55 on the board and tell the class that this is a special number because:

  if you square the number (to get 3025) and split the result into two parts, 30 and 25, then adding the two parts gives the number you started with (55).

  That is, $55^2 = 3025$, $30 + 25 = 55$.
- The puzzle is to find another four digit number with the same property.
- You may wish to give some clues to the solutions such as:

  'two of the solutions include the digits 01';

  'another solution uses the digits 25'.
- The solutions are 9801, 2025 and 0001, although the latter is not strictly a four digit number.

Main lesson activity

- Write on the board an algebraic expression such as $7x$. Ask the class what it is.
- Many will say $7x$, or seven times x, but you want to draw out the answer 'expression' or 'algebraic expression'. (If they can't guess the name you could try playing a part game of hangman in order to get to the word.)
- Explain that the letter x can take any value we wish, and is therefore called a variable. For each different value of x, there will be a different value of the expression.
- Make a simple table of $x \rightarrow 7x$. Write in different values suggested by pupils beneath the heading x (including negative values), and the resulting values of $7x$.
- Explain that in each case we have 'substituted' a number for the variable x.
- Ask the class for a suggestion of another expression and repeat the table.
- Ask if these tables look familiar, and link back to functions and mappings.
- Repeat with the expressions $\frac{x}{2} + 2x$ and $3a + 5b$, including negative values of the variables each time.
- Repeat with a quadratic expression, such as $3x^2$.

- **The class can now do Exercise 10D from Pupil Book 2.**

Plenary

● Write the fraction $\frac{A}{B}$ on the board.

● Ask the class what we know about the values of A and B if this expression is:

 i equal to 1   (A and B are equal, could be negative)
 ii less than 1   (A is smaller than B)
 iii equal to 2   (A is twice as big as B)
 iv greater than 3   (A is more than 3 times the size of B)

 If you mention the possibility of A and B being negative, then use the terms 'larger' and 'smaller' rather than 'greater than' and 'less than'. This distinguishes the relative magnitude of A and B from their relative position on the number line, that is, –4 is less than –1, but larger in magnitude.

Homework

1 If $a = 3$ and $b = 5$ find the value of each of the following.

 a $2a + b$ **b** $3a – b$ **c** $2(b + 3a)$ **d** $4(2b – a)$

2 If $c = 7$ and $d = –1$ find the value of each of the following.

 a $5c + d$ **b** $8c – 3d$ **c** $2(4d + 5c)$ **d** $2(5c – 2d)$

3 If $e = 6$ and $f = –2$ find the value of each of the following.

 a $e^2 + f^2$ **b** $e^2 – f^2$ **c** $ef + 4e^2 – 3f^2$ **d** $e(9 – f^2)$

Homework **Answers**

1 **a** 11 **b** 4 **c** 28 **d** 28
2 **a** 34 **b** 59 **c** 62 **d** 74
3 **a** 40 **b** 32 **c** 120 **d** 30

Framework objectives – Substituting into formulae
Substitute integers into simple formulae, including examples that lead to an equation to solve; substitute positive integers into expressions involving small powers, for example, $3x^2 + 4$ or $2x^3$.

Oral and mental starter

- This is a puzzle that is best thought about individually.
- I was in a shop the other day when the man in front of me asked for:
    'Some 20p balloons, six times as many 10p balloons and make up the rest in 25p balloons.'
    He handed over £6 with the statement 'No change please.'
- How did the shop keeper sort out the number of balloons?
- Ask the pupils to find the solution, reminding them that there must be no change and no overcharging.
- The solution is five 20p balloons, thirty 10p balloons and eight 25p balloons.
- A strategy to help find the solution using algebra is to let the number of 20p balloons be x, then you have $6x$ balloons at 10p and the rest at 25p. Therefore the cost of the 20p balloons is $20x$, the cost of the 10p balloons is $60x$. The cost of both together is $80x$.
- The remainder of the £6 must go on 25p balloons, so to generate no change, $80x$ must be a multiple of 25p. Going through the possibilities of $x = 1$, $x = 2$, $x = 3$, etc., it is found that $x = 5$ gives $80x = 400$, which is a multiple of 25p. Therefore the solution is five 20p balloons, thirty 10p balloons and eight 25p balloons.
- Go through the algebraic solution with the class if there is time.

Main lesson activity

- Ask if anyone can remember what a formula is.
- Draw from the class the fact that a formula is an equation for working out a value from some known facts.
- Explain that Celsius (also called Centigrade) and Fahrenheit are two different scales for measuring temperature. The former is gradually replacing the latter in this country. Introduce the notation °C and °F and how these are pronounced.
- Show the formula for converting a temperature in degrees Celsius into degrees Fahrenheit:

$$F = \frac{9C}{5} + 32$$

- Use the formula to convert 35 °C into Fahrenheit:

$$C = 35, \text{ so } F = \frac{9 \times 35}{5} + 32 = 63 + 32 = 95$$

- Ask the class if anyone can think of a formula which uses two variables to work out a third, for example, the formula for the area of a triangle.
- Use the triangle formula (if no one comes up with another), illustrating how to substitute into the formula to calculate one value from two others.
- For example, the area of a triangle is given by $A = \frac{1}{2}bh$ where b is the base length and h the vertical height of the triangle. Calculate the area of a triangle with a base length of 5 cm and a vertical height of 8 cm.

- Show that:

  Area, $A = \frac{1}{2} \times 5 \times 8 = 20 \, \text{cm}^2$

- Go through another example with this formula, but this time, the area and base length are known, and the height must be calculated. ($A = 36 \, \text{cm}^2$ and $b = 8 \, \text{cm}$ gives $h = 9 \, \text{cm}$.) Substitute in the known values before rearranging to find the height.

- **The class can now do Exercise 10E from Pupil Book 2.** The exercise covers Functional Maths skills.

Exercise 10E **Answers**

1 i 56   **ii** 9
2 i 612   **ii** 180
3 i 900   **ii** 1800
4 a i 200   **ii** 142   **b** 3
5 a i 7   **ii** 1.6   **b** 21
6 a i £35   **ii** £55   **iii** £50   **b** $\frac{1}{2}$ hour
7 a i 72 cm²   **ii** 45 cm²   **b** 4 cm
8 a i 113 °F   **ii** 104 °F   **iii** 149 °F   **iv** 212 °F   **b i** 10 °C   **ii** 15 °C   **iii** 5 °C   **iv** –5 °C
9 a 112   **b** 180
10 a 45   **b** 200
11 a i 60 m³   **ii** 94 m²
    b i 27 cm³   **ii** 54 cm² cube
12 a 1, 3, 6, 10, 15   **b** 4950

Extension **Answers**

1 i 20   **ii** –6
2 i 1.2   **ii** 2.67

Plenary

Key words

☐ **formula**
☐ **variable**
☐ **Celsius**
☐ **Centigrade**
☐ **Fahrenheit**

- Ask the class to give you as many formulae to do with perimeter, area, surface area and volume as they can think of, and write these up on the board. They should be able to recall these from Chapter 6 – Geometry and Measures 2. Make sure they know what each letter stands for.

Homework

1 If $M = DV$, find M when: **i** $D = 2$ and $V = 150$ **ii** $D = 2.6$ and $V = 200$

2 If $A = 4rh$, find A when: **i** $r = 15$ and $h = 5$ **ii** $r = 1.5$ and $h = 16$

3 If $n = \dfrac{A + 360}{180}$, find n when: **i** $A = 540$ **ii** $A = 720$

4 If $U = v - ft$, find U when: **i** $v = 80, f = 32$ and $t = 2$ **ii** $v = 120, f = 15$ and $t = 6$

5 If $L = \dfrac{A}{B}$, find L when: **i** $A = 36$ and $B = 4$ **ii** $A = 10$ and $B = 2.5$

6 If $T = \dfrac{P(q - r)}{2}$, find T when: **i** $P = 14, q = 19$ and $r = 11$ **ii** $P = 8.1, q = 17.5$ and $b = 8.5$

7 If $Q = w(k^2 + g^2)$, find Q when: **i** $w = 16, k = 4$ and $g = 3$ **ii** $w = 8, k = 5$ and $g = 10$

5

Homework Answers

1 i 300   **ii** 520
2 i 300   **ii** 96
3 i 5   **ii** 6
3 i 5   **ii** 6
4 i 16   **ii** 30
5 i 9   **ii** 4
6 i 56   **ii** 36.45
7 i 400   **ii** 1000

Framework objectives – Creating your own expressions and formulae
Derive simple formulae.

Oral and mental starter

- This puzzle is best tackled in groups of two or three.
- Draw on the board the 3 by 3 square shown.
- Show that the 3-digit number in the second line is twice that in the top line, the bottom line is three times the top line and that all the digits from 1 to 9 have been used.
- There are three other ways of arranging the digits 1 to 9 like this. Ask the pupils to find them.
- Strategy should include recognising that the first digit in the top left hand corner must be one of 1, 2 or 3.
- Other hints can include, 'Start with the top right-hand digit, which gives you three of the digits.'
- The three other possible starting numbers are 219, 273 and 327.

1	9	2
3	8	4
5	7	6

Main lesson activity

- Start the lesson by asking the question 'Can you give me four consecutive whole numbers that add up to 100?'
- After a few guesses have been given, explain to the class that today we are going to try to create our own equations from a situation. In this way we can then solve some of the problems.
- Take this four consecutive number problem, 'What do four consecutive numbers add up to?'
- Let's start with the first number, and call it n.
- What will the number be that is one more than n? The class should realise it is $(n + 1)$.
- What is the number one more than that? The class should give $(n + 1 + 1) = (n + 2)$.
- Similarly, the fourth number is $(n + 3)$.
- Now add these together, to give $n + (n + 1) + (n + 2) + (n + 3)$.
- So four consecutive numbers added together can be written as
  $n + n + 1 + n + 2 + n + 3 = 4n + 6$.
- To find which four consecutive numbers sum to 100, we write the equation $4n + 6 = 100$, which leads to $4n = 94$. This has the solution $n = 23.5$. In other words, no four consecutive numbers have the total 100.
- Go through another situation. Ask how many months there are in a year (12).
- Ask how many months there are in 5 years ($5 \times 12 = 60$ months).
- Finally ask how many months there are in t years.
- You will need to discuss this question and its answer of $12t$.

- **The class can now do Exercise 10F from Pupil Book 2.**

Exercise 10F Answers

1 a $S = a + b + c$ **b** $P = xy$ **c** $D = a - b$ **d** $S = 4n + 6$ **e** $D = 7W$ **f** $A = \dfrac{(m + n + p)}{3}$
2 a 21 **b** $7w$ **3 a i** 18 **ii** $13 + t$ **b i** 10 **ii** $13 - m$
4 a 60 **b** $30t$ **5 a** 5000 **ii** $1000x$ **6** $60m$ **7** $\frac{b}{2}$
8 $2t$ **9** bk **10 a** 210 pence **b** $35k$ pence **c** kq pence **11 a** $6b$
b $7b + 2y$ **12** $16 + 3x$

Plenary

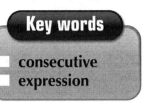

- Ask the class what the first five odd numbers add up to (25).
- Ask them what the first ten odd numbers add up to (100).
- Tell the class that you are super-quick on a calculator and can add up any number of odd numbers on a calculator in, say, 5 seconds.
- Ask the class to set you a target, n, less than 50, and you will add up the first n odd numbers. (The answer is simply n^2.) Write your answer on a piece of paper and give this to a pupil while the rest of the class calculate the total.
- Once a number of pupils have worked out the total for themselves, reveal that your answer is the same. Let them know the formula that you used.

Homework

1 Using the letters suggested, construct a simple formula in each case:

   a The sum, S, of four numbers a, b, c and d.   **b** The product, P, of two numbers A and B.

   c The sum, S, of five consecutive integers. Let the smallest number be n.

2 Give the number of hours in: **a** 4 days **b** d days

3 A boy is now 15 years old.

   a How many years old he will be in: **i** 6 years **ii** t years?

   b How many years old was he: **i** 7 years ago **ii** n years ago?

4 A train is travelling at an average speed of 50 mph. Give how many miles it will travel in:

   a 3 hours   **b** t hours

5 Give how many metres there are in: **a** 7 km **b** y km

6 How many seconds are there in t minutes?

7 Write down the number that is a quarter of M.

8 Write down the number that is three times as big as K.

Homework Answers

1 a $S = a + b + c + d$ **b** $P = AB$ **c** $S = 5n + 10$
2 a 96 **b** $24d$
3 a i 21 **ii** $15 + t$ **b i** 8 **ii** $15 - n$
3 i 5 **ii** 6
4 a 150 **b** $50t$
5 a 7000 **b** $1000y$
6 $60t$
7 $\frac{M}{4}$
8 $3K$

Statistics 2

Overview

11.1 Stem-and-leaf diagrams

11.2 Pie charts

11.3 More about pie charts

11.4 Scatter graphs

11.5 More about scatter graphs

 Football attendances

Context

This chapter builds on previously learnt statistical principles. It extends the pupils' use of data and knowledge of how to interpret statistical diagrams and charts. The way that different types of graphs and charts are used is studied throughout, which is vital for the pupil to appreciate the variety of formats within statistic illustrations.

National Curriculum references

Framework objectives

11.1 Calculate statistics for sets of discrete and continuous data, including with a calculator; recognise when it is appropriate to use the range, mean, median and mode. Construct graphical representations, on paper and using ICT, and identify which are most useful in the context of the problem. Include stem-and-leaf diagrams.

11.2 Interpret tables, graphs and diagrams for discrete and continuous data, relating summary statistics and findings to the questions being explored.

11.3 Construct graphical representations, on paper and using ICT, and identify which are most useful in the context of the problem. Include: pie charts for categorical data; bar charts and frequency; diagrams for discrete and continuous data; simple scatter graphs.

11.4 Construct graphical representations, on paper and using ICT, and identify which are most useful in the context of the problem. Include: pie charts for categorical data; bar charts and frequency; diagrams for discrete and continuous data; simple scatter graphs. Interpret tables, graphs and diagrams for discrete data, relating summary statistics and findings to the questions being explored.

11.5 Construct graphical representations, on paper and using ICT, and identify which are most useful in the context of the problem. Include: pie charts for categorical data; bar charts and frequency; diagrams for discrete and continuous data; simple scatter graphs. Interpret tables, graphs and diagrams for discrete data, relating summary statistics and findings to the questions being explored.

 Calculate statistics for sets of discrete and continuous data, including with a calculator and spreadsheet; recognise when it is appropriate to use the range, mean, median and mode and, for grouped data, the modal class.

Key concepts

Critical understanding

- Recognise that a situation can be represented using mathematics and that it can be represented in different ways, and make connections between these representations

Creativity

- Pose questions and developing appropriate lines of enquiry

Key processes

Representing

- Selecting statistical information appropriately

Analysing

- Working logically towards results and solutions, recognising the impact of constraints and assumptions

Communicating and reflecting

- Communicating findings in a range of forms

Route mapping

Exercise	Levels	
	5	6
11A		1–4
11B	1–6	
11C		1–2
11D		1–5
11E		1–3

LESSON

11.1

Framework objectives – Stem-and-leaf diagrams

Calculate statistics for sets of discrete and continuous data, including with a calculator; recognise when it is appropriate to use the range, mean, median and mode.

Construct graphical representations, on paper and using ICT, and identify which are most useful in the context of the problem. Include stem-and-leaf diagrams.

Oral and mental starter

- Using a counting stick, tell the pupils that, for example, the number 6 is at one end and 20 is at the other end. Ask them for the range. To vary the task, change the numbers, and introduce negatives, fractions and decimals.

- Write the numbers 1, 2, 2, 4, 4, 4, 4 on the board. Ask the class what the mode is, and how they found it. Repeat this procedure for the median and mean. Ask them which average they think best reflects the data. Obviously, it depends on what the data are about.
- Change the middle number to 3. Ask the class for the mode and median. Ask if the mean will go up, down or stay the same. This could be repeated several times, but at this stage keep the numbers in order.
- Now use the same numbers, but change the order. Ask them if changing the order makes any difference.
- Ask the class what happens to the mode, median, mean and range if each number is increased by one.
- Ask the class what happens to the mode, median, mean and range if the numbers are doubled.

Main lesson activity

- Tell the class that they are going to look at larger sets of data and a different way to present data sets so they are easy to analyse.
- Explain that it is quite straightforward to obtain a mode or median from a list of, say, seven numbers, but as the list becomes longer it is easier to make a mistake.
- Write 31 numbers between 25 and 45 on the board in a random order, with some numbers repeated, and ask the pupils to sort them into the following groups: 20s, 30s and 40s. Then ask them to put these groups into numerical order on three separate lines in their books.
- Now, tell them that using a stem-and-leaf diagram reduces the amount of writing.
- Draw the stem on the board and ask one pupil to read out his/her numbers in order. Write the numbers on your diagram and let the pupils copy it into their books. Explain that it is important to line up the columns of numbers.

$$
\begin{array}{c|ccccc}
2 & 0 & 1 & 1 & 3 & \dots \\
3 & 1 & 1 & 2 & 4 & \dots \\
4 & 0 & 2 & 3 & 4 & \dots \\
\end{array}
$$

- Explain that to make sense the diagram will need a key. Use the first value for the key. For example, 2 | 0 represents 20.

© HarperCollins*Publishers* Limited 2008

● Ask them to use the diagram to write down the mode, median and range.

● **The class can now do Exercise 11A from Pupil Book 2.**

Exercise 11A **Answers**

1 a 35   **b** 24   **c** 23   **d** 24
2 a 10   **b** 5   **c** 31   **d** 19
3 a 75   **b** 375   **c** There are insufficient data
4 a 1│1 2 2 5 7 7 7 9
　　2│2 3 3 3 3 4 5 6
　　3│1 1 2 4 6 6 8 9
　　4│2 5 7 7 8 9
　　Key: 1│2 represents 12 years old
　b 23   **c** 38

Plenary

● Remind the class that when creating a stem-and-leaf diagram it is important that they put the data into numerical order, especially as they will need to use the diagrams to find the range, the median and the mode.
● Reinforce that the diagram needs to be presented neatly with the numbers lined up in columns, so that it is easy to see which is the largest group.

Key words

- range
- median
- mode
- modal class
- modal group
- mean
- average
- stem-and-leaf diagram

Homework

Put the following sets of data into stem-and-leaf diagrams. Remember to give a key. In each case write down the range, the mode and the median.

a

22	45	36	32	32	33	27	42	41
37	29	31	34	30	44	42	29	30
44	32	25	26	32	29	41	22	32

b

72	91	83	77	92	92	84
83	70	77	87	95	77	94
91	78	85	93	77	78	87

c

3	14	25	36	6	31	22	27	8	4	4	26
21	25	4	25	32	5	4	27	23	23	28	33
38	4	30	10	31	11	29	34	4	34	24	29

Homework Answers

a 2│2 2 5 6 7 9 9 9
　3│0 0 1 2 2 2 2 2 3 4 6 7
　4│1 1 2 2 4 4 5
　Key: 2│2 represents 22　　Range = 23, Mode = 32, Median = 32
b 7│0 2 7 7 7 7 8 8
　8│3 3 4 5 7 7
　9│1 1 2 2 3 4 5
　Key: 7│0 represents 70　　Range = 25, Mode = 77, Median = 84
c 0│3 4 4 4 4 4 4 5 6 8
　1│0 1 4
　2│1 2 3 3 4 5 5 5 6 7 7 8 9 9
　3│0 1 1 2 3 4 4 6 8
　Key: 0│3 represents 3　　Range = 35, Mode = 4, Median = 24.5

6

Framework objectives – Pie charts
Interpret tables, graphs and diagrams for discrete and continuous data, relating summary statistics and findings to the questions being explored.

Oral and mental starter

- Draw on the board a rectangle and divide it into four equal parts.
- Shade in one part and ask the class "What fraction is shaded?" ($\frac{1}{4}$)
- Shade in two parts and ask the class "What fraction is shaded?" ($\frac{1}{2}$)
- Draw another rectangle on the board and divide it into six equal parts.
- Shade in one part and ask the class "What fraction is shaded?" ($\frac{1}{6}$)
- Shade in two parts and ask the class "What fraction is shaded?" ($\frac{1}{3}$)
- Write 60 on the board and ask the class "What is half of 60?" (30)
- "What is $\frac{1}{3}$ of 60?" (20)
- "What is $\frac{1}{4}$ of 60?" (15)
- "What is $\frac{1}{6}$ of 60?" (10)
- Discuss with the class how they worked these out, by splitting 60 up or by dividing.
- Repeat the above for 120, then for 300.

Main lesson activity

- Draw on the board a circle. Tell the pupils they are going to be looking at ways in which a circle can represent data. A circle represents a pie.
- Draw some simple radii in the circle and explain that each category is represented by a sector of the circle (a slice of the pie).
- Draw another circle (pie chart) with a 90 degrees angle. Explain that this pie chart represents the car sales in a showroom one weekend.
- Label the 90-degree sector 'British', saying that, "This sector represents the British cars sold."
- Label the rest 'Foreign', saying, "This sector represents the foreign cars sold."
- Ask, "If 40 cars were sold, how many sold were British?"
- Talk through with the class that the sector shown is one quarter of the pie, and so $\frac{1}{4}$ of the 40 cars sold were British. Ask what $\frac{1}{4}$ of 40 is. (10)
- Then ask, "How many Foreign cars were sold?" This is the rest. (30)
- Draw another pie chart on the board (see example 11.23 in the Pupil Book) and label it. Explain that this represents how a country (which shall remain anonymous) got rid of its environmental waste in 2006.
- Ask, "How much waste was got rid of by:
  a landfill   **b** burning   **c** dumping at sea   **d** chemical treatment."
- Explain that from the pie chart you can see that:
  a $\frac{1}{2}$ of the waste was landfilled = $\frac{1}{2}$ of 3000 kg = 1500 kg landfilled.
  b $\frac{1}{4}$ of the waste was burnt = $\frac{1}{4}$ of 3000 kg = 750 kg burnt.
  c $\frac{30}{360} = \frac{1}{12}$ of the waste was dumped at sea = 3000 ÷ 12 = 250 kg dumped at sea.
  d $\frac{60}{360} = \frac{1}{6}$ of the waste was treated by chemicals = 3000 ÷ 6 = 500 kg treated by chemicals.

- **The class can now do Exercise 11B from Pupil Book 2.**

Plenary

- Explain that all the pie charts looked at today are reasonably straightforward to interpret, with nice fractions. This is not always the case, but we can also estimate numbers by using percentages.
- Sketch on the board a pie chart with random angles, and label the sectors something like 'Blue', 'Red', 'Green', etc. Say this pie chart represents the favourite colour of 100 pupils and get them to estimate the percentage of each sector, hence the number of pupils who had each colour as their favourite.

Homework

1 The pie chart illustrates how 900 m² of a garden was used:

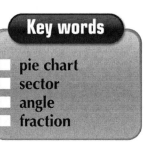

How many square metres were used as:
a flower beds **b** paths **c** shrubs **d** lawn?

2 Katie did a survey about favourite fruit. She asked 120 people. The pie chart illustrates her results:

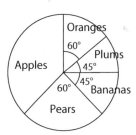

How many of these people's favourite fruit is:
a oranges **b** plums **c** bananas **d** pears **e** apples?

3 The pie chart shows the activities chosen in PE by 240 pupils:

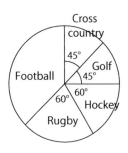

How many pupils opted for:
a rugby **b** hockey **c** golf **d** cross country **e** football?

Framework objectives – More about pie charts
Construct graphical representations, on paper and using ICT, and identify which are most useful in the context of the problem. Include: pie charts for categorical data; bar charts and frequency; diagrams for discrete and continuous data; simple scatter graphs.

Oral and mental starter

- Draw unlabelled angles of 30°, 60° and 120° on the board or on an OHP.
- Tell the class that there is a pattern to the sizes of the angles. Ask them to estimate the size of the angles. Now tell them that the pattern is 'doubling', and let them change their estimates if they want to. Ask them for their answers and write these on the board. Comment on whether the answers are accurate or not.
- Now draw three bars or vertical lines from the same base level, with heights in the ratio $3:4:5$. Tell the class that the height of the first bar represents 15 people, and that, as before, there is a pattern to the heights. Ask the class to estimate the heights the other bars represent.
- Now tell them to think of angles, and that you need three angles that add up to 360°. They need to represent 12 people altogether. Ask the class to work out what angle is needed for four people, then three people and finally five people.
- Ask them to explain how they worked it out, and if anyone did it differently.
- Now tell them that you want three facts about a pie chart (for example, angles add up to 360°, need labels or a key, circular).

Main lesson activity

- Explain to the class that in this lesson they will construct pie charts from data that have already been collected for them. Tell them this type of data is called secondary data. Point out that data collected by themselves is called primary data.
- Draw a circle on the board or OHP and tell them that this represents everyone in the room. Now ask the class how you would show on the pie chart that half the class are boys and half are girls. Then ask them how you would show that one quarter of the class wear glasses and the rest do not wear glasses.
- Now write the number 36 on the board. Tell them that you want a pie chart about 36 people. Ask them how many degrees per person. Keep changing the number of people, but keep using factors of 360 at this stage.
- Ask them to give you some numbers that add up to 36. Write them on the board in a table. Then repeat that there are 10 degrees per person, and ask the class to tell you how big each angle needs to be for the pie chart, such as:

Number of people	Angle
20	200
7	70
6	60
3	30

- Show the class how you want them to set out their working for pie charts, either in a table or as in Pupil Book example 11.5 (p. 152) where the whole calculation is written out each time.
- Let them copy down the above example into their exercise books.

● Finally, explain that if they are given a pie chart they can work the question backwards by using the fraction of 360 to calculate how many items are represented in each sector. Use the example that is already on the board to explain this clearly, such as for the smallest angle in the above example.

● **The class can now do Exercise 11C from Pupil Book 2.**

Exercise 11C — Answers

1 Pie charts drawn with the angles as shown:

a

Subject	Maths	English	Science	Languages	Other
Angle	120	70	80	40	50

b

Food	Cereal	Toast	Fruit	Cooked	Other	None
Angle	99	72	54	81	18	36

c

Goals	0	1	2	3	4	5 or more
Angle	45	60	105	75	60	15

d

Colour	Red	Green	Blue	Yellow	Other
Angle	102	48	126	18	66

2 a 45 **b** 72 **c** 45 **d** 54

Plenary

● Explain to the class that, to make the work easier, the pie charts they have been doing all used numbers that are factors of 360. Explain that this will not always be the case and that they may need to use calculators to do some of the work. This may mean that they will need to round off the angles to, say, the nearest degree.

Homework

Draw pie charts to represent the following data:

a The favourite TV programme of 30 adults

Subject	News	Soaps	Documentaries	Drama
Frequency	8	12	6	4

b The ages of 60 teachers in a school

Age (years)	21–30	31–40	41–50	51–60	Over 60
Frequency	11	19	17	8	5

c The favourite hobbies of 24 pupils

Hobby	Sport	Computing	Games console	Music	Other
Frequency	4	5	8	5	2

Homework Answers

a Subject / angle: News / 96° Soaps / 144° Documentaries / 72° Drama / 48°
b Age (years) / angle: 21–30 / 66° 31–40 / 114° 41–50 / 102° 51–60 / 48° Over 60 / 30°
c Hobby / angle: Sport / 60° Computing / 75° Games console / 120° Music / 75° Other / 30°

6

Framework objectives – Scatter graphs

Construct graphical representations, on paper and using ICT, and identify which are most useful in the context of the problem. Include: pie charts for categorical data; bar charts and frequency; diagrams for discrete and continuous data; simple scatter graphs.

Interpret tables, graphs and diagrams for discrete data, relating summary statistics and findings to the questions being explored.

Oral and mental starter

- Copy this table on to the board or OHP:

Favourite colour	Class 1	Class 2
Blue	9	15
Red	8	5
Yellow	5	6
Other	8	4

- Ask the class to tell you facts about the table. For example, blue is the favourite in both classes, three times as many like blue as red in class 2, twice as many like 'other' in class 1, etc.
- Change the numbers or the headings and repeat.
- Now ask them to draw a blank table the same size and with the same headings, and ask them to try to complete it with these facts (they may work in pairs or groups for this activity):
  - There are 30 pupils in each class.
  - In class 1, 25 did not pick red.
  - In class 1, no one picked yellow.
  - In class 2, three times as many picked red as in class 1.
  - 10 more picked blue than red in class 1.
  - In class 2, only three picked 'other'.
  - In class 2, twice as many picked blue as yellow.
- Now ask how many picked yellow in class 2. You may need to repeat the statements.

Answer	Favourite Colour	Class 1	Class 2
	Blue	15	8
	Red	5	15
	Yellow	0	4
	Other	10	3

Main lesson activity

- Tell the class that in this lesson they will look at pairs of sets of data to see if there are any connections or relationships between them. Ask them what happens to the height of children as they get older.
- Sketch a graph on the board or OHP of height against age and plot a cross near the origin. Tell the class that this cross represents a child who is very young. Ask them to tell you where the cross will be 1 year later. Plot the new cross. Continue with this until you have a few crosses with a positive correlation. Introduce the words correlation and positive correlation. It may be appropriate to discuss why the crosses do not fall on a perfect straight line and talk about strong or weak correlation.
- Now sketch a negative correlation graph on the board and ask them to suggest what the labels could be for the axes, such as Value of a car and Age.
- Discuss the idea of negative correlation and then introduce that of no correlation.
- Summarise by drawing one of each type on the board and asking the class what correlation each one has.

- **The class can now do Exercise 11D from Pupil Book 2.**

Exercise 11D   Answers

1 **a** positive correlation; the higher the temperature, the more deckchairs hired
   b negative correlation; the higher the rainfall, the fewer deckchairs hired
   c positive correlation; the higher the rainfall, the more umbrellas sold
   d negative correlation; the higher the rainfall, the fewer ice creams sold
   e positive correlation; the higher the temperature, the more ice creams sold   **f** no correlation
2 **a** positive correlation; the taller the person, the bigger their shoe size   **b** no correlation
   c positive correlation; the more a person weighs, the bigger their collar size   **d** no correlation
3 **a** positive correlation: the higher the maths A score, the higher the maths B score
   b no correlation   **c** positive correlation: the higher the maths score, the higher the science score
   d negative correlation: the lower the science score, the higher the English score
4 **a** negative correlation: the higher the price, the fewer goals let in   **b** no correlation
   c negative correlation: the higher the price, the fewer goals let in
   d negative correlation: the higher the age, the fewer goals let in
5 **a** no correlation   **b** positive correlation: the higher the weight, the higher the cost
   c positive correlation: the greater the distance, the longer the time   **d** no correlation

Plenary

- Emphasise that there are other types of statistical graphs as well as those already covered. Mention bar charts, frequency diagrams and line graphs, which will be looked at in Chapter 16.
- Say it is important that they choose the graph to use carefully and must be able to justify their choice. Explain that in the next lesson they will look at the data they have already collected and prepare a report.

Key words

- scatter graph
- correlation
- positive correlation
- negative correlation
- interpret

Homework

1 On looking at tests from geography, RE, history and geology, the following scatter diagrams were created:

a

b

c

d

e

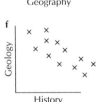
f

Describe the type of correlation and what each graph tells you.

2 After a study of various journeys from Sheffield to London, the following scatter diagrams were created:

Describe the type of correlation and what each graph tells you.

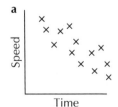
a

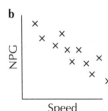
b

Homework Answers

1 **a** no correlation   **b** negative correlation: the higher the history score, the lower the geography score
   c positive: the higher the RE score, the higher the history score   **d** no correlation   **e** positive correlation: the higher the geology score, the higher the geography score   **f** negative correlation: the lower the geology score, the higher the history score was
2 **a** negative correlation: the higher the speed, the less time the journey will take
   b negative correlation: the higher the speed, the less the mpg will be

Framework objectives – More about scatter graphs

Construct graphical representations, on paper and using ICT, and identify which are most useful in the context of the problem. Include: pie charts for categorical data; bar charts and frequency; diagrams for discrete and continuous data; simple scatter graphs.

Interpret tables, graphs and diagrams for discrete data, relating summary statistics and findings to the questions being explored.

Oral and mental starter

- Write on the board or OHP, 'Children eat more junk food than adults.'
- Tell the class to imagine that they have collected lots of data from children and adults to try to prove or disprove this statement.
- Tell them that you have gathered some facts and write these (below) on the board. Ask them what sort of diagrams they could use to show these facts.
  - 75% of the children and 45% of the adults surveyed eat junk food at least once a week.
  - The number of times that the children surveyed eat chips each week is as follows: 3, 3, 2, 4, 4, …
  - Suppose that a table is given to compare age with the approximate number of times people eat junk food each month.
  - Two sets of data, one for children and one for adults, are obtained about how often they go to burger restaurants.
- You may wish to add to the list. Encourage them to give several choices for each one.

Main lesson activity

- Remind pupils about correlation and the different ways of describing it: positive, negative or no correlation.
- Talk to the class about these being the three main types; but of course some correlations are more clearly seen than others, some may be obviously positive, while others show a slight positive correlation only, etc.
- Ask the class to estimate how far from school they live in kilometres and approximately how many minutes it usually takes them to get to school from their homes. Write these on the board in a simple list, for example:

MW	3.5 km	20 mins
AB	1 km	10 mins, etc

- Start to draw a pair of axes on the board to illustrate these data, discussing with the class the labels and the numbers that need to go on the axes. Mark the horizontal time and the vertical distance.
- Plot each pupil on the board with a small cross. (If need be, you can also put the pupils' initials with the crosses.)
- Talk about whatever correlation the graph shows.
- Explain that it is important, when plotting scatter graphs, to do so as accurately on graph paper as possible, using sensible scales.

- **The class can now do Exercise 11E from Pupil Book 2.**

Exercise 11E **Answers**

1 a Scatter graph drawn showing a positive correlation.
  b Older pupils tend to spend more money.
2 a Scatter graph drawn showing a negative correlation.
  b More time spent watching TV means less time spent on homework.
3 a Scatter graph drawn showing a negative correlation.
  b The older the car, the less the value.

Plenary

Key words

- Ask the class for suggestions as to who might use scatter graphs.
- This could generate a useful discussion. Some examples are given below;
  i Teachers, to plot school tests and determine what an absent pupil might have scored.
  ii Researchers, trying to find out links between various factors such as smoking and life expectancy.
  iii Retailers of various commodities such as ice cream or umbrellas.

☐ **scatter graph**
☐ **correlation**
☐ **positive correlation**
☐ **negative correlation**
☐ **interpret**

Homework

1 The test results of 10 pupils are recorded for Maths and Science.

Pupil	1	2	3	4	5	6	7	8	9	10
Maths	50	62	24	35	85	38	42	75	90	56
Science	43	65	18	30	90	38	48	82	95	60

  a Plot the results on a scatter graph:
    Take the x-axis as the Maths result from 0 to 100;
    Take the y-axis as the Science result from 0 to 100.
  b Describe in words what the graph tells you.

2 The table shows the cost of CDs in a record shop sale and the number sold in one day.

CD	A	B	C	D	E	F	G	H	I	J
Cost	£8	£12	£14	£10	£12	£9	£8	£10	£13	£12
Number sold	20	12	8	15	10	18	18	13	7	8

  a Plot the results on a scatter graph:
    Take the x-axis as the Cost from £0 to £20;
    Take the y-axis as the Number sold from 0 to 25.
  b Describe in words what the graph tells you.

Homework Answers

1 a Scatter diagram showing positive correlation.
  b Pupils who score higher in Maths also score higher in Science.
2 a Scatter diagram showing negative correlation.
  b The higher the cost, the fewer CDs sold.

National Tests **Answers**

1 a 36° and 324° **b** Not possible to tell.
2 a angle sizes should be as follows: crime 54°, non-fiction 234°, fantasy 72°
  b 1 pupil = 165 ÷ 11 = 15°; number of pupils = 360 ÷ 15 = 24
3 Before: 46, 12 After: 35, 3
4 a N **b** False: coursework range = 40, test range = 30 **c** 70

Functional Maths – Football attendances

Framework objectives

Calculate statistics for sets of discrete and continuous data, including with a calculator and spreadsheet; recognise when it is appropriate to use the range, mean, median and mode and, for grouped data, the modal class.

Oral and mental starter

Look at the information on the football attendances activity on page 160 of the corresponding Pupil Book. This Functional Maths activity can be introduced once you have covered the previous work on statistics.

- Ask the pupils who they think is the median height of the class? If necessary, remind them of the meaning of median.
- After discussion, ask how they can find out. (All line up in order of size and see who is in the middle.)
- While in the line, can they also see if there is a mode, taking the heights to the nearest centimetre?
- Put four numbers on the board, such as 5, 7, 8, 10. Ask for the median of the numbers. There may be a discussion about no middle number, so explain that the median is the middle of the two middle numbers – or half way between. Here that is $7\frac{1}{2}$.
- Ask the class for the median of the following numbers if the middle two numbers in a ordered list are:

    8, 10 (median 9)   16, 17 (median $16\frac{1}{2}$)   10, 13 (median $11\frac{1}{2}$)
- Continue with other similar examples with only a small difference between the two numbers.

Main lesson activity

- Discuss football attendances. Do the pupils know the typical attendance at a large game involving, say, Manchester United (70,000) and a small crowd at a lower division side (2000–5000)?
- Remind them that some cities, such as Manchester, Birmingham and London, have more than one football team. This is also true of Sheffield, which has two teams: Sheffield Wednesday and Sheffield United. They play home games at different weekends and of course the size of the crowd will usually reflect how well the team is playing and at what level.
- Look at the data shown in the table on page 160 and make sure the pupils know what is meant by:

    level (1 is the top division, 2 is the next division and so on)
    place (the position in the division at the end of the season)
    attendance (the average attendance over the whole season).
- The data handling expected in this spread is:

    reading from a table
    averages, mode, median and mean
    grouped bar chart
    pie charts.
- Ask the class if they can remember what is meant by mode, median and mean.
- **The class can now work through the questions on pages 160–161.**

© HarperCollins*Publishers* Limited 2008

FM Activity — Answers

1 a SW 1, SU 2
2 a SW 2, SU 2
3 a SW 10 310, SU 18 233
4 a SW 24 855, SU 18 031
5 a SW 1.526, SU 1.789
6 a SW 24 373, SU 18 518
7 a The attendances have risen and fallen over the years.
8

Attendances	SW	SU
10 000–15 000	0	4
15 001–20 000	1	10
20 001–25 000	10	4
25 001–30 000	8	0
30 001–35 000	0	1

9 Check pupils' pie charts. Angles are given.

Attendances	SW	SU
10 000–15 000	0	76°
15 001–20 000	19°	189°
20 001–25 000	189°	76°
25 001–30 000	152°	0°
30 001–35 000	0	19°

Level	SW	SU
1	208°	95°
2	114°	246°
3	38°	19°

Plenary

- Ask the pupils whether the average attendances shown in the tables were actually the mode, median or mean. Talk about the mean being the most likely, why? (It is the average that uses every person who attended, allowing for strange distributions.)
- Ask why it is most unlikely to have been made by the mode. (It is very unlikely that more than one attendance in a season is exactly the same as another.)

Homework

Find a similar table of results for Bristol City and Bristol Rovers.

1 Do their attendances vary as the Sheffield teams?

2 Draw a graph of their average attendances, both on the same grid, clearly showing the differences between the two teams.

Homework Answers

Check the pupils' answers.

Number **4**

Context

This chapter builds on previous work on fractions and decimals and then considers more complex calculations. More challenging non-context questions are given for practice and then questions are put in context. Some knowledge of conversions between metric units is required.

National Curriculum references

Framework objectives

12.1 Use the equivalence of fractions, decimals and percentages to compare proportions.

12.2 Add and subtract fractions by writing them with a common denominator. Understand and use the rules of arithmetic and inverse operations in the context of integers and fractions.

12.3 Use the order of operations, including brackets, with more complex calculations.

12.4 Use efficient written methods for multiplication of integers and decimals, including by decimals such as 0.6 or 0.06; understand where to position the decimal point by considering equivalent calculations.

12.5 Use efficient written methods for division of integers and decimals, including by decimals such as 0.6 or 0.06; understand where to position the decimal point by considering equivalent calculations.

FM Use logical argument to interpret the mathematics in a given context or to establish the truth of a statement; give accurate solutions appropriate to the context or problem; evaluate the efficiency of alternative strategies and approaches.

Key concepts

Applications and implications of mathematics

● Understand that basic arithmetical techniques, such as the four rules applied to fractions and decimals and the order of operations, are essential in order to solve models which have been formulated to reflect real problems

Key processes

Representing

● Recognising that a situation has aspects that can be represented using basic arithmetic

Analysing

● Finding results and solutions using appropriate mathematical procedures

Communicating and reflecting

● Interpreting results and solutions

Route mapping

Exercise	Levels	
	5	6
12A	1	2–6
12B		1–6
12C	1–4	
12D	1–4	5–6
12E		1–6

LESSON 12.1

Framework objectives – Fractions
Use the equivalence of fractions, decimals and percentages to compare proportions.

Oral and mental starter

● Have a set of 'Follow me' cards (30 are suggested below) that test the simple cancelling of fractions.

1 START. You are $\frac{4}{8}$

2 I am $\frac{1}{2}$. You are $\frac{4}{14}$

3 I am $\frac{2}{7}$. You are $\frac{30}{40}$

4 I am $\frac{3}{4}$. You are $\frac{4}{18}$

5 I am $\frac{2}{9}$. You are $\frac{10}{12}$

6 I am $\frac{5}{6}$. You are $\frac{4}{12}$

7 I am $\frac{1}{3}$. You are $\frac{16}{18}$

8 I am $\frac{8}{9}$. You are $\frac{6}{20}$

9 I am $\frac{3}{10}$. You are $\frac{8}{20}$

10 I am $\frac{2}{5}$. You are $\frac{20}{32}$

11 I am $\frac{5}{8}$. You are $\frac{2}{8}$

12 I am $\frac{1}{4}$. You are $\frac{6}{10}$

13 I am $\frac{3}{5}$. You are $\frac{8}{18}$

14 I am $\frac{4}{9}$. You are $\frac{10}{15}$

15 I am $\frac{2}{3}$. You are $\frac{4}{40}$

16 I am $\frac{1}{10}$. You are $\frac{4}{20}$

17 I am $\frac{1}{5}$. You are $\frac{8}{10}$

18 I am $\frac{4}{5}$. You are $\frac{6}{14}$

19 I am $\frac{3}{7}$. You are $\frac{14}{16}$

20 I am $\frac{7}{8}$. You are $\frac{60}{70}$

21 I am $\frac{6}{7}$. You are $\frac{5}{45}$

22 I am $\frac{1}{9}$. You are $\frac{10}{18}$

23 I am $\frac{5}{9}$. You are $\frac{14}{20}$

24 I am $\frac{7}{10}$. You are $\frac{5}{40}$

25 I am $\frac{1}{8}$. You are $\frac{10}{14}$

26 I am $\frac{5}{7}$. You are $\frac{70}{80}$

27 I am $\frac{7}{8}$. You are $\frac{6}{36}$

28 I am $\frac{1}{6}$. You are $\frac{81}{90}$

29 I am $\frac{9}{10}$. You are $\frac{5}{35}$

30 I am $\frac{1}{7}$. END

Main lesson activity

● This is mainly a revision lesson on equivalent fractions and mixed numbers.
● Remind the pupils of the method used to convert fractions to mixed numbers, for example, $\frac{24}{7} = 3\frac{3}{7}$. Repeat this using $\frac{11}{3}$ ($= 3\frac{2}{3}$) and $\frac{14}{4}$ ($= 3\frac{2}{4} = 3\frac{1}{2}$).
● Remind the pupils of methods used to convert mixed numbers to fractions, for example, $3\frac{3}{8} = \frac{27}{8}$. Repeat this using $2\frac{2}{5}$ ($= \frac{12}{5}$) and $2\frac{7}{9}$ ($= \frac{25}{9}$).
● Show the pupils what fraction of a metre 345 cm is (a metre is 100 cm, so the fraction is $\frac{345}{100}$, which converts to $3\frac{45}{100}$ and cancels to $3\frac{9}{20}$).
● Show the pupils what fraction of a kilogram 3400 grams is (a kilogram is 1000 grams so the fraction is $\frac{3400}{1000}$, which converts to $3\frac{400}{1000}$ and cancels to $3\frac{2}{5}$).

● **The class can now do Exercise 12A from Pupil Book 2.**

Exercise 12A · Answers

1 a 15 **b** 18 **c** 75 **d** 24 **e** 28 **f** 36 **g** 24 **h** 21 **i** 12
2 a 23 **b** 36 **c** 24 **d** 52
3 a $\frac{23}{6}$ **b** $\frac{9}{2}$ **c** $\frac{12}{5}$ **d** $\frac{52}{9}$
4 a $1\frac{1}{6}$ **b** $1\frac{2}{3}$ **c** $1\frac{1}{7}$ **d** $1\frac{3}{4}$ **e** $1\frac{2}{5}$ **f** $1\frac{2}{5}$ **g** $1\frac{1}{6}$ **h** $2\frac{1}{6}$ **i** $1\frac{5}{6}$ **j** $3\frac{1}{5}$ **k** $1\frac{1}{2}$ **l** $2\frac{1}{7}$
5 a $2\frac{1}{3}$ **b** $2\frac{2}{7}$ **c** $2\frac{2}{5}$ **d** $4\frac{1}{2}$ **e** $2\frac{6}{7}$ **f** $4\frac{4}{5}$ **g** $4\frac{1}{3}$ **h** $2\frac{3}{8}$ **i** $12\frac{1}{6}$ **j** $7\frac{4}{5}$ **k** $4\frac{1}{3}$ **l** $11\frac{1}{3}$
6 a i $2\frac{1}{2}$ **ii** $1\frac{3}{4}$ **iii** $1\frac{1}{5}$ **iv** $1\frac{5}{6}$ **v** $3\frac{1}{4}$ **vi** $1\frac{4}{5}$
  b i $7\frac{3}{20}$ **ii** $2\frac{3}{10}$ **iii** $4\frac{1}{20}$ **iv** $5\frac{4}{5}$ **v** $1\frac{11}{20}$ **vi** $2\frac{1}{4}$
  c i $2\frac{3}{10}$ **ii** $4\frac{1}{20}$ **iii** $7\frac{1}{2}$ **iv** $5\frac{3}{5}$ **v** $1\frac{9}{40}$ **vi** $6\frac{29}{50}$

Extension · Answers

a $3\frac{1}{2}$ **b** $1\frac{1}{4}$ **c** $22\frac{1}{2}$ **d** $5\frac{1}{4}$ **e** $13\frac{1}{2}$ **f** $2\frac{1}{2}$

Plenary

- Discuss the methods for converting improper fractions to mixed numbers.
- Discuss whether it is better to cancel before or after converting to a mixed number. For example, either $\frac{84}{9} = \frac{28}{3} = 9\frac{1}{3}$ or $\frac{84}{9} = 9\frac{3}{9} = 9\frac{1}{3}$.
- Discuss converting top-heavy fractions to decimals (for example, $\frac{13}{4} = 3\frac{1}{4} = 3.25$ and $\frac{19}{8} = 2\frac{3}{8} = 2.375$).
- Repeat with other examples if necessary.

Key words

- top-heavy fraction
- mixed number
- cancelling
- equivalent fraction
- improper fraction

Homework

1 Write these fractions as mixed numbers (cancel down if necessary):

  a nine sixths   **b** fourteen thirds   **c** twelve sevenths   **d** thirteen halves

  e $\frac{22}{6}$ **f** $\frac{34}{7}$ **g** $\frac{31}{3}$ **h** $\frac{22}{8}$

2 a Write the fraction of a full turn that the minute hand of a clock goes through from:
    i 8:15 to 9:45   **ii** 9:25 to 11:10   **iii** 7:12 to 9:36

  b Write the fraction of a metre given by: **i** 675 cm **ii** 4225 mm **iii** 310 cm

  c Write the fraction of a kilogram given by: **i** 3300 g **ii** 4450 g **iii** 8500 g

6

Homework · Answers

1 a $1\frac{1}{2}$ **b** $4\frac{2}{3}$ **c** $1\frac{5}{7}$ **d** $6\frac{1}{2}$ **e** $3\frac{2}{3}$ **f** $4\frac{6}{7}$ **g** $10\frac{1}{3}$ **h** $2\frac{3}{4}$
2 a i $1\frac{1}{2}$ **ii** $1\frac{3}{4}$ **iii** $2\frac{2}{5}$ **b i** $6\frac{3}{4}$ **ii** $4\frac{9}{40}$ **iii** $3\frac{1}{10}$ **c i** $3\frac{3}{10}$ **ii** $4\frac{9}{20}$ **iii** $8\frac{1}{2}$

Framework objectives – Adding and subtracting fractions

Add and subtract fractions by writing them with a common denominator. Understand and use the rules of arithmetic and inverse operations in the context of integers and fractions.

Oral and mental starter

- Draw on the board or have prepared for the OHP the diagram shown.
- Explain the 'Key', which indicates the values to subtract in each direction.
- Point to various cells and ask pupils to give you the value of the cell.
- These could be asked for in order or the cells could be picked at random.
- Other diagrams and 'keys' are:

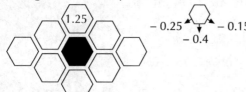

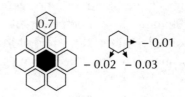

Main lesson activity

- This lesson is a revision of the addition and subtraction of fractions.
- Remind the pupils of the methods used to add fractions with denominators of 2, 4 and 8.
- Remind the pupils how to use the number line.

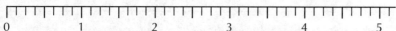

- Work through a couple of examples, such as $2\frac{5}{8} + 1\frac{3}{4} = 4\frac{3}{8}$ and $3\frac{1}{8} - 1\frac{3}{4} = 1\frac{3}{8}$.
- Now remind the pupils of the methods used to add fractions with different denominators.
- Remind the pupils about the Lowest Common Multiple for the denominator.
- Work through a couple of examples, such as:

$\frac{3}{5} + \frac{2}{7} = \frac{21}{35} + \frac{10}{35} = \frac{31}{35}$

$2\frac{3}{10} - \frac{2}{3} = \frac{23}{10} - \frac{2}{3} = \frac{69}{30} - \frac{20}{30} = \frac{49}{30} = 1\frac{19}{30}$

$\frac{1}{5} + \frac{3}{4} + \frac{5}{12} = \frac{12}{60} + \frac{45}{60} + \frac{25}{60} = \frac{82}{60} = 1\frac{22}{60} = 1\frac{11}{30}$

- **The class can now do Exercise 12B from Pupil Book 2.**

Exercise 12B — Answers

1 a $1\frac{1}{8}$ b $1\frac{1}{2}$ c 4 d $3\frac{5}{8}$ e $\frac{1}{8}$ f $1\frac{1}{2}$ g $\frac{3}{4}$ h $1\frac{3}{8}$
2 a $\frac{2}{3}$ b $1\frac{2}{3}$ c $\frac{3}{5}$ d $1\frac{3}{7}$ e $\frac{4}{5}$ f $\frac{1}{3}$ g $\frac{1}{2}$ h $\frac{7}{10}$
3 a $\frac{7}{12}$ b $\frac{1}{2}$ c $\frac{11}{20}$ d $\frac{17}{18}$ e $\frac{17}{30}$ f $1\frac{17}{24}$ g $\frac{5}{6}$ h $1\frac{7}{12}$ i $\frac{1}{12}$ j $\frac{1}{2}$ k $\frac{1}{20}$ l $\frac{13}{18}$ m $\frac{1}{6}$
   n $\frac{1}{24}$ o $\frac{1}{3}$ p $\frac{7}{12}$
4 a $\frac{7}{12}$ b 70 pages
5 a $\frac{2}{15}$ b 120 pupils
6 a $\frac{37}{56}$ b $\frac{19}{56}$

Extension — Answers

a $\frac{15}{16}, \frac{31}{32}, \frac{63}{64}, \frac{127}{128}$ b 1   c $\frac{1}{3}, \frac{4}{9}, \frac{13}{27}, \frac{40}{81}, \frac{121}{243}, \frac{364}{729}, \frac{1093}{2187}, \frac{1}{2}$

Plenary

● Write the following calculation on the board: $2\frac{1}{6} + 3\frac{2}{5}$.
● Discuss how this could be done, that is either convert to top-heavy fractions and then add:

$$\frac{13}{6} + \frac{17}{5} = \frac{65}{30} + \frac{102}{30} = \frac{167}{30} = 5\frac{17}{30}$$

or add the integers and then the fractions:

$$2 + 3 + \frac{1}{6} + \frac{2}{5} = 5 + \frac{5}{30} + \frac{12}{30} = 5 + \frac{17}{30} = 5\frac{17}{30}$$

● Now consider $3\frac{1}{4} - 1\frac{2}{5}$.
● Converting to top-heavy fractions gives $\frac{13}{4} - \frac{7}{5} = \frac{65}{20} - \frac{28}{20} = \frac{37}{20} = 1\frac{17}{20}$.
● Subtracting integers and fractions gives $3 - 1 + \frac{1}{4} - \frac{2}{5} = 2 + \frac{5}{20} - \frac{8}{20} = 2 + -\frac{3}{20} = 1\frac{17}{20}$.
● Discuss which is the better method.

Homework

Convert the following fractions to equivalent fractions with a common denominator, and then work out the answer, cancelling down or writing as a mixed number, as appropriate:

a $\frac{1}{3} + \frac{1}{2}$ b $\frac{1}{7} + \frac{1}{4}$ c $\frac{3}{5} + \frac{3}{4}$ d $\frac{1}{10} + \frac{5}{6}$ e $\frac{4}{15} + \frac{1}{3}$ f $\frac{3}{8} + \frac{1}{6}$ g $\frac{5}{12} + \frac{3}{4}$

h $\frac{3}{8} + \frac{1}{5} + \frac{1}{2}$ i $\frac{1}{2} - \frac{1}{3}$ j $\frac{5}{7} - \frac{1}{3}$ k $\frac{3}{5} - \frac{1}{4}$ l $\frac{7}{10} - \frac{1}{6}$ m $\frac{13}{15} - \frac{3}{5}$ n $\frac{3}{8} - \frac{1}{6}$

o $\frac{5}{12} - \frac{1}{4}$ p $\frac{5}{8} + \frac{2}{5} - \frac{1}{2}$

6

Homework Answers

a $\frac{5}{6}$ b $\frac{11}{28}$ c $1\frac{7}{20}$ d $\frac{14}{15}$ e $\frac{13}{15}$ f $\frac{13}{24}$ g $1\frac{1}{6}$ h $1\frac{3}{40}$ i $\frac{1}{6}$ j $\frac{8}{21}$ k $\frac{7}{20}$ l $\frac{8}{15}$ m $\frac{4}{15}$ n $\frac{5}{24}$ o $\frac{1}{6}$ p $\frac{21}{40}$

Framework objectives – Order of operations
Use the order of operations, including brackets, with more complex calculations.

Oral and mental starter

● Write the following operations on the board:

● Ask the pupils to arrange the operations in any order.
● Ask them to pick a number and work through the operations in the order they have chosen, then subtract the number they thought of. For example, the order as above, starting with 7, gives:

  $7 \rightarrow 12 \rightarrow 24 \rightarrow 20 \rightarrow 10 \rightarrow 3$

  (Note: there are 24 possible arrangements, but only seven answers: –3, –1.5, 0.5, 1, 2, 3, 6.)
● Discuss whether the order matters. In the above example, the answers of 1 all have ÷ 2 and × 2 as consecutive operations.
● Remind the pupils of the mathematical rule for the order of operations in a calculation.
● Pupils should recall BODMAS or BIDMAS, which is the focus of the main lesson.

Main lesson activity

● Continuing from the oral and mental starter, recall the meaning of BODMAS or BIDMAS and discuss what it implies.
● Emphasise the important rules, and that addition and subtraction are of equal worth if there are no other operations in the calculation; the same is true for multiplication and division.
● The normal convention in this situation is to work from left to right.
● Do some examples, in which you demonstrate the order of operations:

  $4 \times 2^2 - 12 \div 4$

Firstly, work out the power or index number	$4 \times 4 - 12 \div 4$
Secondly, the division	$4 \times 4 - 3$
Thirdly, the multiplication	$16 - 3$
Finally, the subtraction	13

  $(5 + 4)^2 \times 4 \div 6$

Firstly, work out the bracket	$9^2 \times 4 \div 6$
Secondly, the power or index number	$81 \times 4 \div 6$
Thirdly, the multiplication	$324 \div 6$
Finally, the division	54

● Introduce the 'nested bracket', for example, $24 \div [5 - (4 - 2)]$.
● The rule is to work out the inside bracket first. Show the pupils some examples:

  $24 \div [5 - (4 - 2)]$

Firstly, work out the inside bracket	$24 \div (5 - 2)$
Then the remaining bracket	$24 \div 3$
Finally, the division	8

  $120 \div [30 \div (20 \div 2)]$

Firstly, work out the inside bracket	$120 \div (30 \div 10)$

Then, the remaining bracket $120 \div 3$
Finally, the division   40

● **The class can now do Exercise 12C from Pupil Book 2.**

Exercise 12C **Answers**

1 a 33 **b** 16 **c** 51 **d** 2 **e** 63 **f** 4 **g** 63 **h** 8 **i** 5 **j** 16 **k** 4 **l** 12
2 a 23 **b** 67 **c** 28 **d** 192 **e** 7 **f** 57 **g** 74 **h** 76 **i** 10 **j** 5 **k** 5 **l** 5
   m −4.7 **n** 6
3 a $3 \times (7 + 1) = 24$ **b** $(3 + 7) \times 2 = 20$ **c** $2 \times (3 + 1) \times 4 = 32$ **d** $(2 + 3)^2 = 25$
   e $5 \times 5 + (5 \div 5) = 26$ **f** $5 \times (5 + 5) \div 5 = 10$ **g** $5 \times [5 + (5 \div 5)] = 30$
   h $(5 \times 5 + 5) \div 5 = 6$ **i** $(15 - 3)^2 = 144$
4 a 5 **b** 6 **c** 29 **d** 50 **e** 23 **f** 2 **g** 27 **h** 4.5 **i** 88

Extension **Answers**

1 a $(4 \times 6) + (4 - 3) \times 8 + 1 = 33$ **b** $4 \times (6 + 4) - (3 \times 8) + 1 = 17$
   c $4 \times (6 + 4 - 3) \times (8 + 1) = 252$
2 a $12 \div (6 - 2) \times (1 + 5) \times 3 = 54$ **b** $[(12 \div 6) - 2 \times 1] + (5 \times 3) = 15$
   c $[(12 \div 6) - 2] \times (1 + 5 \times 3) = 0$

Plenary

Key words

- [ ] **order of operations**
- [ ] **power**
- [ ] **brackets**
- [ ] **index**

● Ask the class 'Which operation comes first: multiplication or division? What about addition or subtraction?' Make sure they understand that neither operation takes precedence within these pairs, but when there is a choice between them they must work from left to right.
● Write a complex calculation on the board, such as:
$$[(2 + 3)^2 - 2] \times 4 + (8 - 6) \div (2^2 \div 16)$$
● Discuss the order of operations and evaluate the above in order (or ask pupils if they can do it):
Firstly, the inside bracket $(5^2 - 2) \times 4 + (8 - 6) \div (2^2 \div 16)$
Secondly, the powers or indices inside brackets $(25 - 2) \times 4 + (8 - 6) \div (4 \div 16)$
Thirdly, each bracket $23 \times 4 + 2 \div \frac{1}{4}$
Fourthly, multiplication and division $92 + 8$
Finally, the addition   100

1 Write the operation that you do first in each of these calculations, and then work out each one:
   a $6 + 2 \times 3$ **b** $(6 + 2) \times 3$ **c** $6 \times 7 - 5$ **d** $6 \times (7 - 5)$

2 Work out the following, showing each step of the calculation:
   a $32 \div 4 + 4^2$ **b** $32 \div (4 + 4)^2$ **c** $2 \times 3 + 2^2$ **d** $2 \times (3 + 2)^2$
   e $\dfrac{100}{2 \times 4}$ **f** $\dfrac{90 - 30}{3 \times 5}$ **g** $\sqrt{(13^2 - 5^2)}$ **h** $\dfrac{(3 + 3)^2}{3 - 1}$

3 Write out each of the following with brackets to make the calculation true:
   a $2 \times 9 - 1 = 16$ **b** $5 + 3 \times 2 = 16$ **c** $2 + 3 \times 1 + 4 = 25$

4 Work out the following (do the inside bracket first):
   a $150 \div [20 - (3 + 2)]$ **b** $150 \div [(25 - 3) - 2]$ **c** $3 + [7 \times (4 - 1)]$

1 a 12 **b** 24 **c** 37 **d** 12
2 a 24 **b** 0.5 **c** 10 **d** 50 **e** 12.5 **f** 4 **g** 12 **h** 18
3 a $2 \times (9 - 1) = 16$ **b** $(5 + 3) \times 2 = 16$ **c** $(2 + 3) \times (1 + 4) = 25$
4 a 10 **b** 7.5 **c** 24

Framework objectives – Multiplying decimals

Use efficient written methods for multiplication of integers and decimals, including by decimals such as 0.6 or 0.06; understand where to position the decimal point by considering equivalent calculations.

Oral and mental starter

- Ask the pupils to think of an odd number and an even number, and then add them together. Ask them if the result is odd or even, and if this is always true.
- Repeat with two odd numbers and two even numbers.
- Repeat with subtraction rather than addition.
- Repeat with multiplication rather than addition.
- Repeat with squaring an odd number and squaring an even number.

Main lesson activity

- This is a revision lesson on multiplying decimals.
- Remind the pupils of the rules for such calculations as 0.3×0.05, that is, $3 \times 5 = 15$ and there are $0.\_ \times 0.\_\_ = 0.\_\_\_$ places in the answer ($= 0.015$).
- Go through some examples with the pupils, such as 0.004×0.03 ($= 0.000\,12$), 0.5×0.007 ($= 0.0035$).
- Remind the pupils of the rules for such calculations as 200×0.007, that is, rewrite these as equivalent calculations until they are simplified as much as possible, $200 \times 0.007 = 20 \times 0.07 = 2 \times 0.7 = 1.4$.
- Go through some examples, such as 300×0.07 ($= 30 \times 0.7 = 3 \times 7 = 21$), 40×0.0008 ($= 4 \times 0.008 = 0.032$).

FM • **The class can now do Exercise 12D from Pupil Book 2.** This exercise covers Functional Maths skills.

Exercise 12D — Answers

1 **a** 0.06 **b** 0.08 **c** 0.36 **d** 0.14 **e** 0.008 **f** 0.032 **g** 0.006 **h** 0.009
i 0.56 **j** 0.0056 **k** 0.27 **l** 0.0054 **m** 0.045 **n** 0.25 **o** 0.004 **p** 0.0018
2 **a** 240 **b** 12 **c** 300 **d** 12 **e** 12 **f** 2 **g** 1.4 **h** 18 **i** 40 **j** 1.2 **k** 3
l 48 **m** 250 **n** 20 **o** 1.5 **p** 0.1
3 £1200
4 3 kg
5 **a** 480 **b** 120 **c** 2.4 **d** 4800 **e** 6.4 **f** 14
6 **a** 0.002 kg **b** 4000 kg

Extension — Answers

a 0.01 **b** 0.001 **c** 0.0001 **d** 0.00001 **e** 0.000001 **f** 0.0000001
g 0.0000000001 **h** 0.04 **i** 0.09 **j** 0.16 **k** 0.25 **l** 0.64 **m** 0.008
n 0.027 **o** 0.064 **p** 0.125 **q** 0.512

Plenary

- This plenary relates to the oral and mental starter.
- Introduce the idea of a counter-example, that is, if someone says 'All square numbers are even', a counter-example is $3^2 = 9$.
- Ask for counter-examples to the following statements:

All numbers have an even number of factors;

$a^2 = 2a$; $(a + b)^2 = a^2 + b^2$;

All multiples of 3 are odd;

All multiples of 9 under 100 have digits that add up to 9;

All prime numbers are odd;

Numbers in the 7 times table do not end in 5.

Key words

- decimal place
- product

Homework

1 Without using a calculator, write down the answer to:

a 0.5×0.7 **b** 0.5×0.2 **c** 0.8×0.8 **d** 0.9×0.3

e 0.03×0.5 **f** 0.6×0.08 **g** 0.07×0.2 **h** 0.5×0.05

2 Without using a calculator, work out:

a 200×0.06 **b** 0.07×300 **c** 0.4×400 **d** 0.03×700

e 0.02×600 **f** 0.003×800 **g** 0.006×800 **h** 0.003×7000

3 Chews cost £0.03. A sweet shop orders 50 000 chews. How much will this cost?

Homework Answers

1 **a** 0.35 **b** 0.1 **c** 0.64 **d** 0.27 **e** 0.015 **f** 0.048 **g** 0.014 **h** 0.025
2 **a** 12 **b** 21 **c** 160 **d** 21 **e** 12 **f** 2.4 **g** 4.8 **h** 21
3 £1500

Framework objectives – Dividing decimals
Use efficient written methods for division of integers and decimals, including by decimals such as 0.6 or 0.06; understand where to position the decimal point by considering equivalent calculations.

Oral and mental starter

41	16	6	15	23
32	27	29	25	34
21	3	31	38	7
19	35	18	9	26
12	13	37	14	39

- Ask pupils to draw a 5 × 5 grid.
- They can then fill in the spaces with 25 numbers from 3 to 41 (but not 30 or 40).
- The numbers can go in any order and should not have any repeats.
- Now throw three dice.

- The first dice is the whole-number part of the mixed number.
- The other two give the fraction part (the larger value is the denominator, and the smaller number is the numerator). If these are the same, throw these again. Do not cancel down mixed numbers, such as $2\frac{4}{6}$.
- Pupils have to work out the numerator of the mixed number (for example, 16) and then cross this off on their grid.
- The first pupil to cross-off five in a row 'wins'.

Main lesson activity

- This is a review lesson on the division of integers and decimals.
- Remind the pupils of the rules used for calculations such as $0.006 \div 0.2$, that is, rewrite the problem as equivalent calculations ($0.006 \div 0.2 = 0.06 \div 2 = 0.03$).
- Repeat the process with $0.4 \div 0.01$ (= $4 \div 0.1 = 40 \div 1 = 40$), and with $0.45 \div 0.009$ (= $4.5 \div 0.09 = 45 \div 0.9 = 450 \div 9 = 50$).
- Remind the pupils of the rules used for calculations such as $300 \div 0.5$, that is, rewrite the problem as equivalent calculations ($300 \div 0.5 = 3000 \div 5 = 600$).
- Repeat the process with $5000 \div 0.002$ (= $50\,000 \div 0.02 = 500\,000 \div 0.2 = 5\,000\,000 \div 2 = 2\,500\,000$), and with $400 \div 0.4$ (= $4000 \div 4 = 1000$).
- Remind the pupils of the rules used for calculations such as $4.8 \div 300$, that is, rewrite the problem as equivalent calculations ($4.8 \div 300 = 0.48 \div 30 = 0.048 \div 3 = 0.016$).
- Repeat the process with $0.38 \div 20$ (= $0.038 \div 2 = 0.019$), and $45 \div 3000$ (= $4.5 \div 300 = 0.45 \div 30 = 0.045 \div 3 = 0.015$).
- **FM** ● **The class can now do Exercise 12E from Pupil Book 2.** This exercise covers Functional Maths skills.

Exercise 12E **Answers**

1 **a** 20 **b** 1.6 **c** 0.6 **d** 30 **e** 20 **f** 3 **g** 0.3 **h** 0.4 **i** 0.8 **j** 40 **k** 8
  l 3 **m** 1 **n** 0.1 **o** 10 **p** 400
2 **a** 500 **b** 1500 **c** 500 **d** 10 000 **e** 300 **f** 1000 **g** 500 **h** 2000 **i** 600
  j 8000 **k** 4000 **l** 20 000 **m** 60 **n** 100 **o** 120 **p** 800
3 **a** 0.16 **b** 0.006 **c** 0.03 **d** 0.04 **e** 0.03 **f** 0.0012 **g** 0.02 **h** 0.04
  i 0.016 **j** 0.0006 **k** 1.2 **l** 0.000 008
4 200 000
5 500 000
6 1 500 000 000

Extension **Answers**

1 **a** 156.4 **b** 15.64 **c** 460 **d** 460
2 **a** 0.1824 **b** 18240 **c** 1824 **d** 0.1824
3 **a** 1540 **b** 2.8 **c** 550 **d** 154

Plenary

Key words

- equivalent
- calculation
- decimal place

- This plenary covers both multiplication and division of decimals.
- Ask pupils to give a number that makes 0.8 smaller when multiplied by it.
- Obtain some examples and write them on the board. What is the common characteristic?
- Establish that any value less than 1 does this.
- What about a value that makes 0.8 larger when multiplied by it?
- Obtain some examples and write them on the board. What is the common characteristic?
- Establish that any value larger than 1 will work.
- Repeat the above procedures with 0.8 divided by a number.
- Establish that values greater than 1 make 0.8 smaller and values less than 1 make 0.8 larger.
- If time is available, test the pupils' understanding by asking for missing values in:
  $0.8 \times \ldots = 8$, $0.8 \div \ldots = 0.08$, $0.8 \times \ldots = 0.08$, $0.8 \div \ldots = 8$

Homework

1 Without using a calculator, work out:
  a $0.6 \div 0.03$ **b** $0.8 \div 0.2$ **c** $0.08 \div 0.1$ **d** $0.8 \div 0.04$
  e $0.5 \div 0.01$ **f** $0.08 \div 0.02$ **g** $0.09 \div 0.03$ **h** $0.12 \div 0.03$

2 Without using a calculator, work out:
  a $600 \div 0.6$ **b** $800 \div 0.2$ **c** $80 \div 0.08$ **d** $600 \div 0.02$
  e $900 \div 0.03$ **f** $20 \div 0.04$ **g** $60 \div 0.1$ **h** $900 \div 0.2$

3 Without using a calculator, work out:
  a $4.2 \div 20$ **b** $2.8 \div 400$ **c** $16 \div 400$ **d** $4.5 \div 90$
  e $32 \div 800$ **f** $80 \div 2000$ **g** $2.1 \div 70$ **h** $4.4 \div 40$

6

Homework Answers

1 **a** 20 **b** 4 **c** 0.8 **d** 20 **e** 50 **f** 4 **g** 3 **h** 4
2 **a** 1000 **b** 4000 **c** 1000 **d** 30 000 **e** 30 000 **f** 500 **g** 600 **h** 4500
3 **a** 0.21 **b** 0.007 **c** 0.04 **d** 0.05 **e** 0.04 **f** 0.04 **g** 0.03 **h** 0.11

National Tests **Answers**

1 $\frac{3}{4}, \frac{7}{12}, \frac{1}{6}$
2 4410, 2.5
3 2, $\frac{7}{8}$
4 6, 12

Functional Maths – Shopping for bargains

> ## Framework objectives
> Use logical argument to interpret the mathematics in a given context or to establish the truth of a statement; give accurate solutions appropriate to the context or problem; evaluate the efficiency of alternative strategies and approaches.

Oral and mental starter

Look at the information given for the supermarket activity on page 172 of the corresponding Pupil Book. This spread is designed partly to look at how supermarkets use special offers to entice people to spend more but also to show how they use fuel discounts to encourage people to shop in the supermarket.

- Ask the pupils to name as many different types of supermarket offers that they can think of, for example, buy one get one free, half price, 50p off, $\frac{1}{3}$ off.
- Look at the supermarket offers on page 172.
- Give pupils a list of prices and ask them to take 10% off, for example £2 (£1.80), £3.40 (£3.06), 50p (45p).
- Give pupils a different list of prices and ask them to take one-third off, for example 60p (40p), £1.50 (£1), £9 (£6).
- Now show the pupils the points system when buying fuel (15 points per complete litre). Ask them a few straightforward questions to check they understand how it works, for example the number of points for 10 litres (150), the number of points for 10.5 litres (still 150).

Main lesson activity

- Continuing on from the oral and mental starter, discuss why supermarkets have special offers (to encourage people to shop there, to encourage people to buy more items than they would if there were no offers).
- Ask the pupils to think of different offers and decide which ones could mean that people would buy more items (for example, buy one get one free, buy 2 for £1).
- Ask the pupils why some items may have the price reduced (for example, supermarket has a large stock of them, items might be near the sell by date, to entice people to try a new product).
- Pupils can now look at the supermarket offers, discussing which ones are most tempting or which offer the best savings.
- If necessary, provide extra questions to supplement, using different offers.
- Alternatively pupils can start by considering the fuel prices. One aim is to allow pupils to discuss and raise awareness of environmental issues.
- Pupils can look at possible alternatives for reducing CO^2 emissions or reducing spending on fuel.
- Check the class have a reasonable understanding.
- **The class can now work through the questions on pages 172–173.**

FM Activity **Answers**

1 a 334 litres **b** £400.80 **c** 12 weeks **d** 1.25%
2 a £52 **b** £13 **c i** £208 **ii** 7.7%
3 a Managing director 1960 kg, Secretary 1600 kg, Delivery driver 2420 kg
 b Managing director 392 kg, Secretary 320 kg, delivery driver 484 kg
4 a Savings per item:
 Chocolate 19p, Mint sauce 55p, Almost Butter £1.38, Milk 50p, Cheese £1, Scotch eggs 23p, Grillsteaks £1.50, Baby shampoo 83p, Luxury Crisps 48p, Yoghurts £1.44
 b Total saving £8.35
5 a £6.60 **b** £13.40 **c** Check pupils' answers, ensuring the total is less than £20 but includes bread, coffee, baked beans and orange juice.
6 Examples of advantages: Saves 30p on cost of driving car, less time consuming.
 Examples of disadvantages: May not get everything you want, have to wait in for the delivery, may not include some in-store offers.

Plenary

- As follow-up work, pupils could look at the internet to carry out research into different vehicles.
- The final question compares the cost of shopping at the supermarket with the cost of home delivery. This considers the advantages and disadvantages. Although part of this is not mathematical it could lead to an enhanced discussion.

Homework

1 A driver has 3500 points saved.
 a How many more points does he need before he receives a £5 voucher?
 b How many litres of fuel will he need to buy before he receives a £5 voucher?

2 A housewife drives her car 9000 km per year. The CO_2 emissions are 150 grams per km.
 Work out the annual amount of CO^2 emissions for the car.
 Give your answer in kilograms.

3 A shopper has £5 to spend on baby shampoo and two grillsteaks. Using the offers how much change will she receive?

Homework **Answers**

1 a 1500 **b** 100 litres
2 1350 kg
3 38p

Algebra **5**

Overview

13.1 Expand and simplify

13.2 Solving equations

13.3 Constructing equations to solve

13.4 Problems with graphs

13.5 Real-life graphs

13.6 Change of subject

FM Train timetable

Context

This chapter builds on previous algebra. Pupils start with expanding and simplifying brackets where the external coefficient may be negative. More complex equations, involving fractions, decimal coefficients and brackets, are solved. Pupils then create and solve their own equations from practical and real-life situations. Previous work on the gradient of a line is recalled and extended. Some real-life graphs are considered. Finally, simple formulae are rearranged to change the subject, involving at most one operation.

National Curriculum references

Framework objectives

13.1 Refine own findings and approaches on the basis of discussions with others; recognise efficiency in an approach; relate the current problem and structure to previous situations. Simplify or transform linear expressions by collecting like terms; multiply a single term over a bracket.

13.2 Solve linear equations with integer coefficients (unknown on either or both sides, without and with brackets) using appropriate methods (for example, inverse operations, transforming both sides in same way).

13.3 Construct and solve linear equations with integer coefficients (unknown on either or both sides, without and with brackets) using appropriate methods (for example, inverse operations, transforming both sides in same way).

13.4 Plot the graphs of linear functions, where y is given explicitly in terms of x.

13.5 Construct linear functions arising from real-life problems and plot their corresponding graphs; discuss and interpret graphs arising from real situations, for example, distance–time graphs.

13.6 Simplify or transform linear expressions by collecting like terms.

FM Identify the mathematical features of a context or problem.

Key concepts

Applications and implications of mathematics

- Know that situations can be modelled using algebra to create equations that can be solved
- Know that relationships between variables can be shown using mapping diagrams, coordinate pairs and graphs

Key processes

Representing

- Expressing relationships symbolically
- Plotting graphs from equations, functions and mapping diagrams
- Rearranging formulae

Analysing

- Knowing how to find the gradient of a line and its relation to the equation of the line
- Using gradients to interpret graphs involving change over time

Communicating and reflecting

- Interpreting graphs that describe real-life situations
- Interpreting problems to create a mathematical model

Route mapping

Exercise	Levels			
	4	5	6	7
13A	1–2	3	4–5	
13B		1–3	4–5	
13C		1	2	
13D			1–5	
13E			1–5	
13F				1–8

LESSON
13.1

Framework objectives – Expand and simplify

Refine own findings and approaches on the basis of discussions with others; recognise efficiency in an approach; relate the current problem and structure to previous situations. Simplify or transform linear expressions by collecting like terms; multiply a single term over a bracket.

Oral and mental starter

- Tell the class the following story.
- A group of prisoners are trying to find their way through a maze of connected cubes inside a larger cube. Each cube is connected to 6 others by a door in each face.
- Each door has a number written on it. If the door's number has a prime number of factors, then the door leads to a safe room, otherwise it is booby trapped.
- Ask the class if the door 24 is safe or not.
- You will need to lead the class through the process of finding pairs of factors, such as 1, 24 and 2,12, etc., until they see eight factors, meaning the room is booby trapped as 8 is not a prime.
- What about door 64, ask them if this is safe or not? (Seven factors, a prime number, so the room is safe.)
- The six doors leading from one room are numbered 84, 77, 25, 36, 100 and 160. How many doors are safe and which are they?
- The correct answer is only one, that is 25, as it has three factors.
- You may wish to take the puzzle further by showing the class that all safe doors have square numbers on them, as these will have an odd number of primes. However, more thought will be needed as to which of the square numbers are safe.

Main lesson activity

- Remind the class of the work done previously on expanding brackets and combining like terms.
- Write on the board $4(2 + 7)$, and ask the pupils what number this will calculate to. (36)
- Discuss with the class the notion of multiplying the 4 over the whole of the bracket.
- Discuss also how different pupils may have done the problem. Some may have added the 2 and 7 so as to calculate $4 \times 9 = 36$. Others may have multiplied first to give $8 + 28 = 36$.
- Make sure each pupil can see that the same answer is found whichever way round you do this.
- Repeat this for a subtraction, for example, $3(8 - 6)$.
- Get the class to show you that the two methods give the same answer, that is $3 \times 2 = 6 = 24 - 18$.
- Now write on the board $3(a + 4b)$ and ask the class how they would multiply the 3 over the whole of the bracket. Explain that this is called expansion.
- Show that this expands to $3a + 12b$.
- Move onto $k(2m - 3n)$; multiply the k over the bracket, noting that the sign will remain the same as we are multiplying by a positive number. This gives $2km - 3kn$.
- Introduce the idea of a negative term in front of a bracket with, for example, $10 - (2 + 5)$, which actually means $10 + -1 \times (2 + 5)$.
- Demonstrate to the class, that $10 - 7 = 3$ is the same as $10 - 2 - 5 = 3$.
- So also then will $10 - (x + y) = 10 - x - y$ (this cannot be simplified).
- Discuss too a negative sign inside the bracket, for example, $4 - (m - p)$.
- This will become $4 - m - -p = 4 - m + p$. You may need to revise some work on negative numbers here. If this is so, then do not leave it; make sure this issue is resolved in this lesson.
- Finish this explanation off by writing on the board an expression that needs expanding and then simplifying, reminding the pupils of like and unlike terms, for example, $8t - 2(5x - 3t) = 8t - 10x + 6t = 14t - 10x$.

- You may need to go over a few more examples on the board with the class for them all to feel confident of expanding and then simplifying, as well as coping with all the negative signs.
- **The class can now do Exercise 13A from Pupil Book 2.**

Exercise 13A — Answers

1 **a** 5a **b** 2b **c** 5c **d** 10d **e** 5x **f** 5t **g** 2m **h** −2d **i** −3t **j** n **k** −9a
l 0
2 **a** 4m + 2k **b** 7p + 3q **c** 3t + 3d **d** 3k + g **e** 7p + 3m **f** 7w + k
g 4m − 2k **h** 8x − 4t **i** 3k + 6m **j** 2t + 4w **k** 5x + 4m **l** 4y + 3p
3 **a** 6a + 9b **b** 8t − 6k **c** 5n + 15p **d** 8q − 4p **e** 3a + at **f** 4b + 3bm
g 5xy − tx **h** 3yx − 2ny **i** am + an **j** 3ap − at **k** 6x + 3xy **l** 2kt − pt
4 **a** 11x + 10 **b** 2a − 15 **c** 6t + 8 **d** 10x − 8 **e** 12 − 3t **f** 4m + 10
g 7k + 18 **h** 11n − 10 **i** 5x + 10
5 **a** 18k + 14 **b** 16x + 15 **c** 27m + 10 **d** 8k + 9 **e** 4 − 3t **f** 6k + 5
g 2 + 6m **h** 8 + 9d **i** 9 + 2k

Extension — Answers

1 Each row and each column should be shown to add up to 3x.

Plenary

Key words

- [ ] **expression**
- [ ] **expand**
- [ ] **simplify**

- Ask the class if anyone can describe what like terms are.
- Write 5m on the board, ask for other terms that are like terms to 5m; write a few of these up on the board also.
- Ask the questions 'What can we do with these like terms?', 'Can we add them?', 'Can we subtract them?', 'Can we multiply them?', 'Can we divide them?'
- The last point will need some discussion. You will need to try some divisions out via substitution to convince pupils that like terms can be divided.

Homework

1 Simplify the following:
   a 7m + 3k + 2m   **b** 5p + q + 3p   **c** 6t + 2d − t   **d** 8k + 5g − k
2 Expand the following:
   a 2(3a + 4b)   **b** 3(5t − 2k)   **c** 6(n + 2p)   **d** 5(2q − p)
   e q(7 + w)   **f** a(5 + 2m)   **g** n(3y − t)   **h** y(2x − 3n)
3 Expand and simplify the following:
   a 4x + 3(2x + 3)   **b** 9a − 2(4a + 5)   **c** 17t − 3(4t − 1)   **d** 5x + 3(2x − 5)
   e 9t − 4(2t − 2)   **f** 17m − 3(5m − 4)
4 Expand and simplify the following:
   a 2(4k + 1) + 3(5k + 1)   **b** 4(3x + 2) + 3(2x + 3)   **c** 4(2m + 3) + 5(2m + 3)
   d 6(3k + 2) − 3(k + 5)   **e** 5(4t + 3) − 2(6t + 3)   **f** 3(7k + 6) − 4(3k + 5)

Homework Answers

1 **a** 9m + 3k   **b** 8p + q   **c** 5t + 2d   **d** 7k + 5g
2 **a** 6a + 8b   **b** 15t − 6k   **c** 6n + 12p   **d** 10q − 5p   **e** 7q + qw   **f** 5a + 2am   **g** 3ny − nt   **h** 2xy − 3ny
3 **a** 10x + 9   **b** a − 10   **c** 5t + 3   **d** 11x − 15   **e** t + 8   **f** 2m + 12
4 **a** 23k + 5   **b** 18x + 17   **c** 18m + 27   **d** 15k − 3   **e** 8t + 9   **f** 9k − 2

4
5
6

LESSON 13.2

Framework objectives – Solving equations

Solve linear equations with integer coefficients (unknown on either or both sides, without and with brackets) using appropriate methods (for example, inverse operations, transforming both sides in same way).

Oral and mental starter

- Draw on the board the circles shown.
- Tell the class that the numbers in each circle follow the same rule. Can they work out the missing number in the third circle?
- A hint can be 'differences'.
- Eventually someone will give you the correct answer, either as a guess or because they have worked it out. Get them to tell you (quietly) if they know how to work it out, and then put the correct answer into the space. (3)
- Ask the pupil (or team) who found the correct answer to give you another circle with a missing number in the bottom right-hand side, for the rest of the class to try to solve.
- If all, or some, of the class are struggling, go through the differences between the numbers and ask if they notice any special numbers. Hopefully they will recognise that the difference between the top and left-hand numbers is a square number in each case. The right-hand number is the square root of this difference.
- The problem can be extended to involve cubed roots for those who find the rule quickly.

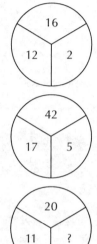

Main lesson activity

- Write the equation $3x = 15$ on the board, and ask the class to solve it. Remind them that when we solve an equation we are looking for the value of the unknown.
- When you are given the answer $x = 5$ (do not accept 5 on its own!), ask how this was found out.
- You are looking for the response 'divide both sides by 3'.
- Now write the equation $3 = \dfrac{12}{n}$ on the board, and ask the class to solve it.
- The important discussion here is not on what the answer is, but on how to find the answer. Many pupils will be able to see by inspection that 4 is the right answer, but this won't help if the numbers are not so convenient.

  How would they solve $11 = \dfrac{209}{n}$, for example?

- Go through the same process as normal. We have an equation, like a balance, so what we do to one side, we must do to the other.

  Starting with $11 = \dfrac{209}{n}$, we need to multiply both sides by n to obtain $11n = 209$.

  This gives a familiar equation type that can be solved by dividing both sides by 11 to give $n = 19$.

- If the pupils start to see shortcut routes to the answers, this should be encouraged, but you must ensure they know why these work. (A learnt trick, with no understanding, is easily forgotten.)
- Write another equation on the board, $4t - 3 = 17$, and ask the pupils how to solve it.

- Go through this with the whole class, using their suggestions. Add 3 to both sides to give $4t = 20$, which again gives the type of equation we started with, that can be solved to $t = 5$.
- Now, write on the board an equation with a bracket, for example, $3(2x + 4) = 54$. You may wish to show both methods of solution as follows.
- Divide both sides by 3, to get $2x + 4 = 18$, which can be solved to $x = 7$.
- Multiply out the bracket, to get $6x + 12 = 54$, which can be solved to $x = 7$.
- It is important that the pupils see both methods and are encouraged to try both for themselves.
- **The class can now do Exercise 13B from Pupil Book 2.**

Exercise 13B Answers

1 **a** $x = 3$ **b** $x = 6$ **c** $m = 7$ **d** $n = 5$ **e** $x = 3.5$ **f** $m = 5.5$ **g** $x = 0.8$
 h $x = 1.3$ **i** $x = 0.6$ **j** $x = 1.6$ **k** $x = 4.2$ **l** $x = 3.75$
2 **a** $n = 3$ **b** $x = 3$ **c** $m = 6$ **d** $x = 3$ **e** $x = 5$ **f** $m = 5$ **g** $x = 9$ **h** $n = 3.5$
 i $k = 12.5$ **j** $x = 1.7$ **k** $x = 2.6$ **l** $n = 4.25$
3 **a** $x = 1.2$ **b** $x = 2.5$ **c** $m = 3.5$ **d** $k = 1.5$ **e** $n = 3.6$ **f** $t = 6.5$ **g** $x = 4.5$
 h $x = 1.5$ **i** $m = -3.5$
4 **a** $t = 3$ **b** $m = 3$ **c** $m = 4$ **d** $k = 4$ **e** $t = 6$ **f** $x = 3$ **g** $t = 2$ **h** $x = 3$
 i $k = -2$ **j** $m = -3.5$ **k** $x = -4$ **l** $x = -2.5$
5 **a** $x = 4$ **b** $x = 5$ **c** $x = 3$ **d** $x = 4$ **e** $x = 2.5$ **f** $x = 3.5$

Extension Answers

1 -4 2 0.8 3 3.5 4 -1

Plenary

- Discuss with the class how to solve equations with brackets in.
- Is it better to expand the brackets first, then solve, or is it easier to divide both sides first?
- Might it depend on what the numbers are? If so, what might be special about the numbers to suggest one way or the other would be better?
- You do not need to make any actual judgement here, just raise the question. It is a personal preference at this stage and we do not want to be prescriptive.

Key words
- solve
- variable
- unknown

Homework

1 Solve the following equations:
 a $4x = 16$ **b** $3x = 30$ **c** $2m = 18$ **d** $5n = 35$

2 Solve the following equations:
 a $6 = \dfrac{18}{n}$ **b** $4 = \dfrac{24}{x}$ **c** $2 = \dfrac{8}{m}$ **d** $9 = \dfrac{27}{x}$

3 Solve the following equations:
 a $2.5x + 1.7 = 7.4$ **b** $4.6x + 9.3 = 25.4$ **c** $2.6x - 5.1 = 6.6$

4 Solve the following equations:
 a $4(3t + 1) = 28$ **b** $3(4m + 5) = 33$ **c** $4(5m + 3) = 72$ **d** $5(2k + 3) = 60$
 e $3(3t - 5) = 12$ **f** $5(2x - 3) = 30$ **g** $4(2t - 5) = 36$ **h** $6(8 - 3x) = 12$

5 Solve the following equations:
 a $2(x + 2) + 3(x - 4) = 27$ **b** $5(x + 4) + 2(x - 3) = 42$
 c $5(3x + 4) + 4(2x - 2) = 127$ **d** $6(2x + 4) - 3(2x + 3) = 45$

Homework Answers

1 **a** $x = 4$ **b** $x = 10$ **c** $m = 9$ **d** $n = 7$
2 **a** $n = 3$ **b** $x = 6$ **c** $m = 4$ **d** $x = 3$
3 **a** $x = 2.28$ **b** $x = 3.5$ **c** $x = 4.5$
4 **a** $t = 2$ **b** $m = 1.5$ **c** $m = 3$ **d** $k = 4.5$ **e** $t = 3$ **f** $x = 4.5$ **g** $t = 7$ **h** $x = 2$
5 **a** $x = 7$ **b** $x = 4$ **c** $x = 5$ **d** $x = 5$

4
5
6

LESSON 13.3

Framework objectives – Constructing equations to solve

Construct and solve linear equations with integer coefficients (unknown on either or both sides, without and with brackets) using appropriate methods (for example, inverse operations, transforming both sides in the same way).

Oral and mental starter

- Write on the board $A \times A = B$ and $A + A = B$.
- Ask the class if anyone can find what numbers A and B can be. There is only one answer, $A = 2$ and $B = 4$
- Tell the class that 2 is a very special number because $2 \times 2 = 4$ and $2 + 2 = 4$.
- There is no other number like this, but there are pairs of numbers that will multiply together and add together to give the same answer, that is, $A \times B = C$ and $A + B = C$. Can anyone find such a pair?
- If there are no correct pairs given, start giving some starters such as:

    3 (with 1.5) or
    5 (with $1\frac{1}{4}$) or
    11 (with 1.1)

- Note: There are an infinite number of possibilities, given by the relationship

$$A = \frac{B}{B-1}.$$

Main lesson activity

- Draw on the board Jim and Jim's Grandad.
- Write down that Grandad is 4 times older than Jim.
- Their ages add up to 105. What are their ages?
- When the class starts to suggest ages, stop them.
- Tell them you want them to find the solution by using algebra. This is the tool that mathematicians use to solve many different problems.
- To solve this problem, we need to start by letting Jim's age be something, say m, and then work out Grandad's age in terms of m. Lead the pupils to $4m$, and away from trying to simply choose another letter!
- If their ages add up to 105, ask if anyone can give an equation to describe the situation.
- Help the class to see that $m + 4m = 105$, and hence $5m = 105$.
- This can now be solved to give $m = 21$, so what are their ages? (21 years and $4 \times 21 = 84$ years.)
- After this, give them another problem, 'Three consecutive even numbers add up to 102, what could the numbers be?'
- Again, start by letting one of the numbers be some variable. Let the smallest even number be N.
- Then the next consecutive even number will be $N + 2$ and the one after that will be $N + 4$.
- If their total is 102, then $N + (N + 2) + (N + 4) = 102$.
- This simplifies to give $3N + 6 = 102$, which will solve to give $N = 32$.
- Hence the three consecutive even numbers that add up to 102 are 32, 34 and 36.

Jim's grandad   Jim

- **The class can now do Exercise 13C from Pupil Book 2.**

Exercise 13C **Answers**

1 **a** $100 - x$ **b** $y + 8$ **c** $18 - p$ **d** $8t$ **e** $n + 2$
2 **a** $4x = 48$, $x = 12$ **b i** $(n + 2) + (n + 4) + (n + 6)$ **ii** 5 **c** 26 and 28
   d 103 and 105 **e** 94 kg **f** 14 and 56 **g** $8x + 3(20 - x) = 110$, so $x = 10$ **h** 24
   i 25

Extension **Answers**

1 735
2 7
3 44
4 24

Plenary

Key words

☐ **equation**
☐ **expression**

● Tell each pupil to think of a number, which they must not tell anyone.
● Double that number.
● Add on 10.
● Halve the answer.
● Take away the number first thought of.
● Write on the board 5, which is the number they should all have.
● Tell the class that they can make these little tricks up using algebra. Show how you did the first one with algebra:

Think of a number	n
Double the number	$2n$
Add on 10	$2n + 10$
Halve the answer	$n + 5$
Take away the first number	5

● Ask the class to make up their own trick and try it out.

Homework

1 Grandma is seven times as old as her grandson is now. If their ages add up to 96, how old is Grandma? Let Grandma's age be x.

2 If n is an even number:

   i Write, as simply as possible, an expression for the sum of the next four consecutive even numbers.

   ii If the sum of these four numbers is 84, find n.

3 The sum of two consecutive odd numbers is 152; find the numbers. Let the smallest number be n.

4 Mark weighs 7 kg more than his brother. Their total weight is 71 kg. How much does Mark weigh? Let Mark's weight be w.

5 Phoebe's Auntie Ann is three times as old as Phoebe. If the sum of their ages is 52, find their ages. Let Phoebe's age be x.

6 I think of a number, add 8 to it, double the answer, subtract 10 and I end up with 16.

   i If the number I first thought of was n, write down an equation that involves n and 16.

   ii Solve the equation to find the number I first thought of.

6

Homework Answers

1 84 years
2 **i** $4n + 20$ **ii** 16
3 75 and 77
4 39 kg
5 13 and 39 years
6 **i** $2n + 6 = 16$ **ii** 5

Framework objectives – Problems with graphs

Plot the graphs of linear functions, where y is given explicitly in terms of x.

Oral and mental starter

- Ask the class if anyone can tell you how many factors 8 has. The answer is four (1, 2, 4, 8).
- Now ask them how many factors 28 has. The answer is six (1, 2, 4, 7, 14, 28).
- Now ask if they think 128 has more or fewer factors than 28. It actually has more, but how many? It has eight altogether (1, 2, 4, 8, 16, 32, 64, 128).
- Now set them a challenge, 'Which three-digit number has the most factors?'
- They could work together in groups of two or three on this problem.
- Do encourage them to start from the factors, that is, what numbers have the factors 1, 2, 3, 4, 5, 6, 7, etc?
- The correct answer is 840 with 32 factors (1, 2, 3, 4, 5, 6, 7, 8, 10, 12, 14, 15, 20, 21, 24, 28 and their respective partners.)

Main lesson activity

- Write the equation $y = mx + c$ on the board. Remind the class that this is the equation that fits every straight-line graph.
- Can anyone tell you what m and c represent? (The gradient and y-intercept respectively.)
- Draw on the board a pair of axes labelled from –1 to 10, with a straight line that goes through the points (0, 1) and (3, 7).
- Ask the pupils if they can find out what the gradient of this line is.
- Go through the process with the class, from their responses, and explain that we need to find how much the vertical rise is for one unit horizontally. This is the gradient. Show that if this is done for the line drawn on the board, the gradient is 2.
- Show, too, how this idea works for any vertical rise divided by the corresponding horizontal run. Show the best way to measure this by drawing a right-angled triangle against the line. This, in effect, gives the rise for one unit along, but is more accurate.
- Now, ask the class what the equation of this line is. As it cuts through the y-axis at $y = 1$ and has a gradient of 2, the equation is $y = 2x + 1$.
- If there are any doubts then draw another straight line through (0, –1) and (3, 8). This has a gradient of 3, and an equation of $y = 3x - 1$.
- Now draw a line on the board with a negative gradient, through (0, 10) and (5, 0).
- Ask the class what the gradient of this line is. They should say 2 from the previous explanations. Ask if the equation of this line is $y = 2x + 10$? No it is not.
- Discuss the difference between this line and the previous line, which also had a gradient of 2 (the difference is that they slope different ways). Explain that we need to show the difference between each direction of slope. This is done by giving a positive gradient to those lines sloping from the bottom left to the top right, and a negative to those sloping from the top left to the bottom right (uphill is a positive gradient and downhill is a negative gradient).
- Hence the equation of the second line on the board is $y = -2x + 10$.
- Explain that it could be written as $y = 10 - 2x$, as some mathematicians do not like an equation or a formula to start with a negative sign if they can help it.

- **The class can now do Exercise 13D from Pupil Book 2.**

Exercise 13D   Answers

1 **a** –3 **b** –2 **c** 4 **d** –1 **e** 6 **f** –4
2 **a** 4, 1 **b** 3, –1 **c** 5, 0 **d** –2, 3
3 **a** $y = 3x + 2$ **b** $y = 4x - 3$ **c** $y = -2x + 5$ **d** $y = -4x - 1$ **e** $y = 4x$ **f** $y = 8$
4 **a** 1, 2, $y = x + 2$ **b** –2, 5, $y = -2x + 5$ **c** –3, 7, $y = -3x + 7$ **d** 3, –1, $y = 3x - 1$
  e –1, 5, $y = -x + 5$ **f** 0, 4, $y = 4$
5 **a** $y = x$ **b** $y = 2x + 5$, $y = 2x - 3$ **c** $y = 3x + 2$, $y = 2 - x$ **d** $y = x$
  e $y = 3x + 2$ and $y + 5 = 3x$; $y = 2x + 5$ and $y = 2x - 3$

Extension   Answers

1 **a i** 3 **ii** 3 **iii** $y = 3x + 3$ **b i** 3 **ii** –1 **iii** $y = 3x - 1$
  c i –6 **ii** 22 **iii** $y = -6x + 22$ **d i** –3 **ii** 18 **iii** $y = -3x + 18$
  e i 3 **ii** 5 **iii** $y = 3x + 5$ **f i** –5 **ii** –7 **iii** $y = -5x - 7$
2 **a** gradient 2, intercept 3 **b** gradient 3, intercept –2 **c** gradient –2, intercept 6

Plenary

Key words

☐ **gradient**
☐ **intercept**
☐ **horizontal run**
☐ **vertical rise**

● Ask the class whether we can now find the equation of any straight line that can be drawn on a grid. The answer should be yes, although some of the gradients and *y*-axis intercepts will be fractions or decimals.
● Now ask the question the other way round, 'Can we draw a graph for any written linear equation?'
● The responses will vary and the pupils may not know until they've tried a few!
● Give them the linear equation $3x - y = 10$, and ask if we can draw this.
● You can show that we can easily find some coordinates that fit the equation, for example, (4, 2), (5, 5), (6, 8), and hence we can draw it. But can we tell from the equation what the gradient and the *y*-axis intercept will be?
● Tell the pupils that one of the later lessons is to look at this type of equation and to change it round so that we have *y* = ….

6

Homework

1 Find the gradient of the straight line that joins the following pairs of coordinates. Plot the points on the coordinate grid.

   a (1, 4) and (2, 8)   **b** (1, 8) and (3, 0)   **c** (1, 9) and (3, 3)

2 Find the gradient and the *y*-axis intercept of each of the following equations:

   a $y = 5x + 3$ **b** $y = -3x + 2$ **c** $y = 3x$ **d** $y = -4x - 7$

3 Write equations for lines in the form $y = mx + c$, where:

   a $m = 4$ and $c = 3$ **b** $m = 5$ and $c = -2$ **c** $m = -3$ and $c = 7$ **d** $m = -5$ and $c = -2$

   e $m = 6$ and $c = 0$ **f** $m = 0$ and $c = 9$

4 Find the gradient, the *y*-intercept and the equation of each linear graph shown below:

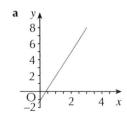 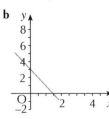 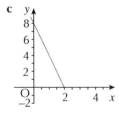 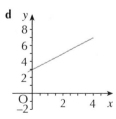

Homework Answers

1 **a** 4 **b** –4 **c** –3
2 **a** 5, 3 **b** –3, 2 **c** 3, 0 **d** –4, –7
3 **a** $y = 4x + 3$ **b** $y = 5x - 2$ **c** $y = -3x + 7$ **d** $y = -5x - 2$ **e** $y = 6x$ **f** $y = 9$
4 **a** 3, –1, $y = 3x - 1$ **b** –2, 3, $y = -2x + 3$ **c** 1, 2, $y = 2x + 1$ **d** 1, 3, $y = x + 3$

Framework objectives – Real-life graphs

Construct linear functions arising from real-life problems and plot their corresponding graphs; discuss and interpret graphs arising from real situations, for example, distance–time graphs.

Oral and mental starter

- Tell the class they are to do a simple problem that is best worked on individually.
- A specialist pet-shop owner only deals in cats and budgies.
- The owner has 72 animals altogether (cats and budgies).
- These animals have a total of 200 legs between them.
- How many cats and how many budgies are there at the pet shop?
- Encourage the class to write down some equations, that is, $4c + 2b = 200$, which implies that $2c + b = 100$, and also $c + b = 72$ ($b = 72 - c$).
- Let the class start this problem on their own, then after a short while let them work together in pairs to discuss what they have done and progress further.
- Logical trial and improvement or solving equations will both lead them to the solution.
- The solution is 28 cats and 44 budgies.

Main lesson activity

- Draw a sketch graph on the board with the pair of axes as temperature (horizontal) from 0 to 30 °C and deckchairs (vertical) from 0 to 100.
- Give the class the scene. 'At Whitby (or your local seaside resort), will a deckchair attendant hire out more deckchairs when it is hot or cold?' You should get the response 'hot'.
- Draw a cross on the sketch grid at (30, 100), and ask if this is about right. Be prepared to alter it slightly if the suggestion is sensible.
- Now draw a cross at (5, 0) and ask if this is sensible. Again, alter this in response to a sensible suggestion.
- Draw in a straight line between the two and ask if this shows the likely link between temperature and number of deckchairs.
- This could prompt a discussion about how it would not be exactly like that, but it probably shows the correct trend.
- Explain that we can use sketch graphs like this to illustrate trends. They are not necessarily exactly correct, but close to reality.
- Ask if anyone could draw a sketch to illustrate how a hot cup of coffee might cool down over half an hour.
- You should get a few volunteers ready to illustrate this with axes showing time and temperature, and a graph showing coffee starting with a high temperature, which decreases over time. A straight line is fine for this purpose, but more accurately it would be a curve (reciprocal shape). Do not discuss this with the class unless they ask at this time.
- Ask the volunteer how they decided which axis to use for time and which for temperature. They may simply be used to putting time on the horizontal axis. Ask the class to suggest a more general way of deciding which variable to put on which axis.
- Establish that this is to do with which variable is 'in control'. Illustrate this with the above examples, that is, the temperature controls the number of deckchairs, so the temperature goes on the horizontal axis. Similarly, the coffee's temperature depends upon how much time has passed, so the horizontal axis represents time.

- **(FM)** **The class can now do Exercise 13E from Pupil Book 2.** This exercise covers Functional Maths skills.

Exercise 13E Answers

1

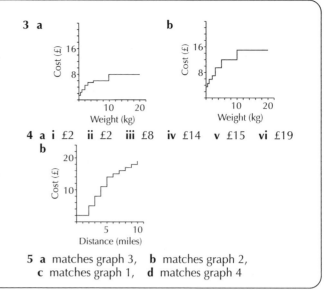

2 a i £1 **ii** £1 **iii** £2 **iv** £2 **v** £5 **vi** £5
  b i Up to 1 hour **ii** Up to 3 hours **iii** Up to 6
  hours
  c It looks like a series of steps

3 a   **b**

4 a i £2 **ii** £2 **iii** £8 **iv** £14 **v** £15 **vi** £19
  b

5 a matches graph 3, **b** matches graph 2,
  c matches graph 1, **d** matches graph 4

Extension Answers

1 i F **ii** G **iii** D **iv** A **v** B **vi** E **vii** I **viii** H **ix** C **2** Graphs like these:

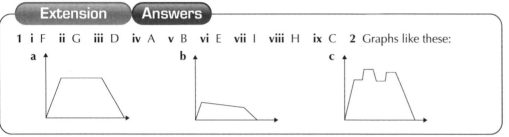

Plenary

● Ask if any of the pupils would like to illustrate their journey to school with a
  diagram on the board. Give them the scales of time and distance from school.
● Discuss the following: where to put starting and ending points; how to
  show time spent waiting; how to show different speeds.

Homework

1 An express parcel delivery agency charges £5 for any delivery up to a mile, then another £4 for each
  mile after that up to 4 miles. For journeys over 4 miles they charge an extra £1 per mile over the 4.
  a How much is charged for the following journeys:
    i half a mile **ii** 1 mile **iii** 2 miles **iv** 4 miles **v** 7 miles **vi** 12 miles?
  Draw a step graph to show the charges for journeys up to 12 miles.
2 Match the following situations to the graphs right:
  a Mary is having a bath. Halfway through she gets out to get a flannel.
  b A delivery truck leaves the depot and makes 5 deliveries.
  c An oven is turned on. Soon after the door is opened whilst food is
    put in. It reaches the required temperature. Later the oven is
    turned off.
  d Tim has a savings account into which he puts money every
    month for 6 months. Some time later he takes half the money out
    to buy a car.

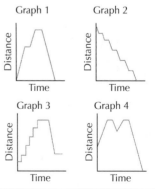

6

Homework Answers

1 a i £5 **ii** £5 **iii** £9 **iv** £17 **v** £20 **vi** £25
2 a matches graph 4, **b** matches graph 2, **c** matches graph 1, **d** matches graph 3

LESSON 13.6

Framework objectives – Change of subject
Simplify or transform linear expressions by collecting like terms.

Oral and mental starter

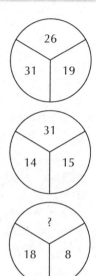

- Draw on the board the circles shown.
- Tell the class that the numbers in each circle follow the same rule. Can they work out the missing number in the third circle?
- A hint can be 'Add pairs up – do you notice anything?'
- Eventually, someone will give you the correct answer, either as a guess or because they have worked it out. Get them to tell you (quietly) if they know how to work it out, and then put the correct answer into the space. (6)
- Ask the pupil (or team) who found the correct answer to give you another circle with a missing number at the top for the rest of the class to try to solve.
- If all or some of the class are struggling, go through the totals of the adjacent pairs of numbers and ask if they notice any connection with the total and the other number. Hopefully, they will recognise that one pair is exactly three times the other number. Ask the class what total the left and top numbers must be to give the number on the right.
- The problem can be extended to involve dividing by other numbers for those who find the rule quickly.

Main lesson activity

- Write on the board the equation $3x - y = 10$.
- Explain that a few lessons ago you were talking about this equation and wanted it to be put into a different form of $y = \ldots$. This is called making y the subject of the equation or expressing y in terms of x.
- Let $x = 4$ and $y = 2$, and write the resulting expression on the board $(3 \times 4 - 2 = 10)$, explaining the substitution you have made. Can we arrange this expression to write $2 = \ldots$?
- Go through the following routine with the class, and ensure they follow every step:

$$3 \times 4 - 2 = 10$$

Add 2 to both sides $\qquad 3 \times 4 = 10 + 2$ (check: $12 = 12$)
Subtract 10 from both sides $\quad 3 \times 4 - 10 = 2$ (check: $10 = 10$)
We can rewrite this the other way round to give $2 = 3 \times 4 - 10$

- Now show how exactly the same routine will transform $3x - y = 10$ into $y = 3x - 10$.

$$3x - y = 10$$

Add y to both sides $\qquad\qquad 3x = 10 + y$
Subtract 10 from both sides $\qquad 3x - 10 = y$
Turn it round to give $\qquad\qquad y = 3x - 10$
y is now the subject of the equation.

- Write on the board the formula $P = 3m - 7$ and ask the pupils for suggestions as to how they would change the formula so that m is the subject.
To make m the subject, start by adding 7 to both sides to give $P + 7 = 3m$
and then divide both sides by 3 to give $\frac{P+7}{3} = m$.
Turn this around to get $m = \frac{P+7}{3}$.

- **The class can now do Exercise 13F from Pupil Book 2.**

Exercise 13F   Answers

1 a $k = \frac{A}{2}$ b $h = 2A$ c $r = C + 5$ d $x = A - 2$
2 a $d = \frac{C}{\pi}$ b $a = P - 1$ c $h = S + 2$ d $h = 3A$
   e $t = \frac{S}{5}$
3 a $E = 83$ b $n = \frac{E - 8}{5}$ c $n = 3$
4 a 10   b $a = S - 3$ c 21
5 a 0   b $x = y + 2$ c 7
6 a 5   b $R = 4T$ c 64
7 a 60   b $t = \frac{V}{12}$ c 3
8 28

Extension   Answers

1 $r = \sqrt{\frac{A}{\pi}}$ 2 $r = \sqrt[3]{\frac{3V}{\pi h}}$ 3 $r = \sqrt{\frac{A}{4\pi}}$

Plenary

● Explain to the pupils that this particular skill is a very useful one that they will be called upon to use on many occasions, not only in mathematics, but also in science and maybe other subjects as well.
● Ask if they see any similarities between this skill and solving equations.
● These two aspects use identical skills of manipulation. They may notice shortcuts they can use, but try to avoid teaching the pupils shortcuts before they have had the opportunity to see how the manipulation works, and to find the shortcuts for themselves.

Key words

☐ subject
☐ transform
☐ change of subject
☐ express in terms of

Homework

1 Rewrite each of the following formulae as indicated:

 a $A = 2K$
   Make K the subject of the formula.

 b $T = 3m$
   Make m the subject of the formula.

 c $F = k + 5$
   Make k the subject of the formula.

 d $V = 6l$
   Make l the subject of the formula.

 e $Q = g - 7$
   Make g the subject of the formula.

2 $d = p - 3$
 a Find d when $p = 11$.
 b Make p the subject of the formula.
 c Find p when $d = 53$.

3 $T = m + 3$
 a Find T when $m = 6$.
 b Make m the subject of the formula.
 c Find m when $T = 23$.

4 $y = x - 1$
 a Find y when $x = 3$.
 b Make x the subject of the formula.
 c Find x when $y = 17$.

Homework Answers

1 a $K = \frac{A}{D}$ b $m = \frac{T}{3}$ c $k = F - 5$ d $l = \frac{V}{6}$
   e $g = Q + 7$
2 a 8   b $p = d + 3$ c 56
3 a 9   b $m = T - 3$ c 20
4 a 2   b $x = y + 1$ c 18

National Tests   Answers

1 $y = 5, k = 3$
2 $8x + 31$
3 0.5
4 Answer should be $6a + 3$
5 $b = a - 4$, $d = \frac{C}{4}$, $m = 4k + 3$
6 $54x^2$

CHAPTER 13
FM

Functional Maths – Train timetable

Framework objectives
Identify the mathematical features of a context or problem.

Oral and mental starter

Look at the information on the timetable activity on page 186 of the corresponding Pupil Book. It shows part of a rail timetable.

● Go through the main features. All rail timetables are in the 24-hour clock. Times are *departure* times. In reality, trains arrive a minute or two before. Dashes mean that the train does not stop at that station. Refer pupils to the 'Notes'.

● Remind pupils that when working with time there are 60 minutes in an hour so calculators cannot be used. A number line can be useful when subtracting times.

Main lesson activity

● Ask pupils to extract data from the sheet. (What time if the first train? What time does the 0704 get to Darton? Does the 0751 stop at Wombwell?)

● Ask pupils to work out the times of some journeys. (How long does the 0808 take to get to Leeds?)

● Continue asking questions until pupils are sufficiently familiar with the timetable.

● **The class can now work through the questions on pages 186–187.**

FM Activity　Answers

1　1 hour 14 minutes
2　1 hour 19 minutes
3　27 minutes
4　Lockwood
5　21 minutes
6　0516 and 0725
7　**a** 4　**b** 39 minutes　**c** 10
8　0656 at the latest
9　Through train from Retford
10　38 minutes
11　1012
12　0855
13　0631 then change at Barnsley to the 0701
14　0905
15　42 minutes

Plenary

● Review progress periodically and assist with any problems.

Homework

This table shows the opening hours of a fish and chip shop.

Day	Open	Close
Saturday	1130	1930
Sunday	Closed	
Monday		
Tuesday	1730	2000
Wednesday	1730	2100
Thursday	1700	2100
Friday	1700	2330

1 For how many hours each week is the fish and chip shop open?

2 On Friday the shop has an average of 50 customers per hour, how many customers is this in total?

3 Janis works in the shop on Saturday. She is paid £5.25 per hour. How much does she earn?

4 These are the prices of the meals in the shop.

  Fish and Chips   £4.99
  Pie and Chips   £4.25
  Burger and Chips   £3.75

  a Freda orders two fish and chips, a pie and chips and a burger and chips. How much change will she get from a £20 note?

  b On Tuesday night there is a 3 for the price of 2 special. If 3 meals are ordered the cheapest is free. The Fisher family of 6 order two fish and chips, one pie and chips and three burgers and chips. How much will the bill be?

  c The next week on Tuesday, the Fisher family want the same order, so mum sends in little Tommy to order two fish and chips and a pie and chips and a few minutes later sends in little Timmy to order three burgers and chips. How much does she save by doing this?

Homework Answers

1 $24\frac{1}{2}$ hours
2 325
3 £42
4 a £2.02   b £17.98   c 50p

CHAPTER 14

Solving Problems

Overview

14.1 Number and measures

14.2 Using algebra, graphs and diagrams to solve problems

14.3 Logic and proof

14.4 Proportion

14.5 Ratio

Context

This chapter takes pupils through a range of problems within different areas of mathematics. It encourages them to identify which aspect of mathematics they will need to solve this problem and how to give a suitable answer to word problems.

National Curriculum references

Framework objectives

14.1 Within the appropriate range and content: make accurate mathematical diagrams, graphs and constructions on paper and on screen; calculate accurately, selecting mental methods or calculating devices as appropriate; manipulate numbers, algebraic expressions and equations, and apply routine algorithms; use accurate notation, including correct syntax when using ICT; record methods, solutions and conclusions; estimate, approximate and check working.

14.2 Identify the mathematical features of a context or problem; try out and compare mathematical representations; select appropriate procedures and tools, including ICT. Use graphs and set up equations to solve simple problems involving direct proportion.

14.3 Use logical argument to interpret the mathematics in a given context or to establish the truth of a statement; give accurate solutions appropriate to the context or problem; evaluate the efficiency of alternative strategies and approaches. Conjecture and generalise; move between the general and the particular to test the logic of an argument; identify exceptional cases or counter-examples; make connections with related contexts.

14.4 Apply understanding of the relationship between ratio and proportion. Enter numbers and interpret the display in different contexts (extend to negative numbers, fractions, time).

14.5 Simplify ratios, including those expressed in different units, recognising links with fraction notation; divide a quantity into two or more parts in a given ratio; use the unitary method to solve simple problems involving ratio and direct proportion.

Key concepts

Competence in mathematical procedures

- Apply mathematical processes and algorithms accurately to a widening range of familiar and unfamiliar contexts within the classroom and beyond

Creativity

- Make connections between different areas of mathematics and between mathematical techniques and problems or situations
- Use existing mathematical knowledge to create solutions to unfamiliar problems

Critical understanding in using mathematics

- Use deductive reasoning as a tool for solving problems

Key processes

Representing

- Identifying the mathematical aspects of the situation or problem

Analysing

- Using knowledge of related problems
- Working logically towards results and solutions, recognising the impact of constraints and assumptions
- Reasoning deductively and deducing

Interpreting and evaluating

- Being aware of strength of empirical evidence and appreciating the difference between evidence and proof

Route mapping

Exercise	Levels	
	5	6
14A	1–3	4–10
14B	1–4	5–10
14C	1–9	10–13
14D	1–9	10–13
14E	1–8	

Framework objectives – Number and measures

Within the appropriate range and content: make accurate mathematical diagrams, graphs and constructions on paper and on screen; calculate accurately, selecting mental methods or calculating devices as appropriate; manipulate numbers, algebraic expressions and equations, and apply routine algorithms; use accurate notation, including correct syntax when using ICT; record methods, solutions and conclusions; estimate, approximate and check working.

Oral and mental starter

- Put the numbers 3 and 5 on the board. Ask the class to tell you ways of making as many different numbers as they can using +, –, × or by writing the numbers side by side; for example, $3 + 5 = 8$, 53, $5 \times 3 = 15$, etc.
- Repeat with different numbers and then introduce a three-number problem, say 2, 4 and 7; for example, $24 \times 7 = 168$, $72 \times 4 = 288$, 742, etc. (Obviously, the class may need help to find the answer for more difficult calculations.)
- Ask the class to tell you the smallest and largest answers that they can find.
- Now give the class four numbers and an answer value, for example 1, 2, 3, 4 and an answer of 50. Tell them they have to make a number as near to 50 as possible using only the three rules and possibly digits combined to make two digit numbers; for example $41 + (2 \times 3) = 47$.

Main lesson activity

- Explain that the objective of this section is to see whether the class can solve a variety of problems involving measures and the properties of numbers.
- Tell the class that there is often no right or wrong method for solving a problem. With each one they should ask themselves: 'Can I spot a pattern?'; 'Can I see a short cut to save working out many unnecessary calculations?'; 'Can I figure out a method for myself?'
- Do they know approximate conversions between imperial and metric units? Tell the class that they should know that 8 km ≈ 5 miles, 1 litre ≈ 1.75 pints, 1 kg ≈ 2.2 lb, and 1 foot ≈ 30 cm. You may want them to write these conversions into their books for reference.
- Tell the class that you know that the distance to a nearby town is 20 km to the nearest kilometre. Ask them what the minimum possible distance could be (19.5 km). Tell them that 19.5 is also called the lower bound. Explain that, although the upper bound is technically 20.49 recurring, it is acceptable to use 20.5 as the upper bound.
- Pupils may also need to be reminded of the meaning of the word consecutive.

- **The class can now do Exercise 14A from Pupil Book 2.**

Exercise 14A — Answers

1 24, 25, 26

2 41 × 43   **b** 71 × 63 = 4473

3

4	3	8
9	5	1
2	7	6

2	9	4
7	5	3
6	1	8

6	2	7
6	5	4
3	8	4

4 a dog 8 seconds, cat 12 seconds

  b when cat has run twice and dog three times round

5 a

3^5	243	3
3^6	729	9
3^7	2187	7

  b 1

6 15 years old

7 a 4.5 × 2.5 = 11.25 km   **b** 2.5 km

8 7 lb, as 3 kg is approximately 6.6 lb

9 10 miles, as 10 miles is approximately 16 km

10 1 square mile, as 1 mile (1.6 km) is greater than 1 km

Plenary

- Remind the class of the metric to imperial conversions. You may even test them in a forthcoming lesson.
- Explain to the class that the problems encountered in this lesson are all related to number and measure, but the next lesson will look at problems that involve algebra and using graphs, which are very useful when solving problems. For example, they could have created a formula to solve some of the conversion questions in this section, or used a conversion graph. The same question can often be solved in many different ways.

Key words

- [ ] **solve**
- [ ] **problems**
- [ ] **investigate**
- [ ] **consecutive**
- [ ] **digit**
- [ ] **product**
- [ ] **number**
- [ ] **measure**

Homework

1 Each of these measurements is given to the nearest centimetre. Write down the lowest possible measurement for each one.

  a 7 cm   **b** 15 cm   **c** 45 cm   **d** 105 cm

2 A rectangle has length 4 cm and width 3 cm. Each measurement is to the nearest centimetre. What is the smallest possible perimeter?

3 Find two consecutive numbers for which the product is 756.

4 A map has a scale of 1 cm to 4 km. The distance between two places on the map is 2.5 cm. What is the actual distance between the two places?

5 Which is the greater length, 3 feet or 1 metre? Explain your answer.

6 Which is the greater, 9 pints or 5 litres? Explain your answer.

7 Which is the greater mass, 4 kg or 9 pounds? Explain your answer.

5

6

Homework Answers

1 a 6.5 cm   **b** 14.5 cm   **c** 44.5 cm   **d** 104.5 cm

2 12 cm

3 27 and 28

4 10 km

5 1 metre, as 3 feet = 90 cm

6 9 pints, as 5 litres = 8.75 pints

7 9 pounds, as 4 kg = 8.8 lb

LESSON 14.2

Framework objectives – Using algebra, graphs and diagrams to solve problems

Identify the mathematical features of a context or problem; try out and compare mathematical representations; select appropriate procedures and tools, including ICT.

Use graphs and set up equations to solve simple problems involving direct proportion.

Oral and mental starter

- Sketch a conversion graph for two currencies on the board or overhead projector (OHP). Briefly state the approximate conversion factor you are using to show how you arrived at your graph.
- Ask the class to give you some approximate conversions from your graph. Ask them how they worked out their value, and what would happen to the line if the exchange rate changed.
- Now draw a flow diagram for two rules, say 'add 5' and 'double'. Give them an input number and ask for the output. As they give you the answer, write down the algebraic expression, $(n + 5) \times 2$.
- Keep changing the rule and writing down the expression.
- Finally, ask the class to give you the expression that goes with your rule.

Main lesson activity

- Tell the class that the aim of this lesson is to solve problems using algebra or by using graphs or other diagrams.
- Leading on from the starter, ask the pupils to each think of a number and then double it and add 3. Write on the board '$2x + 3 =$', and ask a pupil for his or her answer. Write it in the space, for example $2x + 3 = 17$. Ask the other pupils to tell you what the original number was, and how they found it. You could, if needed, show them the flow chart method, as illustrated in Example 14.3 in the Pupil Book.
- Now say to the class that this could be turned into a window-cleaning problem. A window cleaner has a fixed charge of £3 and he charges £2 per window. If the total bill is £17, how many windows does he clean?
- Show the class the equation $2x + 3 = 17$.
- Ask them how the equation changes as the fixed charge is changed or as the rate per window is changed.
- Before the class starts the exercise, you may need to check that they remember the definition of upper and lower bounds, and also the terms sum and difference.
- **The class can now do Exercise 14B from Pupil Book 2.** This exercise covers Functional Maths skills.

Exercise 14B Answers

1 84.5 – 11.5 = 73 kg
2 19 and 24
3 a $C = 12 + 5n$ **b** £62 **c** fixed charge = £10, daily rate = £2
4 a **b** 15 **c** Add on the pattern number to the previous total

5 a $2x + 1 = 33$ **b** 16
6 a $x^2 – 5 = 31$ **b** 6 or –6
7 a $2x + 5 = x – 12$ **b** 7
8 a £550 **b** $100 + 50(n – 1)$ or $50n + 50$
9 2^{99} p
10 31, because 31 teams are knocked out.

Extension Answers

4 and 9; formula is n^2; pattern is square numbers

Key words

- algebra
- algebraic
- graph
- representation
- sum
- difference
- equation
- flow chart
- expression
- formula
- example

Plenary

- Point out to the class that in graph questions, the graph will sometimes be drawn for them, but sometimes they will have to draw their own.
- Tell the class that pattern spotting is an important technique for solving problems or puzzles. Explain that much of mathematics has a pattern to it. Show them how in the Fibonacci sequence (1, 1, 2, 3, 5, 8, etc.), the adjacent numbers are approximate conversions of miles to kilometres. for example 5 miles is approximately 8 kilometres, 8 miles is approximately 13 kilometres.

Homework

1 The sum of two numbers is 27 and the difference is 5. What are the two numbers?

2 The sum of two numbers is 41 and the difference is 7. What are the numbers?

3 Two parcels weigh 12 kg altogether. The heavier parcel weighs 3 kg more than the lighter parcel. How much does each parcel weigh?

4 Two pieces of wood are made from a plank 6 m long. One piece is 50 cm shorter than the other piece. How long is each piece?

5 I think of a number, double it and add four to give an answer of 26:

  a Write down an equation to represent this information. **b** What is the number?

6 I think of a number, square it and add seven to give an answer of 43:

  a Write down an equation to represent this information. **b** What is the number?

7 I think of a number, double it and subtract two. The answer is the same as the number plus seven:

  a Write down an equation to represent this information. **b** What is the number?

5

6

Homework Answers

1 16 and 11
2 24 and 17
3 7.5 kg and 4.5 kg
4 2.75 m and 3.25 m
5 a $2x + 4 = 26$ **b** 11
6 a $x^2 + 7 = 43$ **b** 6 or –6
7 a $2x – 2 = x + 7$ **b** 9

Framework objectives – Logic and proof

Use logical argument to interpret the mathematics in a given context or to establish the truth of a statement; give accurate solutions appropriate to the context or problem; evaluate the efficiency of alternative strategies and approaches.

Conjecture and generalise; move between the general and the particular to test the logic of an argument; identify exceptional cases or counter-examples; make connections with related contexts.

Oral and mental starter

- Pupils can use 'show me' boards, number fans or a sheet of paper to show their answers.
- Ask them to show you: a multiple of 3, a multiple of 4, a multiple of 3 and 4, a multiple of 3 and 4 the digits of which add up to 6.
- Repeat this for several values.
- Now ask them, in pairs, to show you: two consecutive numbers, two consecutive numbers with a sum of 21, two consecutive numbers with a product of 20, two consecutive odd numbers with a sum of 16, two consecutive odd numbers with a product of 35.
- Give the class a fairly large number, say 72, and ask them to give you ways of forming it from two other numbers. Try to get examples with each operator.

Main lesson activity

- This lesson aims to reinforce knowledge of terms such as multiple, factor and consecutive, as well as to look at logical solutions to problems, the use of proof and best-value problems.
- Explain to the class that many of these problems can be solved by different methods, including trial and improvement or trial and error.
- Show that, for example, in a subtraction a conventional method could be used or they could build up to their answer on a number line.
- Show the class that for a division the problem can be turned around to build up by repeated addition or multiplication.
- Explain that when solving a 'missing number' problem, as at the start of the exercise, they could figure it out part by part or they could use a calculator to experiment. Warn them that using a calculator could be a lengthy process.
- Ask the class to add together any two even numbers they choose in their heads. Ask them to put up their hands if their answer is even. Tell them that they will need to know facts like even + even = even. They could make a list in their books of the four combinations for addition and the four combinations for multiplication, as shown:

even + even	even
even + odd	odd
odd + even	odd
odd + odd	even
even × even	even
even × odd	even
odd × even	even
odd × odd	odd

© HarperCollins*Publishers* Limited 2008

- Finally ask the pupils how they would work out a best-value problem; for example, 3 items for £9 or 4 items for £10.
- Write out a valid method on the board for them to use as an example.
- **The class can now do Exercise 14C from Pupil Book 2.** This exercise covers Functional Maths skills.

Exercise 14C · Answers

1 **a** $452 + 97 = 549$ **b** $816 - 57 = 759$ **c** $43 \times 12 = 516$
2 For example, $1 + 3 + 5 = 9$.
3 All other even numbers are a multiple of 2.
4 Odd × even = even
5 **a** 4, 9, 25 **b** square numbers
6 1, 2, 3, 6, 9, 18
7 1, 2, 3, 4, 5, 6, 10, 12, 15, 20, 30, 60
8 250 ml 29p
9 **a** 6 litres for £7.50 **b** 4.5 kg for £1.80 **c** 300 g for £2.10
   d Four chocolate bars for 90p
10 Even + odd = odd, or $2n + 2n + 1 = 4n + 1$; $4n$ is even, and therefore $4n + 1$ is odd.
11 The three numbers contain a multiple of 2 and a multiple of 3, and therefore the product will contain a multiple of 6.
12 1200 g
13 **a** $111^2 = 12\ 321$ **b** $41^2 = 1681$ **c** $\sqrt{15\ 129} = 123$

Plenary

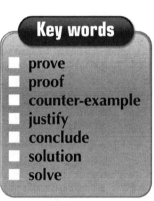

Key words
- prove
- proof
- counter-example
- justify
- conclude
- solution
- solve

- Sum up the lesson by telling the class that there are many different types of proof or disproof. Point out that a good way of disproving something is by finding a counter-example, but finding examples that work for a statement does not necessarily mean that it works all the time.
- Explain that in best-value problems they should not assume the biggest is always the cheapest. Supermarkets may lead you to believe this, but sometimes it is a marketing ploy to encourage you to buy larger quantities than you need.

Homework

1 Copy and complete the following number problems, filling in the missing digits:

a
```
  □2□
+  □3
─────
3 1 6
```
b
```
  □3□
−  □4
─────
7 1 9
```
c
```
   □9
×  1□
─────
2 2 8
```
d $3□^2 = 11□6$

2 Give an example to show that the sum of two odd numbers is always even.

3 Give an example to show that the sum of three consecutive whole numbers is a multiple of 3.

4 Find the three factors of 25.

5 Find the four factors of 15.

6 Which is the better value for money:

a 5 pies for £3 or 6 pies for £3.50? b 12 pencils for £1.44 or 10 pencils for £1.18?

Homework Answers

1 **a** $223 + 93 = 316$ **b** $733 - 14 = 719$ **c** $19 \times 12 = 228$ **d** $34^2 = 1156$
2 For example, $3 + 7 = 10$
3 For example, $3 + 4 + 5 = 12$ (3×4)
4 1, 5, 25
5 1, 3, 5, 15
6 **a** 6 pies for £3.50 **b** 10 pencils for £1.18

Framework objectives – Proportion

Apply understanding of the relationship between ratio and proportion.
Enter numbers and interpret the display in different contexts (extend to negative numbers, fractions, time).

Oral and mental starter

● Use a counting stick as shown:

● Tell the class that **one** section is equal to 5 km. Ask them what distance three sections are equal to. Repeat for different numbers and different units.

● Now tell the class, for example, that five sections are worth £15. Ask them what six sections are worth. Repeat this for many different values, but use appropriate numbers so that any divisions can be done mentally.

● This activity could be developed by using fractions; for example, telling the pupils that $\frac{2}{3}$ of the stick weighs 40 kg and asking what the stick weighs.

Main lesson activity

● The aim of this lesson is to use proportions to solve practical, everyday problems. In addition, the class needs to recall some of the conversions given in Lesson 14.1.

● Ask them which conversions they can remember. Write these on the board (8 km ≈ 5 miles, 1 litre ≈ 1.75 pints, 1 kg ≈ 2.2 pounds, 1 foot ≈ 30 cm).

● Ask them to look at, say, 8 km ≈ 5 miles and give you a related fact; for example, 16 km ≈ 10 miles. Now ask the class how they would work out the number of miles in 20 km. Encourage the pupils to offer different methods.

● Now tell them that sometimes the numbers work out easily, but sometimes they do not. Show them how to use the unitary method, with a calculator, to convert, say, 7 km into miles. Get the class to do several such conversions for you.

● Now ask if anyone can give you the conversion factor to turn miles into kilometres by this method. Once this is established as 1.6, ask individual pupils to do various mile to kilometre conversions with a calculator.

● **The class can now do Exercise 14D from Pupil Book 2.**

Exercise 14D Answers

1 **a** 6 litres blue and 14 litres yellow **b** 1.5 litres blue and 3.5 litres yellow
2 **a** 15 miles **b** 40 km
3 **a** 2.5 feet **b** 1.5 feet
4 £15
5 £12
6 £18
7 **a** 15 miles **b** 75 miles
8 **a** 24 km **b** 36 km **c** 16 km
9 £2
10 16 litres
11 $\frac{1}{5}$ or 0.2 or 20%
12 $\frac{3}{4}$
13 3 : 1

Plenary

- Sum up the lesson by again pointing out that proportion problems can often be solved using many different approaches.
- Explain that, for example, travelling at 60 miles per hour means travelling 60 miles in **one** hour; in other words, one mile every minute.
- Ask the class to explain how they would work out how far you would travel in, for example, 3 hours and 18 minutes.

Key words

- proportion
- fraction
- decimal
- percentage
- ratio
- litres
- volume
- kilogram

Homework

1 A bus travels at 12 miles per hour:
   a How far will it travel in 15 minutes?   **b** How far will it travel in 20 minutes?
   c How far will it travel in 35 minutes?   **d** How far will it travel in 1 hour 20 minutes?
2 Five burgers cost £3.50. What will 15 burgers cost?
3 Three plants cost £18. What will four plants cost?
4 A family spends £30 at the cinema on tickets and £5 on refreshments. What proportion of the spending is on refreshments?
5 10 pens cost £12. What will seven pens cost?
6 1 kg is approximately equal to 2.2 pounds:
   a How many pounds are equal to 4 kg?   **b** How many kilograms are equal to 11 pounds?

Homework Answers

1 **a** 3 miles **b** 4 miles **c** 7 miles **d** 16 miles
2 £10.50
3 £24
4 $\frac{1}{7}$
5 £8.40
6 **a** 8.8 pounds **b** 5 kg

Framework objectives – Ratio

Simplify ratios, including those expressed in different units, recognising links with fraction notation; divide a quantity into two or more parts in a given ratio; use the unitary method to solve simple problems involving ratio and direct proportion.

Oral and mental starter

- Use two target boards:

1:2	1:3	3:2	4:1	5:2
$\frac{1}{2}$	$\frac{1}{3}$	$\frac{1}{4}$	$\frac{2}{3}$	$\frac{3}{4}$

3	5	2	4	1	6	8
10	7	9	12	15	18	20

- Ask the pupils to identify pairs of numbers from the right-hand target board and match them up to ratios or fractions in the left-hand board; for example, 3 and 6 are in the ratio 1:2 or 3 is $\frac{1}{2}$ of 6.
- Now cover the 2nd board and ask pupils to give equivalent ratios or fractions using their own numbers.
- This activity can be developed by adding decimals or percentages to the left-hand target board.
- Pupils could make lists of equivalent ratios or fractions in their exercise books.

Main lesson activity

- Tell the class that the aim of this lesson is to learn how to divide a quantity into a given ratio.
- Ask the pupils to simplify, for example, 6:4. Then ask them to simplify a ratio with mixed units, for example, 1 m:30 cm. Point out that that quantities have to be converted into the same unit before they can be cancelled out. Write an example of each type on the board for them to copy into their books.
- Ask the pupils to explain what they understand by the ratio 1:2. Refer back to the starter with fractions if necessary. Select two girls and one boy. Stand them up and say that you have 30 sweets to share out. Ask how many the girls will get altogether. Now ask the pupils to explain how they worked out their answer.
- Change the number of sweets and the numbers of girls and boys used and repeat.
- Write out an example for the class to show them how you want their solutions presented on paper.
- Now reverse the problem. Again using, for example, two girls and one boy, tell the class that you have already given out coloured pencils to the three pupils equally. Tell them that the girls have 24 pencils altogether and ask the class how many the boy has.
- Change the number of pencils and the numbers of girls and boys used and repeat.

- **The class can now do Exercise 14E from Pupil Book 2.**

Exercise 14E Answers

1 **a** 3:2 **b** 2:5 **c** 3:1 **d** 2:3 **e** 1:4 **f** 4:1 **g** 4:1 **h** 4:3 **i** 1:3
 j 15:7 **k** 5:1 **l** 4:1 **m** 2:5 **n** 1:2 **o** 10:7 **p** 4:3 **q** 4:1 **r** 4:1
 s 2:3 **t** 1:5
2 **a** 24 cm:8 cm **b** 4 kg:16 kg **c** £18:£12 **d** 70 g:50 g **e** £75:£175
 f 16 litres:24 litres **g** 28p:14p:7p
 h 8 million:8 million:4 million
3 44 items
4 140 females
5 100 children
6 48 carp
7 600 brown loaves
8 34 litres

Extension Answers

Volume ratio is cube of side ratio.

Plenary

Key words
- ratio
- unitary method
- divide
- problem
- percentage (%)
- ratio notation
(3 : 2)

- Use this plenary to recap the different types of problem-solving techniques used through the chapter, for example finding patterns, algebra, graphs, proportion and ratio.
- Explain that the ratio method of finding one part is called the unitary method.

Homework

1 Simplify the ratios:

 a 8:4   **b** 5:15   **c** 14:7   **d** 12:9

 e 15:5   **f** 18:12   **g** 3:12   **h** 24 g:18 g

 i 4 cm:16 cm   **j** £10:£7.50   **k** 33 m:3 m   **l** £1:50p

 m 10 kg:4000 g **n** 5 m:1000 mm **o** 1 hour:45 minutes

2 **a** Divide 24 m in the ratio 1:3.   **b** Divide 400 g in the ratio 3:1.

 c Divide £36 in the ratio 5:4.   **d** Divide 150 cm in the ratio 2:3.

 e Divide 60p in the ratio 3:2:1.   **f** Divide 21 000 tonnes in the ratio 1:2:4.

Homework Answers

1 **a** 2:1 **b** 1:3 **c** 2:1 **d** 4:3 **e** 3:1 **f** 3:2 **g** 1:4 **h** 4:3 **i** 1:4 **j** 4:3 **k** 11:1 **l** 2:1
 m 5:2 **n** 5:1 **o** 4:3
2 **a** 6 m:18 m **b** 300 g:100 g **c** £20:£16 **d** 60 cm:90 cm **e** 30p:20p:10p
 f 3000 tonnes:6000 tonnes:12 000 tonnes

National Tests Answers

1 **a** must be even, because even × even = even and even × odd = even
 b could be odd or even as some factors are even (for example, 2, 4, 10, 20) and some are odd (for example, 1, 5)
2 **a** 18 boys, 9 girls **b** 15 boys, 13 girls **c** 9 boys, 18 girls
3 80p
4 **a** (15 × 18) + 75 = £345 **b** (615 − 75) ÷ 15 = 36 words
5 **a** at least one number must be zero **b** 0, 3 + −3 etc
6 **a** 2 × 1 = 2, 2 × 0.5 = 1 **b** 2 − −3 = 5
7 $y = 3x + 1, y = 4x − 3, y = \frac{x}{2} + 11$
8 11

Geometry and Measures 4

Context

This chapter first shows pupils how to draw 2-D representations of 3-D shapes by using plans and elevations. This is then followed by scale drawings. Pupils are then shown how to use coordinates to find the mid-point of a line segment and how to construct a triangle given three sides. They are then introduced to, and shown how to use, the formulae for the circumference and area of a circle, and are then shown how to use three-figure bearings. Finally, pupils are given the opportunity to carry out a geometrical investigation using cubes.

National Curriculum references

Framework objectives

15.1 & 15.2	Use geometric properties of cuboids and shapes made from cuboids; use simple plans and elevations.
15.3	Make scale drawings.
15.4	Find the midpoint of the line segment AB, given the coordinates of points A and B.
15.5	Use straight edge and compasses to construct a triangle, given three sides (SSS). Use ICT to explore this construction.
15.6	Use formulae from mathematics and other subjects; substitute integers into simple formulae.
15.7	Use bearings to specify direction.
15.8	Calculate surface areas of cuboids and shapes made from cuboids.
FM	Identify the mathematical features of a context or problem. Calculate percentages and find the outcome of a given percentage increase or decrease. Use the unitary method to solve simple problems involving ratio. Understand and use the language and notation associated with enlargement. Know rough metric equivalents of imperial measures in common use. Calculate areas of compound shapes. Interpret tables and diagrams.

Key concepts

Applications and implications of mathematics

- Appreciate the everyday use of plans and scale drawings in a wide range of contexts
- Understand the need to draw diagrams accurately
- Know the formulae for the circumference and area of a circle
- Understand the use of bearings in a wide range of contexts

Key processes

Representing

- Using 2-D representations for 3-D shapes
- Using scale diagrams
- Using a ruler and compasses to construct triangles
- Using the formulae to calculate the circumference and area of a circle
- Using bearings to specify direction
- Using an isometric grid to draw cuboids

Analysing

- Recognising the different ways to represent 3-D shapes
- Knowing how to use coordinates to find the mid-point of a line segment
- Knowing which formula to use when finding the circumference or area of a circle
- Recording methods, solutions and conclusions when solving a geometric problem

Communicating and reflecting

- Explaining how to find the mid-point of a line segment
- Explaining how to use the formulae to find the circumference and area of a circle
- Explaining methods when solving a geometric problem

Route mapping

Exercise	Levels	
	5	6
15A		1–6
15B	1–6	
15C	1–4	
15D	1–5	
15E		1–4
15F	1–4	5–6
15G		1–6

LESSONS 15.1 15.2

Framework objectives – Plans and elevations
Use geometric properties of cuboids and shapes made from cuboids; use simple plans and elevations.

Oral and mental starter

- *Imagine* a large cube. How many faces does it have? How many edges does it have?
- Check that the pupils know the correct answers – six faces and 12 edges.
- Now *imagine* a cube on which the top and front faces are coloured red and the other faces are coloured blue.
- How many edges are there where a red face touches another red face?
- How many edges are there where a blue face touches another blue face?
- How many edges are there where a red face touches a blue face?
- The class can be shown a model of the cube to explain the answers: 1, 5 and 6.

Main lesson activity

- The work in this section involves a good deal of complex drawing on isometric paper, which pupils often find difficult. It is therefore suggested that the work should cover two lessons.
- At the start of the lesson the class could be given sheets of centimetre isometric dotted paper and centimetre-squared paper.
- The class should be encouraged to work in pairs or small groups, as pupils can often help each other.
- Multi-link cubes should also be made available for pupils to construct the shapes shown on the isometric grids.

Lesson 15.1
- Explain to the class that the lesson is about how to draw 3-D shapes on isometric paper and how to draw different views of the shapes on squared paper.
- Draw on the board or OHP the 3-D shape shown on the right. The shape could also be made out of multi-link cubes.
- Ask the class to copy it on isometric paper, and show them the correct way to use isometric paper.
- Explain that the dots must always be in vertical columns.
- Explain that a 3-D shape can be viewed from different angles:
    a **plan** is the view of a 3-D shape when it is looked at from above (a bird's eye view).
    an **elevation** is the view of a 3-D shape when it is looked at from the front or from the side.
- The class can now draw the plan and the two elevations, as shown below, on squared paper:

Plan from A

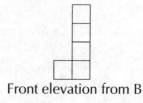

Front elevation from B

Side elevation from C

© HarperCollins *Publishers* Limited 2008

● **The class can now start Exercise 15A from Pupil Book 2.**

Lesson 15.2

● **The class can continue with Exercise 15A from Pupil Book 2.**
● Multi-link cubes and a collection of different 3-D shapes should also be made available for this lesson.

Exercise 15A **Answers**

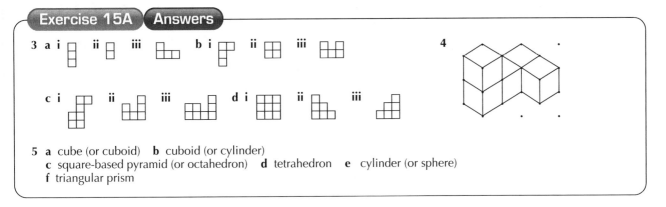

5 **a** cube (or cuboid) **b** cuboid (or cylinder)
c square-based pyramid (or octahedron) **d** tetrahedron **e** cylinder (or sphere)
f triangular prism

Extension **Answers**

1 a E, F, H, I, L **b** the letter must consist of only horizontal and vertical lines

Key words

☐ **elevation**
☐ **isometric**
☐ **plan view**
☐ **triangular prism**
☐ **view**

Plenary

● Ask individual pupils to explain the following terms: plan, front elevation and side elevation.
● Discuss with the class what would happen if they were to view any of the 3-D shapes that they have drawn from below (a worm's eye view) or from the back.

Homework

1 Draw an accurate copy of the cuboid shown on an isometric grid.

6 cm
2 cm
4 cm

2 For each of the following 3-D shapes below, draw on centimetre-squared paper:

i the plan

ii the front elevation

iii the side elevation

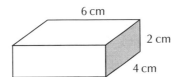

a 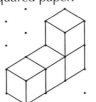 **b** 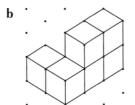 **c**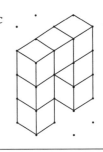

Homework Answers

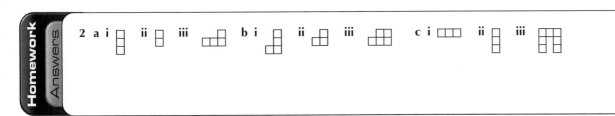

LESSON 15.3

Framework objectives – Scale drawings
Make scale drawings.

Oral and mental starter

- A starter to practice estimating length.
- Pupils will need rulers and possibly a tape measure for this activity. It is best done using individual white boards, but pupils can give their answers orally.
- Ask a pupil to select an object in the classroom.
- Ask the rest of the class to estimate the length of the object and to write their answer on their white boards.
- Ask the first pupil to measure the actual length of the object.
- The pupils can now show their estimates on their white boards. Some discussion of the units used may be a useful exercise.
- The pupil whose estimate is closest to the actual length wins a point.
- The activity can be repeated with a different pupil selecting another object.

Main lesson activity

- Explain to the class that the lesson is about using and making scale drawings.
- Draw on the board or OHP a scale drawing to show the dimensions of a room in school, for example a classroom, the school hall or the gym:

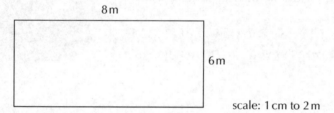

8 m

6 m

scale: 1 cm to 2 m

- Explain to the class the importance of choosing a sensible scale. It might be worth pointing out that if you double the scale, the scale drawing is halved in size.
- Show the class how to find the actual length and width of the room by using the scale.
- **The class can now do Exercise 15B from Pupil Book 2.** This exercise covers Functional Maths skills.
- If time is available towards the end of term, the class can work in groups to complete extra practical work for a display in the classroom. For example, pupils can draw plans for the school playground, the sports field or the staff car park.

Exercise 15B — Answers

1 a 20 m **b** 50 m **c** 35 m **d** 78 m **e** 63 m
2 a 25 m **b** 15 m **c** ≈ 29 m
3 a 1 cm to 2 m **b** 6 m **c** 48 m²
4 a 16 cm **b** 6 cm **c** 2 cm **d** 3 m **e** 2.5 m **f** 1.2 m
5 a i 6 m by 4 m **ii** 4 m by 2 m **iii** 6 m by 4 m **iv** 5 m by 4 m **b** 68 m²

Extension — Answers

3 a 1 : 100 **b** 1 : 400 **c** 1 : 25 **d** 1 : 100 000 **e** 1 : 50 000

Plenary

- Show the class a map of Britain.
- Ask the class to guess the scale for the map.
- Tell the class the answer.
- This can then lead to a discussion of different map scales.

Key words

- [ ] **plan view**
- [ ] **scale**
- [ ] **scale factor**
- [ ] **scale drawing**

Homework

1 The lines below are drawn using a scale 1 cm to 4 m. Write down the length each line represents.

a ─────────── (3 cm)

b ───────────────────── (7 cm)

c ──────────── (4.5 cm)

d ───────────── (5.4 cm)

e ──────────────────────── (8.7 cm)

2 The diagram shown is a scale drawing of Mr Peters' garden:

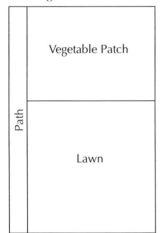

Scale: 1 cm to 2 m

a Find the actual dimensions of the garden.

b Find the actual dimensions of the lawn.

c Find the actual dimensions of the vegetable patch.

d Find the actual area of the path.

3 The length of a netball court is 30 m and its width is 16 m. On centimetre-squared paper, draw a plan of the netball court, using a scale of 1 cm to 4 m.

5

Homework Answers

1 a 12 m **b** 28 m **c** 18 m **d** 21.6 m **e** 34.8 m
2 a 12 m by 8 m **b** 7 m by 7 m **c** 7 m by 5 m **d** 12 m²
3 Scale drawing with sides 7.5 cm by 4 cm

LESSON

15.4

Framework objectives – Finding the mid-point of a line segment

Find the midpoint of the line segment AB, given the coordinates of points A and B.

Oral and mental starter

- This is a revision starter on coordinates, using a practical activity that requires a coordinate grid and two dice of different colours (for example, red and blue).
- Explain to the class that they are going to play the game 'Four in a line'.
- The game can be played in pairs or as a class activity.
- On prepared sheets or OHP, draw a grid with *x*- and *y*-axes going from 0 to 6.
- Explain that one person throws the two dice. The score on the red dice gives the *x*-coordinate and the score on the blue dice gives the *y*-coordinate of a point. The person then plots that point on the grid.
- Another person then throws the dice and plots her point on the grid.
- The game continues until a person wins by plotting four points in a line. The line can be horizontal, vertical or diagonal.

Main lesson activity

- Draw coordinates on the grid shown on the board or OHP.

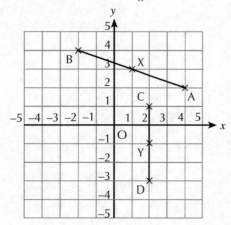

- Ask the pupils to copy it onto centimetre-squared paper.
- Ask the class to give the coordinates of the points A, B, C and D. The points are A(4, 2), B(–2, 4), C(2, 1) and D(2, –3).
- Explain that the point X is the midpoint of the line segment that joins A and B and Y is the midpoint of the line segment that joins C and D. X is usually referred to as the midpoint of AB and Y as the midpoint of CD.
- From the diagram, the pupils should see that the coordinates of X are (1, 3).
- Ask the pupils to give the coordinates of Y.
- The coordinates of Y are (2, –1). Point out that the *x*-coordinates are the same for the three points on the line.

- **The class can now do Exercise 15C from Pupil Book 2.**

Exercise 15C — Answers

1 **a** A(4, 4), B(–2, 4), C(–3, 3), D(–3, –1), E(–2, –4), F(4, –4)
  b i (1, 4) **ii** (–3, 1) **iii** (–2, 0) **iv** (1, –4)
2 **a** P(4, 3), Q(4, –3), R(–2, –3), S(–2, 3)
  b i (4, 0) **ii** (1, –3) **iii** (1, 3) **iv** (–2, 0) **c** (1, 0)
3 **a**

Line segment	Coordinates of the first point on the line segment	Coordinates of the second point on the line segment	Coordinates of the midpoint of the line segment
AB	A(8, 8)	B(2, 8)	(5, 8)
AD	A(8, 8)	D(8, 4)	(8, 6)
BC	B(2, 8)	C(2, 2)	(2, 5)
BF	B(2, 8)	F(4, 6)	(3, 7)
AF	A(8, 8)	F(4, 6)	(6, 7)
CE	C(2, 2)	E(6, 1)	(4, 1.5)

b The *x*-coordinate of the midpoint is half the sum of the *x*-coordinates of the two points and the *y*-coordinate of the midpoint is half the sum of the *y*-coordinates of the two points.
4 **a** (3, 4) **b** (5, 8) **c** (4, 3) **d** (5, 4.5) **e** (1, 2)

Extension — Answers

1 **a** (3, 3) **b** (–1, 3) **c** (–3, 1) **d** (0.5, –3) **e** (3.5, 0)

Plenary

● Draw a grid on the board or OHP.
● Ask individual pupils to plot any two points on the grid and then explain to the class how to find the midpoint of the line segment that joins their two points.

Homework

1 Copy the grid shown and plot the points A, B, C and D.

  a Write down the coordinates of the points A, B, C and D.

  b Using the grid to help, write down the coordinates of the midpoint of each of the following line segments:
   i AD
   ii BC
   iii CD
   iv AB

2 On a grid draw the *x*- and *y*-axes from –5 to 5:

  a Plot the points P(1, 3), Q(4, –1), R(1, –5) and S(–2, –1) and join them to make a quadrilateral.

  b What is the special name given to the quadrilateral?

  c Write down the coordinates of the midpoint of each of the following lines: **i** PR **ii** QS

  d Explain your answer to part **c**.

Homework Answers

1 **a** A(8, 9), B(2, 7), C(2, 1), D(8, 1) **b i** (8, 5) **ii** (2, 4) **iii** (5, 1) **iv** (5, 8)
2 **b** rhombus **c i** (1, –1) **ii** (1, –1) **d** the midpoint of the two diagonals of a rhombus is a common point

Framework objectives – To construct a triangle given three sides

Use straight edge and compasses to construct a triangle, given three sides (SSS).
Use ICT to explore this construction.

Oral and mental starter

- This is a starter to help with spelling and knowledge of mathematical terms.
- Write on the board: Richard Of York Gave Battle In Vain.
- Ask the pupils if they recognise this mnemonic for the colours of the rainbow: Red, Orange, Yellow, Green, Blue, Indigo, Violet (a mnemonic is an aid to help remember facts).
- Ask the pupils to write down the names of all the special quadrilaterals that they have met (square, rectangle, parallelogram, rhombus, kite, arrowhead, trapezium).
- Ask the class to work in pairs and, in five or ten minutes, invent a suitable mnemonic for the names of the quadrilaterals.

Main lesson activity

- Remind the class about the two constructions they used for triangles in Year 7:
    a triangle given two sides and the included angle (SAS):

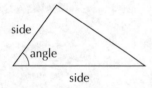

    a triangle given two angles and the included side (ASA):

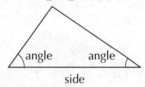

- Explain that the lesson is about how to construct a triangle given three sides (SSS). For this lesson the pupils will require a ruler and compasses.
- Draw a sketch of such a triangle on the board.
- Ask the pupils to draw the triangle shown in stages as described below:

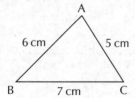

    Draw the line BC 7 cm long.
    Set compasses to a radius of 6 cm and, with centre at B, draw a large arc above BC.
    Set compasses to a radius of 5 cm and, with centre at C, draw a large arc to intersect the first arc.
    The intersection of the arcs is A.
    Join AB and AC to complete the triangle.
    The construction lines should be left on the diagram.

- **The class can now do Exercise 15D from Pupil Book 2.**

Exercise 15D **Answers**

3   A right-angled triangle.
5   The sum of the two shorter sides is smaller than the longest side.

Plenary

● Draw a sketch of this triangle on the board:

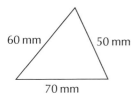

● Ask the class how they would construct the triangle.
● Now draw a sketch of the following triangle on the board:

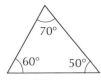

● Ask the class how they would construct this triangle.
● They should say it is not possible, as it could be drawn any size because you do not know the lengths of any of the sides.
● If time allows, it may be possible to discuss the idea of similar shapes.

Homework

1   Construct each of the following triangles (remember to label all the lines):

a
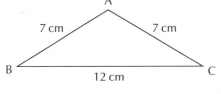

b
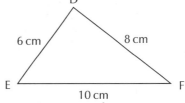

c
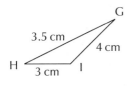

2   Construct the △XYZ with XY = 7.4 cm, XZ = 6.2 cm and YZ = 4.8 cm.
3   Construct an equilateral triangle with sides of length 4 cm.

Framework objectives – Circumference and area of a circle

Use formulae from mathematics and other subjects; substitute integers into simple formulae.

Oral and mental starter

- Describe to the class the route that Carol takes from her house to her local post office:

    Leave home and turn left at the front gate.
    Walk straight on for 100 m.
    The post office is on the left.
- Ask a pupil to describe Carol's route back home.
- Now extend her route.

    Leave home and turn left at the front gate.
    Walk straight on for 100 m.
    Turn left at the crossroads.
    Walk straight on for 50 m.
    The post office is on the left.
- Ask another pupil to describe her route back home.
- Now extend her route again.

    Leave home and turn left at the front gate.
    Walk straight on for 100 m.
    Turn left at the crossroads.
    Walk straight on for 50 m.
    Turn right at the church.
    Walk straight on for 200 m.
    The post office is on the left.
- Ask another pupil to describe her route back home.
- This activity can be changed to suit the ability of the class.

Main lesson activity

- Draw a circle on the board or OHP. Explain the words **radius, diameter** and **circumference**.
- Explain that it is possible to find the circumference and area of the circle by using formulae, and that in Year 9 they will be shown how to find the formulae.
- The formula for the circumference of a circle is given by $C = \pi d$, where C is the circumference and d is the diameter of the circle. π (pronounced pi) is a special symbol used with circles and is a Greek letter. The value of π cannot be written down exactly, so approximate values are used. It is usual to take π as 3.14 to two decimal places or use the π key on a calculator.
- The formula for the area of a circle is given by $A = \pi r^2$, where A is the area and r is the radius of the circle. Explain to the class that πr^2 is the same as $\pi \times r \times r$ and care must be taken when using the formula on a calculator.
- Draw two circles and show the class how to calculate the circumference and area, given either the diameter or the radius.

    Examples:

    given the diameter   given the radius

    $d = 6$ cm $r = 4$ cm

$d = 6$ cm, so $r = 3$ cm $\qquad r = 4$ cm, so $d = 8$ cm

$C = \pi d$ $\qquad\qquad\qquad\quad C = \pi d$

$\quad = \pi \times 6$ $\qquad\qquad\qquad = \pi \times 8$

$\quad = 18.8$ cm (to 1 dp) $\qquad = 25.1$ cm (to 1 dp)

$A = \pi r^2$ $\qquad\qquad\qquad\quad A = \pi r^2$

$\quad = \pi \times 3 \times 3$ $\qquad\qquad = \pi \times 4 \times 4$

$\quad = \pi \times 9$ $\qquad\qquad\qquad = \pi \times 16$

$\quad = 28.3$ cm^2 (to 1 dp) $\qquad = 50.3$ cm^2 (to 1 dp)

- **The class can now do Exercise 15E from Pupil Book 2.**

Exercise 15E | Answers

1 **a** 25.1 cm **b** 31.4 cm **c** 50.3 cm **d** 18.8 cm
   e 12.6 cm **f** 28.3 cm
2 **a** 3.1 cm^2 **b** 78.5 cm^2 **c** 50.3 cm^2 **d** 3.1 cm^2
   e 19.6 cm^2 **f** 30.2 cm^2
3 30.2 cm
4 530 mm^2

Extension | Answers

1 25.7 cm, 39.3 cm^2
2 36.6 cm, 89.1 cm^2

Plenary

- Draw a circle on the board. Ask the pupils to write down the formulae to find the circumference and area of the circle.
- Emphasise the need to learn these formulae, as they are not given in examinations.

Key words

- radius
- diameter
- circumference
- area
- π

Homework

Take $\pi = 3.14$ or use the π key on your calculator.

1 Calculate the circumference of each of the following circles. Give each answer to one decimal place.

2 Calculate the area of each of the following circles. Give each answer to one decimal place.

3 A circular pond has a diameter of 8 m. Calculate its circumference and area. Give your answers to one decimal place.

Homework Answers

1 **a** 44.0 cm **b** 12.6 cm **c** 34.6 cm
2 **a** 113.1 cm^2 **b** 12.6 cm^2 **c** 7.1 cm^2
3 25.1 m, 50.3 m^2

6

LESSON 15.7

Framework objectives – Bearings
Use bearings to specify direction.

Oral and mental starter

- This is an activity called '180', to make the pupils familiar with pairs of numbers that add to 180.
- The target board shown can be drawn on the board or pupils can be given prepared sheets.
- The aim is to cross off the pairs of numbers that sum to 180 as quickly as possible until one number is left.
- The answer is 72.

104	140	36	112	169
157	89	72	99	125
55	162	47	76	65
81	68	40	11	144
133	115	23	91	18

Main lesson activity

- Start the lesson by reminding the pupils of various facts about angles:
    The angles on a straight line add up to 180°.
    The angles in a complete turn add up to 360°.
    In parallel lines, alternate angles are equal.
- Show the class a compass or draw on the board the main compass points.
- Explain to the class that the four main directions on a compass are north (N), south (S), east (E) and west (W). These are examples of **compass bearings**. A **bearing** is a specified direction in relation to a fixed line. The line that is usually taken is due north, the symbol for which is:

The pupils will have probably seen this symbol on maps in Geography.

- Explain that bearings are mainly used for navigation purposes at sea and in the air, and in sports such as orienteering. (Fell walkers will probably also use them when walking in mist and fog!)
- The class can copy this into their books: 'A bearing is measured in degrees (°) and the angle is always measured **clockwise** from the **north line**. A bearing is always given using three digits and is referred to as a **three-digit bearing**. For example, the bearing for an easterly direction is 090°.' (This is pronounced as 'a bearing of zero nine zero'.)
- Draw the diagram shown on the board, and explain that the three-figure bearing of B from A is 040° and the three-figure bearing of A from B is 220°:

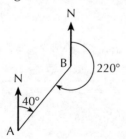

- Draw the diagram to the right on the board and explain how to find the bearing of Leeds from Manchester and the bearing of Manchester from Leeds:

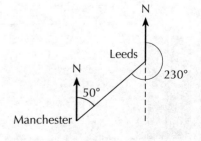

The bearing of Leeds from Manchester is 050° and the bearing of Manchester from Leeds is 230°. To find the bearing of Manchester from Leeds, use the dotted line to find the alternate angle of 50° and then add 180°. The difference between the two bearings is 180°. These are often referred to as 'back bearings'.

● **The class can now do Exercise 15F from Pupil Book 2.**

Exercise 15F   Answers

1 **a** 180°   **b** 270°   **c** 045°   **d** 225°
2 **a** 064°   **b** 008°   **c** 097°   **d** 300°
3 **a** 045°   **b** 020°   **c** 258°   **d** 321°
4 sketches of bearings: **a** 030°   **b** 138°   **c** 220°   **d** 333°
5 **a i** 042°   **ii** 222°   **b i** 074°   **ii** 254°
6 **a** 14.25 km
   b i 081° (±2°)   **ii** 150° (±2°)   **iii** 282° (±2°)

Extension   Answers

1 **b i** 165 km (± 5 km)   **ii** 027° (±2°)
2 **b i** 137° (±2°)   **ii** 190° (±2°)

Plenary

Key words
☐ **bearing**
☐ **three-figure bearing**
☐ **scale drawing**

● Ask individual pupils to explain the difference between compass bearings and three-figure bearings.
● Ask them to convert from one to the other by giving a few examples.

Homework

1 Write down each of the following compass bearings as three-figure bearings:

   a north   **b** east   **c** north-west   **d** south-east

2 Write down the three-figure bearing of B from A for each of the following:

a 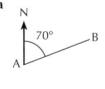   **b**    **c**   **d**

3 Draw a rough sketch to show each of the bearings below (mark the angle on each sketch):

   a From a ship P, the bearing of a harbour Q is 070°.

   b From a helicopter S, the bearing of a landing pad T is 100°.

   c From a rocket R, the bearing of the Moon M is 225°.

   d From an aeroplane Y, the bearing of an airport Z is 310°.

4 The diagram shows the positions of a tanker at sea, a light-house and a harbour:

   a Find the bearing of the tanker from the light-house.

   b Find the bearing of the tanker from the harbour.

   c Find the bearing of the harbour from the light-house.

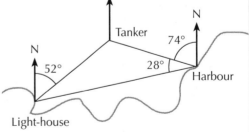

Homework Answers

1 **a** 000°   **b** 090°   **c** 315°   **d** 135°
2 **a** 070°   **b** 163°   **c** 265°   **d** 340°
3 Sketches of bearings: **a** 070°   **b** 100°   **c** 225°   **d** 310°
4 **a** 052°   **b** 286°   **c** 078°

LESSON
15.8

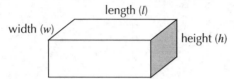

Framework objectives – A cube investigation
Calculate surface areas of cuboids and shapes made from cuboids.

Oral and mental starter

● On the board, draw a cuboid similar to the one shown.

length (*l*)
width (*w*)
height (*h*)

● Ask the class to write down the formula for the volume of the cuboid. Check
their answers. Make sure they use the correct notation for the formula, that is:
$V = lwh$

● Now ask the class to write down the formula for the total surface area of the cuboid.
Check their answers. Make sure they use the correct notation for the formula, that is:
$A = 2lw + 2lh + 2hw$

Main lesson activity

● A cube investigation.

● This investigation focuses on the pupils' ability to represent 3-D shapes
on isometric paper and to explain their methods when solving a problem.
The pupils can work in pairs or in groups. Each pair or group will require
a collection of cubes and centimetre isometric dotted paper (multi-link
cubes are ideal for this investigation).

● The problem is outlined in Pupil Book 2 on page 213 and repeated here.
Two cubes can only be arranged in one way to make a solid shape:
    Copy the diagram onto isometric dotted paper.
    The surface area of the solid is 10 cm².

Three cubes can be arranged in two different ways.
    Copy the diagrams onto isometric dotted paper.
    The surface area of both solids is 14 cm².

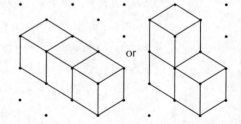

Here is an arrangement of four cubes.

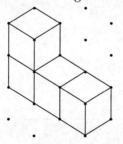

The surface area of the solid is 18 cm².
How many different arrangements can you
make using four cubes?
Draw all the different arrangements on isometric
dotted paper.
What is the greatest surface area for the different
solids you have made?
What is the least surface area for the different
solids you have made?

Make a table to show your results and write down anything you notice.
What do you think is the greatest and least surface area of a solid made
from five cubes?

● **The class can now do Exercise 15G from pupil book 2.**

Exercise 15G **Answers**

There are seven different arrangements:

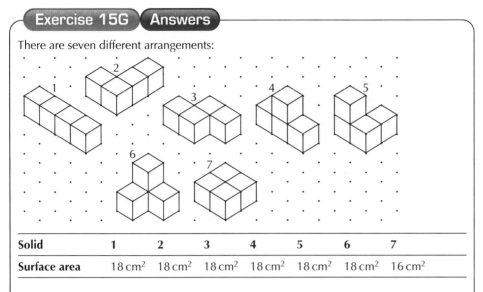

Solid	1	2	3	4	5	6	7
Surface area	18 cm²	18 cm²	18 cm²	18 cm²	18 cm²	18 cm²	16 cm²

Solid 7 has the least surface area and the rest have the same surface area.
The solid with the least surface area has four pairs of faces touching, whereas the other six have three pairs of faces touching.
For all the solids in this investigation, the surface area is an even number of square centimetres.
Two cubes have 12 faces in total, so if one pair of faces are touching, then 10 faces are exposed.
Three cubes have 18 faces in total, so if two pairs of faces are touching, then 14 faces are exposed.
A solid made from four cubes must have three or four pairs of faces touching, so either 16 or 18 faces are exposed.
A solid made from five cubes must have four or five pairs of faces touching, so either 20 or 22 faces are exposed.

Plenary

● Towards the end of the lesson, some discussion of the methods the pupils used to carry out the investigation could take place.

Key words

- [ ] **investigate**
- [ ] **cube**
- [ ] **surface area**

Homework

Complete the write up of the cube investigation, explaining clearly what you have done and how you recorded your results. Remember that if another person reads your work, they should understand exactly what the problem is and what you have done to find the answer.

6

National Tests **Answers**

3 a He should have used Area = $\pi r^2 \times 16$

4

5 a P (60, 60) **b** M (0, 100), N (60, 0)

Functional Maths – Photographs

Framework objectives

Interpret tables and diagrams.

Identify the mathematical features of a contextual problem.

Know rough metric equivalents of imperial measures in common use.

Calculate areas of compound shapes.

Understand and use the language associated with enlargement.

Calculate percentages and find the outcome of a given percentage increase or decrease.

Use the unitary method to solve simple problems involving ratio

Oral and mental starter

Look at the information on the photographs activity on page 216 of the corresponding Pupil Book. This functional mathematics activity consolidates topics previously covered on extracting data, area and ratio.

● Draw the following squares and rectangles on the board or OHP.

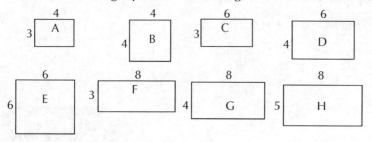

● Ask the class to write down in their books or on mini whiteboards the answers to the following questions.

a Which two shapes have the same perimeter? (E and G)

b Which two shapes have the same area? (D and F)

c Which two shapes have the same value for their perimeter and area? (B and C)

● Check the pupils' answers after each question to ensure they appreciate the difference between perimeter and area.

Main lesson activity

● Encourage pupils to suggest questions which might arise from the data, for example, the use of inches for the dimensions of the prints. Discuss which imperial units are still in common use, for example, weighing vegetables on market stalls, people's weights, etc.

● Discuss the reasons why shops encourage us to buy in bulk.

● It is important that pupils realise that when we refer to 'photograph enlargements', they may not actually be true mathematical enlargements. It may be useful to revise enlargements and scale factors before pupils start question 4.

● Discuss 'best buys' with the pupils. Do people really compare prices in different shops? Ask the pupils for their views. This may well lead on to some discussion about the influence of advertisements on TV and on the internet.

● Before starting the question on Golden Rectangles, it may be useful to revise simplifying ratios.

- The Golden Rectangle appears in paintings and buildings, both ancient and modern. For example, the painting of Salvador Dali's 'The Sacrament of the Last Supper' is a golden rectangle and the exterior of the Parthenon on the Acropolis in Athens is based on the golden rectangle.
- Pupils could be directed to the internet where there is a wealth of information on golden rectangles and the golden ratio, Ø.

$$Ø = \frac{\sqrt{5} + 1}{2} = 1.618\ 039\ 887\ 498\ 948\ 482\ 045\ 868\ 343\ 656\ 381\ 177\ 203\ 091\ 798\ 057\ 6 \dots$$

- **The class can now work through the questions on pages 216–217.**

FM Activity Answers

1 £183.96
2 **a** 5.1″ × 3.5″ and 17.7″ × 11.8″ **b** 6 sq in, 24 sq in, 35 sq in, 48 sq in, 80 sq in, 96 sq in **c** 6″ × 4″ and 8″ × 6″, 8″ × 6″ and 12″ × 8″
3 **a** 13 sq in **b** Frame B – 6″ × 4″, Frame C – 10″ × 8″
4 3″ × 2″ and 6″ × 4″ SF = 2, 6″ × 4″ and 12″ × 8″ SF = 2, 3″ × 2″ and 12″ × 8″ SF = 4
5 **a** 6″ × 4″, 7″ × 5″ and 8″ × 6″ **b** FastPrint, £3.60 c 12p d 10%
6 **a** 3 : 2 = 1.5 : 1, 6 : 4 = 1.5 : 1, 7 : 5 = 1.4 : 1, 8 : 6 = 1.33 : 1, 10 : 8 = 1.25 : 1, 12 : 8 = 1.5 : 1 **b** 3″ × 2″, 6″ × 4″ and 12″ × 8″

Plenary

- Sum up by asking the pupils for the different areas of mathematics they have used during the lesson.
- Pupils could do this by individually writing them on the board or on a flip-chart.

Homework

How to draw a Golden Rectangle:
- Draw a square with sides 4 cm.
- Draw a line from the midpoint of one side of the square to an opposite corner.
- Use that line as the radius to draw an arc that defines the height of the rectangle.
- Complete the golden rectangle as in the diagram below.

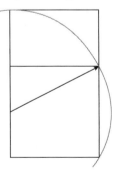

- Measure the length and the width of the rectangle.

  Work out the ratio of the length to the width in the form *n* : 1.

  How close are you to the ratio 1.618 : 1?
- Repeat the construction by starting with a square with sides 6 cm.

Homework Answers

For the 6 cm square, the two Golden Rectangles measurements are 6 cm × 3.7 cm and 9 cm × 5.6 cm.

Statistics 3

Overview

16.1 Frequency tables

16.2 Assumed mean and working with statistics

16.3 Drawing frequency diagrams

16.4 Comparing data

16.5 Which average to use?

16.6 Experimental and theoretical probability

 Questionnaire

Context

This chapter shows how to plan tasks and collect data, and, once it is collected, different ways of using that data. It shows ways of representing the data and then comparing it in a range of contexts. Different approaches to comparison are looked at, finishing with comparing theoretical and experimental probabilities. Links to both statistics and probability are explored.

National Curriculum references

Framework objectives

16.1 Discuss a problem that can be addressed by statistical methods and identify related questions to explore. Decide which data to collect to answer a question, and the degree of accuracy needed; identify possible sources. Plan how to collect the data; construct frequency tables with equal class intervals for gathering continuous data. Collect data using a suitable method (for example, observation, controlled experiment, data logging using ICT).

16.2 Calculate statistics for sets of discrete and continuous data, including with a calculator and spreadsheet; recognise when it is appropriate to use the range, mean, median and mode and, for grouped data, the modal class.

16.3 Construct graphical representations, on paper and using ICT, and identify which are most useful in the context of the problem. Include: bar charts and frequency; diagrams for discrete and continuous data; simple line graphs for time series.

16.4 Interpret tables, graphs and diagrams for discrete and continuous data, relating summary statistics and findings to the questions being explored. Compare two distributions using the range and one or more of the mode, median and mean.

16.5 Recognise when it is appropriate to use the range, mean, median and mode and, for grouped data, the modal class.

16.6 Write about and discuss the results of a statistical enquiry using ICT as appropriate; justify the methods used. Compare estimated experimental probabilities with theoretical probabilities.

 Calculate statistics for sets of discrete and continuous data, including with a calculator and spreadsheet. Interpret the results of an experiment using the language of probability.

Key concepts

Critical understanding

● Know that mathematics is essentially abstract and can be used to model, interpret or represent situations

Key processes

Representing

● Selecting statistical information appropriately

Analysing

● Working logically towards results and solutions

Communicating and reflecting

● Forming arguments based on findings and making general statements

Route mapping

Exercise	Levels	
	5	6
16A		1–4
16B	1–12	
16C		1–2
16D	1–4	
16E	1–3	
16F		1–5

Framework objectives – Frequency tables

Discuss a problem that can be addressed by statistical methods and identify related questions to explore.

Decide which data to collect to answer a question, and the degree of accuracy needed; identify possible sources.

Plan how to collect the data; construct frequency tables with equal class intervals for gathering continuous data.

Collect data using a suitable method (for example, observation, controlled experiment, data logging using ICT).

Oral and mental starter

- Write 0–10, 10–20 and 20–30 on the board or OHP. Tell the class that these represent time intervals for how long pupils spend on a piece of work. Say there is a problem with using these intervals and ask them if they can tell you what it is. They may point out the overlapping time intervals and that you cannot record for more than 30.
- Now change the intervals to 0–10, 11–20, 21–30 and 31+ and ask them if this solves the problem. Hopefully, they will spot that there are now gaps between the classes.
- Ask the class to give you ideas on how to record the times without these problems. Prompt them to use the words inclusive and exclusive.
- Finally, write $0 < \text{time} \leq 10$ on the board and ask them to explain to you what this means. This should lead on to the use of this notation for class intervals. Compare with the meaning of $0 \leq \text{time} < 10$ and point out that they should always check carefully which is being used.

Main lesson activity

- Use the starter as the introduction to the main lesson activity.
- Write on the board or OHP a table, as shown below:

Height of book, h (cm)	Frequency
$22 < h \leq 24$	
$24 < h \leq 26$	
$26 < h \leq 28$	
$28 < h \leq 30$	

- Ask the pupils to measure the height of different books. Record their responses. You may wish to keep a tally alongside the table. Emphasise that the symbol $\leq$ could be the first or second relation, but that this should be kept consistent. Explain to the group again that, for example, 24 will be recorded in the first class.
- Complete the frequency table.
- **The class can now do Exercise 16A from Pupil Book 2.**

Exercise 16A Answers

1 $10 < T \le 20$

2

Height, h (metres)	Frequency
$1.40 < h \le 1.50$	2
$1.50 < h \le 1.60$	4
$1.60 < h \le 1.70$	6
$1.70 < h \le 1.80$	6
$1.80 < h \le 1.90$	2

3

Mass, M (kilograms)	Frequency
$0 < M \le 1$	4
$1 < M \le 2$	2
$2 < M \le 3$	1
$3 < M \le 4$	3
$4 < M \le 5$	2
$5 < M \le 6$	2

4

Temperature, T (°C)	Frequency
$8 < T \le 10$	3
$10 < T \le 12$	5
$12 < T \le 14$	3
$14 < T \le 16$	3
$16 < T \le 18$	2

Plenary

- Explain to the pupils that the next step is to collect large data sets and for them to decide the size of the class interval.
- Point out that it is sensible to keep to a manageable number of classes, but this may depend on the range of the data and the number of pieces of data.
- Finally, summarise the lesson by saying that once they have a frequency table they can go on to record the information diagrammatically in pie charts or histograms.

Key words

- **primary source**
- **secondary source**
- **sample size**
- **frequency table**

Homework

1 Complete a frequency table for the following temperatures, T (°C). Use class intervals of $0 < T \le 10$, $10 < T \le 20$, $20 < T \le 30$ and $30 < T \le 40$.

12	17	32	30	10	22	26	8	16	5
14	33	24	19	6	30	25	40	2	18

2 Complete a frequency table for the ages (years) of a group of people. Use class intervals of $20 \le$ Age < 25, $25 \le$ Age < 30, $30 \le$ Age < 35 and $35 \le$ Age < 40.

24	28	25	36	30	37	33	22	27	39
22	29	34	21	31	30	29	21	32	35

3 Complete a frequency table for the distances d (kilometres) that pupils live from school. Use class intervals of $0 < d \le 1$, $1 < d \le 2$, $2 < d \le 3$, $3 < d \le 4$ and $4 < d \le 5$.

0.1	3.2	4.7	0.8	0.7	1.4	2.5
2.8	1.7	3.3	0.2	0.3	1.0	3.0

Homework Answers

1

Temperature, T (°C)	Frequency
$0 < T \le 10$	5
$10 < T \le 20$	6
$20 < T \le 30$	6
$30 < T \le 40$	3

2

Age (years)	Frequency
$20 \le$ Age < 25	5
$25 \le$ Age < 30	5
$30 \le$ Age < 35	6
$35 \le$ Age < 40	4

3

Distance, d (kilometres)	Frequency
$0 < d \le 1$	6
$1 < d \le 2$	2
$2 < d \le 3$	3
$3 < d \le 4$	2
$4 < d \le 5$	1

Framework objectives – Assumed mean and working with statistics

Calculate statistics for sets of discrete and continuous data, including with a calculator and spreadsheet; recognise when it is appropriate to use the range, mean, median and mode and, for grouped data, the modal class.

Oral and mental starter

- Write the numbers 3, 5 and 7 on the board or OHP.
- Ask the class to tell you the mean of these numbers. Ask them to tell you how they worked it out.
- Change the numbers to 13, 15 and 17. Ask the class to tell you the mean. Ask them to tell you how they worked it out.
- Now try the same with 103, 105 and 107.
- Repeat with different starting numbers, gradually increasing the level of difficulty.

Main lesson activity

- The aim of this main activity is to convince pupils that there are benefits in using an assumed mean, particularly when they carry out non-calculator work.
- Set out a table on the board or OHP, as shown below, for the class to copy and complete. This exercise is better done without using a calculator.

	a	b	c	d
	4	14	24	104
	5	15	25	105
	7	17	27	107
	8	18	28	108
Total				
Mean				

- Repeat this method with different numbers or for, say, five or six values.
- Now work the method backwards using a table as shown below. Choose an assumed mean of 28 and subtract from column **a** to get column **b**:

	a	b
	28	0
	33	5
	41	13
	50	22
Total		40
Mean		10

- By taking the mean of column **b** and adding 28, the mean of column **a** is obtained (38).
- You could now repeat using an assumed mean of 38, as shown:

	a	b
	28	−10
	33	−5
	41	3
	50	12
Total		0
Mean		0

- Explain that adding on numbers or doubling each piece of data alters averages in the same way. Adding on does not affect the range, although doubling will double the range.

- Explain that the assumed mean technique will save on calculations when data consist of large numbers with a fairly small range.

- **The class can now do Exercise 16B from Pupil Book 2.**

Exercise 16B — Answers

1 37.4
2 21
3 116 cm
4 163.25 m
5 600.8 (not a very large sample)
6 6
7 For example 5, 7, 9
8 For example 5, 6, 8
9 For example 3, 5, 7, 10, 10
10 **a** 10 **b** 12
11 **a** 16 **b** 8
12 **a** 7.5 **b** 3

Plenary

- Write x, y and z on the board. Tell the class that the mean of these is 100 and the range is 30.
- Now write $x + 10$, $y + 10$ and $z + 10$. Ask the class what the new mean and range are.
- Now write $2x$, $2y$ and $2z$. Ask the class what the new mean and range are.
- Finally, combine the results. Write $2x + 10$, $2y + 10$ and $2z + 10$. Ask the class what the new mean and range are.
- Repeat with a different set of numbers and use the median or mode instead of mean.

Key words
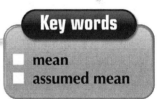

- mean
- assumed mean

Homework

1 Find the mean of 16, 19, 21, 22, 25. Use 20 as the assumed mean.

2 Find the mean of 42, 49, 51, 56, 59. Use 50 as the assumed mean.

3 Find the mean of 22.3, 28.1, 34.2. Use 30 as the assumed mean.

4 Write down four numbers with a mode of 10 and a range of 6.

5 The mean of a set of numbers is 10 and the range is 5. The numbers are now doubled.

   a What is the new mean?   **b** What is the new range?

6 The mean of a set of numbers is 8.4 and the range is 11.1. The numbers are now decreased by 5.

   a What is the new mean?   **b** What is the new range?

Homework Answers

1 20.6
2 51.4
3 28.2
4 For example, 8, 10, 10, 14
5 **a** 20   **b** 10
6 **a** 3.4   **b** 11.1

Framework objectives – Drawing frequency diagrams

Construct graphical representations, on paper and using ICT, and identify which are most useful in the context of the problem. Include: bar charts and frequency; diagrams for discrete and continuous data; simple line graphs for time series.

Oral and mental starter

- Put the words *frequency, table, collect, tally, diagram* and *data* on the board.
- Ask the pupils to sort the words into an order that they can explain, for example, *collect data, tally, frequency table, diagram*. Now ask the class to make the words into a complete sentence. For example, *I am going to collect some data together in a tally chart, which I will then set out as a frequency table and use the information to draw a frequency diagram.*
- You can add other words such as compare, statistic, continuous and discrete.
- This starter can be used to establish a set order of working with statistics, but can also be used as part of the literacy strategy. A further step would be to ask pupils to spell some of the words before putting them on the board.

Main lesson activity

- Sketch a bar chart on the board or OHP. Leave gaps between the bars and label the bars *cats, dogs,* etc.
- Sketch a frequency diagram (with no gaps and equal class intervals) on the board or OHP, labelling the divisions between the bars with continuous data.
- Ask the pupils what the differences are between the two diagrams. They will probably point out the gaps first of all. Ask them why there are gaps on a bar chart. Lead them into talking about discrete data.
- Refer again to the frequency diagram and point out, if necessary, that this diagram has continuous data. State that there should be no gaps.
- Write down a checklist of what is needed for a good frequency diagram for continuous data:
  - A title;
  - Suitable class intervals;
  - Axes labelled, with the horizontal axis labelled at the class boundaries;
  - Neat ruled bars;
  - No gaps.
- Tell the class that, as well as this type of frequency diagram, they will also be required to draw and read from time-series graphs. Show them Example 16.5 and ask them to give you a few facts from the graph. Point out that this type of graph can be used to look at trends.

FM • **The class can now do Exercise 16C from Pupil Book 2.** This exercise covers Functional Maths skills.

1 a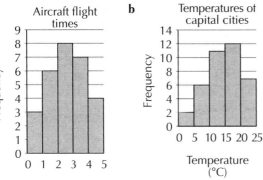

b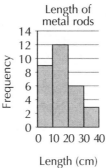

c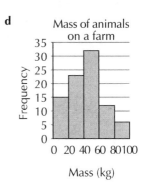

d

Aircraft flight times / Frequency / Time (hours)

Temperatures of capital cities / Frequency / Temperature (°C)

Length of metal rods / Frequency / Length (cm)

Mass of animals on a farm / Frequency / Mass (kg)

2 a City B   **b** City B   **c** 10 months   **d** 15°C

Plenary

- Write four headings on the board: *Time, Temperature, Length, Weight* or *Mass*. Tell the class that these are the most-used categories for continuous data.
- Ask the class to give you units to put into the four columns. Write them in as they give them to you, for example *seconds, °C, miles, kilograms*.
- Summarise the lesson by stressing that continuous data has to have a continuous scale on diagrams.

Key words

- [ ] **bar chart**
- [ ] **line graph**
- [ ] **frequency diagram**
- [ ] **time series**
- [ ] **continuous data**
- [ ] **discrete data**

For each frequency table, construct a frequency diagram.

a Bus journey times:

Time, T (minutes)	Frequency
$0 < T \le 20$	12
$20 < T \le 40$	15
$40 < T \le 60$	9
$60 < T \le 80$	4

b Average temperatures of 37 European Regions:

Average temperature, T (°C)	Frequency
$0 < T \le 5$	4
$5 < T \le 10$	8
$10 < T \le 15$	12
$15 < T \le 20$	9
$20 < T \le 25$	4

c Heights of 50 buildings:

Heights, h (metres)	Frequency
$0 < h \le 10$	25
$10 < h \le 20$	15
$20 < h \le 30$	10

a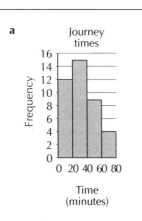

Journey times / Frequency / Time (minutes)

b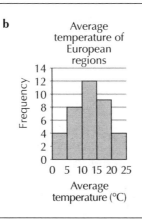

Average temperature of European regions / Frequency / Average temperature (°C)

c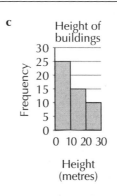

Height of buildings / Frequency / Height (metres)

Framework objectives – Comparing data

Interpret tables, graphs and diagrams for discrete and continuous data, relating summary statistics and findings to the questions being explored.

Compare two distributions using the range and one or more of the mode, median and mean.

Oral and mental starter

- Use a target board as shown:

1	3	5	7	9	11	13
2	4	6	8	10	12	14

- Ask the class to look at the top row and tell you the mean (or average) value. Ask them how they worked it out. Prompt them to refer to the pattern and the symmetry of the line.
- Now ask the class for the mean of the second row, and to compare the first and second rows. Ask them what has happened to each number. Now ask the class for the range of the numbers on the top row and the range of numbers on the bottom row.
- Establish that, although the mean has increased by one, the range is unchanged.
- This starter can be repeated for different second rows, for example, 2, 6, 10, 14, 18, 22, 26.

Main lesson activity

- Write on the board, 'Global warming – Average temperatures will rise by 2 degrees over next 100 years.' Ask the class to explain what will happen to the lowest temperature, the highest temperature and the range.
- Point out that it is unlikely to happen uniformly. Ask them to describe mathematically the effect of the lowest temperature falling and the highest temperature rising. Use terminology such as *more variation* and *less consistent*.
- Now introduce the idea of comparing averages and ranges. Draw a table on the board giving the number of goals by football teams A and B in 6 different matches:

	A	B
	1	0
	0	3
	1	0
	1	7
	1	2
	2	0
Mean	1	2
Range	2	7

- Discuss the differences. Emphasise that they have to compare and not just repeat the data given in the question. Which team would the pupils support?

- **The class can now do Exercise 16D from Pupil Book 2.**

Exercise 16D Answers

1 **a** 15 minutes, 25 minutes, 16 minutes, 8 minutes, 17 minutes   **b** 16.2 minutes
2 **a** 10 °C, 11 °C, 12.5 °C, 13 °C   **b** The further south, the greater the range.
3 Matt did better overall and was more consistent.
4 **a** Mean, range (hours): Everlast 6, 2; Powercell 4, 3; Electro 8.8, 1
   b Any choice if supported by arguments about performance, consistency and price.

Plenary

Key words

- ☐ **comparison**
- ☐ **distribution**
- ☐ **range**
- ☐ **mode**
- ☐ **median**
- ☐ **mean**

- ● Ask the class to explain the advantage of a golf player having a small range on the number of shots taken per hole. Talk about consistency.
- ● Now talk about different pupils spending considerably different lengths of time on their homework. Talk about different average times and less consistency.
- ● Now set the homework!

Homework

1 The table shows the mean and range of a set of golf scores per hole for Emily and Lorna:

	Emily	Lorna
Mean	4.2	6.1
Range	4	3

Compare the mean and range and explain what they tell you.

2 The table shows the median and range of weekly sales of two magazines:

	Teen Mag	*Only 13*
Median	12 000	14 000
Range	1000	3500

Compare the median and range and explain what they tell you.

3 The table shows the mode and range of goals scored by two hockey teams:

	Rotherfield	Shefham
Mode	3	5
Range	1	4

Compare the mode and range and explain what they tell you.

Homework Answers

1 Emily has a better average score, so she will win most holes, but Lorna's scores show less variation.
2 *Teen Mag* sells fewer per week, but sales of *Only 13* fluctuate far more.
3 Shefham generally score more, but are less consistent than Rotherfield.

LESSON 16.5

Framework objectives – Which average to use?

Recognise when it is appropriate to use the range, mean, median and mode and, for grouped data, the modal class.

Oral and mental starter

- Ask the class to give you three numbers with a mode of 5.
- Ask the class to give you three numbers with a median of 6.
- Ask the class to give you three numbers with a mean of 7.
- Ask the class to give you three numbers with a range of 8.
- Ask the class to see if they can make the same three numbers work for more than one statement; for example, 5, 5 and 13 have a mode of 5 and a range of 8.
- Ask the class to give you three numbers and tell you two facts about the numbers; for example, 3, 5 and 10 have a median of 5 and a range of 7.

Main lesson activity

- Explain that this lesson looks at averages, and why sometimes one type of average is better than another.
- Recap the meaning of mode, median, mean and range.
- Explain that for continuous data all the values may be different, and explain this is one reason for putting the data into groups.
- Write down a definition of modal class.
- Put some continuous data, such as a list of times to complete a race, on the board. Ask the pupils to place the data into suitable groups. Perhaps give them the groups to be used.
- Ask them to write down the modal class.
- Ask the class why the mode is not appropriate. Discuss the merits of grouping data.
- Now look at the table of advantages and disadvantages in the pupil book and ask the pupils to write down sets of numbers that satisfy each statement; for example, write down a set of numbers for which the mean would be suitable and a set of numbers for which the mean would not be suitable.
- The class could work in small groups for this activity.
- Explain to the pupils that the guidelines are not set in stone and that some data require caution when deciding which type of average is suitable or not suitable.

- **The class can now do Exercise 16E from Pupil Book 2.**

Exercise 16E Answers

1 a 5.8. Mean is suitable, as the data are evenly distributed.
   b 2. Mode is suitable, as it is a central value.
   c 8. Median is suitable, as it is a central value.
   d 10. Mode may not be suitable, as it is an extreme value.
   e 2. Median may not be suitable, as it is an extreme value.
   f 8.7. Mean may not be suitable, as the data contain an extreme value.

2

Time T (seconds)	Tally	Frequency
$10 < T \le 12$	///	3
$12 < T \le 14$	////	4
$14 < T \le 16$	𝍱 /	6
$16 < T \le 18$	//	2

The ungrouped data all have different values. The grouped data show the most common time interval ($14 < T \le 16$).

3 a 9. The range is suitable, as data are evenly spread.
   b 9. The range could be unsuitable, as one extreme value distorts the result.
   c 9. The range could be unsuitable, as one extreme value distorts the result.
   d 9. The range is suitable, as data are evenly spread.
   e 9. The range is suitable, as much of the data are at both extremes.
   f 12. The range is suitable, as data are evenly spread.

Plenary

Key words

☐ **modal class**
☐ **extreme value**
☐ **appropriate data**
☐ **central value**

● Summarise this lesson by emphasising that there can be more than one valid explanation for why different averages are appropriate.
● Remind the class that they have to be able to write statistical reports which explain why they use a particular measure. Tell them that it is also just as important to say why they do not use a particular measure.

Homework

1 Look at each set of data and give a reason why the chosen average is suitable or not:

   a 1, 3, 4, 8, 10, 11   Mean   **b** 2, 2, 2, 2, 4, 6, 8   Mode
   c 2, 4, 6, 8, 10, 11, 11   Median   **d** 2, 2, 2, 3, 5, 6, 6   Mode
   e 1, 2, 4, 6, 8, 8, 8   Median   **f** 1, 12, 13, 15, 19, 19   Mean

2 Look at each set of data and decide whether the range is suitable or not, and explain your answer:

   a 2, 3, 6, 8, 9, 10   **b** 1, 1, 1, 1, 20   **c** 2, 2, 4, 6, 8
   d 1, 2, 5, 7, 8, 9   **e** 1, 2, 2, 2, 8, 9, 9, 20

5

Homework Answers

1 a Mean is suitable, as the data are evenly distributed.
   b Mode may not suitable, as it is an extreme value.
   c Median is suitable, as it is a central value.
   d Mode may not be suitable, as it is an extreme value.
   e Median may be suitable, although it is numerically closer to one end than the other.
   f Mean may not be suitable, as it has an extreme value.
2 a Range is suitable, as data are evenly spread.
   b Range could be unsuitable, as one extreme value distorts the result.
   c Range is suitable, as data are evenly spread.
   d Range is suitable, as data are evenly spread.
   e Range could be unsuitable, as one extreme value distorts the result.

Framework objectives – Experimental and theoretical probability

Write about and discuss the results of a statistical enquiry using ICT as appropriate; justify the methods used.

Compare estimated experimental probabilities with theoretical probabilities.

Oral and mental starter

- Place 1 black and 3 white pieces of card or counters in a bag. Ask a pupil to pick out a piece without looking. Show it to the class. Ask the class what this tells them about the pieces of card in the bag. Replace it and shuffle the pieces. Repeat 20 times, recording the results on the board.
- Tell the class that there are 4 pieces of card in the bag. Ask a pupil to predict how many black and how many white ones there are.

Main lesson activity

- Continuing from the starter, get a pupil to divide the number of times a black card was picked out of the bag, by the total number of cards picked out. Tell the class that they have calculated an experimental probability of picking a black card from the bag.
- Ask the class a few simple theoretical probability questions. Finish with: 'if there are 4 cards in a bag, 1 of which is black, what is the probability of picking out a black card?'
- Now show the class the contents of the bag and ask if anyone can explain why the theoretical probability differs from the experimental one (assuming it does!).
- Emphasise that if you had carried out the test more times, you would expect the results of the experimental and theoretical probabilities to be closer together, but this may or may not happen.
- For less straightforward events it may be very difficult or impossible to calculate a theoretical probability, so gathering data in an experiment is the only way to estimate the probability of an event occurring again. Illustrate this with an example such as 'the probability of a pupil being late for school'. How would the class work out the experimental probability for this?
- Finish off this part by saying that in the Pupil Book exercise the class will have to devise experiments of their own to compare experimental and theoretical probabilities.

Exercise 16F Answers

1 a $\frac{1}{5}$ 2 a $\frac{1}{6}$ b $\frac{1}{2}$ 3 a $\frac{1}{5}$ 4 a $\frac{1}{2}$

5 a

		First dice					
		1	**2**	**3**	**4**	**5**	**6**
Second dice	**1**	2	3	4	5	6	7
	2	3	4	5	6	7	8
	3	4	5	6	7	8	9
	4	5	6	7	8	9	10
	5	6	7	8	9	10	11
	6	7	8	9	10	11	12

b $\frac{1}{6}$

● **The class can now do Exercise 16F from Pupil Book 2.**

Plenary

● Show the pupils the random-number function on a scientific calculator.
● Tell them that if, for example, the random numbers are from 0 to 0.999, three decimal place values, they could simulate a coin in several ways. They could use the last digit, odd to represent heads and even to represent tails. They could use numbers less than 0.500 for heads and greater than or equal to 0.500 for tails.
● For a dice, they could use the first digit and ignore any values that are not 1, 2, 3, 4, 5 or 6.

Key words

- biased
- event
- experimental probability
- sample
- sample space
- theoretical probability
- theory

Homework

1 a A coin is thrown and an ordinary dice is rolled. Copy and complete the sample space diagram to show all possible outcomes:

	1	2	3	4	5	6
Head	H1	H2				
Tail	T1					

  b What is the theoretical probability of throwing a head and rolling an even number?

  c Design and carry out an experiment to test whether you think the coin and dice are fair.

2 a Complete the list to show all the outcomes for throwing two coins and rolling a dice:

  HH1, HT1, TH1, TT1

  b What is the theoretical probability of throwing two heads and rolling a number 6?

6

Homework Answers

1 a

	1	2	3	4	5	6
Head	H1	H2	H3	H4	H5	H6
Tail	T1	T2	T3	T4	T5	T6

  b $\frac{3}{12}$ or $\frac{1}{4}$

2 a HH1, HT1, TH1, TT1
   HH2, HT2, TH2, TT2
   HH3, HT3, TH3, TT3
   HH4, HT4, TH4, TT4
   HH5, HT5, TH5, TT5
   HH6, HT6, TH6, TT6
  b $\frac{1}{24}$ or 0.042

National Tests Answers

1 a No, because the data is not numeric.
  b Yes, because you can find which sport occurs most frequently.
2 a 6 b 1 and 5 c for example, 1 and 3 and 5 (3 numbers total = 9, range = 4)
3 a $\frac{16}{30}$ b $\frac{3}{30}$ c $\frac{1}{3}$
4 a

8	0.3
14	0.5
6	0.2

  b The probability has decreased.

Functional Maths – Questionnaire

Framework objectives

Calculate statistics for sets of discrete and continuous data, including with a calculator and spreadsheet.

Interpret the results of an experiment using the language of probability.

Oral and mental starter

Look at the information on the questionnaire activity on page 230 of the corresponding Pupil Book. This Functional Maths activity can be introduced once you have covered the previous work on statistics.

- Ask the pupils for the answer to 13×4. (52)
- Ask how they did this. Draw out that they can do this in two parts, $10 \times 4 = 40$ and $3 \times 4 = 12$, then add the two parts together $40 + 12 = 52$. (If someone says it's the number of cards in a four-suited deck, congratulate them and ask them the next one.)
- Now ask for the answer to 13×7. (91)
- Again, get someone to explain how they did it, in two parts $10 \times 7 = 70$ and $3 \times 7 = 21$, add 70 to 21 giving 91.
- Now ask a few more questions, encouraging the pupils to use the technique just shown, for example, 13×5 (65) 13×8. (104)
- Now move on to 15×7, asking for the answer. (105)
- Ask for another explanation, which should be as before, split the sum into two parts and add the answers.
- Ask these questions: 15×5 (75), 16×4 (64), 16×6. (96)

Main lesson activity

- Discuss with the pupils questionnaires they might have been involved in.
- Ask them to suggest questions they might ask on a questionnaire about music and Y8 pupils.
- Look at the data shown in the table on page 230 and make sure the pupils are familiar with the questions being asked to illicit these responses.
- The data handling expected in this spread is:
    reading from a table
    median
    bar charts
    probability.
- You may wish to remind the class of the meaning of median and to ask a few simple probability questions to ensure they remember how to form their answers as fractions and not odds.

- **The class can now work through the questions on pages 230–231.**

1

	frequency	
	Boys	Girls
Arctic Monkeys	10	9
Kate Nash	4	12
Panic! At the Disco	4	4
Spice Girls	0	2
Fall out Boy	8	5
Foo Fighters	14	8

2 Check pupils' pie charts

	Angles	
	Boys	Girls
Arctic Monkeys	90°	81°
Kate Nash	36°	108°
Panic! At the Disco	36°	36°
Spice Girls	0°	18°
Fall out Boy	72°	45°
Foo Fighters	126°	72°

3 a 33 **b** 31.5 **c** 32.5
4 a $\frac{1}{2}$ **b** $\frac{19}{80}$ **c** $\frac{47}{80}$ **d** $\frac{10}{80} = \frac{1}{8}$

Plenary

- Ask the class to suggest a topic for a survey. If they asked similar questions to those given in this exercise, what answers might they have had instead of those shown?
- Ask for a suggestion for a survey questioning their families that evening. It could be anything from favourite TV programmes to the number of minutes spent eating a family meal. If a good suggestion is provided, this can be used for homework.

Homework

Choose one of the following questions.

1 Carry out a survey using the questions suggested at the end of the lesson.

2 Ask your family:

   a How many minutes were taken to prepare the evening meal?

   b How long did it take for the family meal to be eaten, from start to finish?

These results can be put together in a following lesson in order to make a display.

New Maths Frameworking Year 8 Learning Checklists

For use with New Maths Frameworking Year 8 Pupil Book 2

Number and Algebra 1 – Learning Checklist

Level 4

I can write down the multiples of any whole number. ☐

I can work out the factors of numbers under 100. ☐

Level 5

I can add and subtract negative numbers, for example, $-7 + -3 = -10$. ☐

I can write down and recognise the sequence of square numbers. ☐

I know the squares of all numbers up to 15^2 and the corresponding square roots. ☐

I can use a calculator to work out powers of numbers. ☐

I can find any term in a sequence given the first term, say 5, and the term-to-term rule such as 'goes up by 6 each time', for example, the 20th term is 119. ☐

I know that the square roots of positive numbers can have two values, one positive and one negative, for example, $\sqrt{36} = +6$ or -6. ☐

Level 6

I can multiply and divide negative numbers, for example $-5 \times +3 = -15$. ☐

I can find the lowest common multiple (LCM) for pairs of numbers, for example, the LCM of 24 and 30 is 120. ☐

I can find the highest common factor (HCF) for pairs of numbers, for example the HCF of 24 and 30 is 6. ☐

I can write a number as the product of its prime factors, for example, $24 = 2 \times 2 \times 2 \times 3 = 2^3 \times 3$. ☐

I can find any term in a sequence given the algebraic rule for the nth term, for example, for a sequence with an nth term of $6n - 5$ has a 10th term of 55. ☐

I can find the nth term of a sequence in the form $an + b$, for example the nth term of 3, 7, 11, 15, 19, … is $4n - 1$. ☐

I can investigate a mathematical problem. ☐

Geometry and Measures 1 – Learning Checklist

Level 5

I know that the sum of the interior angles of a triangle is 180°. ☐

I can identify the symmetry properties of 2-D shapes. ☐

Level 6

I know that the sum of the interior angles of a quadrilateral is 360°. ☐

I know the angle properties of parallel lines. ☐

I know how to use the properties of quadrilaterals. ☐

I can classify the different types of quadrilaterals. ☐

I know how to devise instructions for a computer to generate 2-D shapes. ☐

I can construct perpendicular lines and bisect angles. ☐

Statistics 1 – Learning Checklist

Level 5

I can calculate probabilities using equally likely outcomes. ☐

Level 6

I can calculate probability from experimental data. ☐

I know what mutually exclusive events are. ☐

I can use the probability of an event to calculate the probability that the event does not happen. ☐

Number 2 – Learning Checklist

Level 5

I can work out least common multiples. ☐

I can calculate a fraction of a quantity. ☐

I can calculate percentages of a quantity. ☐

I can multiply a fraction by a whole number (integer). ☐

Level 6

I can change fractions to decimals. ☐

I can add and subtract fractions with different denominators. ☐

I can calculate one quantity as a percentage of another. ☐

I can use percentages to solve real-life problems. ☐

Algebra 2 – Learning Checklist

Level 4

I can simplify algebraic expressions such as $3 \times 2n = 6n$. ☐

I can solve simple equations such as $4x = 32$. ☐

I can simplify algebraic expressions by collecting like terms, for example $3x + 4y + 2x - y = 5x + 3y$. ☐

Level 5

I know the equivalence of algebraic expressions such as $a + b = b + a$. ☐

I can solve equations with two operations, such as $2x + 5 = 11$. ☐

I can expand a bracket such as $4(2x - 1) = 8x - 4$. ☐

I can write algebraic expressions in a simpler form using index notation, for example, $n \times n \times n \times n \times n = n^5$. ☐

Level 6

I can expand a bracket with a negative sign, for example, $-(3x - 2) = -3x + 2$. ☐

I can expand and simplify expressions with more than one bracket, for example $3(x + 1) - 2(x - 4) = x + 7$. ☐

I can simplify algebraic expressions using index notation, such as $3ab^2 \times 2a^3b^2 = 6a^4b^4$. ☐

Geometry and Measures 2 – Learning Checklist

Level 5

I know how to convert one metric unit into another.

☐

I know how to convert imperial units into metric units using rough equivalents.

☐

Level 6

I can use the approximate formulae to find the area of triangles, parallelograms and trapezia.

☐

I can find the volume of a cuboid.

☐

Algebra 3 – Learning Checklist

Level 5

I can complete a mapping diagram to represent a linear function, for example, $x \rightarrow 2x + 1$.

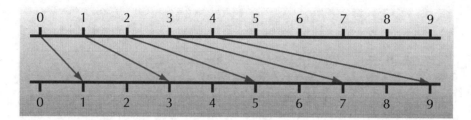

Level 6

I can find the linear function that connect two sets of data, for example, $x = \{1, 2, 3, 4, 5\} \rightarrow y = \{2, 5, 8, 11, 14\}$ is $y = 3x - 1$.

I can complete a table of value for a linear relationship and use this to draw a graph of the relationship.

I can calculate the gradient of a straight line drawn on a coordinate grid and can distinguish between a positive and a negative gradient.

I can draw and interpret graphs that describe real-life situations.

Number 3 – Learning Checklist

Level 5

I can round numbers to one decimal place. ☐

I can use bracket, square and square root keys on a calculator. ☐

I can add and subtract decimals up to two decimal places. ☐

I can multiply and divide decimals up to two decimal places. ☐

Level 6

I can round numbers to two decimal places. ☐

I can multiply and divide by powers of 10. ☐

I can approximate decimals when solving numerical problems. ☐

Geometry and Measures 3 – Learning Checklist

Level 5

I can recognise congruent shapes.

I can recognise and visualise simple transformations of 2-D shapes.

I can solve problems using ratio.

Level 6

I can transform 2-D shapes by a combination of reflections.

I can enlarge a 2-D shape by a scale factor.

Algebra 4 – Learning Checklist

Level 5

I can solve equations of the type $3x + 7 = 10$, for example, where the solution may be fractional or negative.

I can substitute positive and negative numbers into algebraic expressions, for example, work out the value of $4a - 3b$, when $a = 3$ and $b = -2$.

I can substitute positive and negative numbers into formulae, for example work out the value of $A = 2b + 2w$ when $b = 5$ and $w = 3$.

I can devise algebraic formulae to represent simple ideas such as the distance travelled by a car doing 40mph in t hours.

Level 6

I can solve equations of the type $2(3x - 8) = 14$, for example, where the solution may be fractional or negative.

I can solve equations of the type $4x + 9 = 3 + x$, for example, where the solution may be fractional or negative.

I can substitute positive and negative numbers into formulae, for example, work out the value of $A = b^2 + c^2$, where $b = 3$ and $c = 4$.

Statistics 2 – Learning Checklist

Level 5

I can interpret a pie chart.

Level 6

I can interpret stem-and-leaf diagrams.

I can construct a pie chart.

I can understand a scatter diagram and can describe the correlation, if any is shown.

Number 4 – Learning Checklist

Level 5

I can simplify fractions by cancelling common factors. ☐

I can add and subtract simple fractions. ☐

I know the correct order of operations, including using brackets. ☐

I can multiply simple decimals without using a calculator. ☐

Level 6

I can add and subtract fractions by writing them with a common denominator. ☐

I can multiply and divide decimals. ☐

Algebra 5 – Learning Checklist

Level 4

I can simplify algebraic expressions by collecting like terms, for example $3a + 5m + 2a - 3m = 5a + 2m$. ☐

I can solve simple equations of the form $4x = 32$. ☐

Level 5

I can solve equations of the form $6 = \frac{21}{x}$. ☐

I can solve equations of the type $3x + 7 = 10$, for example, where the solution may be fractional or negative. ☐

I can expand brackets such as $4(2a - 1) = 8a - 4$. ☐

I can use algebra to represent a practical situation. ☐

Level 6

I can expand and simplify expressions such as $2(3x + 5) + 2(x - 1) = 8x + 8$. ☐

I can solve equations of the type $2(3x - 8) = 14$, for example, where the solution may be fractional or negative. ☐

I can solve equations of the type $4x + 9 = 3 + x$, for example, where the solution may be fractional or negative. ☐

I can use algebra to set up an equation to represent a practical situation. ☐

I can calculate the gradient of a straight line drawn on a coordinate grid and can distinguish between a positive and a negative gradient. ☐

I can plot the graph of $y = 2x + 1$, for example, using the gradient intercept method. ☐

I can draw and interpret graphs that describe real-life situations. ☐

Level 7

I can solve equations of the type $4x + \frac{3}{x} + 2$, for example. ☐

I can find the equation of a line using the gradient intercept method. ☐

I can change the subject of a formula with at most two variables, for example making a the subject of the formula $b = a + 2$. ☐

Solving Problems – Learning Checklist

Level 5

I can identify the information needed to solve a problem. ☐

I can check a result to see if it is sensible. ☐

I can explain my reasoning. ☐

Level 6

I can solve a complex problem by breaking it down into smaller tasks. ☐

I can justify answers by testing for particular cases. ☐

I can calculate using ratios in appropriate situations. ☐

Geometry and Measures 4 – Learning Checklist

Level 5

I can use coordinates in all four quadrants. ☐

I know how to make a scale drawing. ☐

I know how to use three-figure bearings. ☐

I can construct a triangle given three sides. ☐

Level 6

I know how to draw plans and elevations. ☐

I can calculate the volume and surface area of shapes made from cubes and cuboids. ☐

I can find the circumference and area of a circle. ☐

Statistics 3 – Learning Checklist

Level 5

I can calculate a mean from an assumed mean.

I can compare the range and the mean from two sets of data.

I can decide which average is the best to use in different circumstances.

Level 6

I can construct grouped frequency tables.

I can construct and interpret grouped frequency diagrams.

I can compare experimental and theoretical probability.

New Maths Frameworking Year 8
Practice Book 2 Answers

CHAPTER ① Number and Algebra 1

1A

1 a –4 **b** –1 **c** –7 **d** 16 **d** –12
2 i a 3 **b** 1 **c** –4 **d** 0 **e** 8 **f** 5 **g** 15 **h** 9 **i** 7 **j** 12
   ii a –15 **b** –13 **c** –8 **d** –12 **e** –20 **f** –17 **g** –27 **h** –21 **i** –19 **j** –24
3 a –15 **b** 40 **c** –30 **d** 4 **e** –42 **f** 40 **g** 6 **h** 600
4 a –8 **b** 1 **c** –3 **d** –4 **e** –10 **f** 2 **g** –3 **h** 4
5 a

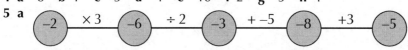

b

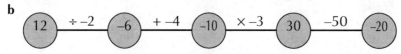

c

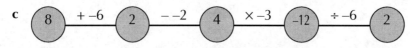

6 Answers will vary. Check calculations. For example:
  a $2 \times -3, -2 \times 3, 1 \times -6, -1 \times 6, -1 \times -2 \times -3$ **b** $5 \div -1, -5 \div 1, 10 \div -2, -15 \div 3, 25 \div -5$
7 a 64 **b** –10 **c** –2 **d** 4 **e** –32 **f** –20 **g** 5
8 a $9 \times (-2 + 1) = -9$ **b** $-4 + (-6 \div -2) = -1$ **c** $5 - (7 + 2) - 4 = -8$

1B

1 a i 3, 6, 9, 12, 15, 18, 21, 24, 27, 30 **ii** 6, 12, 18, 24, 30, 36, 42, 48, 54, 60
  iii 8, 16, 24, 32, 40, 48, 56, 64, 72, 80 **iv** 15, 30, 45, 60, 75, 90, 105, 120, 135, 150
  b i 24 **ii** 30 **iii** 24 **iv** 120
2 a i 1, 2, 3, 4, 6, 12 **ii** 1, 2, 3, 6, 9, 18 **iii** 1, 2, 4, 5, 10, 20 **iv** 1, 2, 3, 5, 6, 10, 15, 30
  b i 6 **ii** 4 **iii** 10 **iv** 2
3 a 8 **b** 30 **c** 56 **d** 36 **4 a** 7 **b** 4 **c** 6 **d** 3

1C

1 a 125 **b** 1331 **c** 1728 **2 a** 576 **b** 3375 **c** 15 625 **d** 43.56 **e** 74.088
  f 389.017
3 a 64 **b** 1024 **c** 4096 **d** 46 656 **e** 6561
4 a 4 **b** 9 **c** 4 **d** 7 **5 a** $x = \pm 7$ **b** $x = \pm 10$ **c** $x = \pm 15$ **d** $x = \pm 1.2$
6 a–d

Number	0.1	0.2	0.3	0.4	0.5	0.6	0.7	0.8	0.9	1
Square	0.01	0.04	0.09	0.16	0.25	0.36	0.49	0.64	0.81	1

7 a&b Answers will vary. **c** Numbers get smaller as power increases because numbers are being repeatedly multiplied by a fraction.
8

Number	0.1	0.2	0.3	0.4	0.5	0.6	0.7	0.8	0.9	1
Cube	0.001	0.008	0.027	0.064	0.125	0.216	0.343	0.512	0.729	1

1D

1 a 50 **b** 24 **c** 294
2 a $6 = 2 \times 3$ **b** $18 = 2 \times 3 \times 3 = 2 \times 3^2$ **c** $32 = 2 \times 2 \times 2 \times 2 \times 2 = 2^5$ **d** $70 = 2 \times 5 \times 7$
  e $36 = 2 \times 2 \times 3 \times 3 = 2^2 \times 3^2$
3 a $14 = 2 \times 7$ **b** $45 = 3 \times 3 \times 5 = 3^2 \times 5$ **c** $96 = 2 \times 2 \times 2 \times 2 \times 2 \times 3 = 2^5 \times 3$
  d $130 = 2 \times 5 \times 13$ **e** $200 = 2 \times 2 \times 2 \times 5 \times 5 = 2^3 \times 5^2$
4 $3 \times 7, 2 \times 11, 23, 2 \times 2 \times 2 \times 3, 5 \times 5, 2 \times 13, 3 \times 3 \times 3, 2 \times 2 \times 7, 29, 2 \times 3 \times 5$
5 a 23, 29 **b** prime numbers **c** 31
6 a $2^3 \times 3 \times 5$ **b** $2^2 \times 3^2 \times 5$ **c** $2^3 \times 3 \times 5^2$

1E

1 a 1, 3, 5, 7, 9, 11, 13, 15, 17, 19, 21 **b** 3, 9, 27, 81, 243
2 a i Start 5, add 3. **ii** Start 2, multiply by 5. **b i** 20, 23 **ii** 1250, 6250
3 a 1, 20, 400, 8000, 160 000 **b** 64, 16, 4, 1, 0.25 **c** –3, 6, –12, 24, –48
4 a i • • • • • • •   • • • • • • • •
     • • • • • •   • • • • • • **ii** 16, 19, 22, 25

    b i   • •   • • **ii** 20, 27, 35, 44
       • • •   • • •
     • • • •   • • • •
   • • • • •   • • • • •
• • • • • •   • • • • • •
   • • • • • •

1F

1 a $a = 6, d = 2$ **b** $a = 30, d = 5$ **c** $a = 100, d = -4$
2 a 7, 13, 19, 25, 31, 37 **b** 2, 4.5, 7, 9.5, 12, 14.5 **c** 8, 3, –2, –7, –12, –17
3 a 2, 6, 18, 54, 162 **b** 20, 17, 14, 11, 8, 5, 2, –1, –4, –7, –10, –13 **c** 1, 3, 7, 13, 21, 31
   d 1, –6, –34, –146, –594, –2386 **e** 500, 50, 5, 0.5, 0.05, 0.005, 0.0005
4 a i 2, 5, 8, 11, 14 **ii** 3 **b i** 7, 9, 11, 13, 15 **ii** 2 **c i** 2, 7, 12, 17, 22 **ii** 5
   d i 20, 30, 40, 50, 60 **ii** 10
5 a $6n + 1$ **b** $3n + 2$ **c** $6n + 2$ **d** $3n - 2$ **e** $7n + 9$
6 Answers will vary. Typical answers shown.
   a $A = -1$, rule: subtract 2 **b** $A = 5$, rule: subtract 2 **c** $A = 300$, rule: divide by 10

1G

1 a 24 slabs **b** Number of slabs = 2 × Pond size + 6
2 Number of matches = 3 × Number of squares + 1
3 a

Number of Saturdays	Account balance, £
1	4
2	8
3	12
4	16
5	20
6	24

   b Account balance = 4 × Number of Saturdays since account opened

CHAPTER ❷ Geometry and Measures 1

2A

1 a *f* and *d* are alternate angles. **b** *c* and *g* are corresponding angles.
   c *e* and *a* are corresponding angles. **d** *c* and *e* are alternate angles
   e *d* and *h* are corresponding angles.
2 a For example: *u* and *s*, *t* and *r*, *e* and *c*, *f* and *d*, *d* and *q*, *a* and *r*, *h* and *u*, *e* and *v*.
   b For example: *a* and *p*, *b* and *q*, *c* and *r*, *d*, and *s*, *e* and *t*, *f* and *u*, *g* and *v*, *h* and *w*.
3 a   **b**

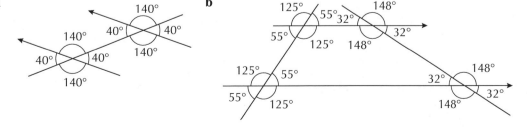

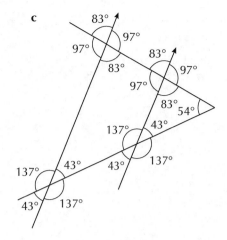

2B

2B

1 $a = 40°$, $b = 140°$, $c = 67°$, $d = 150°$, $e = 53°$, $f = 74°$, $g = 127°$
2 $a = 54°$, $b = 48°$, $c = 37°$ 3 $a = 108°$, $b = 72°$, $c = 89°$ 4 $a = 75°$, $b = 105°$, $c = 55°$

2C

1 $a = 180° - b$, $a = 180° - d$, hence $b = d$
  $d = 180° - a$, $d = 180° - c$, hence $a = c$
2 $e = f$ (isosceles triangles), $b = c$ (congruent triangles), $b + c = 180°$ (angles on a straight line),
  hence $b = c = 90°$
3 $a = d$ (alternate angles), $b = c$ (alternate angles), hence $a + b = c + d$

2D

1

Two pairs of equal angles	Rotational symmetry of order 4	Exactly two lines of symmetry	Exactly two right angles	Exactly four equal sides
square rectangle parallelogram rhombus kite arrowhead	square rhombus	rectangle rhombus	kite trapezium	square rhombus

2 kite   3 kite   4 square, rhombus, kite, trapezium
5 square, rectangle, some kites and some trapezia

2E

1–4 Check constructions.
5   (Not to scale)

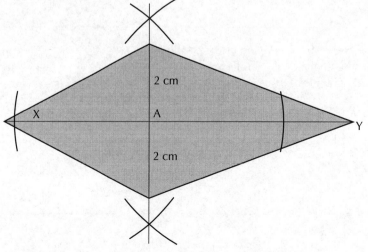

6 Answers will vary. Check constructions and comparisons.

CHAPTER **3** Statistics 1

3A

1

d	a		c		e	b
Impossible	Very unlikely	Unlikely	Evens	Likely	Very likely	Certain

2 Answers will vary.

3 a odd number   **b** equally likely   **c** multiple of 3   **d** triangle number

4 a Picking a shape with a right angle is unlikely.
  b Picking a shape with at least two equal sides is very likely.
  c Picking a shape with four angles is certain.
  d Picking a shape with two acute angles is an even chance.
  e Picking a shape with no equal sides is very unlikely.
  f Picking a shape with three sides is impossible.

3B

1

Event	Probability of event occurring (p)	Probability of event not occurring ($1 - p$)
A	$\frac{2}{5}$	$\frac{3}{5}$
B	0.75	0.25
C	$\frac{5}{8}$	$\frac{3}{8}$
D	0.12	0.88
E	$\frac{19}{20}$	$\frac{1}{20}$
F	0.875	0.125
G	74%	26%

2 0.991   **3 a** $\frac{1}{5}$ **b** $\frac{3}{4}$ **c** $\frac{39}{100} = 0.39$ **d** $\frac{84}{100} = 0.84$
          4 a $\frac{1}{3}$ **b** $\frac{1}{4}$ **c** $\frac{1}{4}$ **d** $\frac{3}{4}$ **e** $\frac{2}{3}$ **f** $\frac{3}{4}$ **g** $\frac{5}{6}$ **5 a** $\frac{9}{10}$ **b** 0.18   **c** 65%

3C

1 a mutually exclusive   **b** not mutually exclusive   **c** mutually exclusive
  d not mutually exclusive   **e** not mutually exclusive   **f** not mutually exclusive

2 a A and B, C, D, H
    B and A, H
    C and A, H
    D and A, F, G
    F and D, H
    G and D, H
    H and A, B, C, F, G

  b A and E, F, G
    B and C, D, E, F, G
    C and B, D, E, F, G
    D and B, C, E, H
    E and A, B, C, D, F, G, H
    F and A, B, C, E
    G and A, B, C, E
    H and D, E

3 (1, 1) (1, 2) (1, 3) (1, 4) (1, 5) (1, 6)   (4, 1) (4, 2) (4, 3) (4, 4) (4, 5) (4, 6)
  (2, 1) (2, 2) (2, 3) (2, 4) (2, 5) (2, 6)   (5, 1) (5, 2) (5, 3) (5, 4) (5, 5) (5, 6)
  (3, 1) (3, 2) (3, 3) (3, 4) (3, 5) (3, 6)   (6, 1) (6, 2) (6, 3) (6, 4) (6, 5) (6, 6)

3D

1 a $\frac{1}{3}$ **b** $\frac{1}{3}$ **c** $\frac{5}{9}$ **d** $\frac{5}{9}$ **e** $\frac{2}{3}$ **f** $\frac{2}{3}$

2 a

Kim	1p	2p	5p	10p	20p	50p	£1
Franz	1p	2p	5p	10p	20p	50p	£1

b i $\frac{1}{14}$ **ii** $\frac{3}{14}$ **iii** $\frac{1}{7}$ **iv** $\frac{13}{14}$ **v** $\frac{5}{7}$

3 a

		Red taxi					
		1	**2**	**3**	**4**	**5**	**6**
	1	2	3	4	5	6	7
	2	3	4	5	6	7	8
Green taxi	**3**	4	5	6	7	8	9
	4	5	6	7	8	9	10
	5	6	7	8	9	10	11

b i $\frac{5}{30} = \frac{1}{6}$ **ii** $\frac{1}{30}$ **iii** 0   **iv** $\frac{6}{30} = \frac{1}{5}$ **v** $\frac{15}{30} = \frac{1}{2}$ **vi** $\frac{6}{30} = \frac{1}{5}$

3E

1 a

Recording period	Number of days of rain	Experimental probability
30	12	0.4
60	33	0.55
100	42	0.42
200	90	0.45
500	235	0.47

b 0.47 based on largest period   **c** 0.53   **d** a greater chance of it not raining.

2 Answers will vary. Ask a friend or classmate to check your results.

CHAPTER ④ Number 2

4A

1 a $\frac{6}{10} = \frac{3}{5}$ **b** $\frac{36}{100} = \frac{9}{25}$ **c** $\frac{65}{100} = \frac{13}{20}$ **d** $\frac{255}{1000} = \frac{51}{200}$ **e** $\frac{25}{1000} = \frac{1}{40}$

2 a 0.26   **b** 0.68   **c** 0.8   **d** 0.15

3 a $\frac{3}{8} = 0.375$ **b** $\frac{2}{7} = 0.\dot{2}8571\dot{4}$ **c** $\frac{9}{25} = 0.36$ **d** $\frac{13}{40} = 0.325$ **e** $0.8\dot{3}$

   f 0.38   **g** $0.\dot{4}$ **h** $0.2\dot{1}4285\dot{7}$ **i** 0.9375   **j** $0.\dot{7}6190\dot{4}$

4 a $\frac{3}{25} = 0.12$, $\frac{1}{7} \approx 0.143$ (larger)   **b** $\frac{11}{18} \approx 0.61$ (larger), $\frac{9}{16} = 0.5625$

   c $\frac{7}{11} \approx 0.636$, $\frac{29}{40} = 0.725$ (larger)

5 $\frac{33}{50} = 0.66$, $\frac{5}{7} \approx 0.714$, $\frac{13}{16} \approx 0.8125$, $\frac{22}{27} \approx 0.815$

6 a i $\frac{8}{9}$ **ii** $\frac{73}{99}$ **iii** $\frac{657}{999}$ **iv** $\frac{1234}{9999}$ **v** $\frac{4}{90}$ **vi** $\frac{36}{990}$ **vii** $\frac{2}{99}$ **viii** $\frac{28}{9900}$ **vii** $\frac{5}{999}$

4B

1 a 10   **b** 24   **c** 6   **d** 30   **e** 36   **2 a** $\frac{9}{10}$ **b** $\frac{17}{24}$ **c** $1\frac{1}{6}$ **d** $1\frac{6}{35}$

3 a $\frac{1}{10}$ **b** $\frac{7}{18}$ **c** $\frac{5}{24}$ **d** $\frac{9}{20}$

4 a $1\frac{2}{21}$ **b** $\frac{13}{24}$ **c** $1\frac{11}{18}$ **d** $1\frac{4}{5}$ **e** $\frac{5}{18}$ **f** $\frac{1}{3}$ **g** $\frac{11}{15}$ **h** $1\frac{1}{12}$ **5 a** $1\frac{1}{2}$ **b** $2\frac{7}{12}$ **c** $\frac{11}{24}$ **d** $1\frac{17}{20}$

4C

1 a 7   **b** 18   **c** 12   **d** 18

2 a 16 kg   **b** 250 ml   **c** 28 cm   **d** 13 km   **e** 18 cm   **f** 35 grams   **g** £48   **h** 560 litres

3 a $1\frac{5}{7}$ **b** $7\frac{1}{2}$ **c** $2\frac{1}{10}$ **d** 6

4 a $\frac{2}{15}$ **b** $\frac{4}{27}$ **c** $\frac{1}{9}$ **d** $\frac{3}{28}$

4D

1 a 76%   **b** 65%   **c** 24%   **d** 6%   **2 a** 61%   **b** 68%   **c** 9%   **d** 46%

3 a 43.75%   **b** 56.25%   **4** Labour 46.4%, Liberal Democrat 29.6%, Conservative 23.9%

5 34.3%, 27.6%, 38.2%

6 a Algebra 28.75%, Number 41.25%, Shape and Space 30%   **b** Total time = 110 minutes; Algebra 20.9%, Number 30%, Shape and Space 21.8%, Extension 27.3%

4E

1 a $48 **b** 190 kg **c** 2.8p **d** 3900 m **e** 333.5 ml **f** £1.14 **2** 81 words per minute

3 John £213, Hans £160, Will £238 (largest)

4 a 299.72 cm² **b** £2.44 **c** 10 500.21 g **d** 0.9694 litres **e** £522 **f** 514.8 kg

5 £84.60 **6 a** 327.68 ≈ 328 **b** Decrease 327.68 by 15% to get 278.528 ≈ 279

7 a 415k **b** 421.8k **c** 504.35k **d** 101.12k (the smallest)

4F

1 a £188 + £3810.40 = £3998.40 **b** £20 001.60 **c** £1666.80 **d** £600.05

   e New salary = £25 680; tax paid = £188 + £4180 = £4368; salary received = £21 312;
    monthly salary after tax = £1776; pension scheme payment = £639.36 per year

2 Amount to be divided between children = £43 005; Derek £15 911.85, Maria £12 471.45,
   Jason £14 621.70

3 Trustworthy Cars £13 320, Bargain Autos £14 364, Future Car Sales £13 092 (cheapest)

4 a £600 **b** £649.96

CHAPTER ⑤ Algebra 2

5A

1 a $\dfrac{x}{5}$ **b** $3b$ **c** $4mn$ **d** $\dfrac{p}{q}$ **e** $2(x-1)$ **f** $5m+3$ **g** $\dfrac{c}{d+2}$ **h** $\dfrac{5t}{4}$ **i** $(a+b)(m-n)$

2 a $6nt$ **b** $15km$ **c** $5gh$ **d** $24tuv$

3 a incorrect **b** incorrect **c** correct **d** incorrect **e** incorrect **f** correct

4 $st+3 = 3+st = 3+t\times s = t\times s+3$ $3\div s+t = t+\dfrac{3}{s}$
   $3s+t = t+s3 = s\times 3+t$ $3\times s\times t = s3t$
   $t\times 3+s = s+3t$

5 a $x=3$ **b** $p=8$ **c** $m=11$ **d** $c=7$ **e** $k=2.75$ **f** $f=15.375$

6 a correct **b** correct **c** incorrect **d** correct **e** incorrect **f** incorrect

5B

1 a $y, 2x, -3$ **b** $4x, 3, 2x$ **c** $\dfrac{4}{t}, -u$ **d** $3x^2, 14x, 2$

2 a $11i$ **b** $5r$ **c** $-2u$ **d** $4h$ **e** $-2y$ **f** $2m$ **g** $-5t$ **h** n **i** $9zt$ **j** $-2ab$ **k** $-ad$ **l** $2f^2$

3 a $10k+3l$ **b** $7h+i$ **c** $13y+2x$ **d** $6p-1$ **e** $-3d+2e$ **f** $3t-2u$ **g** $-w+3x$
   h $5fg+7f$ **i** $4s^2-t^2$

4 a $7q+7i$ **b** $5z+2b$ **c** $11u+7v$ **d** $9j+2k$ **e** $-2m+3n$ **f** $6d-2e$ **g** $5c-d$
   h $2r-11s$ **i** $-g+h$

5C

1 a $2f+2k$ **b** $st-4s$ **c** $8a+12$ **d** $mn+3mr$ **e** $9w-6s$ **f** $2ab-3a$ **g** $5s+5t-5u$
   h $2d-3dr+4dg$

2 a $-p-q$ **b** $-3r+s$ **c** $-4a-4b$ **d** $-2m+2n$ **e** $-10d+15e$

3 a $10f+4g$ **b** $11k-3s$ **c** $-2x+4y$

4 a $9p+11q$ **b** $11i+j$ **c** $10b-12a$ **d** $11m-7n$ **5 a** $2t-3u$ **b** $5m+n$ **c** $-x-4y$

6 a $2h+i$ **b** $9s+8t$ **c** $-2w-11v$

5D

1 a perimeter = $4x+10$, area = $10x$ **b** perimeter = $8n+8$, area = $12n+3$
   c perimeter = $2p+10$, area = $pq+2(5-q) = pq+10-2q$
   d perimeter = $14+2b+2a$, area = $5a-2b$ **e** perimeter = $4m+14$, area = $4m-14$

2 a $5a$ **b** A = 9, B = 6, C = $2a-6$, D = $3a-9$ **c** A + B + C + D = 9 + 6 = $2a-6+3a-9 = 5a$

3 Answers will vary. Typical answers shown.

a   **b**   **c**   **d**

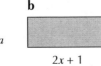

1 a g^6 **b** $9k^2$ **c** $15t^2$ **d** $4r^2$ **e** $8j^3$ **2 a** $8m$ **b** t^5 **c** $3d + e^3$
3 $6w = w + w + w + w + w + w$ $w^6 = w \times w \times w \times w \times w \times w$
4 a $3v + v^2$ **b** $3m^2 - 2mn$ **c** $3DE - 2D^2$ **d** $6s^2 + 9st$
5 a $5ab + 2a$ **b** $2v^2 + 2vt$ **c** $6qz + 2q^2$
6 a $2r^2 + 4rs + s^2$ **b** $3p^2 + 2pq - 5q^2$ **c** $3m^2 - 4n^2$ **d** $3c^2 - 7cd + d^2$
7 a $5g^2 + 4g$ **b** $5d^2 + 3de$ **c** $w - 4w^2$

CHAPTER **6** Geometry and Measures 2

6A

1 a 27 cm² **b** 2 m² **c** 345 mm² **d** 72 m² **e** 44 cm² **f** 72 mm²

2

Base	Height	Area
12 cm	9 cm	54 cm²
8 cm	14 cm	56 cm²
6 mm	7 mm	21 mm²
16 cm	8 cm	64 cm²
10 m	20 m	100 m²

3 Answers will vary. Check areas are 24 cm².
4 A = 6 cm², B = 9 cm², C = 19 cm², D = 6 cm², E = 12 cm², F = 4 cm², G = 6 cm²,
H = 2 cm²

6B

1 a 40 mm² **b** 352 cm² **c** 15 m² **d** 13.75 cm²

2

Base	Height	Area
7 cm	13 cm	91 cm²
9 m	19 m	171 m²
250 mm	70 mm	17 500 mm²
8 m	15 m	120 m²
12 cm	2.5 cm	30 cm²

3 Answers will vary. Check areas are 48 cm².
4 A = 7 cm², B = 6 cm², C = 10 cm², D = 6.5 cm², E = 6 cm², F = 4 cm², G = 5 cm²,
H = 5.5 cm², I = 7 cm², J = 4 cm², K = 3 cm².

6C

1 a 40 cm² **b** 160 mm² **c** 30 cm² **d** 3600 mm²

2

Parallel side a	Parallel side b	Height h	Area
7 cm	9 cm	3 cm	24 cm²
13 m	8 m	5 m	52.5 m²
2 mm	6 mm	8 mm	32 mm²
16 m	4 m	6 m	60 m²
12 cm	38 cm	10 cm	250 cm²

3 Answers will vary. Check areas are 24 cm².
4 A = 7 cm², B = 8 cm², C = 6 cm², D = 7 cm², E = 7.5 cm², F = 10 cm², G = 4 cm²,
H = 5.5 cm², I = 9 cm².

6D

1 a i 76 m² **ii** 1376 cm² **iii** 282 cm² **b i** 40 m³ **ii** 3360 cm³ **iii** 162 cm³
   c i 40 000 litres **ii** 3.36 litres **iii** 162 ml
2 volume = 216 cm³, surface area = 216 cm², capacity = 216 ml
3 a mini 288 cm³, medium 10 368 cm³, giant 38 880 cm³ **b** 3.75 **c i** 36 **ii** 135
   d mini 14 g, medium 518 g, giant 1.944 kg
4 a 1380 cm³ **b** 35 000 mm³

6E

1 a 350 lb   **b** 12 320 yd   **c** 115 in   **d** 7840 lb

2 a 5 lb 3 oz   **b** 177 yd 1 ft   **c** 9 gall 3 pt   **d** 10 ft 5 in   **3 a** 160 st   **b** 5280 ft

4 a 330 g   **b** 432 km   **c** 250 cm = 2.5 m   **d** 3.625 kg

5 a 45 miles   **b** 14 oz   **c** 18 gall   **d** 1 lb 8 oz   **6** 640 in = 53 ft 4 in = 17 yd 2 ft 4 in   **7** $\frac{1}{2}$ pt

8 $1\frac{1}{2}$ lb flour (using 1 lb = 500 g), 12 oz butter (using 1 oz = 30 g), $10\frac{1}{2}$ oz sugar,

   $2\frac{1}{2}$ oz rice flour, $\frac{1}{2}$ oz salt

9 a 1 yd ≈ 90 cm   **b** 1 lb ≈ 480 g   **c** 1 mile ≈ 1584 m

CHAPTER ❼ Algebra 3

7A

1

2

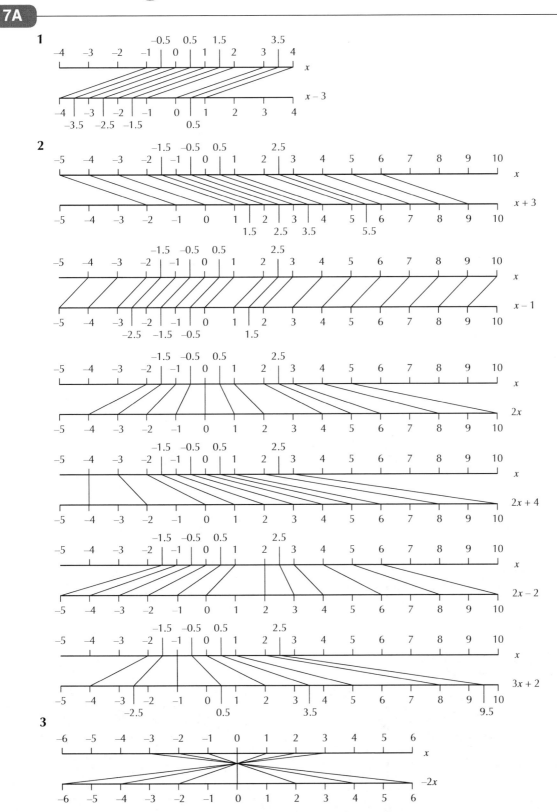

3

7B

1 a $x \rightarrow x + 6$ b $x \rightarrow 2x$ c $x \rightarrow x - 2$ d $x \rightarrow 2x + 1$ e $x \rightarrow 3x - 1$ f $x \rightarrow 2x + 5$
 g $x \rightarrow 4x - 2$
2 a $x \rightarrow 3x - 1$ b $x \rightarrow 3x + 2$ c $x \rightarrow 5x - 3$ d $x \rightarrow 4x$ e $x \rightarrow 2x - 3$
3 a $x \rightarrow 2x + 3$ b $x \rightarrow 3x - 2$ c $x \rightarrow 5x + 1$

7C

1 a

x	−3	−2	−1	0	1	2	3
$y = 3x$	−9	−6	−3	0	3	6	9

b&c *See graph below.*

2 a

x	0	1	2	3	4	5
$y = 4x - 3$	−3	1	5	9	13	17

b&c *See graph below.*

3 a

x	−2	−1	0	1	2	3
$y = x + 2$	0	1	2	3	4	5
$y = 2x + 2$	−2	0	2	4	6	8
$y = 3x + 2$	−4	−1	2	5	8	11
$y = 4x + 2$	−6	−2	2	6	10	14

b&c *See graph below.*

d They all cross the y-axis at $y = 2$. e They have different gradients.

1   b&c

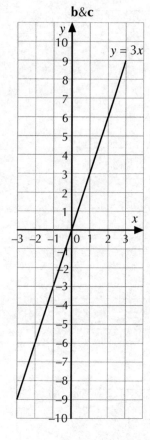

2 b&c

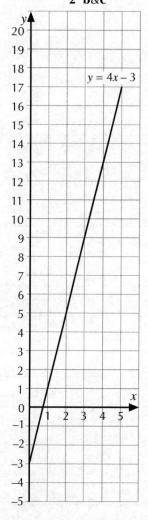

3 b&c

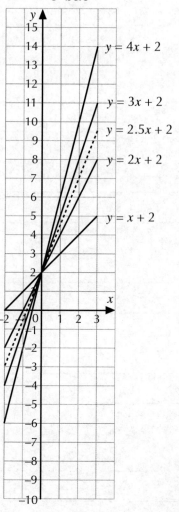

7D

1 a i 3   **ii** 1   **iii** 3   **iv** 2   **b i** 3   **ii** 1   **iii** 0   **iv** 4
2 a $y = 3x + 3$ **b** $y = x + 1$ **c** $y = 3x$ **d** $y = 2x + 4$
3 b 1   **c** (0, 2)   **d** $y = x + 2$

7E

1 a&b

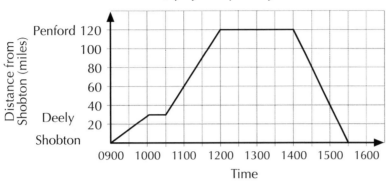

c $120 ÷ 1.5 = 80$ mph

2 a&b

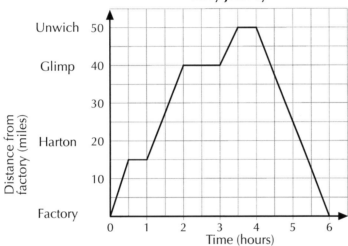

c i 20 mph   **ii** 25 mph

3

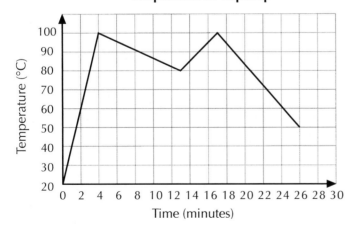

CHAPTER **8** Number 3

8A

1 a 27 000   **b** 500   **c** 380 000   **d** 80   **2 a** 0.73   **b** 0.004   **c** 0.0028   **d** 35.842
3 a 7400   **b** 1 300 000   **c** 0.000 87   **d** 0.174   **e** 6.5   **f** 0.001 94
4 a i 2.8   **ii** 0.28   **b i** 0.006   **ii** 0.0006   **c i** 0.0105   **ii** 0.001 05
  d i 98.51   **ii** 9.851
5 a i 400   **ii** 4000   **b i** 80 000   **ii** 800 000   **c i** 90   **ii** 900   **d i** 6720   **ii** 67 200
6 a 2000 → 200 000 → 200 → 0.2 → 20 → 200 000 → 2 000 000 → 20
  b 7 → 700 → 0.7 → 0.0007 → 0.07 → 700 → 7000 → 0.07
  c 0.6 → 60 → 0.06 → 0.000 06 → 0.006 → 60 → 600 → 0.006
7 a i 8.3   **ii** 8.27   **b i** 4.0   **ii** 3.97   **c i** 0.0   **ii** 0.05
  d i 5.0   **ii** 4.99   **e i** 0.1   **ii** 0.10
8 a 142.81   **b** 639.42   **c** 22.561

8B

1 a Nine hundred and fifty-six thousand, three hundred and forty-eight.
  b Fifteen million, two hundred and thirty thousand, four hundred and twenty-one.
  c Eight million, two thousand and forty.
  d Six hundred and four million, five hundred thousand and two.
2 a 206 107   **b** 50 032 008
3

Hour	Number of shares sold (millions)
9.30 – 10.30	7.2
10.30 – 11.30	5.7
11.30 – 12.30	3.7
12.30 – 1.30	3.3
1.30 – 2.30	3.9
2.30 – 3.30	4.5
3.30 – 4.30	7.8

4 a i 7 250 000   **ii** 7 200 000   **iii** 7 000 000   **b i** 1 950 000   **ii** 2 000 000   **iii** 2 000 000
  c i 650 000   **ii** 600 000   **iii** 1 000 000   **d i** 9 600 000   **ii** 9 600 000   **iii** 10 000 000
5 a Luton, Birmingham   **b** 130 000 000

8C

1 a Last digit should be 3, not 1.   **b** Estimate $60 \times 30 = 1800$ shows answer too small.
  c Estimate $900 \div 10 = 90$ shows answer too small.
2 a $6800 - 500 = 6300$ **b** $30 \times 120 = 3600$ **c** $500 \div 20 = 25$
  d $800 \times 800 = 640000$ **e** $\dfrac{60 + 40}{20} = 100 \div 20 = 5$
3 a 15×22
4 a Yes, because $5 \times £3.71 < 5 \times £4 = £20$.   **b** Last digit should be 0 because $5 \times 8 = 40$.
5 a 6.55   **b** 3.9   **c** –7

8D

1 a 24.13   **b** 1.72   **c** 35.228   **d** 5.355   **e** 116.725
2 a 3.52 m   **b** 1.48 m   **c** 0.645 m   **d** 0.2439 m   **3 a** 2.729 litres   **b** 2.27 litres
4 a 15.259 kg   **b** $10.886 - 4.373 = 6.513$ kg   **5** 25.34 cm

8E

1 a 11.6   **b** 3.8809   **c** 6.25   **2 a** $\frac{11}{18}$ **b** $9\frac{17}{20}$ **c** $23\frac{1}{4}$ **d** $2\frac{1}{4}$ **e** $9\frac{513}{784}$ **f** $\frac{1}{8}$
3 a 2187   **b** 3.1   **c** 240.1   **d** 0.9
e 2.6
4 a $28\frac{19}{60}$ turns in total (or $21\frac{31}{60}$ turns clockwise)   **b** $13\frac{3}{4} \approx 13$ days   **c** £28.96   **d i** $\frac{1}{120}$ **ii** $\frac{14}{375}$ **iii** $\frac{29}{1000}$

8F

1 a 48.36   **b** 25.08   **c** 11.637   **d** 0.3822   **2 a** 5.4   **b** 0.15   **c** 1.3   **d** 3.2   **3** 402.9 cm
4 a £4.76   **b** 20   **c** $18 \times £0.70 = £12.60$, $26 \times £0.24 = £6.24$ (cheaper)

CHAPTER ❾ Geometry and Measures 3

9A

1 A = F, B = E, C = D
2 A = H, B = D = N, C = J = L, E = G = M, F = I, K = O
4 Answers will vary. Check congruence of shapes indicated.

9B

1 a i translation 2 right, 5 down **ii** 180° rotation about origin **iii** reflection in *y*-axis
  iv 90° clockwise rotation about origin **v** translation 4 left, 5 up
  b i reflection in *y*-axis followed by reflection in *x*-axis **ii** translation 4 right, 5 down followed by
  reflection in *x*-axis (or reflection in *x*-axis followed by translation 4 right, 5 up)
  iii 90° anticlockwise rotation about origin followed by translation 5 left, 4 down

2 a–c

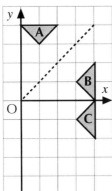

3 a

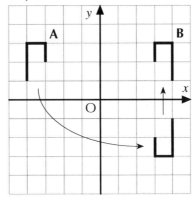

  d 90° clockwise rotation about origin

  b 180° rotation about origin followed by
  reflection in the *x*-axis

4 a 360° rotation about origin
  b any two clockwise/anticlockwise rotations that add up to 360°; two reflections in the same mirror
  line; two translations, e.g. 3 right, 2 up then 3 left, 2 down, etc.

9C

1

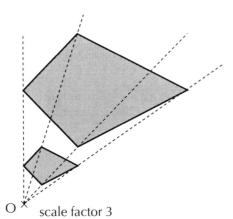

scale factor 3   scale factor 2

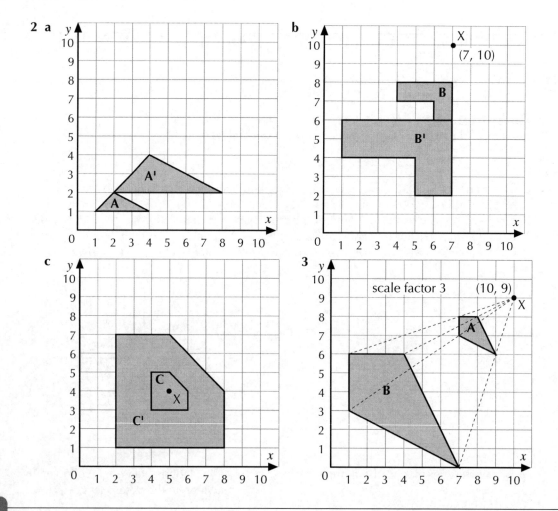

2 a

b X (7, 10)

c

3 scale factor 3 (10, 9)

1 a 9:2 **b** 4:9 **c** 3:4 **d** 9:20 **e** 13:16
2 a 2:3 **b** 2:9 **c** $\frac{2}{9}$ **d** 9:20 **e** B $= \frac{9}{20}$ C; $\frac{9}{20} = 0.45 > \frac{2}{9} = 0.\dot{2}$
3 a 3:2 **b** 40 m^2 **c i** 120 m^2 **ii** 80 m^2
4 a 46 m : 26 m = 23:13 **b** 30 m^2 **c** 120 m^2 – 30 m^2 = 90 m^2 **d** 3:1

CHAPTER ⑩ Algebra 4

10A

1 a $a = 2$ **b** $n = 7$ **c** $v = 10$ **d** $x = 4$ **e** $c = 9$ **f** $y = 3$
2 a $t = 5$ **b** $m = 2$ **c** $d = 5$ **d** $s = 11$ **e** $z = 4$ **f** $i = 8$
3 a $q = 3.5$ **b** $h = 1.2$ **c** $y = 4.8$ **d** $f = 2\frac{1}{3}$ **e** $e = 1\frac{3}{4}$ **f** $w = 2.8$
4 a $n = 5$ **b** $p = 7$ **c** $g = 8$ **d** $r = 2$ **e** $b = 3$ **f** $i = 3$
5 a $r = 7$ **b** $x = 1.4$ **c** $y = 2$ **d** $a = 9$ **e** $h = 4$ **f** $u = 4.5$

10B

1 a $x = -3$ **b** $y = -6$ **c** $a = -1$ **d** $C = -5$ **2 a** $x = -2$ **b** $b = 5$ **c** $m = -3$ **d** $q = -4$
3 a $d = 4$ **b** $x = -5$ **c** $z = -6$ **d** $t = -2$ **4 a** $i = -7$ **b** $H = -2$ **c** $k = 2$ **d** $x = -5$
5 a $x = -3$ **b** $u = -2$ **c** $d = 5$ **d** $m = -4$ **6 a** $s = -1$ **b** $m = 3$ **c** $n = -2$ **d** $y = 5$
7 a $x = -2$ **b** $x = 4$ **c** $f = -3$ **d** $x = -8$ **e** $w = 2$ **f** $d = -4$

10C

1 a $y = 3$ **b** $x = 5$ **c** $u = 5$ **d** $p = 8$ **2 a** $x = 5$ **b** $c = 3$ **c** $d = 6$ **d** $p = 2$
3 a $g = 2$ **b** $i = 3$ **c** $h = 3$ **d** $t = 9$ **4 a** $k = 5$ **b** $x = 4$ **c** $x = 4$ **d** $r = 6.5$
5 a $y = -5$ **b** $k = -2$ **c** $j = -8$ **d** $d = -3$ **e** $r = -3$ **f** $n = -3$
6 a $x = 2$ **b** $g = 4$ **c** $s = 11$ **d** $w = -9$

10D

1 a i $x = 11$ **ii** $x = 31$ **iii** $x = -9$ **b i** $p = -38$ **ii** $p = -2$ **iii** $p = 70$
  c i $d = 49$ **ii** $d = 36$ **iii** $d = 1$ **d i** $s = 18$ **ii** $s = 200$ **iii** $s = 8$
  e i $m = 11$ **ii** $m = -4$ **iii** $m = 11$ **f i** $n = 20$ **ii** $n = -10$ **iii** $n = -85$
2 a 7 **b** 14 **c** 34 **e** 16 **3 a** –1 **b** –8 **c** 15
4 a 12 **b** 20 **c** 32 **d** –44 **5 a** –30 **b** –1 **c** –1 **d** 40

10E

1 a 52.5 kg **b** 72 kg **c** 60 kg **2 a** 36 **b** 460 **c** 6 **3 a** £24 **b** £13.50 **c** £0.72
4 a 3.6 **b** 0.6 **c** 1.2 **5 a** 75 cm² **b** 18.75 cm² **c** 2.43 cm²

10F

1 a $d + 3$ **b** $u - 5$ **c** $7ws$ **d** $\dfrac{m}{3}$ **e** $5f$ **2 a** $12Y$ **b** $\dfrac{x}{100}$

3 a $(H - 5)$ cm **b** $(H + x)$ cm **c** $(S - H)$ cm **d** $\dfrac{S + H}{2}$ cm

4 a i $(c + f)$ pence **ii** $5f$ pence **iii** $(3c + 2f)$ pence
  b i $(200 - c - f)$ pence **ii** $(200 - 5f)$ pence **iii** $(200 - 3c - 2f)$ pence

CHAPTER ⑪ Statistics 2

11A

1 a 38 mph **b** 34 mph **c** 39 mph **d** 18
2 Note: there are only 23 children's ages given, not 25 as stated in the question.
  a 12 **b** 14 children **c** modes are 11 years 9 months and 12 years 10 months; median = 12 years 3 months; range = 1 year, 8 months

3 a

0	8
1	0 6 8
2	3 5 9
3	0 3 8
4	4 5 8 8
5	0 9
6	0 2 3 4 7
7	4 8
8	8
9	0 2 6

Key: 4 | 5 means 45 g

b 48 g **c** 88 g **d** 48 g **e** 11 letters

11B

1 a 150 **b** 125 **c** 125 **d** 200 **2 a** 500 **b** 200 **c** 100 **d** 400
3 a 4 **b** 3 **c** 3 **d** 6 **e** 8 **4 a** 12 **b** 9 **c** 6 **d** 36

11C

1 a Numbers of birds spotted   **b** Sizes of dresses sold in a week

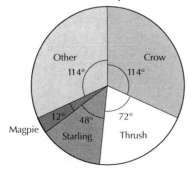

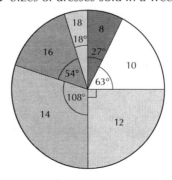

2 a 15 **b** 50 **c** 45 **d** 40

11D

1 a positive correlation: the higher the price, the more goals scored
  b no correlation
  c no correlation
  d negative correlation: the higher the age, the fewer goals scored
2 a positive correlation: the higher the price, the more pages
  b no correlation
  c positive correlation: the more pages, the greater the number of chapters
3 a negative correlation: the higher the age, the fewer hours of sleep needed
  b positive correlation: the higher the age, the greater the height
  c positive correlation: the greater the weight, the more hours of sleep needed
  d no correlation

11E

1 a
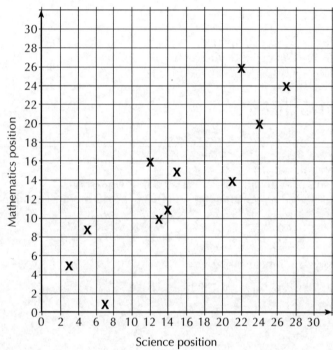

  b The higher a pupil is in the Science class, the higher they are likely to be in the Mathematics class.
  c Positive correlation.

2 a
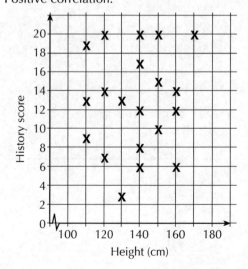

  b There is no relationship between height and History test score.   c No correlation.

CHAPTER ⑫ Number 4

12A

1 a $\frac{9}{4} = \frac{27}{12}$ **b** $\frac{20}{3} = \frac{180}{27}$ **c** $\frac{11}{2} = \frac{99}{18}$ **d** $\frac{32}{7} = \frac{160}{35}$ **e** $\frac{100}{28} = \frac{25}{7}$ **f** $\frac{144}{18} = \frac{24}{3}$
2 a 19 **b** 22 **c** 55 **d** 224
3 a $2\frac{3}{5}$ **b** $10\frac{2}{3}$ **c** $3\frac{1}{9}$ **d** $6\frac{2}{3}$ **e** $7\frac{1}{2}$ **f** $4\frac{2}{3}$ **g** $6\frac{1}{3}$ **h** $4\frac{1}{3}$ **i** $2\frac{1}{4}$
4 a i $3\frac{1}{5}$ litres **ii** $6\frac{9}{20}$ litres **iii** $2\frac{18}{25}$ litres **iv** $9\frac{3}{8}$ litres **b i** $1\frac{2}{3}$ ft **ii** $4\frac{1}{4}$ ft **iii** $8\frac{1}{3}$ ft **iv** $9\frac{1}{2}$ ft

12B

1 a $1\frac{5}{8}$ **b** $4\frac{1}{2}$ **c** $\frac{7}{8}$ **d** $1\frac{7}{8}$ **e** 1 **2 a** $\frac{5}{7}$ **b** $\frac{1}{3}$ **c** $2\frac{1}{5}$ **d** $1\frac{1}{8}$
3 a $\frac{7}{10}$ **b** $\frac{1}{2}$ **c** $1\frac{5}{18}$ **d** $1\frac{11}{24}$ **e** $\frac{5}{12}$ **f** $\frac{1}{6}$ **g** $\frac{4}{9}$ **h** $\frac{1}{5}$
4 a $\frac{3}{10}$ **b** 48 **5 a** $\frac{7}{18}$ **b** red 8 ml, 6 ml, yellow 22 ml

12C

1 a × first; 6 **b** brackets first; 8 **c** × first; 7 **d** – first; 20 **e** square first; 11
f square first; 196
2 a 19 **b** 1 **c** 4 **d** 4 **e** 12 **f** 4 **g** 4.2
3 a $11 - (7 - 1 + 4) = 1$ **b** $1 + (4 + 3)^2 = 50$ **c** $24 \div (2 \times 3) = 4$
d $(6 + 9) \div (12 \div 4) = 5$ **e** $12 - (3^2 - 7) \times 4 = 4$ **4 a** 85 **b** 23 **c** 72 **d** 129

12D

1 a 0.42 **b** 0.81 **c** 0.035 **d** 0.024 **e** 0.16 **f** 0.0036 **g** 0.0018 **h** 0.000 016
2 a 180 **b** 320 **c** 45 **d** 1400 **e** 3.6 **f** 2.8 **g** 360 **h** 6
3 41 g **4 a** 96 **b** 8.4 **c** 0.84 **5 a** 60 km **b** 180 km **c** 0.006 km

12E

1 a 20 **b** 0.4 **c** 9 **d** 2.25 **e** 40 **f** 50 **g** 1.4 **h** 400
2 a 30 **b** 50 **c** 2000 **d** 800 **e** 25 000 **f** 300 000 **g** 10 000 **h** 2000
3 a 0.14 **b** 0.04 **c** 0.004 **d** 0.0004 **e** 0.006 **f** 0.000 02
4 £20 **5** 400 000 hits **6 a** 0.000 000 03 g **b** 0.000 000 000 003 g

CHAPTER ⑬ Algebra 5

13A

1 a $11p$ **b** $6u$ **c** $6d$ **d** $16i$ **e** $4n$ **f** $2h$ **g** $-5f$ **h** $-9y$ **i** $-8d$
2 a $9s + 4t$ **b** $5i + 2j$ **c** $4a + 5b$ **d** $8d + 4y$ **e** $2r + 3h$ **f** $5b - 4d$ **g** $8u + 6a$
h $7d + 3y$ **i** $3k + 2p$ **j** $8t - 7g$
3 a $4x + 32$ **b** $21d - 35$ **c** $8f + 4e$ **d** $3d - du$ **e** $2mr + mc$ **f** $3jh - 2jg$
4 a $5x + 15$ **b** $14d + 12$ **c** $5i - 8$ **d** $u + 9$ **e** $12k + 5e$ **f** $-6a + 11b$
5 a $16i + 14$ **b** $8s + 1$ **c** $18i - 13$ **d** $5s + 6$ **e** $f + 19$ **f** $6 + 20g$

13B

1 a $t = 6$ **b** $u = 8$ **c** $p = 3$ **d** $h = 6.5$ **e** $y = 7.6$ **f** $m = -6$ **g** $x = -5$ **h** $m = 4$
2 a $p = 2$ **b** $b = 4$ **c** $f = 5$ **d** $e = 7$ **e** $y = 3.5$ **f** $w = 4.6$
3 a $x = 5$ **b** $y = 2$ **c** $i = 3$ **d** $n = -4$
4 a $d = 5$ **b** $f = 2$ **c** $s = 2.5$ **d** $g = -4$ **e** $t = 7$ **f** $q = -2$
5 a $d = 3$ **b** $s = 4$ **c** $w = 4$ **d** $k = -2$

13C

1 a £$(8 - x)$ **b** $2j$ years **c** $(T - 4)$ metres
2 a $4x = 112$; cost of tyre = £28 **b** $y + 9 = 16$; Jamie is 7 years old
c $12 - n = 5$; smaller number is 7 **d i** $2p + 12$ **ii** $2p + 12 = 44$; plum weighs 16 g
e i $4m$ **ii** $4m = 32$; cartoon lasts 8 minutes **f** $3n + 3 = 78$; $n = 25$
g $3(x - 4) = 27$; I am 13 years old **h** $4x + 3(15 - x) = 51$; there are 6 large boxes

13D

1 a 4 **b** –1 **c** $\frac{1}{2}$ **d** 2 **e** –3 **f** $\frac{1}{2}$ **g** –2 **2 a** 3 **b** –4 **c** $\frac{1}{2}$ **d** 2 **e** –6

3 a gradient = 3, y-intercept = 5 **b** gradient = –2, y-intercept = 3
c gradient = 0.5, y-intercept = –3 **d** gradient = 3, y-intercept = 0

4 a $y = 5x + 2$ **b** $y = 6x – 3$ **c** $y = –3x + 9$ **d** $y = 1.2x$

5 a gradient = 2, y-intercept = 3; $y = 2x + 3$ **b** gradient = –1, y-intercept = 2; $y = –x + 2$
c gradient = 4, y-intercept = –1; $y = 4x –1$ **d** gradient = 2, y-intercept = –3; $y = 2x – 3$
e gradient = –2, y-intercept = –2; $y = –2x – 2$ **f** gradient = –2, y-intercept = 4; $y = –2x + 4$
g gradient = 0.5, y-intercept = 3; $y = 0.5x + 3$ **h** gradient = – 0.25, y-intercept = –1; $y = –0.25x – 1$

13E

1 a

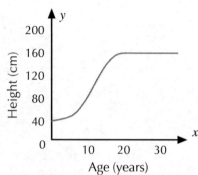

b

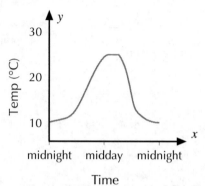

b

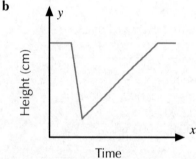

2 a i Square Deal Cars £12,
  Cheap Hire £10
  ii Square Deal Cars £20,
  Cheap Hire £10
  iii Square Deal Cars £27,
  Cheap Hire £31
  b Square Deal Cars: 20p per mile for the first
  100 miles then 5p per mile.
  Cheap Hire: £10 plus 15p for every mile
  over 100 miles.
  c Cheap Hire is cheaper than Square Deal
  Cars when the distance travelled is between
  50 and 200 miles.

3 a iii **b** iv **c** ii **d** i

4

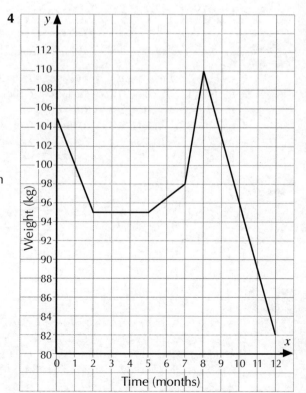

13F

1 a $D = T - 4$ **b** $d = 5m$ **c** $T = \frac{P}{6}$
   d $s = 7 - R$
2 a $p = \frac{A}{9}$ **b** $x = y - 5$ **c** $A = C - 5$
   d $c = y - 8$ **e** $m = \frac{T}{4}$
3 a 9 **b** $a = P - 5$ **c** 32
4 a 36 **b** $u = v - 16$
5 a 9 **b** $a = A - 4$ **c** 14

CHAPTER ⑭ Solving problems

14A

1 Pen = 14 cm, pencil = 21 cm; total length = 119 cm
2

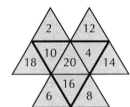

3 330 km ÷ 1.6 = 206.25 miles; 124 + 206 = 330 > 320 miles, so he has to stop for petrol.
4 a 36, 38, 40 **b** 32, 34
5 7 kg × 2.2 = 15.4 lb so French bag is heavier
6 a 11 o'clock **b** 6 days, i.e. 12 × 12 hours

14B

1 a 60 days
   b $D = 240 - 2n$
2 $3x - 24 = 27$; $x = 17$
3 a $W = 500 + 200n$
   b&c See graph to right.
   d A bowl of 3 oranges weighs the same as a bowl of 3 apples; 1100 g
4 $5x = 3x + 16$; $x = 8$
5 a $3 \times 2 = 6$
   b $3 \times 2 \times 2 = 12$
   c $N = 3 \times 2^n$
   d $3 \times 2^5 = 96$
   e $3 \times 2^7 = 384$; i.e. 7 times

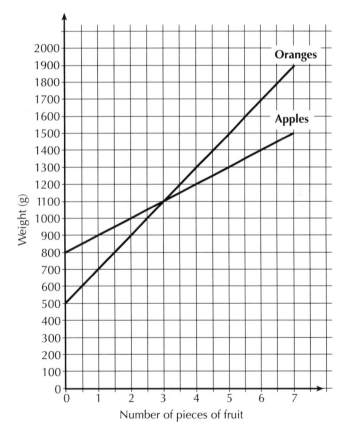

14C

1

	a				b				c	
		2 5 9				3 7			$77^2 = 5959$	
	+	1 8 7			×	2 4				
		4 4 6				8 8 8		d	$(10 + 4)(5 + 8) = 182$	

2 a 24 hours **b** 48 hours **c** 16 hours
3 A mug holds 18 cl. A glass holds 20 cl. So a glass holds more.

4 a Answers will vary, e.g. $3 \times 5 \times 7 = 105$ **b** The product of the first two numbers is odd. So the product of this product and the third number is also odd.

5 a Answers will vary, e.g. $3 \times 3 \times 4 \times 4 = 144$ **b** The product of two even numbers is even. The product of two odd numbers is odd. The product of an even and an odd number is always even. Hence the product of two odd and two even numbers is always even.

6 a 1, 3, 7, 21   **b** The factors multiply together to give an odd number. Only odd numbers multiply to give an odd number. So the factors must be odd. Or: if one of the factors of an odd number were even, then multiplying it by any other numbers would give an even number, which is a contradiction.

14D

1 a $\frac{1}{4}$ **b** 1:3 **c** 3 **2 a** 480 litres **b** 120 litres **3** £18 **4** 39
5 a 14 gallons **b** 33.75 litres **6 a** 11.2 g **b** 46.875 cm
7 photo : enlargement = 108:180 = 3:5

14E

1 a 4:3 **b** 8:15 **c** 3:7 **d** 16:3 **e** 14:3 **f** 3:20 **g** 20:7
2 a 35 cm : 5 cm **b** 330 mm : 270 mm **c** 1875 people : 3125 people **d** £8 : £28 : £40
3 72 hot meals **4** 84 children **5** 150 000 000 km²

CHAPTER ⓯ Geometry and Measures 4

15A

1

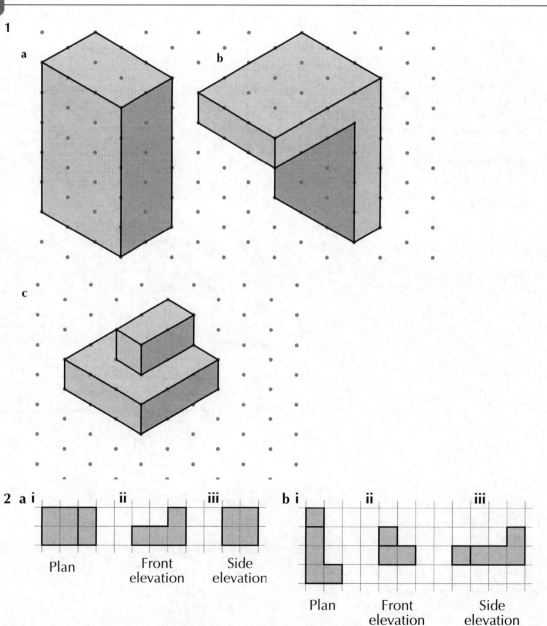

2 a i / **ii** / **iii** Plan / Front elevation / Side elevation   **b i** / **ii** / **iii** Plan / Front elevation / Side elevation

3

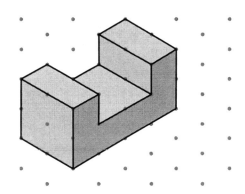

15B

1 a 105 cm **b** 5 m **c** 7.91 m **d** 10.5 m
2 a 900 m **b** 504 m **c** 453 600 m²
3

	Scale	Scaled length	Actual length
a	1 cm to 2 m	12 cm	24 m
b	1 cm to 5 km	9.2 cm	46 km
c	2 cm to 7 miles	12 cm	42 miles
d	5 cm to 8 m	30 cm	48 m

4

Part of supermarket	Length, cm	Width, cm	Area, cm²	Area, m²
Deliveries	3.3	1.3	4.29	670.3125
Chemist	4.0	1.3	5.2	812.5
Checkout area	5.3	0.9	4.77	745.3125
Non-foodstuff	2.0	0.8	1.6	250
Bakery	1.5	2.5	3.75	585.9375
Delicatessen	2.6	2.1	5.46	853.125
Packaged food	3.3	1.2	3.96	618.75
Wine	2.0	2.1	4.2	656.25
Frozen food	4.0	2.9	11.6	
	0.5	2.5	+ 1.25 = 12.85	2007.8125
Fresh food	2.7	2.1	5.67	
	1.4	2.1	+ 2.94 = 8.91	1392.1875

15C

1 a A(5, 5), B(5, 1), C(0, 5), D(–4, 5), E(–4, –1), F(4, –1), G(1, 1), H(2, –5)
b

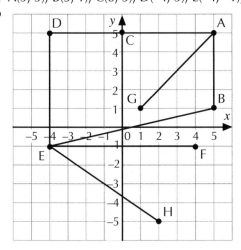

c&d AB (5, 3), AD (0.5, 5), DE (–4, 2),
EF (0, –1), EH (–1, –3), BE (0.5, 0)
2 a C(1, 1) **b** E(3, –3) **c** G(–3, –3)
d (–5, 1) **e** (5, –1)
3 a (3, 5) **b** (2.5, 6) **c** (–2, 3) **d** (–2, –3)

15D

Check measurements are correct to within ±2 mm.

15E

1 a 50.3 cm   **b** 18.8 cm   **c** 44.0 cm   **d** 34.6 cm
2 a 201.1 cm² **b** 153.9 cm² **c** 63.6 cm² **d** 10.2 cm²
3 37.7 cm, 113.1 cm²

15F

1 a 038°   **b** 157°   **c** 339°
2 a 130°   **b** 333°   **c** 221°
3

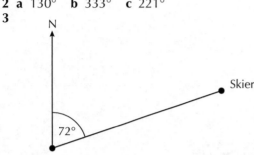

a

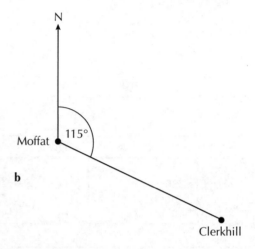

b

4 a 122°   **b** 302°   **c** 040°   **d** 220°   **e** 97°   **f** 277°

CHAPTER 16 Statistics 3

16A

1 a $4.5 \leq L < 5$ **b** 13   **c** 8   **d** 25   **e** 9
2

Volume of liquid (*V* cl)	Tally	Frequency
$10 \leq V < 10.5$	//	2
$10.5 \leq V < 11$	ⅢⅡ	5
$11 \leq V < 11.5$	///	3
$11.5 \leq V < 12$	//	2
$12 \leq V < 12.5$	////	4
$12.5 \leq V < 13$	////	4

3

Length of telephone call (minutes)	Frequency
$0 < t \leq 10$	17
$10 < t \leq 20$	9
$20 < t \leq 30$	2
$30 < t \leq 40$	0
$40 < t \leq 50$	1
$50 < t \leq 60$	1

16B

1 a $250 + 3.5 = 253.5$ **b** $72 + 0.4 = 72.4$ **c** $58\,280 + 3.6 = 58\,283.6$
2 5, 9   **3** 7, 10, 10   **4** 1, 1, 6, 12
5 a Mode and mean increased by 10.   **b** Range unaffected = 10.
6 a mean = £350, range = £130   **b** £300
   c mean increases to £330, range stays the same = £130   **d** Both will increase by 10%.

16C

1 a

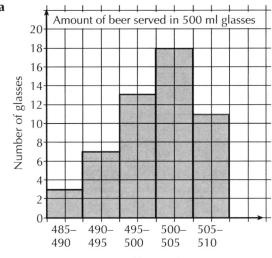

b

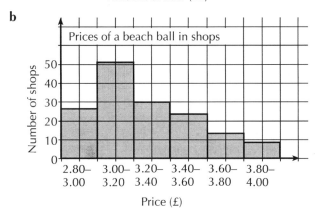

2 a

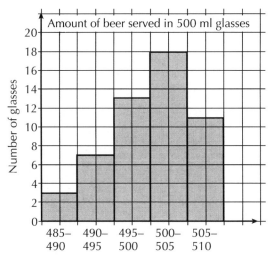

b 25 ml and 70 ml   **c** 1.625 m
d 40 ml (50 ml would be wasteful)
e 0, 10, 80, 90, 100, 110 ml

16D

1 a QuickDrive: mode 3 days, median 3 days, range 7 days.
  Ground Works: modes 2 days and 3 days, median 2 days, range 3 days.
 b Ground Works has lower median, indicating that it lays drives more quickly or that it lays smaller
  drives than QuickDrive.
 c QuickDrive range = 7 days, Ground Works range = 3 days; confirms **b**.
2 a Jerry: mean 376 g, range 620 g. Aditya: mean 296 g, range 170 g.
  Marion: mean 175 g, range 360 g   **b** Aditya, smallest range
 c Jerry (greatest total weight and greatest mean weight) or Marion (greatest number of fish caught)
 d Jerry (greatest mean weight and heaviest fish)
3 Although Tutu has the smaller mean weekly rainfall, it has a greater range, indicating that the climate
  has greater extremes.

16E

1 a mode = 9; unsuitable (it is an extreme value)   **b** mean = 30; suitable (no extreme values)
   c median = 16; suitable   **d** mean = 1.9; unsuitable (two extremely small values)
   e median = 170; unsuitable (doesn't represent top three values)
2 a 170, suitable   **b** 53, unsuitable (extremely small value)   **c** 20, suitable
3 a mean = 25.4 (to 1 d.p.), median = 26, mode = 6   **b** mean, median
   c mode (extreme value)
   d

Points awarded, p	Tally	Frequency
$0 \leq p < 10$	///	3
$10 \leq p < 20$	//	2
$20 \leq p < 30$	卌 ///	8
$30 \leq p < 40$	///	3
$40 \leq p < 50$	///	3

   e i $20 \leq p < 30$ **ii** yes
4 a Periwinkle
   b Unsuitable because of extreme value 30. Omitting this gives Jenny's the greater range.

16F

1 b $\frac{1}{3}$ **c** Answers will vary. Check comparison of theoretical and experimental probabilities.
2 a 0.5   **b** Answers will vary. Check comparison of theoretical and experimental probabilities.

Your notes

Your notes

Your notes

William Collins' dream of knowledge for all began with the publication of his first book in 1819. A self-educated mill worker, he not only enriched millions of lives, but also founded a flourishing publishing house. Today, staying true to this spirit, Collins books are packed with inspiration, innovation and practical expertise. They place you at the centre of a world of possibility and give you exactly what you need to explore it.
Collins. Freedom to teach.

Published by Collins
An imprint of HarperCollins*Publishers*
77–85 Fulham Palace Road
Hammersmith
London W6 8JB

Browse the complete Collins catalogue at
www.collinseducation.com

10 9 8 7 6 5 4 3
ISBN-13 978-0-00-726620-3

Keith Gordon, Kevin Evans, Brian Speed and Trevor Senior assert their moral rights to be identified as the authors of this work.

British Library Cataloguing in Publication Data
A Catalogue record for this publication is available from the British Library

Commissioned by Melanie Hoffman and Katie Sergeant
Project management by Priya Govindan
Covers management by Laura Deacon
Edited by Brian Ashbury
Project edited by Letitia Luff
Proofread by Amanda Dickson
Design and typesetting by Newgen Imaging
Covers by Oculus Design and Communications
Illustrations by Derek Lee and Newgen Imaging
CD mastering by Infuze
Printed and bound by Hobbs the Printers, Hampshire, UK
Production by Simon Moore

Every effort has been made to trace copyright holders and to obtain their permission for the use of copyright material. The authors and publishers will gladly receive any information enabling them to rectify any error or omission at the first opportunity.

Mixed Sources
Product group from well-managed
forests and other controlled sources
www.fsc.org Cert no. SW-COC-1806
© 1996 Forest Stewardship Council

FSC is a non-profit international organisation established to promote the
responsible management of the world's forests. Products carrying the FSC
label are independently certified to assure consumers that they come
from forests that are managed to meet the social, economic and
ecological needs of present and future generations.

Find out more about HarperCollins and the environment at
www.harpercollins.co.uk/green